CUSTOMIZING AutoCAD®

The Complete Guide to AutoCAD Menus, Macros, and More

Joseph Smith and Rusty Gesner

With Technical Assistance from Patrick Haessly

 New Riders Publishing, Thousand Oaks, California

CUSTOMIZING AutoCAD ®

A Complete Guide to AutoCAD Menus, Macros, and More

By Joseph Smith and Rusty Gesner

Published by:

New Riders Publishing
Post Office Box 4846
Thousand Oaks, CA 91360 USA

First Edition, 1988
Second Edition, 1989

Printed in the United States of America

Library of Congress Cataloging-in-Publication Data

```
Smith, Joseph (Joseph J.)
   Customizing AutoCAD : the Complete Guide to AutoCAD Menus, Macros,
and more / Joseph Smith and Rusty Gesner : with technical assistance
from Patrick Haessly. -- [2nd ed.]
     p.   cm.
 ISBN 0-934035-45-8 : $27.95
 1. AutoCAD (Computer program)   I. Gesner, Rusty.  II Haessly,
Patrick.
T385.S624  1989
620'.00425'02855369--dc19
                                                          89-30313
                                                          CIP
```

Warning and Disclaimer

Trademarks

About the Authors

Joseph Smith

Joseph J. Smith is president of ACUWARE, Inc., in Portland, OR. His company provides an AutoCAD-based application program called AUTOPE for structural engineering drafting. He has used AutoCAD since Version 1.4 and writes about AutoCAD customization from the standpoint of a user and a developer producing commercial application packages.

Before moving to the west coast, Mr. Smith was a product manager with MiCAD Systems, Inc., in New York. He was in charge of AutoCAD systems development and provided corporate training for customized AutoCAD systems. Mr. Smith is trained as a civil engineer with a B.S. degree from Villanova University, Villanova, PA. Prior to joining MiCAD Systems, he worked as an engineer with James T. Smith & Co., Philadelphia, PA, and Piasecki Aircraft Corp., Philadelphia, PA.

Rusty Gesner

B. Rustin Gesner is Director of Technical Applications for New Riders Publishing and heads New Rider's office in Portland, OR. He is responsible for New Rider's technical applications books and software products. He has used AutoCAD since Version 1.1 and writes about AutoCAD from the standpoint of a long-time user and from customizing AutoCAD for architectural applications.

Prior to joining New Riders, Mr. Gesner was president of CAD Northwest, Inc., Portland, OR. He was responsible for the sale, installation, and support of AutoCAD systems. Mr. Gesner is a registered architect. Before forming CAD Northwest, he was a practicing architect in Portland. He attended the College of Design, Art and Architecture at the University of Cincinnati, and Antioch College.

Patrick Haessly

Patrick Haessly is Senior Technical Developer at New Riders Publishing in Portland, OR. He provided support and assistance to the authors in developing the book and contributed to many of the exercises, menus and AutoLISP routines used in the book.

Mr. Haessly has used AutoCAD since Version 1.3. Prior to joining New Riders, he was the AutoCAD Systems Manager for A to Z Steel Systems, Inc., a structural steel detailing company in Wilsonville, OR. He was responsible for developing and maintaining customized AutoCAD systems.

Acknowledgments

Rusty would like to thank Kathy, Alicia, and Roo for their patience, encouragement, and good cheer when the going was rough, and to thank his parents for support in the endeavors which led to this book.

Joe wishes to thank his parents, Jim and Rita, for giving him an abundance of love, support, and a chance at every passing opportunity, most recently this book.

Joe, Rusty, and Pat wish to thank Harbert Rice for making this project possible, and Jon DeKeles for his continual support. Thanks to Carolyn Porter and Todd Meisler for overseeing page layout and production. Thanks to Christine Steel for editing, rewriting, and laying out the book.

The authors wish to thank Tom Mahood, Mauri Laitinen, Duff Kurland, Eric Lyons, John Sergneri, Keith Marcelius, Dave Kalish, Robert Wenig, John Forbes, and many others from Autodesk, Inc., for their help and support over the years.

Special thanks to Robert Palioca and all the staff at KETIV Technologies, Inc., for invaluable help, advice, review, and computing equipment used in developing the book.

Special thanks to Keith McIntyre, PE, for ideas, support, and his review of the book, and to Dorothy Kent, Synergsis, Inc., for her review.

Thanks also to Dan Stone, Ken Eichler, Dan Belmont, Eugene Jones, Bill Work and the rest of the people at MiCAD Systems, Inc., for their many ideas and techniques that contributed to material in the book. Thanks to the people at Smith Engineering for serving as the testbed of application experiments.

Autodesk, Inc. supplied AutoCAD, Xerox Corp. supplied Xerox Ventura Publisher. Microsoft Corp. supplied Microsoft Word. Michael Cuthbertson of Symsoft provided copies of Hotshot and Hotshot Plus. Thanks to Barry Simon and Richard Wilson, the developers of CTRLALT.

Special thanks to SUN Microsystems Inc. for providing a SUN 386i computer system, which runs both DOS and UNIX applications. Verticom Inc. provided a 2Page Display System for Ventura Publisher displays. Verticom also provided H256e and M256e Video Display System displays. Vermont Micro Systems provided a VMI1024 Video Display System for AutoCAD displays. CALCOMP provided Model 2300 and 2500 Digitizers.

CONTENTS

PART II. BASIC TOOLS

CHAPTER 5   *The Anatomy of a Menu*

CHAPTER 6   *A Menu System*

PART III. SUPPORT LIBRARIES, FONTS, AND HATCHES

PART IV. APPLYING AUTOLISP AND MENUS TO APPLICATIONS

CHAPTER 10   *Customizing for 3D*

CHAPTER 11   *Efficient Dimensioning With AutoCAD*

APPENDIX A — *Menu Macros*

APPENDIX B — *Setup, Memory and Errors*

APPENDIX C — *Reference Tables*

APPENDIX D — *The Authors' Appendix*

INDEX

INTRODUCTION

Welcome to the most creative part of using AutoCAD, CUSTOMIZING AutoCAD. The goal of this book is to bring you the information and tools to make AutoCAD do what you want it to do. From simply adding a few menus and macros, to designing a sophisticated menu-controlled user interface, to writing a complete *system* that executes your application with AutoLISP assistance, CUSTOMIZING AutoCAD will give you the knowledge you need to make AutoCAD work for you.

Second Edition

The first edition of CUSTOMIZING AutoCAD was one big book! With the increased power and 3D capabilities of AutoCAD Release 10, the need for customization is greater than ever. As AutoCAD has grown, so has our task of showing how to customize AutoCAD. Therefore, to thoroughly cover customizing we have expanded our coverage to two books. CUSTOMIZING AutoCAD now includes more menu, macro, support library, and introductory AutoLISP material. It features new chapters on dimensioning and 3D drawing. We have broadened our coverage of AutoLISP in our second book, INSIDE AutoLISP.

INSIDE AutoLISP picks up where CUSTOMIZING AutoCAD leaves off by explaining the full scope of AutoLISP. Using LISP, it provides the external programming tools and techniques that you need to develop a well-integrated and controlled application system and includes the original advanced applications material.

Scope of Personal Applications

Most users adapt AutoCAD to their own needs at some level. They start by writing macros which they add to their screen menus. Writing and using menu macros is a natural extension of AutoCAD. Many users move on to a second stage of customizing AutoCAD, making their macros more efficient with AutoLISP expressions, or adding new drafting and calculation functions, commands, and subroutines to their systems. They integrate these commands and functions into their menus. Finally, some users and groups move on to developing *full-blown* integrated application systems. These systems do everything from developing complete user interfaces for AutoCAD to integrating and running external programs.

CUSTOMIZING AutoCAD addresses the key issues you encounter in planning, developing, programming, and testing a professional AutoCAD application system. Whether you are a user entering the first stages of customization, or a developer putting a complete custom application together, CUSTOMIZING AutoCAD will help you assess your application needs and choose the best avenues for customizing. The book provides menu macros and AutoLISP-enhanced macros to help you gain greater control over AutoCAD and better access to your programs and data. The book helps you develop a user interface, allowing you to create your own prompts, input questions, and default options. The book addresses issues like integrating drawing standards and drawing scales to take full advantage of AutoLISP, creating the robust controlled programs and applications you need to go further into an application.

Checklist for Customization

Here is a checklist of things that you need to do to customize AutoCAD. We will help you to:

☐ Set your application goals. You need to know what tasks you want AutoCAD to do.

☐ Lay out your customization plans. Determine how to do your applications in AutoCAD.

☐ Develop your macros. Get them tested and working.

☐ Develop your menus and integrate your macros.

☐ Develop the AutoLISP macros that you need and integrate these into your menu system.

How CUSTOMIZING AutoCAD Is Organized

CUSTOMIZING AutoCAD is organized into four parts. Think of the book as four handy reference guides in one place. These four guides take you from setup all the way through a set of applications.

PART I. SYSTEM ORGANIZATION gives you the basic organization of your MS-DOS and AutoCAD environments for customizing an AutoCAD application. Chapter 1 starts off by showing you a little AutoLISP, then gives the book's bootup and DOS directory structures. Chapter 2 leads you through making a startup batch file for CUSTOMIZING AutoCAD, and using AutoCAD's SHELL to integrate your text editor to do program development. Chapter 3 sets out the book's structure of AutoCAD colors, layers, and linetypes. CUSTOMIZING AutoCAD's basic working environment is designed to give you and the book a common jumping-off point for custom development, and to let you work through the exercises without interfering with your other AutoCAD applications.

PART II. BASIC TOOLS gives you a set of working menu tools to help you with the customizing process. Chapter 4 shows you how to build menu macros. Chapter 5 leads you through AutoCAD's menu system, demonstrating how to use popup (pull-down) menus and icons. Chapter 6 shows you how to organize and integrate a menu system.

PART III. SUPPORT LIBRARIES, FONTS, and HATCHES. Many custom applications require support libraries. Chapters 7 and 8 show you how to build custom libraries for AutoCAD's text styles, fonts, hatches, linetypes, and fills. Chapter 8 also has a process for making hatch patterns that can be automated.

PART IV. APPLYING AUTOLISP AND MENUS TO APPLICATIONS has three chapters. These chapters will give you both the theory and the practical AutoLISP tools that you will need to develop custom applications. Chapter 9 shows you how to build and integrate AutoLISP routines into your menu system and discusses AutoLISP's program structure and data types. After you have worked through this introductory chapter on AutoLISP, you will have a basic understanding of AutoLISP and a core set of AutoLISP functions that you can use in your own applications. Chapter 10 customizes 3D by developing menus and AutoLISP routines to fill in the gaps in AutoCAD's 3D toolkit. 3D, like any other application, needs customization for efficiency and control. Chapter 11 finalizes what you have learned about menus and AutoLISP by developing a mini-application: a custom dimensioning system. Advanced menu development, page toggling techniques, and AutoLISP expressions are used to customize many of the settings that control the way AutoCAD drawings are dimensioned.

APPENDICES. There are four appendices. Appendix A describes the menus and macros used in the book. Appendix B covers common problems and solutions encountered in setting up and using AutoCAD in a DOS environment. Appendix C provides two invaluable reference tables, a complete AutoCAD system variables table and a descriptive table of all AutoLISP functions and their syntax. Appendix D discusses the system setups and software used to produce this book, along with the authors' comments on software and information sources helpful to customizing AutoCAD.

How to Use CUSTOMIZING AutoCAD

There are three ways to use CUSTOMIZING AutoCAD. First, you can read it front to back. Second, you can set up the CUSTOMIZING AutoCAD environment in Chapters 1 and 2, then pick and choose the menus, macros, and AutoLISP programs you want to learn and use. Third, you can just pick and choose what customizing skills you wish to acquire from the chapters that interest you.

Pick and Choose

Obviously, CUSTOMIZING AutoCAD provides you with a wealth of information about how to customize AutoCAD. We expect that you will go through parts of the book several times, using it as a reference and as a source for macros and AutoLISP routines. The book tries to make your access to the material easy by providing lists of both tools and customization skills in each chapter. Each chapter starts with a How-To Skills Checklist like the one shown below. The example checklist is taken from Chapter 11 on dimensioning. Pick the skills that you want to gain by looking at the skills checklist in each chapter.

Sample How-To Skills Checklist

The exercises on dimensioning show you how to:

❏ Plan a menu system, organize the contents of a menu, and develop it.

❏ Overlay pages of menus on the same screen to dynamically update menu options.

❏ Read and understand how AutoLISP processes a LISP expression.

❏ Use AutoLISP to create intelligent macros which are sensitive to user settings in the current drawing.

❏ Build informative prompts that give defaults and show current values.

After the skills checklist, each chapter has a list of menus, macros, and AutoLISP routines to be used in the chapter. We call this list the *toolkit*. These toolkits are re-indexed in Appendix A. By looking at the toolkits in each chapter, you can decide what menus and programs you want to acquire. A typical toolkit looks like the one shown below. This toolkit is taken from Chapter 10 on 3D applications.

Sample Menus, AutoLISP Tools, and Programs

MENUS

**3D is the main menu for working with the book's 3D macros and tools.

**P2-END-SAVE is a pull-down menu with standardized save and end routines.

**P1-3DVARS is a pull-down menu providing instant access to the AutoCAD system variables which control 3D mesh creation.

MACROS

[Const 2D] creates plan, side, and front view reference drawings for simultaneous viewing or individual plotting.

[3DVpoint] is a replacement macro for the VPOINT command. It uses DVIEW to provide enhanced control of eye-to-target viewing.

[Bracket] shows how a simple macro can create complex 3D parts. The macro controls the 3DMESH command to create any size bracket.

[Cylinder] is an effective tool and a demonstration of how to use UCS, point filtering, and a little AutoLISP to make cylinders. Cylinders are common to many piping, industrial, and mechanical applications. A series of 3D intersection cylinders and a method of determining intersections are also incorporated into the 3D menu.

[Entity:], **[On/Off]** and **[Reset]** are related macros that selectively turn entities on and off during 3D edit operations. They operate much the same way as turning layers on and off.

Building a Customized Menu

If you follow the book front to back, you will build a complete, custom menu system. The CUSTOMIZING AutoCAD menu has a dozen major AutoCAD menu pages. After you set up your initial screen menus with the BASIC TOOLS in PART II, you add a menu page (or more) with most chapters. These menu pages are illustrated at the end of each chapter. You can follow the overall menu plan used in the book by looking at these menu pages. A chapter screen menu page looks like the one shown below. This menu page is taken from Chapter 10 on 3D.

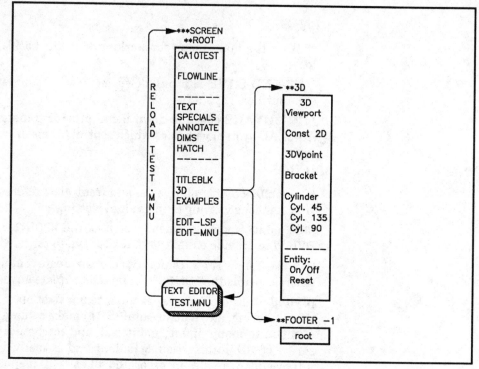

Sample Menu Illustration

Learn By Doing

Learning to use AutoLISP may look like a formidable task. It isn't. You may also harbor the suspicion that you have to be a programmer to use AutoLISP to develop a custom AutoCAD application. You don't. We have written CUSTOMIZING AutoCAD for typical AutoCAD users like you (and us).

How Exercises Are Shown

The following example exercise will show you the book's format and syntax for representing AutoCAD commands. To get started, all you need to know is how to start up AutoCAD. AutoLISP should be loaded. The following table shows how the book represents drawing settings. When you come across these tables, change your settings to the appropriate values shown. In the sample below, you would set your snap to 0.1, your grid to 1 unit, and turn ortho on. The table tells you to set your limits to 0,0 and 11,8.5 and to make a new layer named OJB02.

SNAP	GRID	ORTHO
0.1	1	On
LIMITS	Set limits from 0,0 to 11,8.5.	
LAYER	Make OBJ02 and leave it current.	

Sample Drawing Settings

The book uses the full width of the page for exercises. Look at the following exercise example. Commands and instructions are shown at the left. In the sequence below, "Start up AutoCAD, then:" is an instruction step. The "Command:" prompt demonstrates how we show all AutoCAD prompts, including those that you will create with AutoLISP. Prompts are shown as they will appear on your screen. Boldface type indicates input that you need to type in.

Example Drawing Exercise

Start up AutoCAD, then:

Enter selection: **1**   Begin a NEW drawing named CA.

Make the settings shown in the Sample Drawing Settings table above.

Command: **ZOOM**
All/Center/Dynamic/Extents/Left/Previous/Window/<Scale(X)>: **L**
Lower left corner point: **<RETURN>**
Magnification or Height <9.0000>: **8.5**

Command: <Coords on>   Toggle coordinates on with <^D> or <^F6>.
Select **[DRAW] [LINE]**   Pick absolute point 1,1 then polar point @2<90 and
                              type relative point @2,0. <RETURN> to end.

The exercise's right-hand section provides *in-line* comments and instructions about the command sequence. Menu picks are shown in boldface with brackets, like "*Select* **[DRAW] [LINE]**." All you need to do in an exercise is follow the command sequence, refer to any in-line instructions that are provided, and input any text shown in bold.

Things to Watch in the Exercises

The book's routines were tested by us and by our reviewers. Here are three things we suggest you watch for in the exercises:

The printing font used in the exercises doesn't distinguish clearly between zero and the letter O, and the number one and lower case letter L. You need to watch these closely:

0   This is a zero.
O   This is an upper case letter O.
1   This is the number one.
l   This is a lower case letter l.

How Screens Are Illustrated

Pure, uninterrupted lines of command sequences can become mesmerizing. To help you with the hands-on exercises, the book provides illustrations and "screen shots" of what you should see on your screen at key points. Remember, we had to do the exercises too! We captured our screens as we tested the prompt sequences and AutoLISP routines for the book. A typical screen shot is shown below.

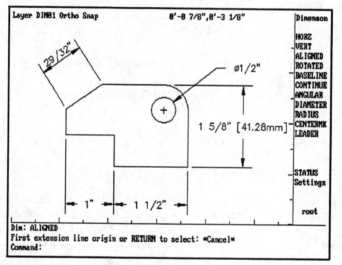

Sample Screen Shot

The CUSTOMIZING AutoCAD DISK

A disk, called the CUSTOMIZING AutoCAD DISK (or CA DISK for short), is available for use with the book. The disk includes all the menu .MNU files, batch .BAT files, symbol and example .DWG files, and other support files used in CUSTOMIZING AutoCAD.

While not absolutely essential for most exercises, the CA DISK will save you time and energy. Using the CA DISK ensures that your customization menus, macros, and AutoLISP routines are accurate. The

CA DISK also releases you from tedious typing. This lets you focus your attention on the real material when you work through the exercises. The back of the book includes an order form for the CUSTOMIZING AutoCAD DISK. Instructions on installing and using the disks are given in the first chapter.

To help you with the exercises, the book provides some simple disk icons showing you when to use files from the CA DISK.

A pointing finger icon indicates material that will be important to a later chapter. These icons are shown below.

 Do "this" if you have the CA DISK.

Do "this" if you don't have the CA DISK.

☞ Do "this" whether or not you have the CA DISK. You need the material for later chapters.

When you are using the CA DISK menus with the exercises, the disk will show the completed menu or file as it will appear at the end of the chapter. You can follow the chapter's menu macro edits by examining the menu with your text editor.

Prerequisites for CUSTOMIZING AutoCAD

The hardest part of CUSTOMIZING AutoCAD is typing accurately. If you have problems with your typing, we recommend that you get the CUSTOMIZING AutoCAD DISK. This simplifies the typing by eliminating most of it.

DOS Experience and Version

You need PC or MS-DOS 3.0, or a later DOS version on your system. If you have MS-DOS 2.0, you can still use the book, but refer to our Appendix B. You should be familiar with the major DOS commands: CD, CHKDSK, COPY, DEL, DIR, DISKCOPY, FORMAT, MD, PATH, REN, RD, and TYPE. You should also know how to make a text file with your word processor.

➡ *TIP: Update your operating system to at least DOS version 3.1. It is easy to remember to keep the AutoCAD software up-to-date, but it is easy to forget to update PC-DOS or MS-DOS. DOS versions 3.1 and later offer valuable features for a customizing environment, including a better ability to deal with environment space limitations. DOS 4.0 allows some of the environment memory consumption to be moved into expanded RAM, freeing up more of the 640K RAM for AutoCAD. We recommend updating your operating system.*

UNIX Users

Although the exercises are shown in DOS example format, we have made them compatible with UNIX-based AutoCAD systems, and have tried to point out important distinctions between DOS-based and UNIX-based systems where the differences are important.

AutoCAD Experience, Version, and Equipment

To use this book, you should have enough experience to feel comfortable using AutoCAD. If you have worked through any of New Riders' AutoCAD books like INSIDE AutoCAD or STEPPING INTO AutoCAD, you should have no problem using this book. You should be familiar with most of AutoCAD's commands, but you do not need to be an expert. You should know how to configure your AutoCAD system. Beyond that, you just need a desire to make your AutoCAD system more effective and productive.

You don't need a fast or fancy AutoCAD system. However, if your system is not running at IBM-AT speed, you may find some parts a little slower than you'd like. A hard disk, or equivalent, is required. You will need 640K of RAM to utilize AutoLISP. Extended or expanded RAM is nice, but not required. A mouse is OK, but a digitizer tablet is preferable, and a tablet is required to do the tablet and button menu examples. The menu exercises covering popups and icon menus require a video driver that supports the advanced user interface (AUI). If you aren't sure about popups, you can test your video display now.

Testing for POPUPS and ICONS

```
Command: SETVAR
Variable name or ?: POPUPS
POPUPS = 0 (read only)
Command: QUIT
```

ADI 3.0 or later video driver from your video board manufacturer. If your video board is really outdated, you may need to buy a new one. If you don't care about using icon and popup menus, don't worry.

The following sequence will check your version of AutoLISP and verify that it is enabled.

Checking Your Version of AutoLISP

```
Command: (ver)                               Type (ver) and hit <RETURN>.
Lisp returns: "AutoLISP Release 10.0"        Or your version number.
```

Lisp returns: is used to call your attention to AutoLISP's backtalk. You won't see the *Lisp returns:* on your screen, but what follows it should appear on your screen as shown in the book.

If you got "AutoLISP Release 10.0" or higher, you're in great shape. If you got "AutoLISP Release 9" and you are using this book's companion disk, you'll have to make some adjustments. Although the CA DISK was developed on and supports AutoCAD Release 10, most of the material will work in Release 9. You'll need to edit some menus and LISP files to remove or revise commands exclusive to Release 10. See the CA DISK for more information.

You should also check to see that AutoLISP is not disabled by insufficient memory or the configuration menu option "Configure operating parameters."

Moving On With a Little LISP

Let's get our feet wet by playing around with a few simple AutoLISP routines in Chapter 1, then we'll organize the DOS system environment for CUSTOMIZING AutoCAD.

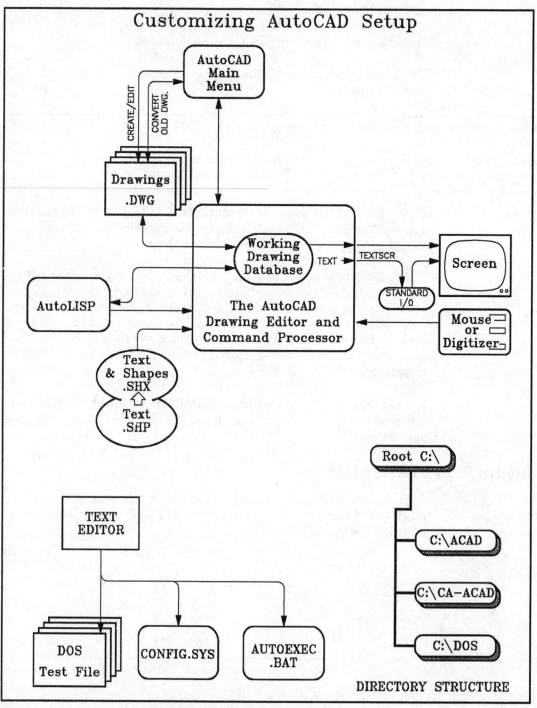

System Organization for Customizing AutoCAD

CHAPTER 1

Getting Started

A LITTLE LISP AND ORGANIZING DOS

CUSTOMIZING AutoCAD is built around structuring menus, writing macros and organizing your computer to do better drawings faster. This chapter demonstrates how easy it is to automate repetitive work with AutoLISP, a powerful customizing tool. Then you'll see how to organize your system environment for CUSTOMIZING AutoCAD. If you haven't already, go back and read the introduction before you start working through this chapter. The introduction contains important information about how to use the book that will help you avoid mistakes.

The Benefits of a Well-Organized System

Macros make customizing AutoCAD a straightforward process. AutoCAD's menus make it possible to turn your macros and AutoLISP programs into your own application system.

Creating a well-organized system environment makes development and management easier. Using subdirectories to organize your files into groups is a key to good file management. A well-managed system helps you, AutoCAD, and other programs find your application files. Setting up system resources properly will also improve AutoCAD's performance.

Your text editor is your key developer's tool. You will use it to develop your menus, macros, AutoLISP programs, and other support files. This chapter will help you test your text editor and help you set up your operating system for customizing AutoCAD.

How-To Skills Checklist

Here are the skills that you will acquire in this chapter. You will learn how to:

❑ Use simple AutoLISP routines interactively at the keyboard to automate tedious AutoCAD tasks.

❑ Set up and test your text editor.

❑ Configure your operating system environment using the DOS CONFIG.SYS and AUTOEXEC.BAT files, or UNIX setup files.

❑ Structure subdirectories suitable for customizing AutoCAD.

❑ Set a directory path for programs to search and make the operating system prompt display the current path.

❑ Install the CA DISK.

Operating System Programs and Files

☞ You will need to create or verify your operating system programs and files to use the book. We will show you how to do this later in this chapter.

DOS Files

CONFIG.SYS is the DOS root directory file that sets the general DOS environment.

AUTOEXEC.BAT is a DOS batch program that initializes DOS environment settings when you boot the system.

A Little LISP

Before we get into the nitty-gritty of system setup, let's look at a little AutoLISP. To do this exercise you need to start a new drawing. Type in the boldface text shown below and follow the comments on the right-hand side of the exercise. The book assumes that your hard disk is C: and that AutoCAD is in the \ACAD directory. If your drive and directory names are different, use your own.

You are going to make the ZOOM command do a ZOOM Limits. Try it!

Don't panic if AutoLISP returns a 1>. It is just AutoLISP's way of telling you that you need another right parenthesis. Type) and a <RETURN>, then hit a <^C> and try again. The hardest part of AutoLISP is getting matching pairs of parentheses and quotation marks!

Doing an AutoLISP ZOOM Limits Command

```
C:\ACAD> ACAD              Start AutoCAD normally.
Enter selection: 1         Begin a NEW drawing named TEST=
                           The = forces all ACAD default settings.

Command: ZOOM              Zoom to lower right quarter of the screen.

Command: STYLE             Name it ROMANC. Use the ROMANC font. Default all options.

Command: TEXT              Set height to 0.5 and type "Customizing AutoCAD" as text.

Command: (command "ZOOM" "W" (getvar "LIMMIN") (getvar "LIMMAX"))

ZOOM                       AutoLISP is in control now.

All/Center/Dynamic/Extents/Left/Previous/Window/<Scale(X)>: W
First corner: Other corner:          It Zooms to the limits.
Lisp returns: nil

Command: ERASE             Clean up. Erase the text.
```

That was easy. Now let's try an AutoLISP routine to automate a tedious task. Manually entering a column of numbers is normally slow and error prone. AutoLISP can do it for you.

AutoLISP Automated Row Numbers

AutoLISP Automation

```
Command: SETVAR
Variable name or ?: TEXTEVAL
New Value for TEXTEVAL <0>: 1

Command: (setq inc 0  num (getint "Enter number of lines: "))
Enter number of lines: 12
Lisp returns: 12
```

Command: **TEXT**   Start the command and use AutoLISP to enter text.
Start point or Align/Center/Fit/Middle/Right/Style: Pick a point at top left.
Height <0.5000>: **.25**
Rotation angle <0>: **<RETURN>**

Text: **(repeat num (command (strcat "A" (itoa (setq inc (1+ inc)))) "" ""))**
A1   AutoLISP enters the text "A1" and continues.
Command:
TEXT Start point or Align/Center/Fit/Middle/Right/Style:
Text: A2
Command:
TEXT Start point or Align/Center/Fit/Middle/Right/Style:
                                     And so on until "A12" is entered.

Text: A12
Command:
TEXT Start point or Align/Center/Fit/Middle/Right/Style:
Text: nil   Finally, AutoLISP returns nil.
Text: **<RETURN>**   Finish with a <RETURN>.

Command: **QUIT**   And exit AutoCAD to your operating system.
C:\ACAD> **CD**   Return to your root directory.
C:\>

➡ *NOTE: If you make a mistake and try again, be sure to use (setq inc 0) before doing the (repeat num . . .) expression.*

All the text commands, prompts and AutoLISP should scroll on by and you should be left with a screen like the AutoLISP Automated Row Numbers illustration. AutoLISP took the integer you entered and stored it under the variable name NUM. After you started the text command, the AutoLISP REPEAT expression took over and looped 12 times. Each loop incremented the INC variable, converted it to a text string value with the ITOA function, and combined it with the string "A" with the STRCAT function.

If you had to type custom routines like this each time you used them, it wouldn't be worth the trouble. Later you will store them with menu macros, or as AutoLISP programs and commands. Then you will have them at your fingertips for immediate use, improving your system's versatility and flexibility.

Now that you are back in good old DOS, let's start setting up the workstation for AutoCAD development.

Necessary Directories

A good directory structure provides flexibility in organizing files. It increases efficiency if you limit the number of files in each directory to a reasonable number, say 100 to 200. AutoCAD provides good support for directory use by allowing you to set search paths for program and support files. The book's directory structure also ensures that the book's exercises will not interfere with your current AutoCAD setup.

CUSTOMIZING AutoCAD assumes that your hard disk is C:, and that you have a directory structure like that shown in the Directory Structure illustration. The exercises show a DOS style prompt that includes a path. A *path* is a set order of directories that DOS searches for programs or batch files when you execute them. This allows you to execute programs from a directory that is different from the one you're currently in.

You may be using another type of operating system or your drive letter or subdirectory names may vary from those shown. If so, you need to substitute your prompt, drive letter and names wherever you encounter the C:\PATH prompt, C: drive, or various directory names in the book.

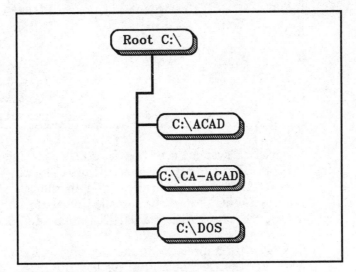

Customizing AutoCAD Directory Structure

The CA-ACAD, ACAD and operating system directories are necessary for this book and for its companion disk's application environment to work. We will assume your operating system directory is named DOS. Use the following exercise to make the current directory CA-ACAD. Then take a look at your directory names and at the book's directory names. Make sure drive C: is the current drive, then:

Subdirectory Setup

```
C:\> MD \CA-ACAD
```

```
C:\> DIR *.
```
                        This lists directories and little else. The book's directories are:

```
Volume in drive C is DRIVE-C
Directory of C:\

ACAD      <DIR>  12-01-88    11:27a
DOS       <DIR>  12-01-88    11:27a
CA-ACAD   <DIR>  12-01-88    11:27a
3 File(s)   8753472 bytes free
```
                        AutoCAD program, config. and standard files.
                        All of the operating system files.
                        CUSTOMIZING AutoCAD support files.
                        Your list will be different, and show others.

➡ *NOTE: On a UNIX system, we assume you will create the CA-ACAD directory in your home directory. Throughout the book, you will have to substitute appropriate UNIX commands and paths for the DOS commands and paths shown, for example:*

DOS	UNIX	Purpose
CD \	cd ~	Change to root (DOS) or home (UNIX) directory.
MD \CA-ACAD	mkdir ~/ca-acad	Make books directory.
DIR filename	ls -l filename	List directory for filename.
DIR *.	ls -d */	List directories.

Some UNIX systems may vary from these examples. Also, you will have to do a search and replace to substitute the path ~/ca-acad/ for the path /CA-ACAD/ for all menu files later in the book. Depending on your system, AutoCAD may be installed in /usr/acad, /files/acad, or ~acad directories. Check with your UNIX system administrator.

The CA-ACAD directory is the working and support directory for the book. For the DOS operating system, the DOS, ACAD, and CA-ACAD directories are the minimum directories necessary for the book.

If your operating system files are not in a directory named DOS, they need to be in some other directory in your system's path. Paths are generally set in your AUTOEXEC.BAT file, as shown later in this chapter.

If your AutoCAD directory is not named ACAD, you will have to make sure your AutoCAD directory name is in the book's startup batch file's path. The book's startup batch file is called CA.BAT. You will create this startup batch file in the next chapter.

➡ *TIP: It helps to keep each program and group of data files that you use in their own subdirectories. File access is faster. Files don't get mixed up, and future program upgrades are easier to install.*

AutoCAD Program and Support Files

AutoCAD is a big program, one of the biggest running on microcomputers. The ACAD.EXE file executes AutoCAD and loads core functions, but most of AutoCAD's program code is contained in several overlay files (ACADPP.OVL, ACADPL.OVL, ACADDS.OVL, and ACADDG.OVL). In addition, AutoCAD uses several support files, such as text fonts, linetypes, and hatch patterns. If you are unfamiliar with AutoCAD's file structure, take a look at the program files list in the AutoCAD Installation and Performance Guide that accompanied your software. Understanding these files will help you understand why and how things happen in AutoCAD.

Setting Up AutoCAD's Configuration Files

The book assumes that AutoCAD's support files are in the \ACAD subdirectory. Besides support files, AutoCAD also requires device driver, *.DRV, files during configuration. These drivers are used by the device configuration overlay files. Configuration also creates a configuration file (ACAD.CFG) that stores the settings and configuration-related system variables used by AutoCAD. After configuration, the drivers are no longer needed.

In order not to disturb established systems, we won't change your existing AutoCAD setup when you work through this book. Use the following exercise to establish a separate configuration for CUSTOMIZING AutoCAD by copying AutoCAD configuration files to the \CA-ACAD directory. Copy the configuration overlay and ACAD.CFG files to the CA-ACAD directory to run the book's AutoCAD environment.

Copying AutoCAD Files to the CA-ACAD Directory

```
C:\> CD \ACAD
C:\ACAD> COPY ACADP?.OVL \CA-ACAD\*.*
ACADPL.OVL                              Plotter overlay file.
ACADPP.OVL                              Printer/plotter overlay file.
2 File(s) copied

C:\ACAD> COPY ACADD?.OVL \CA-ACAD\*.*
ACADDS.OVL                              Display (video) overlay file.
ACADDG.OVL                              Digitizer (or mouse) overlay file.
2 File(s) copied

C:\ACAD> COPY ACAD.CFG \CA-ACAD\*.*
1 File(s) copied                        General AutoCAD configuration file.
```

ADI Drivers

ADI drivers are memory resident TSR (Terminate and Stay Resident) programs or DOS device drivers for plotters, printers, digitizers and video cards. If you are using an ADI (Autodesk Device Interface) driver, you must install this type of driver prior to starting AutoCAD. You can install an ADI driver in your AUTOEXEC.BAT file or your AutoCAD startup batch file unless they are designed to be installed by the CONFIG.SYS file. See Appendix B for more information on ADI drivers.

Installing the CUSTOMIZING AutoCAD Disks

Now you are ready to install the CUSTOMIZING AutoCAD disks. If you don't have them yet, see the order form in the back of the book. We recommend getting the disks. They will save you a lot of typing and debugging time.

You need to copy the CA DISK files into the \CA-ACAD directory. To conserve disk space, the disk files are merged into the single CA-LOAD.EXE file which automatically copies all files into the current directory.

Installing the CUSTOMIZING AutoCAD DISKS

Put the CA DISK in your diskette drive A:

```
C:\> CD \CA-ACAD
C:\CA-ACAD> A:CA-LOAD
```

➡ *NOTE: To install the CA DISK on a UNIX system, you can first install it on a DOS system on your network, then copy the files across the network into your ~ca-acad directory.*

Selecting Text Editors

This chapter, and most of the book, depends on the use of a text editor. We used Norton's Editor to develop the book's files, but any good text editor will work. Make sure that your text editor will work for menu and AutoLISP development. Norton's Editor, Sidekick, PC Write (a "shareware" editor), Wordstar in non-document mode, the Word Perfect Library Program Editor, and the DOS program EDLIN all produce the standard ASCII file format that you will need. EDLIN is awkward and we recommend its use only as a last resort, or for temporary use until you settle on an editor.

If your text editor stores any of its format settings or modes, or cannot accept file paths, you need a separate non-document configured copy in your CA-ACAD directory. If so, make a copy of your text editor in your CA-ACAD directory and permanently configure it for non-document mode so that you can use it without switching directories. This avoids any conflicts in the text files that you will create for your development application. Be sure to keep word wrap off. The book assumes your editor is in CA-ACAD. If not, you may need to modify commands which access your editor.

Your editor must create standard ASCII text files. AutoCAD can handle either DOS or UNIX ASCII formats. The CA DISK files are in DOS format. UNIX users need to strip the <RETURN>s. We assume that you have a suitable editor at hand. If you have doubts about a DOS editor's ability to produce ASCII files, test it with the following steps.

Text Editor Test

`C:\> ` **CD \CA-ACAD**

Install and configure a copy of your editor in the \CA-ACAD directory.

Load your text editor. Get into its edit mode and make a new file named TEXT.TXT.

Write a paragraph of text and block copy it to get a few screens full.

Save the file and exit to DOS. Then test it:

```
C:\CA-ACAD> COPY TEXT.TXT CON
```
All the text you entered scrolls by if your editor produced a standard ASCII file.

```
C:\CA-ACAD> DEL TEXT.TXT
```

Your text editor is OK if "COPY TEXT.TXT CON" showed text identical to what you typed in your editor with no extra åÇäÆ characters or smiling faces! If you got any garbage, particularly at the top or bottom of the copy, then your text editor is not suitable, or is not configured correctly for use as a development editor. If you are unsure of your editor or want better alternatives, see Appendix D.

➡ *NOTE: **You need a suitable text editor to continue.** A good text editor is invaluable in customizing AutoCAD. It helps if your editor is comfortable, compact, quick, and easy to use, but there are three essential things that your editor must do. It must create pure ASCII files, including the ASCII <ESCAPE> character. It must be able to merge files. And it must allow you to turn word wrap off.*

➡ *NOTE: If you are using a UNIX text editor, you will find that the book's text files end each line with a <^M> and each file with a <^Z> due to their DOS text format. You may need to strip these <^M> and <^Z> characters. See your system administrator for help.*

The DOS Bootup Environment

When the computer starts up, it reads COMMAND.COM and two hidden files named IBMBIO.COM and IBMDOS.COM. Then, it looks around for some more environment information. It gets its environment information from two important files: CONFIG.SYS and AUTOEXEC.BAT.

You need a CONFIG.SYS file and an AUTOEXEC.BAT file, like those shown below, as a minimum base for using the book. (These files are not used in UNIX systems.)

CONFIG.SYS

CONFIG.SYS is the place to install *device drivers* that tell the computer how to talk to devices like disk drives, RAM disks, and unusual video cards. It is also the place to put instructions that will improve your system performance and increase your environment space for customization.

CONFIG.SYS must be located in the root directory. It is read automatically when your computer boots up. You may never even know it is there. We recommend that your file include the following lines. If you have a CONFIG.SYS file, display your file to examine it.

CONFIG.SYS

```
C:\CA-ACAD> CD \
C:\> COPY CONFIG.SYS CON
```
This assumes your drive is C:
Copies the file to the CONsole, the screen.

The recommended minimum includes:

```
BUFFERS=32
```
Use a number from 20 to 48.
```
FILES=24
BREAK=ON
SHELL=C:\COMMAND.COM /P /E:512
```
Allows <^C> and <BREAK> to break whenever possible.
/E:512 is for DOS 3.2 or 3.3.
Use /E:32 for DOS 3.0 or 3.1.
```
DEVICE=C:\DOS\ANSI.SYS
```
Allows use of extended character set.

```
C:\> COPY CONFIG.SYS *.OLD
```
Back up your original file, if any.

 COPY \CA-ACAD\CONFIG.CA to \CONFIG.SYS and edit it, or edit your existing CONFIG.SYS file.

 Edit your CONFIG.SYS file. If you do not have a CONFIG.SYS file, create one.

Edit or create your CONFIG.SYS in your root directory using your tested ASCII text editor. Include lines similar to those above. Use the discussion below to help you make any modifications.

The BUFFERS line allocates more RAM to hold your recently used data. If a program frequently accesses recently used data, buffers reduce disk accesses and increase speed. Each two-buffer increment steals 1K from the DOS memory available to your programs. You may have to use a smaller number if AutoCAD runs short of memory.

The FILES line allocates more RAM to keep recently used files open. This reduces directory searching and increases data access speed. FILES uses very little memory, and a large value helps with AutoCAD and AutoLISP.

The SHELL line ensures adequate space for DOS environment variables. DOS allocates a small portion of RAM to store environment variable settings and information. AutoCAD and AutoLISP use several of these. You will need at least 256 bytes. We recommend allocating at least 512 bytes with DOS 3.2 and DOS 3.3. If you use DOS 2.n, you will probably get an "Out of environment space" error and need to upgrade to DOS 3.n or later. If you get errors with DOS 3.n, see Appendix B on operating system errors and problems.

The ANSI.SYS line is necessary for some of the routines that you will develop in the book. It provides the full 256 ANSI character set, including all characters like åÇäÆ£Ü and Ç. It enables other functions, like screen cursor control and key redefinition, to work. You need to have the DOS file ANSI.SYS in your DOS directory, or you need to change the path in the ANSI.SYS line to wherever your ANSI.SYS file is located.

AUTOEXEC.BAT

AUTOEXEC.BAT is a batch file like any other, with one important exception: it is automatically executed every time the system is turned on. Like CONFIG.SYS, it must be in the root directory.

The AUTOEXEC.BAT file is the place to install your TSR programs like Prokey, Sidekick, and Superkey. It also is the place to install the other setup commands and DOS environment settings that you need to complete your application environment. Examine your AUTOEXEC.BAT file. We recommend that it include the following lines.

AUTOEXEC.BAT

Be sure you are in the root C:\ directory.

`C:\>COPY AUTOEXEC.BAT CON`   Examine it.

The following are DOS environment modifiers.
```
PROMPT $P$G
PATH C:\;C:\DOS;
```
Other information may follow.

`C:\> COPY AUTOEXEC.BAT *.OLD`   Back up your original file, if any.

Edit your AUTOEXEC.BAT file. If you do not have one, create one.

Edit or create your AUTOEXEC.BAT in your root directory, using your tested ASCII text editor. Include the PROMPT and PATH lines similar to those above. Use the discussion below to help you with any modifications.

PROMPT PG is extremely valuable. It causes the DOS prompt to display your current directory path so you don't get lost.

PATH is essential for automatic directory access to programs and DOS commands. The C:\ root and C:\DOS paths are necessary for this book's setup. If your DOS files are in a different directory, include your directory.

You should use whatever is relevant to your setup. Your path will probably contain additional directories.

Reboot

The CONFIG.SYS and AUTOEXEC.BAT changes do not take effect until you reboot your computer.

Reboot to test your configuration and batch file.

If you have problems setting up your environment, or want information about setting up more complex environments, see Appendix B.

If you wish to install a more advanced autoexec batch file, a more extensive example file is given in Appendix D, the Authors' Appendix.

This completes the initial setup for the book's operating system environment. Next, we move on to setting up AutoCAD.

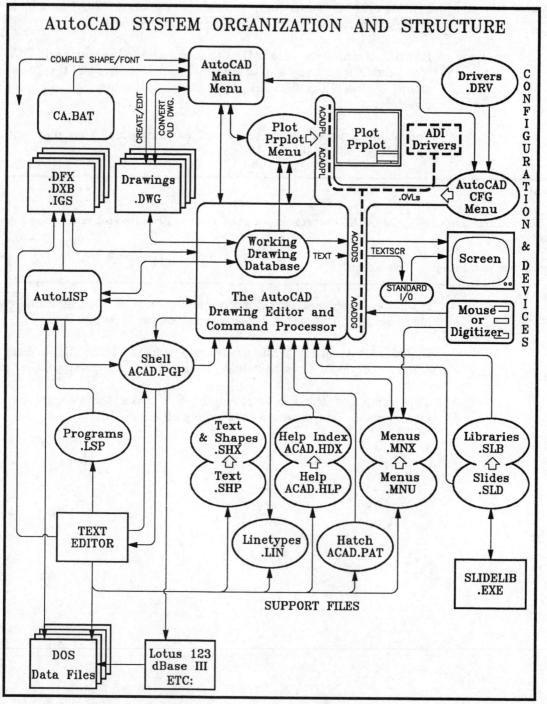

AutoCAD System Organization and Structure

CHAPTER 2

Your AutoCAD System

ORGANIZING AutoCAD AND CRACKING THE SHELL

Getting the right system environment is half the battle in customizing AutoCAD. Setting your AutoCAD system environment with a DOS batch file or UNIX script is a key element in custom applications development. Interactively using your text editor in DOS via AutoCAD's SHELL command is another key element. This chapter shows you how to set up AutoCAD and how to use SHELL to run other programs without leaving AutoCAD. You will also create a prototype drawing to use with the rest of the exercises in the book.

The Benefits of Organizing AutoCAD's Environment

There are three main benefits to organizing your AutoCAD setup. First, controlling AutoCAD's operating system environment lets you make more efficient use of subdirectories and lets you run multiple applications and development configurations. Second, with the help of AutoCAD's SHELL command, you can flip back and forth between developing your custom routines with your text editor and testing them in AutoCAD. Finally, using a customized prototype drawing eliminates the need for inputting most AutoCAD drawing settings and allows you to standardize your drawings.

How-To Skills Checklist

In this chapter, you will learn to:

□ Set the AutoCAD DOS environment variables with a startup batch file.

□ Use SHELL to suspend AutoCAD in the background while you run DOS programs.

□ Add new *commands* to AutoCAD using the ACAD.PGP file.

□ Make a prototype drawing.

Programs and Files

☞   You need to create or verify your CA.BAT and ACAD.PGP files, and configure AutoCAD with the CA-PROTO.DWG file for use with the book.

PROGRAMS

CA.BAT sets AutoCAD's DOS environment variables and starts up AutoCAD.

FILES

ACAD.PGP defines the link between AutoCAD commands and DOS programs.

CA-PROTO.DWG is the prototype drawing used in the book.

A Common Base for Jumping Into the Book

You have already created part of your system environment with the AUTOEXEC.BAT and CONFIG.SYS files. Now you need to crack AutoCAD's SHELL.

PGP: Cracking the SHELL

You can run other programs, utilities, or DOS (or UNIX) commands without having to end AutoCAD or reload your drawing. A few predefined *external commands* are included with AutoCAD to do this. They are set in the ACAD.PGP file. The PGP stands for ProGram Parameter file. To see how SHELL fits into AutoCAD, look at the AutoCAD System Organization and Structure illustration at the beginning of the chapter.

The next exercise will show you how to set up AutoCAD's SHELL to jump directly into a test menu and AutoLISP files. This setup provides the development cycle that you can use throughout the rest of the book.

AutoCAD's standard SHELL features are set in the ACAD.PGP file, giving direct access to DOS commands. This access can be a general purpose access or a predefined jump to a specific DOS command or program. If you have the CA DISK, you have a custom ACAD.PGP file in the \CA-ACAD directory. Otherwise, you will copy the ACAD.PGP file from your \ACAD directory.

➡ *NOTE: UNIX and other multi-tasking environments generally make the need for the SHELL command and the PGP file unnecessary. You may still find this section useful, particularly if you need to adapt any third party software that expects to be in a DOS environment. You might need to replace the DOS utility command names with UNIX utilities.*

Try SHELL with some standard DOS commands. Start with a simple directory command:

PGP Going Outside AutoCAD.

`C:\> CD \CA-ACAD`   Change to the book's directory.

Do NOT copy ACAD.PGP.   You have custom ACAD.PGP file.

`C:\CA-ACAD> COPY \ACAD\ACAD.PGP`   Copy your original PGP file.

`C:\CA-ACAD> \ACAD\ACAD`   Start up AutoCAD.
`Enter selection: 1`   Begin a NEW drawing named EGGS.

`Command: SHELL`   The general SHELL DOS access command.
`DOS Command: DIR ACAD*.*`
`Volume in drive C is DRIVE-C`
`Directory of  C:\CA-ACAD`   The files you copied in the first chapter:

```
ACADPP    OVL     1314    7-06-88   11:53a
ACADPL    OVL     9555    7-16-88    8:22p
ACADDG    OVL     2461    9-04-88    4:07p
ACADDS    OVL    13842    9-14-88    5:21p
ACAD      CFG     1516    9-14-88    5:28p
ACAD      PGP      501   10-19-88    9:00a
```
                                                            And possibly other files. Your file sizes and
                                                            dates will vary.
`6 File(s)   2838528 bytes free`

The PGP File

AutoCAD freed some memory, permitting DOS to run the DIR command. Although the DIR command is not a true AutoCAD command, you can enter it as if it were. Its execution is enabled by its definition in the ACAD.PGP file.

Let's take a look at the contents of the PGP file with another PGP *command*, the DOS command TYPE:

```
Command: TYPE
File to list: ACAD.PGP


CATALOG,DIR /W,30000,*Files: ,0
DEL,DEL,30000,File to delete: ,0
DIR,DIR,30000,File specification: ,0
EDIT,EDLIN,42000,File to edit: ,0
SH,,30000,*DOS Command: ,0
SHELL,,127000,*DOS Command: ,0
TYPE,TYPE,25000,File to list: ,0
```

If your ACAD.PGP listing does not include these lines, you need to find and copy the ACAD.PGP file from your original AutoCAD diskettes.

Each line in the file defines one PGP command, and uses five fields of information. Each field is a piece of information separated by a comma. Look at the last line, which defines the TYPE command. Let's examine the parts of the PGP specification.

Example PGP Fields:

TYPE is the **AutoCAD Command**. The first field tells AutoCAD what name you want to use for the command at the AutoCAD command prompt.

TYPE is the **External Command**. The second field is what AutoCAD feeds to the DOS command line prompt, but it is not displayed inside AutoCAD. The external command field may include spaces and a path. If the external command field is blank, as in the SH and SHELL lines, it is not fed to DOS. DOS is fed only what you enter as input in response to the prompt. UNIX users should refer to the note and table following this section.

30000 is the **Memory Reserve**. This number sets the amount of memory (in bytes) that you want AutoCAD to release for DOS use. Depending on your DOS version, it requires 30000 bytes or more. Memory reserve is the total RAM available under AutoCAD, less a few Kbytes. Certain resident devices, like mice, may interfere with large settings. If you get errors, see Appendix B. UNIX systems ignore the memory reserve setting and can run larger programs. The ACAD default is 30000.

File to list: is **The Prompt**. AutoCAD uses the fourth field as a prompt for user input. It adds the input to the external command field and feeds the combined string to DOS. If an asterisk precedes the prompt, AutoCAD accepts spaces in the input line, but it requires an actual <RETURN> to enter the input.

0 is the **Return Code**. The final item tells AutoCAD which screen to return to in a single screen system. A 0 returns to the text screen, while a 4 returns to whatever screen was displayed just before the PGP command was issued. For information on the other return codes, see the AutoCAD Reference Manual on DXB files.

So, when you entered TYPE and hit <RETURN>, AutoCAD released 30000 bytes of its memory, jumped out to DOS, and issued the text string "TYPE ACAD.PGP" exactly as if you had typed it at the C:\CA-ACAD> DOS prompt. Then, AutoCAD returned directly to the AutoCAD text screen and the command prompt.

➡ *NOTE: For UNIX in the external command field, edit the file and substitute the following:*

DOS	UNIX
DIR /W	ls
DEL	rm
DIR	ls
EDIT	(depends on system)
TYPE	cat

Now, let's add some new utility commands to the PGP file and integrate a text editor.

The following exercise sets up AutoCAD's SHELL to interact easily and effectively. While it is possible to set up a multi-tasking environment, the book uses AutoCAD's SHELL because it is clean, simple, reasonably quick, and available to everyone.

SHELLing Out to DOS

While you are in the EGGS drawing, SHELL out to DOS.

```
Command: SHELL              Remember, SHELL sends DOS only what you enter on
DOS Command: <RETURN>       this prompt line. If you enter nothing with a <RETURN>,

Type EXIT to return to AutoCAD          it simply dumps you into DOS:

The IBM Personal Computer DOS
```

```
Version 3.30 (C)Copyright International Business Machines Corp 1981, 1987
(C)Copyright Microsoft Corp 1981, 1986

C:\CA-ACAD>>
```

Most PGP commands jump into DOS and straight back to AutoCAD without ever showing you a DOS C:\> prompt. If you use the SHELL command and hit a <RETURN>, you simply get a DOS C:\>> with a subdirectory. The double >> indicates that AutoCAD still lurks in the background. You can run as many DOS commands and programs as you want before going back to AutoCAD with EXIT.

If you have the CA DISK, examine your custom ACAD.PGP file and read on. Otherwise, use your text editor to examine and modify the original ACAD.PGP file you copied, as shown below:

Integrating the Text Editor

You should still be SHELLed out to DOS.

 Modify the ED, LSP, and MNU lines to accommodate your text editor.

Enter the following lines. If you need to, modify the ED, LSP, and MNU lines.

Load your editor with the file ACAD.PGP. For Norton's Editor, the book uses:

```
C:\CA-ACAD>> NE ACAD.PGP
```

Add these lines to the end of the copied ACAD.PGP file:

```
SHMAX,,480000,*DOS Command: ,0
REN,RENAME,30000,*Oldname Newname: ,0
DWGS,DIR *.DWG,30000,,0
DUP,COPY,30000,*SOURCEfile(s) TARGETfile(s): ,0
ED,NE,130000,File to edit: ,4
LSP,NE TEST.LSP,60000,,4
MNU,NE TEST.MNU,130000,,4
SHOW,MORE <,30000,File to list: ,0
```

Save the file and exit your editor.

```
C:\CA-ACAD>> EXIT                        Takes you back to AutoCAD.
```

➥ *NOTE: Make sure you use the correct command to start your text editor in the ED, LSP, and MNU lines. Include any command line parameters your editor needs. If your editor requires additional memory, increase the 130000 value in the ED line until your editor works. See Appendix B for more information.*

➥ *TIP: UNIX users should be careful in the use of EXIT. If you are running AutoCAD in the background, EXIT can terminate your parent process and leave AutoCAD stranded. Consult your system administrator.*

➥ *NOTE: UNIX users can use their text editors concurrently with AutoCAD, and can omit the three NE lines. The other lines can be changed as follows:*

```
DOS                        UNIX
RENAME                     mv
DIR *DWG                   ls -l *.dwg
COPY                       cp
MORE <                     more (omit the <)
```

➥ *NOTE: The \ACAD\ACAD.PGP is the factory standard file. AutoCAD only recognizes the name ACAD.PGP, so your file needs to have the same name. Be careful not to mix your files. Keep backup copies of PGP files under unique, unusable names like ACAD-10.PGP for the Release 10 standard file, or CA-ACAD.PGP for the one you just created for this book.*

The book's additions to the PGP file are:

SHMAX runs a maximum size SHELL. You may need to adjust the 480000 size. Make it your available DOS memory less about 10 Kbytes. You can determine the maximum amount of RAM available in your system by running a CHKDSK in DOS.

REN implements the standard DOS command REName, with a prompt.

DWGS lists all drawings in the current directory.

DUP is the DOS command COPY.

ED starts the text editor for use.

LSP starts the text editor and edits TEST.LSP, a testbed AutoLISP file that the book uses.

MNU starts the text editor and edits a testbed menu file.

SHOW is an improved TYPE command, which pauses for pages.

AutoCAD loads the PGP file when it starts a drawing, so you'll have to force it to reload the new PGP file to test it. Quit your drawing, then come back in and test the file. Type ED and a file name at the command line and your text editor will automatically start.

```
Command: QUIT              Yes.
Enter selection: 1         Begin a NEW drawing (again) named EGGS.

Command: ED
File to edit: TEST         Starts your editor in TEST.
```

Quit your text editor and try the other PGP commands you added:

```
Command: SHMAX             <RETURN> to go to DOS, then type EXIT back to AutoCAD.
Command: SHOW              Enter ACAD.PGP and it should display it.
Command: DUP               Test DUP. Back it up for safekeeping.

SOURCEfile(s) TARGETfile(s): ACAD.PGP CA-ACAD.PGP

Command: LSP               Starts editor with new file TEST.LSP. Exits back to AutoCAD.
Command: MNU               Edits a new file TEST.MNU. Exits to AutoCAD.
Command: DWGS              Lists .DWG files, if any.
```

➡ *NOTE: Throughout this book, wherever we use the ED, LSP, and MNU commands, UNIX users should execute their editors directly, then reload any modified files as needed.*

If your editor doesn't automatically load files when you use it, you may have to <RETURN> at the "File to edit:" prompt, and manually load files. If SHMAX fails, reduce its memory reserve slightly. See Appendix B on DOS if you encounter other problems.

➡ *TIP: Customize your ACAD.PGP file by adding additional commands, utilities, or programs that you would like to access from AutoCAD.*

You are nearly finished setting up. All that's left is to clear any possible conflict from any ACAD.LSP file your system may have and to make a CA.BAT startup batch file and a CA-PROTO.DWG prototype drawing.

Avoiding ACAD.LSP Conflict

If your system already has an ACAD.LSP file, AutoCAD automatically loads it at the start of each drawing edit session. Your existing ACAD.LSP file may interfere with the book's setup. If you have the CA DISK, you have its dummy ACAD.LSP in your CA-ACAD directory. Otherwise, play it safe and make a dummy ACAD.LSP file.

Making a Dummy ACAD.LSP File

```
Command: ED
File to edit: ACAD.LSP        Enter the following line:

(prompt "CA empty ACAD.LSP . . . OK.")
```
Save the "empty" file and exit back to AutoCAD.

This empty dummy ACAD.LSP will load instead of any other ACAD.LSP file.

Starting ACAD With a DOS Batch File

AutoCAD lets you preset several of its startup settings. These control its memory usage and support files search order. The book's CA.BAT startup batch file sets memory allocations, file search order, and loads AutoCAD automatically.

Creating a CA.BAT File

 Use or modify the CA.BAT file from the CA-ACAD directory.

Create a new CA.BAT file.

You should still be in EGGS.DWG.

```
Command: ED              Start up your text editor.
File to edit: CA.BAT     Load or create the file, CA.BAT.
```

The CA.BAT file assumes your AutoCAD path is \ACAD. If not, substitute your path.
Enter or modify these lines where applicable:

```
SET ACAD=\ACAD
SET ACADCFG=\CA-ACAD
```

```
SET ACADFREERAM=20
SET LISPHEAP=25000
SET LISPSTACK=10000
C:
CD \CA-ACAD
\ACAD\ACAD %1 %2
CD\
SET ACADCFG=
SET ACAD=
```

Save the CA.BAT file, exit your editor to AutoCAD.

Command: **DUP**   Copy CA.BAT to your root directory, or elsewhere on your PATH.
SOURCEfile(s) TARGETfile(s): **CA.BAT \CA.BAT**

Command: **QUIT**   Then exit to DOS.

➡ *NOTE: The book assumes you will use the CA.BAT file. Type CA when you want to start AutoCAD. If you do not use the CA.BAT file, you may get incorrect DOS environment settings. UNIX users can create an equivalent CA script, described later in this chapter.*

➡ *TIP: Run CHKDSK /F at the DOS prompt on a regular basis. It will verify your hard disk file structure and free up lost clusters. Lost clusters are created when programs crash. Answer N when it asks if you want to convert the clusters to files. Do not run CHKDSK /F in AutoCAD or it will crash.*

The CA.BAT file settings:

SET ACAD= tells AutoCAD where to look if it doesn't find a needed support file in the current directory. AutoCAD searches the current directory first, then this specified support directory, then the program directory. The program directory is the directory where ACAD.EXE was started.

SET ACADCFG= tells AutoCAD where to look for configuration files. Creating several configuration directories and startup batch files is useful if you need to support more than one environment or more than one device, like different plotters.

SET ACADFREERAM= reserves RAM for AutoCAD's working storage. The default is 14K, the maximum depends on the system, usually about 24-26K. If you get "Out of RAM" or other errors, see Appendix B for more information on setting memory use.

SET LISPHEAP= allocates memory for AutoLISP functions and variables (nodes). If you use many AutoLISP programs, or if you use large AutoLISP programs, you may need to increase this value. More HEAP space increases AutoLISP speed by reducing the swapping (paging) of functions. If you have extended memory, using Extended AutoLISP gives you practically unlimited HEAP space.

SET LISPSTACK= defines AutoLISP's temporary working data area during execution. Complex AutoLISP programs using many arguments, recursive and/or nested routines, or large amounts of data may require more stack space.

➡ *TIP: HEAP and STACK space combined cannot exceed 45000 bytes. They reduce memory that otherwise is available to AutoCAD for free RAM and I/O page space. If you encounter problems running large programs, you have to adjust these settings to achieve a working balance. Don't be alarmed. It is not hard. If it works, use it. If it's broken, change your settings until it works.*

➡ *NOTE: Spaces cause errors in DOS variable names and their assigned values:*

```
SET ACADCFG=\CA-ACAD    is acceptable, however
SET ACADCFG = \CA-ACAD  won't work.
```

These set environment settings do not affect memory outside AutoCAD.

➡ *NOTE: If you have Extended AutoLISP, you can install it in the startup batch file. The startup file can also include settings for control of extended memory (SET ACADXMEM=), expanded memory (SET ACADLIMEM=), and extended AutoLISP memory allocation (SET LISPXMEM=). If your system has more than 2 Mb of extended or expanded memory, you may find that limiting its use may improve performance. AutoCAD must use normal memory to implement extended or expanded. Too much extended or expanded memory starves the system for normal I/O page space and free RAM, and can actually reduce performance. See your Installation and Performance Guide for more information.*

That's all there is to the settings. See our Appendix B, your AutoCAD Reference Manual, and the AutoCAD Installation and Performance Guide for more details. The rest of the CA.BAT batch file is made up of the following startup DOS commands.

CA.BAT DOS Commands:

C: ensures that you are on the right drive. If your drive isn't drive C: substitute the appropriate letter.

CD \CA-ACAD changes the current directory to \CA-ACAD.

\ACAD\ACAD %1 %2 executes ACAD. If \ACAD is on your path, you could use ACAD alone here, but specifying the directory avoids having DOS search the path. It also avoids conflict with an ACAD.BAT file, if any exists. The %1 and %2 are replaceable parameters that you will use later in the book when you run CA.BAT. For example, to run a script with the name, NAME, you would enter CA X NAME and CA.BAT would execute this line as \ACAD\ACAD X NAME to run the script.

CD returns you to the root directory.

➡ *TIP: Use SET ACAD= and SET ACADCFG= to clear any SET ACAD=name and SET ACADCFG=name settings that you make in a startup batch file like CA.BAT. It is always good practice to have batch files clear their settings so your other AutoCAD applications will not be directed to the wrong configuration and support files. If you use EXTLISP, you may also clear its memory for other programs with REMLISP.*

Starting ACAD With a UNIX Script

The syntax and process of creating the UNIX equivalent of the CA.BAT file depends on what shell your system is using. Consult your system administrator, and refer to your AutoCAD Installation and Performance Guide for syntax. You can omit all memory settings, such as ACADFREERAM and LISPHEAP, however you need to set ACAD and ACADCFG. You also need to add the appropriate entries to change directories and start up AutoCAD.

Prototype Drawing

AutoCAD uses a default prototype drawing named ACAD.DWG to establish its drawing environment defaults for new drawings. You can modify ACAD.DWG to create your own default setup. You can also configure AutoCAD to use any other drawing as its prototype.

To follow the book, you need a drawing setup that is consistent with ours. The easiest way to achieve this is to create a new standard prototype drawing for use with our customization exercises and configure AutoCAD to use it. This CA-PROTO.DWG establishes a common drawing base.

Drawings and Scale

Unlike drawings on the drafting board, computer drawings are drawn at full scale. But before you start any drawing, you need to know what scale the drawing will be plotted at. Once a scale is known, you derive a *scale factor*. The scale factor is used in various AutoCAD settings and commands. A scale factor is critical to standardizing AutoCAD and is used to determine:

- Limits (sheet size).

- Line width.

- Text height.

- Symbol size.

- Linetype scale.

- Dimension appearance.

- Display controls (snap, grid, and axis).

You determine a scale factor as a multiple of your drawing scale. For example, if a drawing has a scale of 3/8"=1'-0", your scale factor is 32.

```
3/8:12/1 or 1:96/3 for a scale factor of 32.
```

The CA-PROTO drawing is going to be set up for 1/8"=1'-0" scale on a 36" x 24" plotted sheet size. Using the above formula gives you a scale factor of 96. We will explain how to use scale factors in more detail throughout the book. For now, make the CA-PROTO drawing and examine how the settings were determined.

First, start with fresh defaults. Then set your units, limits and a viewport configuration, along with some dimension settings. Finally, set the layer and style conventions for CA-PROTO. If you have the CA DISK, you already have CA-PROTO.DWG.

Cleaning the Slate With CA-PROTO

 Just read this exercise.

 Create CA-PROTO.

`C:\CA-ACAD> CA`	Use CA.BAT to start up.
`Enter selection: 1`	Begin a NEW drawing named CA-PROTO=.
	Make the following settings:
`Command: UNITS`	Set Arch. (4), Denom. 64, Angular frac. 2. Default the rest.
`Command: GRID`	Set to 96. This is 1" at a plot scale of 1:96.
`Command: SNAP`	Set to 24. This is 1/4" on the plot.

```
Command: AXIS          Set to 48. This is 1/2" on the plot. This is optional.
Command: LTSCALE       Set to 36 (0.375 x 96).
Command: LIMITS        Set to 0,0 and 288',192'. That's feet!
Command: ZOOM          Zoom All.
Command: VIEW          Save a view named A, for All.

Command: VPORTS        Split it into three vertical viewports.
Save/Restore/Delete/Join/SIngle/?/2/<3>/4: 3
Horizontal/Vertical/Above/Below/Left/<Right>: V
Regenerating drawing.

Command: VPORTS        Join the right-hand pair.
Save/Restore/Delete/Join/SIngle/?/2/<3>/4: J
Select dominant viewport <current>: <RETURN>
Select viewport to join:  Pick the middle viewport.

Command: ZOOM          Zoom All.

Command: VPORTS        Click on left viewport and trisect it.
Save/Restore/Delete/Join/SIngle/?/2/<3>/4: 3
Horizontal/Vertical/Above/Below/Left/<Right>: H

Command: VPORTS        Join the top left pair.
Save/Restore/Delete/Join/SIngle/?/2/<3>/4: J
Select dominant viewport <current>: <RETURN>
Select viewport to join:  Pick middle left viewport.

Command: VPORTS        Save them.
Save/Restore/Delete/Join/SIngle/?/2/<3>/4: S
?/Name for new viewport configuration: CA
```

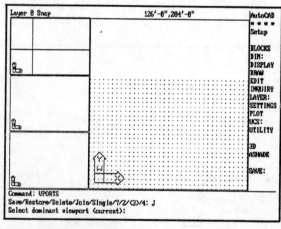

Intermediate Viewports

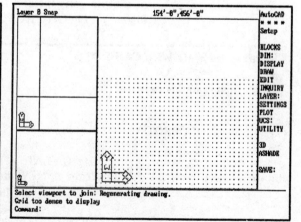

Finished Viewport Configuration

```
Command: VPORTS                 Set a single current.
Save/Restore/Delete/Join/SIngle/?/2/<3>/4: SI

Command: VIEW                   Restore view A.
Command: UCSICON                Set to off.

Command: DIM                    Reset the following dimension variables.
```

Type these in regardless of the defaults shown:

DIMSCALE	96	DIMASZ	3/16	DIMCEN	1/16	DIMEXO	3/32
DIMDLI	3/8	DIMEXE	3/16	DIMTXT	1/8		

```
Dim: EXIT
Command: MENU                   Enter period for none! You will set a menu later.
Command: <Coords on>
```

➡ *NOTE: If you work in a consistent set of limits, or in 3D, you may want to set additional viewports, viewpoints, and UCSs in your prototype drawing.*

DIMSCALE is set to the plot:drawing scale with DIMSCALE=96. DIMASZ will plot a 3/16-inch arrowhead. You need to type in the dimension variable settings regardless of the apparent defaults because the defaults are rounded off. For example, DIMASZ's default is 0.1800, but architectural units misleadingly rounds off the display to 3/16 inch. DIMTXT works the same way, but your fixed height text styles will override it.

CA-PROTO's default limits are set to get started. When you create different size drawings in the customization exercises, you can adjust these limits and scale settings. Later, you will create a menu and an AutoLISP-based setup routine to automatically handle all these drawing setups.

Layering and Style Conventions

Let's establish the layers and text styles for the book's exercises. Unless you have the CA DISK, create the following layers, colors, and linetypes.

Layer Name	State	Color	Linetype
0	Current	7 (white)	CONTINUOUS
ANN02	On	4 (cyan)	CONTINUOUS
ANN03	On	6 (magenta)	CONTINUOUS
CEN31	On	2 (yellow)	CENTER
DSH11	On	3 (green)	DASHED
HID21	On	3 (green)	HIDDEN
OBJ01	On	3 (green)	CONTINUOUS
OBJ02	On	1 (red)	CONTINUOUS
OBJ12	On	1 (red)	DASHED
REF00	On	9 (varies)	CONTINUOUS
REF01	On	2 (yellow)	CONTINUOUS
TXT01	On	3 (green)	CONTINUOUS
TXT02	On	1 (red)	CONTINUOUS

Layer Settings Table

Command: **LAYER**   Create the layers from the table above.

Enter ? * to list and verify all the layers.
Make sure the current layer is 0.

Style Name	Font Files	Height
STANDARD	TXT	0'-0"
STD3-16	ROMANS	1'-6"
STD1-4	ROMANS	2'-0"
STD3-32	ROMANS	0'-9"
STD1-16	ROMANS	0'-6"
STD1-8	ROMANS	1'-0"

Style Settings Table

Command: **STYLE**   Create the text styles in the table above.
All settings are defaults except height.

Set STD1-8 last to leave it current.

QUIT to the Main Menu.

END to save CA-PROTO.

➡ *NOTE: The book's macros and AutoLISP routines assume a fixed height text style. AutoCAD does not prompt for height in TEXT and related commands if you use a fixed height. Some macros and AutoLISP will require modification if you need to use them on variable height styles. The prototype drawing initially fixes text height for a 1:96 plot scale (1/8"=1'-0").*

Establishing a Layering Convention

Customization requires a common layering scheme to automate drawing setups with menu macros. To do this, you need to establish your conventions in advance so that macros can be written for them.

DOS uses wildcard characters to filter file names. AutoCAD uses them to filter layer names, using the same "?" and "*" syntax. The book's layer names are designed for filtering. The names distinguish text from material components, and dimensions from annotations, using names like TXT01 or DIM01 and CEN02. Here is the naming convention:

Objects on Layer	Layer Names
Text	TXT01 thru TXT03
Components, assemblies, and materials	OBJ01 thru OBJ93
Dimensions	DIM01 thru DIM03
Symbols and annotations	ANN01 thru ANN93
Title sheets or forms	REF01 thru REF93
Linetypes – dashed, center, hidden...	DSH01, CEN01, HID01
	thru DSH93, CEN93, HID93
DON'T PLOT reference layers	REF00

Layer Naming Conventions

The first three characters tell you *what* you are dealing with. The two digit code describes the *appearance*. The first appearance code keys to layer linetype. The second keys to plotting 1, 2, or 3 line weight, using the color assigned to the layer. The book groups the standard seven colors and assigns them to three pens. Following are two more tables, showing codes for linetype and pen weight.

LTYPE Code	AutoCAD Linetype	LTYPE Code	AutoCAD Linetype
0	Continuous	5	Dot
1	Dashed	6	Dashdot
2	Hidden	7	Divide
3	Center	8	Border
4	Phantom		

Weight Code	AutoCAD Color	Pen Weight	Pen Size
1	2 (yellow)	Fine	0.25mm
1	3 (green)	Fine	0.25mm
1	5 (blue)	Fine	0.25mm
2	1 (red)	Medium	0.35mm
2	4 (cyan)	Medium	0.35mm
3	6 (magenta)	Bold	0.60mm

Ltype Code and Pen Weight Code Table

There are many alternative layering conventions. For example, OBJ12 is an objects layer using a dashed linetype with a weight code of 2 (color red) which plots with a medium pen. This is a simple yet flexible layering scheme. Feel free to adopt and modify it.

Configuring and Testing CA-PROTO

Your AutoCAD setup probably uses the default name ACAD.DWG as its automatic prototype drawing. New drawings will start up using this default prototype drawing unless you instruct AutoCAD to use a different prototype.

Because you set up a separate configuration for Customizing AutoCAD in the CA-ACAD directory, you can change the default without affecting your normal AutoCAD setup. Do this whether you have the CA DISK or not. You should be in the Main Menu.

Configuring CA-PROTO as the Default Drawing

```
Enter selection: 5                        Configure AutoCAD.
Press RETURN to continue: <RETURN>

Enter selection <0>: 8                    Configure operating parameters.
Enter selection <0>: 2                    Initial drawing setup.
```

```
Enter name of default prototype file for new drawings
or . for none <ACAD>: CA-PROTO
```

Enter selection <0>: **<RETURN> <RETURN> <RETURN>**   3 times to save and exit to
                                               Main Menu.

Enter selection: **1**   Begin a NEW drawing named TEST.
                           It should start up identically to the CA-PROTO you saved.

Command: **QUIT**   And if OK, exit to DOS.

Now you should be on common ground with the book's starting environment. We have a common bootup environment, a common DOS environment for AutoCAD, and a common AutoCAD prototype drawing, CA-PROTO. It's time to move on to creating some symbols and parts to use in customizing AutoCAD.

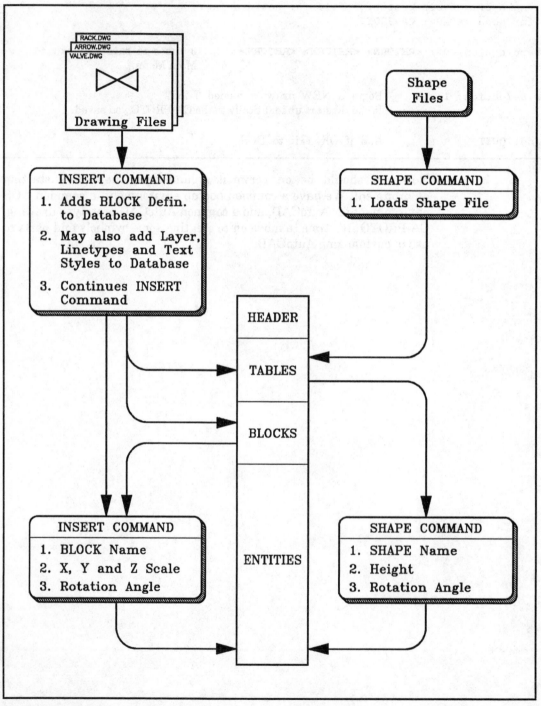

AutoCAD Blocks, Files, Inserts and Shapes

CHAPTER 3

Scaling and Block Management

SYMBOLS and PARTS

Most users build their customized drawing applications around a set of standard symbols and parts. You create and manage symbols and parts by using AutoCAD's block commands. The block commands store the entities that make up symbols and parts as a single definition in a drawing file or as completely new drawings on your hard disk, enabling you to quickly reproduce the symbols and parts you need. This chapter shows you how AutoCAD's block structure works and illustrates a simple layering scheme for managing blocks.

The Benefits of Well-Organized Blocks

There are three main benefits to using blocks to define symbols and parts. First, a well-managed symbol library can reduce your time and effort by allowing you to reuse, modify, redefine and nest blocks. Second, your symbols gain flexibility when you exploit the block features of AutoCAD. Third and most important, you can control visual effects, giving a standardized, custom look to every drawing you make.

How-To Skills Checklist

In this chapter, you will learn how to:

- Make a block, understand where it is stored and how AutoCAD manages the block's definition.

- Draw your symbols so that they work with any plotted scale.

- Control your symbol colors, linetypes, and layer assignments to get both flexibility and control over your drawing.

- Create nested blocks.

Simple Is Better

For typical fixed purpose blocks, like *parts* and *single purpose symbols*, we recommend using BYLAYER entity settings on named layers. This provides good control over your symbols and parts. You can organize data by layers and use layer control to sort data for evaluation. You can control line thickness through layer color so that different layers are plotted by different width pens.

For *multipurpose symbols,* we recommend that you use BYLAYER on layer 0, and control the appearance of your blocks by controlling the layer you insert them on. If you use *pseudo-entities,* like unit-scaled rectangles and ellipses, we recommend that you use layer 0 with color and linetype defined BYBLOCK. This will place your blocks on the current layer with the current color and linetype settings.

Symbols, Parts and Blocks

Let's define *symbols* and *parts.* Then, let's look at AutoCAD's blocks and block commands to make sure that we have a common understanding of how AutoCAD treats blocks.

SCALE	PARTS	SYMBOLS
1/2" = 1'–0"	INSERTED FULL SCALE	INSERTED 24X PLOT SIZE
1/4" = 1'–0"	INSERTED FULL SCALE	INSERTED 48X PLOT SIZE
1/8" = 1'–0"	INSERTED FULL SCALE	INSERTED 96X PLOT SIZE

Plotted Scale of Parts and Symbols

Symbols represent intangible objects. A symbol in the drawing requires a size adjustment based on the plotting scale. For example, a 1/4 inch annotation bubble would have to be 24 inches in your drawing so it would plot 1/4 inch in a 1/8"=1'-0" plot.

Parts represent real objects. A chair is a part. So is a tank, column, window or desk. Parts are drawn or inserted in AutoCAD at full scale, their actual dimensions in the real world.

Unit parts are blocks drawn at a one-unit scale and stretched by their insertion scale to represent sizes of real objects. Examples include doors, hex bolt heads, or a simple 1 x 1 square that can be stretched to represent any rectangular object.

Use AutoCAD's BLOCK command to make symbols and parts.

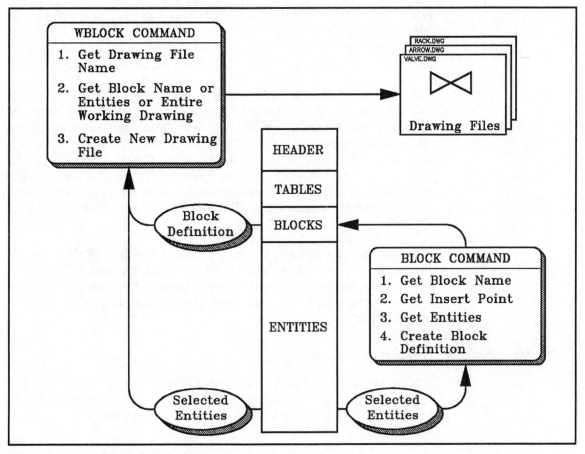

BLOCK and WBLOCK Commands

Block Commands and Block Definitions

When you use the BLOCK command, the selected entities are erased. BLOCK does not create a visible entity, it creates what we'll call a block definition or block def in the AutoCAD drawing. There is no such thing as an *entity* called a block. A block definition invisibly holds a record of the original entities. Use the INSERT command to duplicate an image of the block's entities.

The INSERT command places an entity called an insert in the drawing. However, the LIST command confusingly lists it as a block reference. Block reference is a more apt description than insert, but AutoLISP and DXF use insert. We refer to the entity as a block insert, or just an insert. A block insert is a very simple entity. It references, by name, the block def from a table of definitions. It inserts an image of the block's entities, not an actual duplicate set of entities. Each insert is modified by the scale, rotation, and location of its insertion. However, if you insert a block with *name, AutoCAD does not create an insert. INSERT*name inserts an actual duplicate copy of the block def's entities. When you insert a drawing, all blocks defined in it become defined in your current drawing.

When you use WBLOCK, you create a new drawing file, or you overwrite an existing drawing file. There is no such thing as a wblock. The WBLOCK command does not create a block def, but you can insert any drawing file, including those created by WBLOCK, into a drawing. An inserted drawing becomes a block def in the current drawing. Any block def can be BLOCKED or WBLOCKED, and any drawing file can be INSERTed to create a block def in the current drawing. If you insert a drawing with *name, it does not create a block def. It inserts a copy of the drawing entities.

It doesn't matter whether you create a block def with BLOCK or INSERT. The block def may contain a single entity within a complex drawing. It may contain many entities with many layers and linetypes. It may itself contain another block def. But if you create many blocks, you need to organize them.

How to Organize Blocks

You can create many individual drawing files for use as block inserts and store them in a directory. Or you can create and store many block defs in a single drawing and insert the whole drawing when you need one of the block defs.

We recommend that you combine both methods of block organization in your customization. In this book, we create a group of related symbols in a single *library* drawing, then export each to separate files with WBLOCK for insert use. This allows you to update them easily by editing the library drawing and WBLOCKing the modified blocks again.

Your block defs will grow rapidly as you develop your application. Keep your block library drawings in separate subdirectories. Later, you can subdivide these into other categories based on your application. If you have more than a hundred blocks in a subdirectory, it is a good idea to subdivide the blocks further.

To actually use symbols and parts, you need to scale them in your drawing. Let's look at scaling.

Scaling Parts and Symbols

Scaling parts is easy because you build and insert them at full scale.

To see how symbol scaling works, consider the Pointing Arrow illustration shown below. It's designed for insertion at the end of a leader line. What size should it be?

You have two basic options in scaling symbols. You can base your symbols on an insertion factor of 1.0, and define one set of symbols for each plot scale that you use. Or you can define your symbols at the exact plotted size that you want on the final output. This scale is 1:1 to the plotted paper. You scale it by the drawing's scale factor when you insert it.

Both scale methods work, but working at 1:1 to the paper output lets you think and program to the paper size. We recommend creating symbols at 1:1 scale to the paper. You only need one defined block for each symbol, and you can adjust the size of an inserted symbol with scale factors.

Create the arrow. To help you visualize symbol creation at the actual plot size, draw a polyline to represent an 11" x 8 1/2" plot sheet in a viewport. The 88 by 68 foot limits will plot 11" x 8 1/2" at 1/8"=1'-0". Create the arrow with a polyline, WBLOCK the arrow (unless you have the CA DISK), and insert it at a drawing scale of 96.

LIMITS	Set limits from 0,0 to 88',68'.
VPORTS	Restore CA viewports.
In the Lower Left Viewport:	
SNAP	Set snap to 1/16"
GRID	Set the grid to 1"
UCSICON	Turn the icon off
ZOOM	Window from 0,0 to 11",8-1/2"
In the Right Viewport:	
UCSICON	Turn the icon off
ZOOM	Window from 0,0 to 88',68'

Symbol Scale and Plot Scale Settings

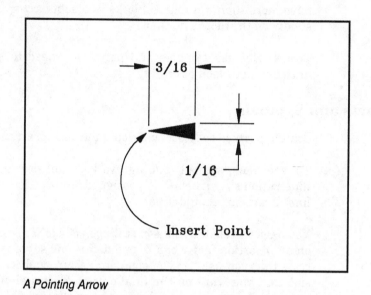

A Pointing Arrow

Symbol Scale and Plot Scale

```
C:\CA-ACAD> CA                 Use CA.BAT to start ACAD.
Enter selection: 1             Begin a NEW drawing named BLOCKS.
```

Make the settings shown in the table above.
Make the right viewport active.

```
Command: PLINE                 Draw an 88' x 68' rectangle with lower left corner at 0,0.
                               This outlines our full scale drawing area.
Command: PLINE                 Draw an 11" x 8 1/2" rectangle with lower left corner at 0,0.
```

The large rectangle represents an 11" x 8 1/2" sheet at 1/8" scale. The grid represents 1" at 1/8" scale. The small rectangle, magnified in the lower left viewport, represents the same sheet as it would appear when plotted. Use the exercise sequence below to draw the arrow in the lower left viewport at the exact size it would appear when plotted. Then insert the arrow in the right viewport to represent the same arrow at the scale required for the electronic drawing.

Make the lower left viewport active.

```
Command: PLINE                 Draw the ARROW.
From point:                    Pick absolute point 2,2.
```

```
Arc/Close/Halfwidth/Length/Undo/Width/<Endpoint of line>: W
Starting width <'-0">: <RETURN>
Ending width <'-0">: 1/16
Arc/Close/Halfwidth/Length/Undo/Width/<Endpoint of line>: @3/16,0  The arrow head.
Arc/Close/Halfwidth/Length/Undo/Width/<Endpoint of line>: <RETURN>  Exit pline.
```

 Do not Wblock the arrow. Skip to the INSERT below.

Continue the exercise with the BLOCK and OOPS command.

Command: **WBLOCK**	Wblock it to ARROW, with the insertion base point at 2,2 to the arrow's point.
Command: **OOPS**	Oops it back for comparison.

Make the right viewport active.

Command: **INSERT**	ARROW at 16',48', scale 96, rotation 0.
Command: **DIM1**	Draw a leader for comparison.
Dim: **LEA**	
Leader start:	Pick absolute point 16',28'.
To point:	Pick absolute point 24',36'.
To point:	Pick absolute point 28',36'.
To point: **<RETURN>**	
Dimension text <>: **TEXT**	

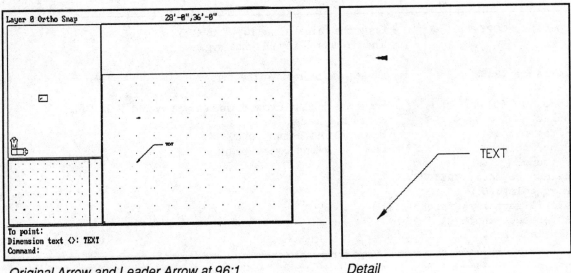

Original Arrow and Leader Arrow at 96:1   *Detail*

The arrows look proportionately the same, but the arrow in the right viewport is actually 96 times larger than the arrow in the lower left. If your DIMSCALE is correct, the block and leader arrows will look the same. DIMSCALE should be 96, the same as the scale factor. Finish the exercise below to see exactly how scale works. First copy the arrows to the lower left viewport to compare their size. Then use the SCALE command to simulate the plot process.

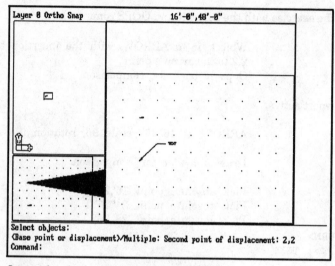

Comparing the Inserted Arrow to the Original

Command: **COPY**

Copy the arrow from 16',48' to 2",5".
The arrow is clearly 96 times larger.

Command: **ERASE**

Erase last to remove the arrow.

Command: **SCALE**
Select objects: **C**
First corner:
Other corner:
3 found.
Select objects: **<RETURN>**
Base point: **0,0**
<Scale factor>/Reference: **R**
Reference length <1>: **96**
New length: **1**

Scale the leader arrow down, as you would if plotting.
Select the leader.
Pick the first corner point.
Pick the second corner point.

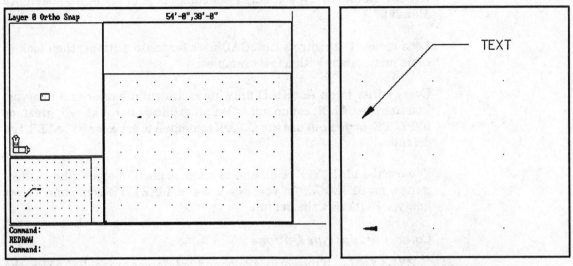

Screen After SCALE   *Detail of Lower Left Viewport*

The arrow and leader appear in the lower left viewport at the correct plot scale. If you examine the text, you will find it is exactly 1/8" high.

Original arrow size	1/16" x 3/16"
Insertion scale factor	96
Arrow size in AutoCAD drawing	6" x 18"
Plotting scale	1:96
Final size on paper	1/16" x 3/16"

The Scale Process

You will use the WBLOCKed arrow to make some leader macros in later exercises.

Now that you understand the book's convention for scaling blocks, let's look at some layer/color/linetype issues that you will encounter in customization.

Layers/Colors/Linetypes and Blocks

Symbols and parts frequently contain entities with a variety of layers, colors and linetypes. In fact, AutoCAD is so flexible that layer, color and linetype settings in blocks can become complicated and confusing. We assume you are familiar with AutoCAD's ways of controlling layers, colors and linetypes, but if you need to refresh your memory, refer to

INSIDE AutoCAD (New Riders Publishing) or your AutoCAD Reference Manual.

Let's review the controls AutoCAD uses for these settings, then look at some interactions with a few examples.

Every entity in an AutoCAD drawing is drawn in a color and linetype. You use the COLOR command to set an explicit color, like red, green or BYBLOCK, or you can use the COLOR command to set color BYLAYER, the default.

You use the LINETYPE command to set an explicit linetype, like dashed, center, or BYBLOCK, or you can use the LINETYPE command to set linetype BYLAYER, the default.

Color and Linetype Options

BYLAYER — If the entity's color and/or linetype are set BYLAYER, the LAYER command settings control the entity's color and/or linetype. For example, the ARROW block was created on layer 0, with both color and linetype settings set BYLAYER. Each inserted ARROW shows up on the layer that is current when it is inserted, with the color and linetype current for that layer. If you change the ARROW's layer, the color and linetype change to the settings of the new layer.

Explicit Entity Color/Linetype — If you explicitly set or assign an entity color and/or an entity linetype, it overrides the default settings for the layer. The entities are *molded* or *modified* by the explicit settings. CHPROP is the AutoCAD command that can modify them further. If you make a setting explicit, AutoCAD stores the setting with the entity.

BYBLOCK — is treated as an explicit setting. Color BYBLOCK is stored as color 0. BYBLOCK means *not yet established*. It is similar to the action of Layer 0.

Layer 0 — Although not actually an option, it helps to think of layer 0 as layer BYBLOCK. Blocks created on layer 0 float to the layer current at the time of their insertion.

Blocks with color and linetypes BYBLOCK also adopt the current settings at the time of their insertion, whether the current setting is BYLAYER or explicit. Layer 0 blocks with settings BYBLOCK act exactly like primitive entities. These make good general purpose blocks, like one-unit squares and circles that are stretched to insert as rectangles and ellipses.

➡ *NOTE: The color and linetype shown by the LIST command for a block insertion are confusing. You can't see an insert, just the entities within it. But the LIST command shows the properties of the insert, and not those of the inner entities.*

Let's see how some of these block combinations work.

Layers, Colors and Linetypes

Continue in the previous BLOCKS drawing.

Command: **VPORTS**	Set lower left viewport to SIngle.
Command: **ZOOM**	Center at 40'3",32' and 13 inches high.
Command: **SNAP**	Set snap to 1".
Command: **CIRCLE**	Draw a 1" radius circle with the center at 39'10,32'. It's white and continuous.
Command: **LAYER**	Set HID21 current.
Command: **CIRCLE**	Draw a 2" radius circle. It's green and HIDDEN.
Command: **LTSCALE**	Set the linetype scale to 1.
Command: **COLOR**	Set color to red.
Command: **LINETYPE**	Set linetype to DIVIDE.
Command: **CIRCLE**	3" radius. It's red and linetype's DIVIDE, though on layer HID21.
Command: **COLOR**	Set color BYBLOCK.
Command: **LINETYPE**	Set linetype BYBLOCK.
Command: **CIRCLE**	4" radius. It's white and CONTINUOUS.

The circle's explicit settings overrode the current layer's defaults. The four-inch BYBLOCK explicit settings also overruled the layer for the new circle. You can verify these with the LAYER and STATUS commands.

➡ *NOTE: LTSCALE was set to 36 in the prototype drawing. That is an appropriate scale for plotting at 1/8"=1'0". But we set it to 1 so we could see the linetypes better in this exercise.*

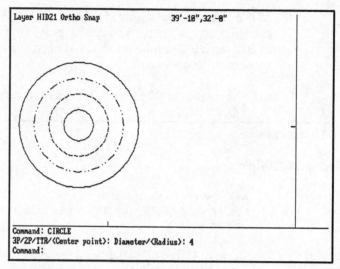

Layer HID21 Ortho Snap   39'-18",32'-8"

```
Command: CIRCLE
3P/2P/TTR/<Center point>: Diameter/<Radius>: 4
Command:
```

BYLAYER, Explicit and BYBLOCK Circles

Command: **STATUS**	Look at the settings.
Command: **LIST**	Select all circles and examine.
Command: **LAYER**	Enter ?. It shows the current layer as HID21, (green and HIDDEN).
Command: **BLOCK**	Block all to CIRCLES, insertion base at center.
Command: **INSERT**	Insert CIRCLES at 39'10,32'. They're unchanged except the 1" layer 0 circle floated to current layer HID21, green and HIDDEN.
Command: **ERASE**	Erase the CIRCLES block.
Command: **COLOR**	Set color to blue.
Command: **LINETYPE**	Set linetype to DIVIDE.
Command: **INSERT**	Insert CIRCLES at 39'10,32'. The 4" BYBLOCK circle adopted the current explicit settings.
Command: **COLOR**	Set color to BYLAYER.
Command: **LINETYPE**	Set linetype to BYLAYER.
Command: **LAYER**	Set layer REF01 current.
Command: **INSERT**	Insert CIRCLES at 40'8,32'. Now the 1" layer 0 BYLAYER circle and the 4" BYBLOCK circle adopted the current settings, the layer defaults.
Command: **CHPROP**	Change the first insert to layer REF01. The 4" BYBLOCK remains blue DIVIDE, but the 1" BYLAYER becomes yellow CONTINUOUS.
Command: **END**	You will need the drawing later.

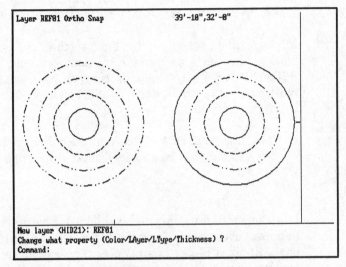

```
Layer REF01 Ortho Snap          39'-18",32'-8"




New layer <HID21>: REF01
Change what property (Color/LAyer/LType/Thickness) ?
Command:
```

BYBLOCK vs. BYLAYER

If the four-inch BYBLOCK circle originally had been inserted with current settings BYLAYER, it would have become BYLAYER and CHPROP would affect it.

An entity that looks red on the screen can be explicitly red, or can be set BYLAYER with a layer color of red. The screen display is the same. However, these settings have an important effect on the organization and ease of updating blocks in customization.

If you organize your entities BYLAYER, you can manipulate a group of entities using the layer on/off and freeze/thaw options. If a layer's color and/or linetype is changed, it changes all entities on the layer unless they have overriding explicit colors or linetypes. If properties are explicit, say red dashed, you can still freeze/thaw and turn the layer on/off, but you can't reset entity color or linetype within a block.

BYLAYER entities within the block def do not have explicit colors and linetypes. They become chameleons and assume the insert's properties, adopting the time-of-insertion defaults of the current layer.

Deciding to use BYLAYER, BYBLOCK, or explicit colors and linetypes is important to your block construction. Once the block is defined, explicit settings are locked in. This means you can't easily change them unless you redefine the block! However, if you set color and linetype BYLAYER, you can change them easily by changing the default for the layer. Organizing your drawings BYLAYER imposes a structure you can easily control by turning layers on/off and freezing/thawing them. Simple schemes for blocks are usually better than complex schemes.

Mixing explicit settings with layers settings can be confusing. For typical blocks, like parts and single purpose symbols, we recommend using BYLAYER entity settings to control your symbols and parts. For multipurpose symbols, use BYLAYER on layer 0, and control your blocks by layer insertion.

➥ *TIP: Use BYBLOCK if you need the colors and linetypes of entities to vary, like a primitive entity from one insertion to another.*

3D Blocks

Drawing in 3D is more complex than 2D. How you use and manage blocks becomes even more important for efficient production. The use of one-unit-sized blocks is a popular time-saving technique. For example, you can insert a 1 x 1 square at varying X,Y scales to create any size rectangle. The copying, arraying and mirroring of such blocks also drastically reduces the number of entities in complex drawings. The following exercise demonstrates the use of a 1 x 1 x 1 unit-scaled 3D block in quickly building a cylindrical joint.

Layers in 3D take on a new meaning. A *layer* becomes an organizational concept and loses its 2D similarity to overlay drafting. Any layer may include any entity anywhere in 3D space. When you examine the following block, you will see that it includes snap node points and construction lines on a layer named REF3D. This layer is normally frozen or turned off. It may be turned on if needed for object snapping points, or if the block is exploded and edited.

Cylindrical objects vary widely in size and may meet a plane or other cylinders at any angle. However, any joint between equal-sized cylinders or a cylinder and plane can be quickly constructed from three or fewer 1 x 1 x 1 unit blocks.

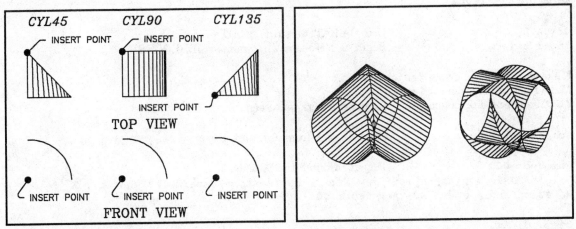

Unit Cylindrical Blocks in Plan View   Joint Constructions

To build the CYL45 block, create a quarter arc and elliptical polyline on a construction layer. The polyline is formed by converting a 3D line and tangent curve fitting it. Then use RULESURF to create the mesh. Use layer 0 so it will float to the current layer on insertion. Work in the right viewport and use the upper left viewport for a 3D view.

VPORTS	Restore CA viewports.
LIMITS	Set limits from 0,0 to 4,3.
LAYER	Make REF3D, color blue, leave current.
In the Right Viewport:	
SNAP	Set snap to 0.1
GRID	Set grid to 1
ORTHO	Turn ortho on
SETVAR	UCSFOLLOW to 1
ZOOM	Center 0,0 Height 4
In the Top Left Viewport:	
VPOINT	Set point of view to 1,-2,1
GRID	Set grid to 1
ZOOM	Center 0,0 Height 4

3DBLOCKS Drawing Settings

Creating a 3D Block

```
C:\CA-ACAD> CA                    Use CA.BAT to start ACAD.
Enter selection: 1                Begin a NEW drawing named 3DBLOCKS.
```

Make the settings shown in the table above.
Make the right viewport active.
ZOOM as needed throughout exercise to keep work on screen.

```
Command: LINE                     Draw in 3D from 0,1,1 to 1,0,0.

Command: UCS                      Tilt up around the X axis.
Origin/ZAxis/3point/Entity/View/X/Y/Z/Prev/Restore/Save/Del/?/<World>: X
Rotation angle about X axis <0.0>: 90

Command: ARC
Center/<Start point>: C
Center: 0,0
Start point: 1,0
Angle/Length of chord/<End point>: 0,1

Command: UCS                      Rotate Y axis -45 degrees into plane of the line.

Command: PEDIT                    Turn line into 1/4 ellipse.
Select polyline:                  Pick the line.
Entity selected is not a polyline
Do you want to turn it into one? <Y> <RETURN>
Close/Join/Width/Edit vertex/Fit curve/Spline curve/Decurve/Undo/eXit <X>: E
Next/Previous/Break/Insert/Move/Regen/Straighten/Tangent/Width/eXit <N>: T
Direction of tangent:             Pick any point at an angle of 0 degrees.
Next/Previous/Break/Insert/Move/Regen/Straighten/Tangent/Width/eXit <N>:<RETURN>
Next/Previous/Break/Insert/Move/Regen/Straighten/Tangent/Width/eXit <N>: T
Direction of tangent: 270
Next/Previous/Break/Insert/Move/Regen/Straighten/Tangent/Width/eXit <N>: X
Close/Join/Width/Edit vertex/Fit curve/Spline curve/Decurve/Undo/eXit <X>: F
Close/Join/Width/Edit vertex/Fit curve/Spline curve/Decurve/Undo/eXit <X>: X

Command: UCS                      Return to World.
Command: SETVAR                   Set SURFTAB1 to 12.

Command: POINT                    Add a node point for future osnaps.
Point: 0,0

Command: LAYER                    Set 0 current.

Command: RULESURF                          Finally, create the mitered surface.
Select first defining curve:               Select arc near intersection.
Select second defining curve:              Select pline near intersection.
```

```
Command: SELECT            Preselect before freezing the REF3D entities.
Select objects: C          Select all four entities.

Command: LAYER             Freeze REF3D.

Command: WBLOCK
File name: CYL45
Block name: <RETURN>
Insertion base point: 0,1

Select objects: P          Previous even gets the frozen construction lines.
4 found.
Select objects:<RETURN>

Command: SAVE
```

➤ *TIP: You can quickly build the CYL90 and CYL135 blocks by modifying the CYL45 block. For example, to create CYL135, INSERT *CYL45, thaw REF3D, regenerate, ERASE the mesh, ROTATE the polyline ellipse 90 degrees, RULESURF and WBLOCK.*

Now, see how quickly you can build a cross joint using only CYL45.

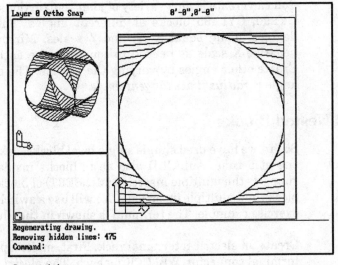

Cross Joint

Building With 3D Blocks

```
Command: INSERT
Block name (or ?): CYL45    At 0,0 with scale .75 (3/4" radius) and rotation 0.


Command: MIRROR                         Select Last, then:
First point of mirror line: 0,0
Second point:                           Pick a point 90 degrees above the first.
Delete old objects? <N> <RETURN>


Command: ARRAY              Create the full top half. Select Last and Previous, then:
Rectangular or Polar array (R/P): P
Center point of array: 0,0
Number of items: 4
Angle to fill (+=ccw, -=cw) <360>: <RETURN>
Rotate objects as they are copied? <Y> <RETURN>


Command: UCS                Rotate the UCS 90 degrees around X.
Command: MIRROR             Mirror everything down horizontally, creating the bottom half.


Click upper left viewport to make it active.


Command: HIDE               Take a look.
```

You can create a wide variety of joint contructions by combining CYL45, CYL90, CYL135 blocks at different angles. The default angle is 45 degrees, using equal X, Y, and Z scales. Mirror the blocks or use a negative X scale as needed to construct the entire cylindrical section. Create other angles by varying the Y scale. The correct Y scale for any angle is *radius times tangent angle*.

Multiple and Nested Blocks

So far, we have used simple single level blocks, asking you to insert them one at a time. AutoCAD also nests blocks inside other blocks. And it supports the multiple insertion (MINSERT) of blocks. Let's look at nested blocks and multiple insertions. We will use a switchboard terminal as the exercise example. The terminal is shown in the illustration below.

Create an electrical terminal rack. First, make a positive and a negative terminal connector, WBLOCKing each. The electrical rack needs 16 rows of terminals, one POSitive and one NEGative per row. Insert the top row and add "1" for the text number. Then, array the three objects downward.

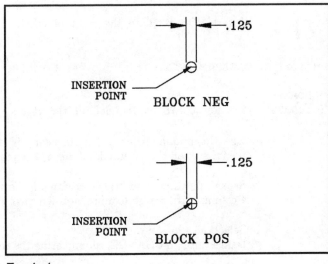

Terminals

SNAP	GRID	ORTHO
.0625	.5	On

LIMITS	Set limits from 0,0 to 11,8.5
LAYER	Make OBJ02 current
ZOOM	Zoom Window from 0,0 to 3,2.5

Terminals Drawing Settings

Nesting Blocks

Enter Selection: **1**   Begin a NEW drawing named TERM-BLK=.

Make the settings shown in the table above.

Command: **SAVE**   Save the drawing settings for later.
Do not SAVE again or END it later.

 You have the terminal blocks on the disk.

 Create the blocks from the illustration above.

Command: **INSERT**   Insert NEG at 1:1 scale in the upper left screen corner.

Command: **INSERT**   Insert POS @.5,0 to the right of NEG.

Command: **STYLE**
Text style name (or ?) <STANDARD>: **STD3-32**   Create for full scale.
New style.
Font file <TXT>: **ROMANS**
Height <0.0000>: **.09375**   Set for .09375 at 1:1, default the rest.

Command: **TEXT**   Use the middle point option to center the start
                                       point between the terminals. Enter a "1" as text.

Command: **ARRAY**   Select all three and use a rectangular array. Use 16 rows,
                                       1 column with a unit distance between rows of -.125 (minus .125).

Command: **CHANGE**   Select all the text.
                                       Dance through CHANGE, renumbering the terminals 1 thru 16.

Command: **WBLOCK**   Make this into one block called RACK. Pick the insertion
                                       base point just above top center and select all 48 entities.

Two RACK Inserts

Command: **STATUS**   Note the number of entities in the drawing, about 54,
                                       but erasures and errors count!
Command: **INSERT**   Hit a "?" to see the defined blocks list, only POS and NEG.
Command: **QUIT**   Quit the drawing. You saved it before.

```
Enter selection: 2            Edit the TERM-BLK again.

Command: STATUS              No entities yet.
Command: INSERT              Hit a "?" to see that no blocks are defined.

Command: INSERT              Insert the RACK in the top left of the drawing.
Command: STATUS              Compare the number of entities to before. Sixty now.
Command: INSERT              Hit a "?" to see defined blocks list: RACK, POS and NEG.

Command: INSERT              Insert another RACK in the top center of the drawing.
Command: STATUS              Compare the number of entities. Only one more than above.
```

Remember, blocks are not entities. When you WBLOCKed RACK, the entities that made it up were erased, but they temporarily remain in the drawing database until you re-edit it. Deleted blocks are purged from the drawing database when you reload an existing drawing. The block RACK was not yet defined in the current drawing's block definitions.

When you re-edited the drawing and inserted RACK, AutoCAD put the definition, as well as the nested NEG and POS, in the block definitions. AutoCAD counts each of the items within the block definition in the entity count, even though they don't occur in the drawing as individual entities.

Your nested block RACK contains 16 copies of the NEG block insert, 16 copies of the POS block insert, as well 16 text entities. If RACK, POS and NEG were not blocks, the AutoCAD drawing would store 32 circles, 48 lines and 16 text entities, a total of 96 entities.

Nesting blocks makes drawing files smaller. The first insertion of RACK added 60 entities. Without nesting, it would have added 96 individual entities. When you insert additional RACKs, AutoCAD adds only one more entity, the RACK insert, and simply *looks up* the RACK data. This is why there is only one definition allowed per block in any one drawing. Since all definitions are stored in a table, only one description can exist for each named block.

MINSERTs of Blocks

For repetitive block insertions, AutoCAD provides a more compact way of storing the data, the MINSERT command. MINSERT is like a combined INSERT and ARRAY command. MINSERT inserts the block, but it also prompts for the number of rows and columns.

MINSERTed RACKs

Reconstruct your RACK, using MINSERT for the top positive and negative symbols.

Command: **EXPLODE**	Explode one of the RACKs.
Command: **ERASE**	Erase the other RACK and each of the 16 POS and NEG inserts in the exploded RACK, leaving only the 16 text entities.
Command: **STATUS**	Note the number of entities in the drawing.

```
Command: MINSERT
Block name (or ?) <RACK>: NEG
Insertion point:                     Pick point .25 to the left of the 1.
                                     Default scale to 1 and rotation to 0.

Number of rows (---) <1>: 16
Number of columns (|||) <1>:
Unit cell or distance between rows (---): -.125      That's minus .125.
```

Command: **MINSERT**	Repeat the minsert with the POS block and same parameters. It should look identical to original RACK.
Command: **STATUS**	Note the number of entities. Only two more, not 32!

MINSERTed Rack

Command: **WBLOCK**	WBlock it to RACKM.
Command: **INSERT**	Insert RACKM at the left. The duplicate definitions are ignored.
Command: **STATUS**	Note entity number. Twenty-one more, not 60 like RACK.

Command: **INSERT**	*RACK to make a comparison.
Command: **ERASE**	Erase the terminals.
Command: **WBLOCK**	All of the text to file name RACKTEXT.
Command: **DIR**	Do a DIRectory of RACK*.* and compare the files.
Command: **QUIT**	You can also delete files RACK*.DWG.

Compare the file sizes. RACKTEXT is the base file size. RACKM is about 880 bytes larger, and RACK is about 1640 bytes larger. You can see from the file size of RACKM that MINSERT is about twice as efficient. RACK contains 32 insert entities. RACKM contains two MINSERTs. Both contain the same text.

➡ *TIP: Use MINSERT for very regular, fixed patterns that will not be edited.*

Side Effects of Blocks

There are drawbacks to using blocks. You cannot edit inserted entities as easily as individual entities. You can scale, rotate, copy, move or change them to different layers. But if you have to change a part of the internal structure of the insert, you're out of luck unless you can EXPLODE it.

EXPLODE breaks down an insert one nest level at a time. It replaces the insert entity with the first level of the block definition's individual entities, including any nested blocks. Exploding an insert allows easy editing of its components, but it has one small, often annoying side affect: the entities are put back to their original layers of definition. Inserts with different X,Y,Z scales cannot be exploded.

Blocks vs. Shapes

While we are looking at blocks, let's look at shapes. AutoCAD has an older command called SHAPE. SHAPE stores symbols in a compact form. AutoCAD's text fonts are special shape files. Many AutoCAD users are curious about shapes and wonder about using them in applications, but haven't played with them. We have included a shape file, called CA.SHP, on the CA DISK. You can use this file to compare the difference in speed and file size in drawing with shapes versus blocks.

AutoCAD thinks in vectors when displaying and plotting, not lines, arcs, and circles. Entities are groups of data used to determine how to draw vectors. Shapes are hexadecimal-coded vector lists that tell AutoCAD how far and in which direction to draw. Since shapes are already defined in vector format, AutoCAD handles and draws them faster. AutoCAD stores each shape as a single reference in a drawing. The actual makeup of the shape is stored outside the drawing file in a file saved with the .SHX extension. The .SHX file is a binary file compiled from the .SHP definition file before use. You can globally update shapes in all drawings by modifying and recompiling the shape definition file.

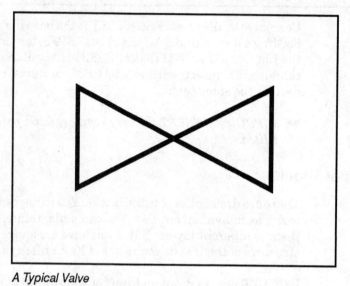

A Typical Valve

Are You In SHAPE? A Performance Test

The CA DISK includes a file named CA.SHP which is a typical valve symbol.

If you don't have the CA DISK, just read along. Skip doing the exercise.

Enter selection: **7**	AutoCAD Main Menu option 7 to compile shape file CA.SHX.
Enter NAME of shape file (default term-blk): **CA**	
Enter selection: **1**	Begin a NEW drawing named SHAPES.
Command: **LOAD**	Load shape file CA.
Command: **SHAPE**	
Shape name (or ?): **VALVE**	Pick a point in the center. Drag its height so it's big enough to see, and use 0 rotation. Notice that it scales equally X,Y.
Command: **LINE**	Trace another symbol over the shape. It doesn't need to be exact for the test results to be valid.
Command: **BLOCK**	Block the lines only to the name VALVE.
Command: **ARRAY**	Do a large array, 24 x 20 or more, of the shape VALVE.
Command: **ZOOM**	All.

Command: **REGEN**	Time it.
Command: **WBLOCK**	Wblock all the shape valves to VALVE-S.
Command: **INSERT**	Insert the block VALVE.
Command: **ARRAY**	Do the same array, 24 x 20 or more, of the block VALVE.
Command: **REGEN**	Time it.
Command: **WBLOCK**	Wblock the array of blocks to VALVE-B.
Command: **DIR**	Do a directory of VALVE*.* and compare file size.
Command: **QUIT**	You can also delete VALVE-?.DWG.

An Array of Valves

The test shows something like a 25 percent faster drawing regeneration, and a 30 percent smaller file size. The proportional file size savings is actually greater, since an empty drawing file is about 2000 bytes.

Shapes are more efficient than blocks when the drawings you produce contain few insertions of complex symbols. Why doesn't everyone use shapes? Shapes have no flexibility in editing. You can't break, stretch, or assign multiple colors to shapes. You can't explode them, and they only support one osnap mode, insert. Finally, shapes are difficult to create. Blocks are easy.

➡ *TIP: Consider using shapes if you have standardized, complex symbols that are never edited in a drawing.*

This completes the basic setup tour of AutoCAD. It's time to start making some menu macros.

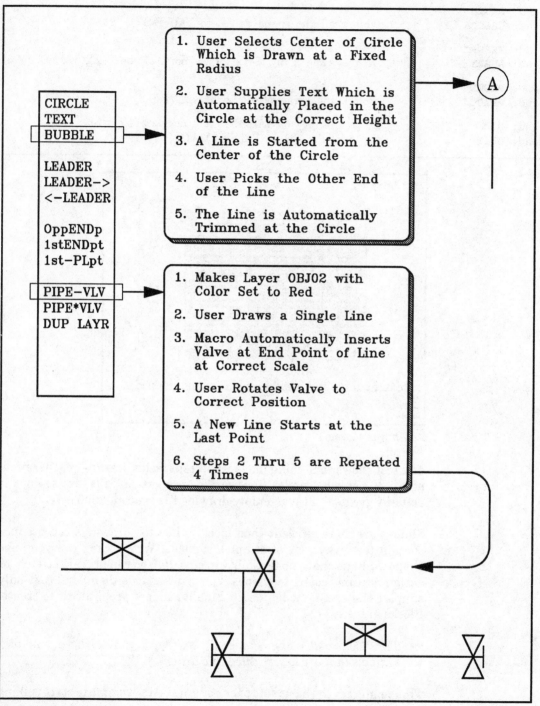

CIRCLE
TEXT
BUBBLE

LEADER
LEADER–>
<–LEADER

OppENDp
1stENDpt
1st–PLpt

PIPE–VLV
PIPE*VLV
DUP LAYR

1. User Selects Center of Circle Which is Drawn at a Fixed Radius

2. User Supplies Text Which is Automatically Placed in the Circle at the Correct Height

3. A Line is Started from the Center of the Circle

4. User Picks the Other End of the Line

5. The Line is Automatically Trimmed at the Circle

A

1. Makes Layer OBJ02 with Color Set to Red

2. User Draws a Single Line

3. Macro Automatically Inserts Valve at End Point of Line at Correct Scale

4. User Rotates Valve to Correct Position

5. A New Line Starts at the Last Point

6. Steps 2 Thru 5 are Repeated 4 Times

Screen Menu Macros

CHAPTER 4

Menu Macros

A LITTLE MACRO GOES A LONG WAY

Like most computer programs, you can use typed commands to control AutoCAD's drawing editor. However, typing your input is tedious and prone to error. This chapter introduces you to the AutoCAD menu system. Customizing your menus is another key to customizing AutoCAD.

The Standard AutoCAD Menu

Although AutoCAD's standard menu is fine for beginners, it becomes cumbersome to wade through as you become a more experienced user. You use 20 percent of the AutoCAD commands 80 percent of the time. If you create your own commands using menu macros, your custom menu system will be an enormous time saver and an easy way to automate repetitive drawing procedures. We do not rely on AutoCAD's standard menu in this book. Instead, we will help you learn how to make menus that are designed for your own unique needs.

Basic Macro Skills

A *macro* is a series of AutoCAD commands and parameters put together to perform a task. Macros can call AutoCAD commands, pause for input from the user, and draw or edit objects on the screen. Macros also can automatically repeat.

Macros are found in menu files. A *menu* is an ASCII text file listing the commands and macros for each box of the screen, tablet, buttons, pull-down, and icon menus. A typical screen menu displays a list of macro choices beside the drawing area. Although the actual body of the menu item is never seen on the screen, it is similar to what echoes to the command line. What echoes is the same as what you would type at the command prompt if manually executing the sequence.

The Benefits of Using Menu Macros

A customized menu gives you important advantages over keyboard style input. Using a menu for input is faster and offers fewer chances for error when issuing complex instructions to AutoCAD. At its simplest, a menu system is a super typist. Additionally, macros help you increase productivity by reducing drawing steps. They help you set drafting standards and control consistency. And they allow you to add new *commands* with drawing features that would be too tedious to use without menu customization.

How-To Skills Checklist

This chapter will show you how to:

❑ Put AutoCAD commands in a menu file.

❑ String commands together to form a basic macro.

❑ Make macros pause for input from a user.

❑ Use special characters in a macro to toggle snap, grid, ortho and several other AutoCAD modes.

❑ Use object snaps in macros, including using the QUIck modifier to filter points.

❑ Use labels for macros.

❑ Use path names in macros.

❑ Repeat entire macros automatically using an * modifier, and repeat individual commands using the MULTIPLE command modifier.

Menus and Macros

MACROS

These are the macros that you will create in this chapter:

[BUBBLE] draws column line grids and bubbles, then puts in text.

[LEADER] is a straight line annotation leader with an arrow block.

[LEADER->] is a single entity leader that uses a polyline to create a straight segment and arrow end.

[<-LEADER] starts with an arrow and can have unlimited curved and/or straight leader segments.

[OppENDpt] gets the opposite endpoint of an entity.

[**1stENDpt**] gets the first endpoint of an entity, not necessarily the closest.

[**1st-PLpt**] gets the starting point of a selected polyline.

[**PIPE-VLV**] initializes layer controls, draws pipe flow lines and puts in valve symbols.

[**DUP LAYR**] duplicates a set of entities on another layer.

MENUS

In this chapter, you will also create three menu files:

CA04.MNU is this chapter's example menu.

TEST.MNU is your scratch working menu file.

MAIN.MNU is a standard menu template file.

How to Make Menu Files With the CA DISK

 This disk icon identifies your critical points.

The book uses menu files from the CUSTOMIZING AutoCAD companion disk (CA DISK). The disk contains the menus, example drawing files, and symbol libraries used in the hands-on exercises. Each chapter uses a working TEST.MNU file. At the beginning of each chapter, we will ask you to copy the CAxx.MNU chapter file to a file called TEST.MNU. When the exercises ask you to "Add such and so to your TEST menu . . ." you can *edit* the TEST.MNU by simply *examining* its code.

At the end of each chapter, you delete your TEST.MNUs. This method lets you experiment in the TEST.MNU file. But the CAxx.MNU menus insure that you are on common ground with the book when you start each new chapter.

How to Make Menu Files Without the CA DISK

This no-disk icon identifies your critical points.

If you don't have the CA DISK, we will ask you to make a new TEST.MNU with each chapter. Later, we will make this task easier by creating and copying a *template* file called MAIN.MNU. You will copy the MAIN.MNU file to create the TEST.MNU for each chapter. At the end of each chapter, you will rename TEST.MNU to names like MY04.MNU. The book will instruct you each step of the way. The exercise sequences are written as if you *don't* have the CA DISK.

Writing a Simple Menu Item

First, make a new menu file called TEST.MNU. Even if you have the CA DISK, type this one as shown. This first test menu makes sure your menu editing process is OK, and tests the MNU command you added to the PGP file. Just follow our sequence.

A Simple Menu Item

`C:\> CA`	Use the CA.BAT batch file to start ACAD.
`Enter selection: 1`	Begin a NEW drawing named CA04.
	It should look like CA-PROTO.DWG, grid and all. If not, refer to previous chapters and check your CA.BAT, DOS directories, and the "Initial drawing setup" in your AutoCAD configuration.
`Command: MNU`	This is the PGP command you made.

If everything is set up right, you're now in your text editor. If your text editor didn't automatically create a new TEST.MNU file in the CA-ACAD directory, please start one now. Some editors can't automatically load files. From now on we will assume that your editor loads the file automatically.

Type the next two lines into the TEST.MNU file.

```
CIRCLE
TEXT
```

If you have the CA DISK, your menu shows additional commands and parameters. Save the file and exit your editor. Go back to AutoCAD.

`Command: MENU`	Load the menu TEST.
`Menu file name or . for none <.>: TEST`	
`Compiling menu C:\CA-ACAD\TEST.mnu...`	[CIRCLE] and [TEXT] should appear at the top of the menu.

Select **[CIRCLE]**	Works just as if typed at the Command: prompt.
`Command: CIRCLE 3P/2P/TTR/<Center point>:`	Draw a circle to test it:

Select **[TEXT]**	Test it also.

```
Command: ERASE              Wipe them out. Then make a bubble using the new menu:
Command: ZOOM               Zoom Center with a height of 16'.
Command: SNAP               Set to 2".
Command: GRID               Set to 1'.

Select [CIRCLE]             Pick a point centered on the screen:
Command: CIRCLE 3P/2P/TTR/<Center point>:
Diameter/<Radius>: 24                    That's 1/4" at 1:96 plot scale.

Select [TEXT]                            And you get:
TEXT Start point or Align/Center/Fit/Middle/Right/Style: S
Style name (or ?) <STD1-8>: STD3-16
Start point or Align/Center/Fit/Middle/Right/Style: M
Middle point: @           The @ lastpoint is the center of the circle.
Rotation angle <0.00>:    Default to 0.
Text: A                   Just the letter A.
```

➥ *NOTE: When you edit menus, input characters exactly as the book shows them. Do not use tabs, invisible trailing spaces, or blank lines.*

This first example menu was simple. Each item sends a single command to AutoCAD and terminates, letting the user do the rest. Text didn't prompt for height because our style is set at a preset height.

Special Characters in Menus

Macros need automation. Stringing together multiple commands that can be interrupted for user input requires special characters. The backslash \ is the most important of these special characters. It makes AutoCAD pause for input, then resume execution with more commands or options. This *pause* is the menu feature that makes automation possible.

Repeat the bubble sequence. Write down each character of each step, ignoring the prompts. Use a blank space to represent each <SPACE> or <RETURN> that you enter at the keyboard. Use a \ to mark where you pick a point or type input.

Repeat the previous bubble sequence with CIRCLE and TEXT.

Write this sequence down as you repeat the bubble.
```
CIRCLE \24 TEXT S STD3-16 M @ 0 \
```

Next, let's input this sequence to make a macro that creates circles with centered text. This macro starts the CIRCLE command, pauses for location, draws a 24-inch circle, and waits for text before automatically putting the text into the center of the circle. The exercise shows additions to the existing menu in boldface type.

Command: **MNU**   Your PGP command to edit the TEST.MNU file.

Add the following below the TEXT and CIRCLE lines:

```
TEXT
CIRCLE
CIRCLE \24 TEXT S STD3-16 M @ 0
```

Save and exit back to AutoCAD.

Command: **MENU**   Enter TEST. After editing, you must reload the menu
                                     or the old menu gets used. We'll automate this later.

Select **[CIRCLE \]**   Pick a point and type a character.

Your screen should show a circle with text. Using the macro to draw the bubble only took three steps compared to the nine manual steps previously used.

➡ *TIP: If you make an error, use Undo. Any error in a menu item crashes the rest of the item, but Undo cleans it up.*

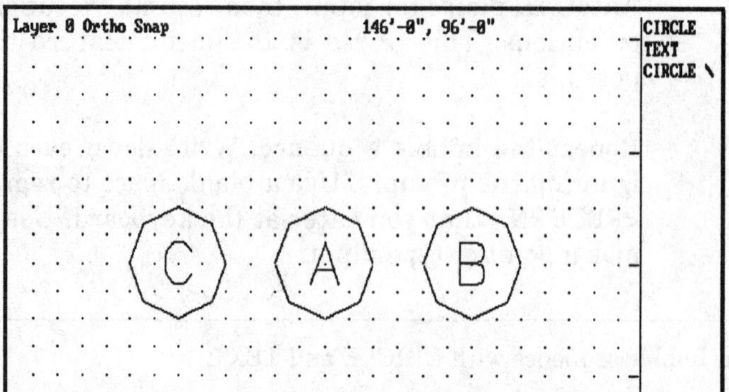

Circles With Text

A single backslash tells AutoCAD to wait for a single piece of input. In the circle-with-text macro, it pauses for the circle's center point. Without a backslash, AutoCAD would continue taking its input from the macro and would pass the next item along to the command processor. It would read the 24 as the center point and get confused because it isn't a coordinate point. A redundant second backslash is omitted at the end of the macro since the TEXT command is waiting for input anyway.

➡ *NOTE: Each backslash pauses for exactly one item of input. Count your backslashes carefully. The menu item resumes as soon as the backslash gets any form of input. It doesn't care whether it's correct or not.*

You may wonder why we specified the style with "S STD3-16" when it was already set. You never know what was used last in macros. It is good practice to explicitly set modes and settings, like style, if they are important for your macro to function.

Backslash, <SPACE> and Special Characters

Backslashes and spaces are two of the control characters that you use in menus. AutoCAD automatically places a space at the end of a menu line, unless the line ends with a special character. When AutoCAD encounters a special character at the end of a menu line, it *never* adds an automatic space.

The following table lists the special menu characters. The @ (lastpoint) is not listed as a special character because it does not share in the special treatment by the AutoCAD menu interpreter. Here is the list of special characters:

```
                    SPECIAL MENU CHARACTERS
\    Pauses for input              ;     Issues RETURN
+    Continues to next line        []    Encloses Label
*    Autorepeats, or marks page    ^B    Toggles SNAP
^D   Toggles COORDS                ^E    Toggles ISOPLANE
^G   Toggles GRID                  ^H    Issues BACKSPACE
^C   *Cancel*                      ^O    Toggles ORTHO
^P   Toggles MENUECHO              ^Q    Toggles Printer Echo
^T   Toggles Tablet                ^M    Issues RETURN
^X   *Delete* input in buffer      <SPACE>
^Z   Suppresses automatic SPACE at end of line
```

Special Menu Characters

Enter control characters, like Ctrl-B, into a menu file as two characters. Use a caret ^ followed by an upper case letter, like ^B. This coding avoids conflicts with any use your text editor makes of control characters.

Semicolons Are a Special Case

Let's look at the semicolon by adding extension lines to the new bubble macro. The semicolon is the special character for <RETURN>. The bubble macro uses more backslashes and the QUAdrant osnap mode. Again, we show the *additions* to the existing menu lines in boldface.

Command: **MNU**   Edit TEST.MNU. Add the boldface part to the end of the macro:

CIRCLE \24 TEXT S STD3-16 M @ 0 **\LINE QUA \\;**

Save and exit to AutoCAD.

Command: **MENU**   Reload the menu.

Select **[CIRCLE \]**
Command: CIRCLE 3P/2P/TTR/<Center point>:   **Pick a point.**
Diameter/<Radius>: 24
Command: TEXT   The TEXT command scrolls by:
Text: **CC**   Enter two characters.
Command: LINE From point: QUA of   Pick the QUA point anywhere on circle.
To point: Pick a point.
To point: Macro issues ; as a <RETURN> and ends.

The \\ made the command pause for two input points after the LINE command, then the last semicolon terminated it. You must supply one backslash for each entry that you want to make.

The last character is a semicolon. You commonly can use semicolons and spaces interchangeably in macros, like the returns and spaces typed from the keyboard. In macros, spaces act like the <SPACE> key on the keyboard and semicolons act like the <RETURN> key. Unless there is a special character at the end of the line, AutoCAD will execute the macro as if there is a trailing space. The above macro ends with a backslash, a special character, so we need to use the semicolon. It is best to terminate a macro with a semicolon which you can see, rather than with an *invisible* trailing space.

➡ *TIP: Never use two spaces in a row. You can't see them to count them. Use one space and then use semicolons for subsequent <RETURN>s.*

Command: **MNU**   Add these two lines.
                                           Note the A1 LINE vs. the A2;LINE:

CIRCLE \24 TEXT S STD3-16 M @ 0 A1 LINE QUA \\;
CIRCLE \24 TEXT S STD3-16 M @ 0 A2;LINE QUA \\;

Reload your menu and test both items. Which one works?

You would think that both lines would put their text label, A1 or A2, in their bubbles. The first line tries to use the space after the A1 while the second line uses the semicolon for a <RETURN>. Only the A2 item works.

Since you must be able to type spaces in the middle of text strings, AutoCAD's menu interpreter treats them as true spaces in your text, not equivalent to <RETURN>s. If you want the macro to continue after text input, as in the A1 example above, you need some way to tell AutoCAD that the string of text is complete. You can't use the automatic space in the macro line following text. Again, the semicolon is your best bet.

Putting a Semicolon in Menu Text Strings

Except for spaces, all special characters act exactly the same whether they are in the middle of a text string or not. You can use a semicolon anywhere to issue a <RETURN>. The sacrifice you make is that the only way to enter a real semicolon within a text string created by a menu is to use ASCII codes. The AutoCAD menu interpreter doesn't recognize ASCII codes, but the text string does.

You are familiar with AutoCAD's underscores in text, such as the %%u which underscores a text string. The %% is the "escape" character in fonts. ASCII 59 is the ASCII code for the semicolon. If you imbed a %%59 in a text string, you get a semicolon. For example, "Word%%59 item, stuff" becomes "Word; item, stuff." This is the text method for special characters and text modes. The %%nn works for any character where nn is the ASCII code number.

Labeling Macro Commands

Now that you have several macros on your screen, it is hard to distinguish what each command does. You can control what is displayed on the screen by putting macro labels in [SQUARE BRACKETS]. Only eight characters display on the typical screen menu, but you can make labels longer for documentation. The extra characters just won't display, unless you have an ADI display driver that exceeds eight characters. Labels can include letters, numbers, and any displayable character. Control and extended ASCII characters are simply ignored. The square brackets identify the label to AutoCAD's menu interpreter.

Let's add labels to the menu. Don't leave any blank spaces between your screen labels and the body of the macros. AutoCAD treats everything that follows the label as an instruction, so a space will cause an error.

Making a Menu Label

 Copy CA04.MNU to TEST.MNU to replace the one already created.

Continue editing TEST.MNU.

Command: **MNU** Add these labels and delete the other items:

```
[CIRCLE] CIRCLE
[TEXT  ] TEXT
[BUBBLE] CIRCLE \24 TEXT S STD3-16 M @ 0 \LINE QUA \\;
```

Save, exit and reload the menu. See the screen differences.

Your screen should display the screen menu labels shown in the screen shot. If you have the CA DISK, you will also see additional labels.

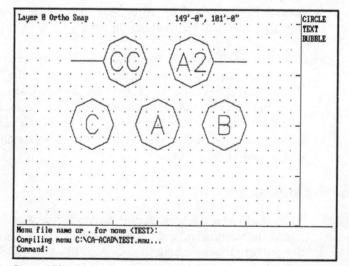

Screen Menu Labels

➡ *TIP: Give all menu items [LABELS]. Use empty square brackets for blank menu items and as placeholders to visually orient you in the menu.*

➡ *TIP: The INSert key makes selections from the screen menu. Begin your macro labels with unique characters to make <INS> work effectively.*

Using Special Characters and Path Names

The next exercise shows you how to use more special control characters while you make a series of [LEADER] macros. The exercise also shows how to use directory path names in macros.

The first [LEADER] draws a two-segment polyline and inserts an arrow block at the end. The macro uses the ARROW block that you created in an earlier chapter. The macro rotates the arrow to the midpoint of the line, using osnap MIDpoint.

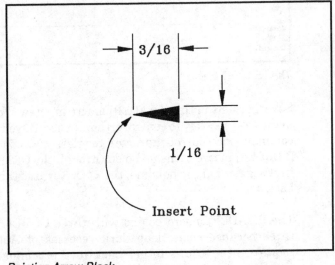

Pointing Arrow Block

Making a [LEADER] Macro

Command: **MNU**   Edit TEST.MNU. Add the following:

`[LEADER    ]^C^C^CORTHO ON PLINE \\^O\ INSERT /CA-ACAD/ARROW @ 96 ;MID @ ^O`

Save, exit and reload the menu.

Command: **ERASE**   Erase the bubbles to clean up the screen.

Select **[LEADER]**   Try it. The ortho, pline and block commands scroll by and
                            it ends with <Ortho on>, leaving a two-polyline leader and arrow.

Your screen should show the two-polyline leader.

The LEADER Macro

Several items in this [LEADER] macro are new. You are probably used to
using the <F8> key to control ortho. In menus, you need to use the ORTHO
command or control-character toggles. <^O> is the ortho toggle. The
[LEADER] macro turns ortho on through the ORTHO command. After the
first segment of the polyline, the <^O> turns ortho off. Later it flips ortho
back on.

The [LEADER] macro begins with three Ctrl-Cs. We recommend using
three because some deep dark recesses of AutoCAD and AutoLISP
require three <^C>s to get back to the command prompt. It is good
practice to begin command macros with <^C>s to cancel anything that is
pending.

Look at the directory path name for the ARROW being inserted in the
[LEADER] macro. The slashes are forward slashes /, not the backslashes
that you are used to in the DOS operating system. We used a path in this
macro to show you how to handle path names. The macro didn't really
need a path since ARROW was in the current directory. But when macros
do need path names, you have to use the forward slash. There is no

exception. Backslashes make menus pause! UNIX systems also require forward slashes for their paths.

The [LEADER] macro used the @ symbol to recall the lastpoint at the end of the polyline during the block insertion. The macro then fed the X scale value of 96 (plot scale). The semicolon in "96 ;MID" defaulted the Y scale factor to equal the X. When you accept default values, show them with a semicolon.

Last, the [LEADER] macro osnapped the block rotation with "MID @." Since the @ lastpoint is at the end of the polyline, the MIDpoint orients the ARROW symbol to the angle of the line. This is why ARROW was created pointing to the left with its insertion point at the arrow point.

Now, try a few macro tricks. Create an entire leader, including its arrow, as a single polyline. The advantage of this [LEADER->] is that you can select it as a single entity. First draw interactively with AutoCAD, writing down the characters and picks, then write the macro.

Making a Single Entity [LEADER->]

```
Command: ORTHO
ON/OFF <Off>: ON
Command: PLINE
From point:                                              Pick a point.
Current line-width is 0'-0"
Arc/Close/Halfwidth/Length/Undo/Width/<Endpoint of line>: W
Starting width <0'-0">: 0                       Make sure it is 0 width.
Ending width <0'-0">: 0
Arc/Close/Halfwidth/Length/Undo/Width/<Endpoint of line>:          Pick a point.
<Ortho off>                                     Toggle with ^O and pick another point.
Arc/Close/Halfwidth/Length/Undo/Width/<Endpoint of line>: W
Starting width <0'-0">: 0
Ending width <0'-0">: 6
Arc/Close/Halfwidth/Length/Undo/Width/<Endpoint of line>: L
Length of line: -18                             Yes, that's minus 18.
Arc/Close/Halfwidth/Length/Undo/Width/<Endpoint of line>: W
                                                Reset width to 0. <RETURN> to exit.
```

Collect all your typed input and picks. String them together to make the [LEADER->] macro.

```
Command: MNU                      Edit the TEST.MNU and add this line:

[LEADER->]^C^C^CORTHO ON PLINE \W 0 0 \^O\W 0 6 L -18 W 0 0 ;
```

Save, exit and reload the menu.

Select **[LEADER->]**   Pick points when it pauses, in the same sequence as above.

Command: **LIST**   List it. It is a single polyline.

Your screen should show a single entity leader.

A Single Entity Leader

The label [LEADER->] *graphically* indicates the direction of the leader. Since you can't predict the incoming default polyline width, your polyline macros should always set the width explicitly, as in "W 0 0 ." Remember that backslashes and control characters, like <^O>, do not need a <SPACE> or <RETURN> to execute. "W 0 6 " sets the width to draw the arrowhead.

The "L" length parameter draws the 18-inch long arrow segment by using a negative length polyline trick. It folds the polyline back upon the previous polyline segment with "L -18 ."

The last leader macro starts with the arrow. Its label is [<-LEADER]. The macro uses a PEDIT trick to reset the @ lastpoint to the start point of a polyline. This lets the macro start with an arrow, but you must repick the second point. You can finish it up with as many line or arc polyline segments as you like.

Making a Multi-Segment [<-LEADER] Macro

Command: **MNU**   Edit TEST.MNU and add the following line:

[<-LEADER]^C^C^CPLINE \\;PEDIT L E M @ X ;ERASE L ;PLINE @ W 0 6 L 18 W 0 0 L 1

Save, exit, reload the menu.

Select **[<-LEADER]**   It executes PLINE:
Command: PLINE   Pick two points.
                                  Many PLINE and PEDIT prompts scroll by, then:

```
Arc/Close/Halfwidth/Length/Undo/Width/<Endpoint of line>:
```
                    Re-pick the second point, a third point, and <RETURN> to end.

Your screen should show a multi-segment polyline leader.

Multi-Segment Polyline Leader

The "PLINE \\;" draws a single segment that establishes a starting direction for the arrow. The "PEDIT Last Edit Move @" is the key trick used in the macro. It doesn't actually move the vertex, but the @ resets the lastpoint to the start of the polyline.

The "X ;" exits PEDIT. Then "ERASE L ;" erases the temporary polyline. The macro starts the real polyline with an arrow at the lastpoint with "PLINE @ ." The "W 0 6 " sets the arrow width so you can draw it with the length parameter using "L 18 ." The "W 0 0" sets width back to 0. Add a small length segment with "L 1 " to keep the next segment from distorting the arrow. If you don't, it miters the arrow base relative to the angle of the next segment. The macro leaves you in the polyline command. Re-pick the second point and draw line segments, hit an A to draw arcs, or <RETURN> to end.

Making Long Macros

Menu items can get very long, too long for one line. You can continue a macro for many lines by ending each line with a plus sign. Let's continue with the [BUBBLE] macro. As it gets too long for one line, continue the macro with a + sign.

Explore some more osnap features, making the [BUBBLE] macro require just two picks. Use SELECT, an AutoCAD command seldom used outside macros, to enhance the [BUBBLE]'s features.

Making a [BUBBLE] Macro Using the SELECT Command

Command: **MNU**   Edit the [BUBBLE] item in the TEST.MNU.

Edit the menu to get the following two lines.
Edit the TEST.MNU lines even if you have the CA DISK.

```
[BUBBLE ]^C^C^CCIRCLE \24 SELECT L ;TEXT S STD3-16 M @ 0 \+
LINE @ \;ID MID,QUI @ TRIM P ;ENDP,QUI @ ;
```

Save, exit, reload the menu.

```
Select [BUBBLE]
Command: CIRCLE 3P/2P/TTR/<Center point>:          Pick a point.
Diameter/<Radius>: 24
Command: SELECT                          This "saves" the last circle as Previous.
Select objects: L 1 found.
Select objects:                          ; <RETURN>s to end selection.
Command: TEXT          The text command scrolls by with "S STD3-16 M @ 0 ", then:
Text: A3                                  Enter some text.
Command: LINE From point: @              Starts at circle's center.
To point:                                Pick a point.
To point:                                ; ends the line.
Command: ID Point: MID,QUI @             Saves line's midpoint as lastpoint.
X = 130'-0"  Y = 128'-0"  Z = 0'-0"
Command: TRIM
Select cutting edge(s)...
Select objects: P 1 found.               Selects the circle SELECT saved as Previous.
Select objects:
Select object to trim: ENDP,QUI @        Trims end at the saved lastpoint.
Select object to trim:                   And it's done.
```

Look at the end of the first macro line. When AutoCAD sees a + at the end of the line, it treats the next line as part of the same item. The most important thing to remember about + is that you cannot put a space or semicolon after the + character.

The osnap trick "ID MID,QUI @" uses the harmless ID command to reset lastpoint to the MIDpoint of the line, which is picked by @. QUIck mode makes the macro find the most recently entered nearby MIDpoint, instead of the closest MIDpoint. Since you just drew the line, you know it will be most recent. This avoids MID finding the wrong line in heavy traffic. QUIck also speeds up osnap. Use it when osnapping an entity that you are sure is more recent than its neighbors. This is a frequent case in macros.

To trim off the extra bit of the line, "TRIM P ;" selects the circle as a cutting edge, then "ENDP,QUI @" picks the line to trim. The macro uses ENDPoint to select the correct end, and @ to pick the lastpoint that ID saved. The final semicolon exits TRIM and ends the macro. The macro uses ENDP (not END) to avoid accidentally ENDing the drawing.

Although both ends of any line are equidistant from its midpoint (your lastpoint in the macro), AutoCAD is never random. AutoCAD will always find the first endpoint of the line if you osnap ENDP from the midpoint of the line. You may not normally worry about the difference between the ends of lines, but you will have to consider it when using AutoLISP.

You can use the same techniques to form three handy stand-alone macros to find the opposite end of a line, first end of a line, or the first end of a polyline. Add these new macros to your menu.

Command: **MNU**   Edit TEST.MNU and add the following three macros.

```
[OppENDpt]^C^C^CLINE \MID @ ;ROTATE L ;@ 180;+
ID MID,QUI @ ID ENDP,QUI @ ERASE L ;ID ENDP @
[1stENDpt]^C^C^CID MID \ID ENDP @
[1st-PLpt]^C^C^CPEDIT \E M @ X X
```

Save, exit, and reload the menu. Draw some lines and polylines. Play with the macros.

Notice how the [OppENDpt] rotates, flipping a line 180 degrees, then osnaps to *walk* down it.

Layers and Macros

The next [PIPE-VLV] macro shows you how to control layer names, color, and linetype settings with a menu macro. Rather than assuming that a layer was created in a prototype drawing or by a setup routine, assume that it doesn't exist. Have the macro create the layer that it will use. This type of macro control avoids the problem of a user accidentally purging unused layers from a drawing.

The macro [PIPE-VLV] contains several AutoCAD commands. It makes a layer, draws a line, then inserts a block named VALVE. If you have the CA DISK, you already have the VALVE.DWG file. Otherwise you need to make and WBLOCK a VALVE. If you are unfamiliar with the syntax of AutoCAD's LAYER command, test and record the macro sequence in AutoCAD.

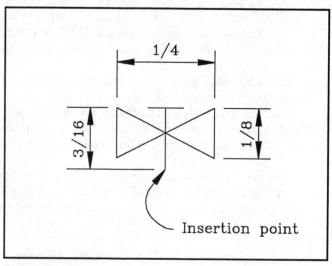

Pipe Flow Valve

[PIPE-VLV] Piping Macro With Layer Setup

  Use VALVE.DWG on the disk.

  Draw a valve as shown. Wblock it to VALVE.

Command: **MNU**   Edit the TEST.MNU
Add the following:

```
[PIPE-VLV]^C^C^CLAYER M OBJ02 C RED ;;+
LINE \\;INSERT VALVE @ 96 ;DRAG
```

Save, exit, and reload the menu.

Command: **ERASE**   Erase the screen before going on.
Select **[PIPE-VLV]**   Pick two points. The layer, line, and insert commands scroll by. Drag rotation and pick a point to set it.

Command: **ZOOM**   Zoom in to see it better.
Command: **ERASE**   Erase it.
Command: **ZOOM**   Zoom Previous.

Here is how the [PIPE-VLV] macro works. "LAYER M OBJ02 C RED ;;" sets the layer and its color. Instead of Set, the macro uses M (Make) to set the layer current. This works even if the layer doesn't exist. With "RED ;;" the space enters RED, the first semicolon defaults the current layer to RED, and the second semicolon exits the layer command. The plus sign continues the macro to the next line.

Next, "LINE \\;" draws a single pipe line when you pick two endpoints, and terminates the line command with the semicolon. To "INSERT VALVE," the "@ 96 ;" places the insert at the lastpoint with an X scale of 96 and with a semicolon defaulting the Y scale equal to X. Finally, "DRAG" ensures that Drag is on while you rotate the insert. Although your default is Drag Auto, some users may have it turned off. If a macro depends on Drag to show the user orientation, you should explicitly drag to be sure.

➡ *TIP: Long macros, particularly ones that change settings or layers, may corrupt your AutoCAD environment if they fail due to an error or <^C>. Putting an UNDO Mark at the beginning of macros allows an UNDO Back to restore the previous condition cleanly.*

Repeating Macros and Multiple Commands

A little automation always calls for more. Why should you have to repeatedly reselect a macro from the screen if you want to use it several times? Let's improve the [PIPE-VLV] macro, making the macro command repeat five times. Add " \+" to the last line. Then, add four more lines.

Command: **MNU**   Edit the TEST.MNU item [PIPE-VLV] to:

```
[PIPE-VLV]^C^C^CLAYER M OBJ02 C RED ;;+
LINE \\;INSERT VALVE @ 96 ;DRAG \+
LINE ;\;INSERT ;@ 96 ;DRAG \+
LINE ;\;INSERT ;@ 96 ;DRAG \+
LINE ;\;INSERT ;@ 96 ;DRAG \+
LINE ;\;INSERT ;@ 96 ;DRAG
```

Save, exit, and reload the menu.

Select **[PIPE-VLV]**   It works as before, but draws five segments.

You could fit this repeating macro on fewer lines, but this format makes it easier to see what it does. The original macro didn't need a backslash after ending DRAG at the rotation prompt of the INSERT command. However, since each subsequent line starts with another LINE command, you have to fill the rotation prompt with a pause. The last line of an item never gets a plus sign continuation character, nor does the last line need a backslash.

Note the differences between the second line and the successive lines. The repetitive lines start with "LINE ;\" instead of "LINE \\," using a semicolon to default the new start point to the end point of the previous line. The macro is more efficient after the initial line/valve set is placed because you do not need to repeat the first line and the block name. The layer is already set and the INSERT command has a default block from the first insert. The repetitive inserts replace "VALVE" with a semicolon. Of course, if you want to draw less than five sections, you can always cut the macro short with a <^C>.

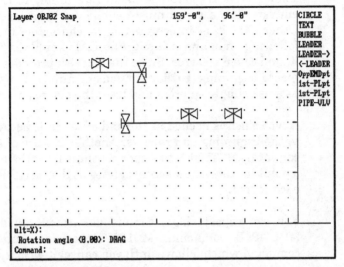

Pipe Lines and Valves

Indefinitely Repeating Macros and Commands

If you have AutoCAD Release 9 or 10, you can repeat macros indefinitely by placing an asterisk as the first character of the macro. If you use a screen [LABEL], put the asterisk immediately after the closing right bracket.

Make [PIPE*VLV] a repeating macro, using the Release 9 and 10 asterisk feature for macros. Put an asterisk in the [PIPE*VLV] label too as a reminder that it is a repeating macro.

Making Commands and Macros Repeat

Command: **MNU**   Copy the previous [PIPE-VLV] and edit it.

```
[PIPE*VLV]*^C^C^CLAYER M OBJ02 C RED ;;+
LINE \\;INSERT VALVE @ 96 ;DRAG \
```

Save, exit, and reload the menu.

Select **[PIPE*VLV]**   It works like the first one but repeats until <^C> cancels it.

The asterisk triggers the menu interpreter to repeat the macro in its entirety. The asterisk must be followed by at least one <^C> or a <^X>. Otherwise, it is interpreted as a character and interferes with the following command or input. AutoCAD would see *LAYER, not recognize it, and cause an error. Since the asterisk precedes the typical "^C^C^C" macro beginning, earlier versions of AutoCAD that don't recognize the asterisk simply ignore it and treat the macro as a standard single macro.

A backslash is needed at the end of the line, because the macro returns to the beginning and repeats. Another feature of this macro is that you can hit a <RETURN> to either continue from the previous line or to pick a point to start a new string of lines at the "LINE From point:" prompt of each repeat.

You can repeat single commands without an asterisk by using the MULTIPLE command. MULTIPLE causes AutoCAD to repeat the command which follows until you cancel it with a <^C>. MULTIPLE only repeats a single command, ignoring any options or parameters used in the first execution. You can make your original CIRCLE and TEXT commands repeat automatically using MULTIPLE.

Command: **MNU**   Change the CIRCLE and TEXT entries to:

```
[CIRCLE    ]^C^C^CMULTIPLE CIRCLE
[TEXT      ]^C^C^CMULTIPLE TEXT
```

Save the file and reload your menu.

Select **[CIRCLE]**   It keeps drawing circles, repeating like the DONUT command.
Select **[TEXT]**   It repeats, but you have to reenter the parameters each time.

MULTIPLE works for simple menu items like [CIRCLE] and [TEXT]. However, if you tried to make TEXT automatically repeat a mode like "M" for Middle, it would use the mode the first time, then ignore the mode on repeats. "^C^C^CMULTIPLE CIRCLE 3P" would draw a single three-point circle, then repeat with normal prompts. Anything like "^C^C^CMULTIPLE CIRCLE \\LINE" causes an error as the "LINE" tries to input to the repeat. MULTIPLE is intended primarily for on-the-fly keyboard use or single commands. We find the asterisk method works best for macros.

Macros That Use Selection Sets to Edit

Selection sets give you a hand as a macro-writer. Selection sets let you control how your user selects objects. AutoCAD editing commands always ask for a set of entities before any edit tasks can begin. This limits your macro writing by allowing only a fixed number of picks. Whether you use Window, Last, or another selection mode, you still need to predefine one backslash per pick. AutoCAD's SELECT command is indispensable in macros because it has the unique feature of pausing the macro indefinitely until the entire selection process is complete. It pauses even when other commands follow. Let's try an example.

Building Selection Sets in Advance

Make a Duplicate-to-Another-Layer macro, called [DUP-LAYR].

Command: **MNU**   Edit TEST.MNU and add the macro:

[DUP LAYR]^C^C^CSELECT \COPY P ;0,0 ;CHPROP P ;LA \;

Reload your menu. Try it on existing entities, or draw a few new ones to use.

Select [DUP LAYR]   It pauses for the new layer name. Use ANN02.
Command: **LAYER**   Switch the current and ANN02 layers On/Off to see.

As you see in [DUP-LAYR], SELECT doesn't *do* anything except create a selection set of entities allowing an indefinite number of picks. This is invaluable because you can use a subsequent command, like COPY, to select that selection set with a P (Previous). CHPROP also uses a P in [DUP-LAYR], but it is technically reselecting COPY's set.

Notice the use of "0,0 ;" to do the copy with 0,0 displacement. Many users are unaware that a <RETURN> in response to COPY's "Second point of displacement:" prompt causes it to take the first point as an actual relative displacement, 0,0 in this case. The same <RETURN> response applies to MOVE.

➡ *NOTE: You should always use CHPROP instead of CHANGE when changing properties. CHANGE will reject many entities if they are 3D or you are laying in skewed UCSs.*

Selection Set Modes

Other selection modes besides the old standbys, Window, Last, Crossing, Add, Remove, Multiple, Previous, and Undo are:

SIngle. Stays in selection mode until an object or set is successfully picked.

BOX. Acts like either Crossing or Window, depending on the order of the two points picked.

AUto. If the first point finds an object, AUto picks it. Otherwise AUto acts like BOX.

Combine SIngle with other modes, like Crossing or AUto. You also can use it with SELECT if you want to force the creation of a Previous set with only a single selection. But, before you assume SIngle solves the problem of a missed pick ruining or aborting a menu macro, read on. Although SIngle ends object selection when an object or set is picked, it doesn't suspend the rest of a macro. SIngle will work for simple macros like:

```
[STRETCH1]*^C^C^CSTRETCH SI C
```

SIngle keeps you from having to hit a <RETURN> to end the selection process. However, if you miss your first selection and any additional commands or parameters follow, SI will try to use them as input. For example, this macro changes an entity to yellow:

```
[C-YELLOW]^C^C^CCHANGE SI \PROP C 2 ;
```

This macro works fine if you don't miss the entity, but if you do miss, SI tries to use PROP as object selection input.

We recommend using BOX for macros. Except for the STRETCH command, you should probably forget about using Window and Crossing in macros. Just use BOX. Play with it and get used to the order of picks. We think you will agree that BOX is clean and simple. Pick left-to-right for a Window and right-to-left for a Crossing.

AUto also is useful. It gives the most flexibility, combining picking by point with the BOX mode. If your first point misses, you go into BOX mode. Otherwise, AUto selects the entity at the first pick point. This causes one quirk in menus if the macro has other parameters following it:

```
[C-YELLOW]^C^C^CCHANGE AU \\;PROP C 2 ;
```

This macro needs two backslashes for Crossing/Window. It works fine if you use it as Window or Crossing. However, if your first pick finds something, AUto is satisfied, but the macro is still suspended by the second backslash. Hit the button again at the same point. The macro will find the same object by pointing again. AUto is a good candidate for everyday editing and selection commands on the digitizer buttons.

Menu Macro Cleanup

It is time for a little cleanup to put your menu items in an easier-to-read format.

Improving the Menu Format

Command: **MNU**   Edit **TEST.MNU** to make it look like this:

```
[CIRCLE   ]^C^C^CMULTIPLE CIRCLE
[TEXT     ]^C^C^CMULTIPLE TEXT
[BUBBLE   ]^C^C^CCIRCLE \24 SELECT L ;TEXT S STD3-16 M @ 0 \+
LINE @ \ ID MID,QUI @ TRIM P ;END,QUI @ ;
[]
[LEADER   ]^C^C^CORTHO ON PLINE \\\^O\ INSERT /CA-ACAD/ARROW @ 96 ;MID @ ^O
[LEADER-> ]^C^C^CORTHO ON PLINE \W 0 0 \^O\W 0 6 L -18 W 0 0 ;
[<-LEADER ]^C^C^CPLINE \\;PEDIT L E M @ X X ERASE L ;PLINE @ W 0 6 L 18 W 0 0 L 1
[]
[OppENDpt ]^C^C^CLINE \MID @ ;ROTATE L ;@ 180 +
ID MID,QUI @ ID END,QUI @ ERASE L ;ID END @
+
[1stENDpt ]^C^C^CID MID \ID END @
[1st-PLpt ]^C^C^CPEDIT \E M @ X X
[]
[PIPE-VLV ]^C^C^CLAYER M OBJ02 C RED ;;+
LINE \\;INSERT VALVE @ 96 ;DRAG \+
LINE ;\;INSERT ;@ 96 ;DRAG \+
LINE ;\;INSERT ;@ 96 ;DRAG \+
LINE ;\;INSERT ;@ 96 ;DRAG \+
LINE ;\;INSERT ;@ 96 ;DRAG
+
[PIPE*VLV ]*^C^C^CLAYER M OBJ02 C RED ;;+
LINE \\;INSERT VALVE @ 96 ;DRAG \
+
[DUP LAYR ]^C^C^CSELECT \COPY P ;0,0 ;CHPROP P ;LA \;
```

Save, exit, and reload the menu.

Test each menu item to insure it works properly. Then save the menu for your own use.

Select [   ]   Select and test each item to be sure it is error free.

Command: **QUIT**

Save TEST.MNU for the next chapter.

Copy TEST.MNU to MY04.MNU. Save TEST.MNU for the next chapter.

Make sure all menu items begin with ^C^C^C. We recommend spacing the closing label brackets over to column 11. It is easier to read menu items if they are aligned and if there is at least one space at the end of the label. The extra spaces have no other effect since they are within the label. We added the three empty []s to separate items and indicate blank lines.

You can also indicate a blank line with a solitary plus sign. The + before [1stEndPt], tells AutoCAD to continue to the next line. This + has no effect on the menu. While this is not the intended use of the +, it does make the file easier to read by providing a visual break. AutoCAD ignores the solitary plus sign.

Summary

These aren't perfect macros. You will make more efficient, flexible and dependable macros with help from AutoLISP, but these macros show that you need to know AutoCAD's command and macro syntax to write good macros.

It also helps to pay attention to the graphic structure of entities, their on-screen behavior, and the start points and endpoints that you can use as osnappable points. Your macro and AutoLISP dependability will benefit. Play a little. It loosens up your imagination. The idea for the [OppENDpt] rotation trick came from play, making a worm walk across the screen!

Experiment. Look for tricks that you have picked up using AutoCAD, like the sequence "LINE;^C" that resets the lastpoint to the end of the last line drawn. It is great for inserting blocks at the end of a line. Look for ways to use osnaps as tools in macros, like rotating block inserts to get correct angles. Remember, the SELECT command automatically pauses for a selection set. Use SELECT to make the set and then pass the set to other editing commands like COPY via the Previous option.

When you write complex menu items, your command syntax must be exact. Use the drawing editor interactively as a testbed so that you know what options and input parameters are expected in your macros. Write your sequences down. Make your mistakes in the drawing editor, not in your text editor.

Now that you have a few menu macros under your belt, let's look at how to put menus together.

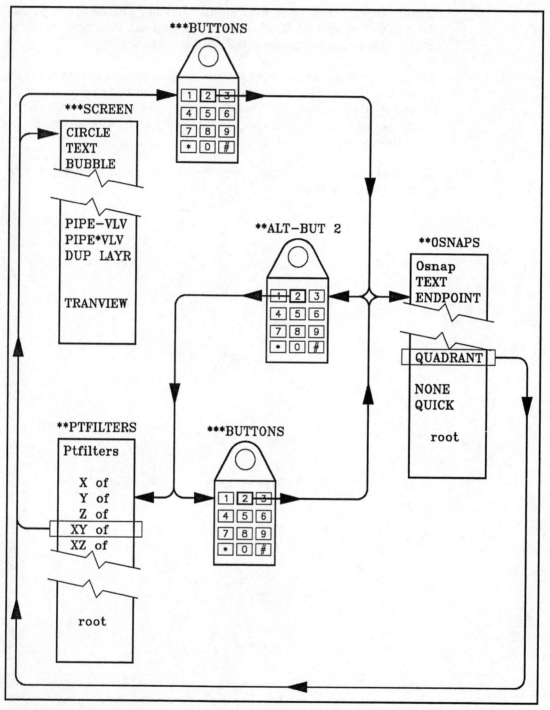

Buttons and Screen Toggling

CHAPTER 5

The Anatomy of a Menu

ELEMENTS OF MENU CONSTRUCTION

So far, you have been using a single screen menu for your macros. As you add more commands to your menu, you will need a way to organize and structure your menu system. This chapter will show you how.

Pages of Macros

AutoCAD's menu works with *pages* of macros and commands. A *menu page* is simply a group of macros that follow a given label. AutoCAD uses this label to find and activate the menu macros as a set.

The Benefits of a Well-Organized Menu

Using menu pages helps you organize and integrate your commands in a logical, intuitive way. You will be able to inform users of program settings as well as control your program's operation by the page structure. You will find that using pages of symbols makes inserting symbols into the drawing faster and more accessible for the user. And you will be able to design your menu pages to group macros by application task instead of AutoCAD functions. This will make drawing straightforward and efficient. Finally, designing your menu system pages to use screen, tablet, buttons, pull-down and icon menus will allow you to take advantage of the different features offered by each device.

How-To Skills Checklist

Here are the menu skills that you will acquire. You will learn how to:

☐ Put your symbols on screen menus.

☐ Create menu pages and direct them to different devices.

☐ Establish default pages for devices, using page and device labels.

☐ Make menu label toggles for interactive menus.

☐ Overlay a section of a menu with different macros.

☐ Use pull-down and icon menus.

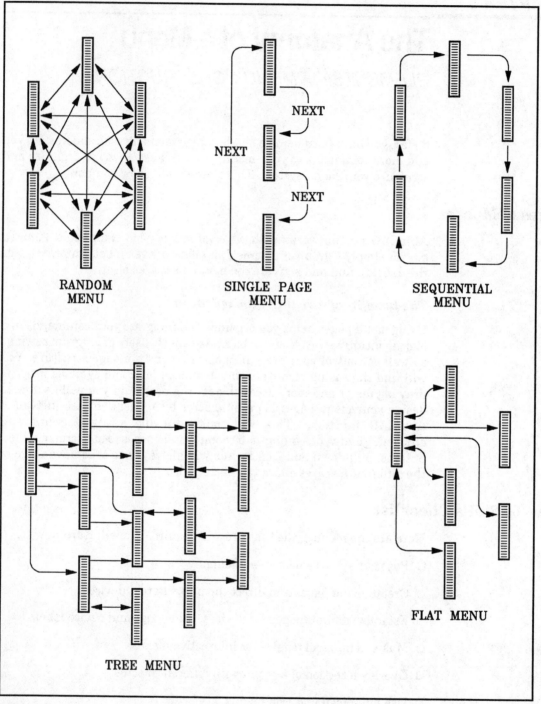

RANDOM
MENU

SINGLE PAGE
MENU

NEXT

NEXT

NEXT

SEQUENTIAL
MENU

TREE MENU

FLAT MENU

Types of Menus

Macros, AutoLISP Tools, and Programs

Menu Pages

These are the menu pages that you will create in this chapter.

***BUTTONS is a device name, but it also serves as the default page name for a set of command entries, osnaps, toggles and returns.

**FLOWSYMB is a full page of symbols for your basic library.

**OSNAPS is a menu page containing the object snap modes.

**PTFILTERS is a menu page with point filters.

**TRANVIEW is a page illustrating the use of transparent commands like 'ZOOM, 'PAN and 'VIEW.

**P1-SETVARS is a pull-down menu page. It contains transparent system variable settings, like APERTURE size and MIRRTEXT for mirroring text.

**POINTS is an icon screen menu that presents AutoCAD's point options. The macros set the point mode and size.

Menu Layouts

There are five basic ways to lay out menus: single page, tree, flat, sequential, and random. A menu structure is created by dividing the menu into *pages* identified by special labels. The five structures are created by controlling the page changes. You change pages by having menu items reference the special labels.

The *single page* structure is the default; it uses simple NEXT paging.

The *tree* structure is the most common layout. The tree structure is useful when you need access to a library of interrelated macros. Each branch can apply to a single task or application. Branches for flow diagrams, schedules, and site plans are good examples. Specific branches often incorporate flat and sequential menus.

The *flat* structure is rarely used for an entire menu system, although it is frequently used in parts of a large menu. A flat structure works well to present specific command options or subcommand parameters. A typical item in the page of a flat menu executes a command, pulls down a list of choices, waits for the user to make a selection, then returns automatically to the calling page.

A *sequential* structure is used for applications that follow a strict pre-determined order, like an assembly process. You program the menu to enforce this order. You might use a sequential menu to force the order for drawing gears for a clock or cogs for an engine. A page of a sequential menu can pause for any number of steps, but can only change to a predetermined NEXT page for the continuation of the process.

It is easy to create a *random* structure menu system. Yes, random menus can be useful. They permit the change from one screen menu to any other screen menu in the system. They are handy for notational menus, like special dimensioning routines, leader macros, text input macros, or any small frequently used set of items.

Which menu structure should you use? You should have them all! The tools you use to create them are the same. How you organize your menu pages makes the difference. To start working with menu pages, we need enough macros to fill a couple of menu pages. Let's add a group of symbols.

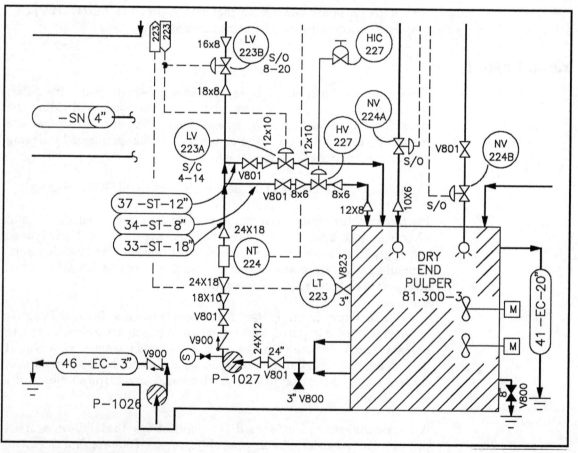

A Process Flow Diagram

Adding Some Symbols

You will create two screens of menus in the following exercise. In the process, you will develop a small symbol library, making macros to insert the symbols. These symbols are process flow symbols from the flow diagram shown in the illustration, but the menu procedures that you will use are the same for any application that you choose to develop.

If you have the CA DISK, you already have a set of symbol drawings. Otherwise, create one or two of the symbols shown below in a single *scratch* drawing to test the menu.

SYMBOL	FILE NAMES	SCREEN LABELS
	FLOWSMVL	SM VALVE
	FLOWARRO	ARROW
	FLOWPUMP	PUMP
	FLOWGATO	GATEOPEN
	FLOWXMTR	METER
	FLOWDRAN	DRAIN
	FLOWAGIT	AGITATOR
	FLOWMOTR	MOTOR
	FLOWCHKV	CHECK V
	FLOWSHOW	SHOWER
	FLOWDOT	DOT
	FLOWGATC	GATECLOS
	FLOWRED	REDUCER
	FLOWINC	INCREASE
	FLOWSAMP	SAMPLER

Symbols, Files, and Labels

Let's look at the steps involved in doing the first symbol. Draw and WBLOCK each symbol to a file name. Scale the dimensions. The file names and screen labels for the symbols are shown in the illustration. The first symbol is shown in detail in the Small Valve illustration.

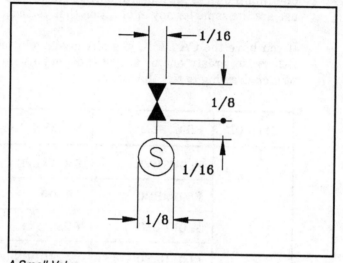

A Small Valve

Adding Symbols to a Menu

```
Enter selection: 1        Begin a NEW drawing named CA05.
Command: MENU             Load TEST, the menu from the previous chapter.

Command: LIMITS           0,0 to 36,24. A 1:1 schematic sheet size.
Command: ZOOM             Zoom window 0,0 to 2,2. Get close for these small symbols.
Command: GRID             Set to 1/2.
Command: SNAP             Set to 1/32.
Command: AXIS             Reset to 1/4 if you use axis lines.
Command: LAYER            You should be on layer 0. If not, check and fix CA-ACAD.DWG.
Command: STYLE            Redefine STD1-16 to set height to 1/16 for 1:1 scale.
```

 Skip to the menu writing part of the exercise where you add [SM VALVE].

Draw and Wblock the valve as shown:

Command: **SOLID**   Deliberately draw a "bow tie" by picking points clockwise.
Command: **LINE**   Then the vertical line.
Command: **CIRCLE**   It's easiest with a two-point circle, starting at the line.
Command: **TEXT**   Use style STD1-16, middle justified, and enter an S.

Command: **WBLOCK**   To file FLOWSMVL, insertion base point top of the "bow tie."

Command: **INSERT**   Insert FLOWSMVL at 1:1 to test.
Command: **ERASE**   Then erase it.

                                    Create a few more symbols if you wish, then write the menu:

Command: **MNU**   Edit TEST.MNU from Chapter 4, even if you have the CA DISK.
                                    If you skipped Chapter 4, copy CA04.MNU to TEST.MNU to continue
                                    this sequence.

Add the following [SM VALVE] to the end of your menu. Add the [FlowSymb] line as an identifying header. Use a [--------] line below [FlowSymb] to separate the label from [SM VALVE].

```
[DUP LAYR ]^C^C^CSELECT \COPY P ;0,0 ;CHANGE P ;P LA \;
[]
[FlowSymb ]
[-------- ]
[SM VALVE ]^C^C^CINSERT FLOWSMVL \1 ;\COPY L ;M @
```

Save, exit, and reload the TEST menu.

Select **[SM VALVE]**   Test it.
Command: INSERT FLOWSMVL   Insert command scrolls by as you pick points.
Command: COPY   Copy scrolls by, selecting last and leaves you in:
Second point of displacement: Pick any number of points. It is copy multiple.

Here is how the [SM-VALVE] macro works. The first \ pauses for the insertion point, then the macro sets the X,Y scale to 1 with "1 ;." The second \ pauses for rotation, then "COPY L ;M @" automatically copies it multiple times.

Your screen should show inserted valves.

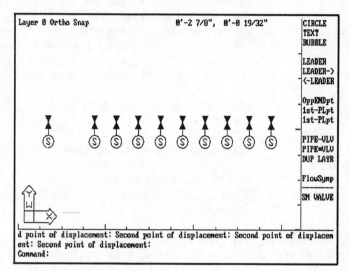

Inserted Valves

[SM VALVE] is a typical symbol menu item, using an insert macro. You need to copy and edit it to create a full page of similar symbol macros for the following menu.

Add the lines shown below to your TEST.MNU by duplicating the first line 14 more times. Then go back and change the [LABEL] and symbol block names. Enter them in alphabetical order. This order places the original [SM VALVE] last.

Command: **MNU**   Even if you have the CA DISK, edit the TEST.MNU to read:

```
[]
[FlowSymb ]
[-------- ]
[AGITATOR ]^C^C^CINSERT FLOWAGIT \1 ;\COPY L ;M @
[ARROW    ]^C^C^CINSERT FLOWARRO \1 ;\COPY L ;M @
[CHECK V  ]^C^C^CINSERT FLOWCHKV \1 ;\COPY L ;M @
[DOT      ]^C^C^CINSERT FLOWDOT \1 ;\COPY L ;M @
[DRAIN    ]^C^C^CINSERT FLOWDRAN \1 ;\COPY L ;M @
[GATECLOS ]^C^C^CINSERT FLOWGATC \1 ;\COPY L ;M @
[GATEOPEN ]^C^C^CINSERT FLOWGATO \1 ;\COPY L ;M @
[INCREASE ]^C^C^CINSERT FLOWINC \1 ;\COPY L ;M @
[METER    ]^C^C^CINSERT FLOWXMTR \1 ;\COPY L ;M @
[MOTOR    ]^C^C^CINSERT FLOWMOTR \1 ;\COPY L ;M @
[PUMP     ]^C^C^CINSERT FLOWPUMP \1 ;\COPY L ;M @
[REDUCE   ]^C^C^CINSERT FLOWRED \1 ;\COPY L ;M @
```

```
[SAMPLER  ]^C^C^CINSERT FLOWSAMP \1 ;\COPY L ;M @
[SHOWER   ]^C^C^CINSERT FLOWSHOW \1 ;\COPY L ;M @
[SM VALVE ]^C^C^CINSERT FLOWSMVL \1 ;\COPY L ;M @
[]
```

Save, exit, and reload the menu.

Command: **ERASE**   Erase the valves from the screen.

Select [**NEXT**]   Select [NEXT] at the bottom of the screen menus a few times.

Your screen should look similar to the illustration below.

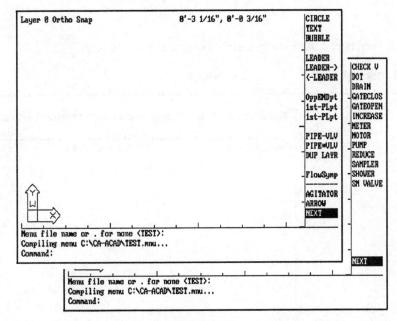

Screen Menu With Automatic NEXT Paging

You won't see all of the entries immediately if your menu exceeds one page. Instead you will see a NEXT at the bottom of the screen. AutoCAD automatically paginates the screen menu for you, creating a NEXT option.

When you select NEXT, another page of the macros appears. NEXT is a continuous loop with any number of pages. When you reach the last page, NEXT brings you to the first page. Notice that AutoCAD is smart enough to make the NEXTs come up in the same place on each page.

➡ *NOTE: There are 35 items in the menu. Most video displays support 20 to 30 items per page, but a few video displays support as many as 80 items per screen. If your display shows the entire menu, the next exercise will force the menu over onto a second page.*

Place a leading asterisk before a menu [LABEL] to control where a new menu page begins.

Command: **MNU**   Edit the menu to force a new page. Add * to [FlowSymb]:

```
[]
*[FlowSymb ]
[-------- ]
```

Save, exit, and reload. All Flow items are forced to the second page.

Select **[NEXT]**   Test NEXT.

Your screen should show the screen menu split at [FlowSymb].

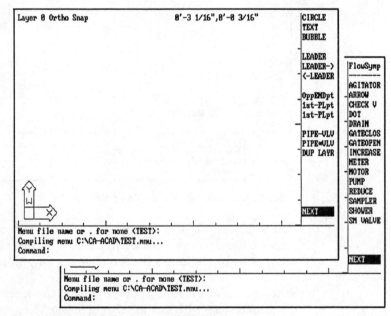

Screen Menu With Controlled NEXT Paging

Single page menus serve simple applications. You can also use them for quick, temporary menus. Most applications need more extensive, structured menus.

Naming Menu Pages

You can break menus into named pages of commands and macros by labeling each page with a unique name. You distinguish this page name or label from other lines in a menu by two leading asterisks. The format is **name, where *name* is any name you like.

Let's break out the flow symbols as a menu page.

Labeling and Switching Pages

Command: **MNU**   Edit TEST.MNU

Insert the **FLOWSYMB page name above the [FlowSymb] label.
Remove the asterisk from [FLOWSYMB].
**FLOWSYMB

[FlowSymb]

Save, exit, and reload the menu.

Now you can't get to the symbol page, and the automatic [NEXT] is gone. To get to the symbol page, you need to tell AutoCAD which page to load on the device. You do this via the "$" menu special character code. Since you are working with a screen menu, you use a $S. The format is $S=*name*, where *name* is the page you are going to load. To make the menu switch to the FLOWSYMB page, add a line to the bottom of your first page.

➡ *NOTE: When using **page names, single asterisks, like *[FlowSymb], must be removed.*

Command: **MNU**   Edit TEST.MNU.

Add [FLOWSYMB] and three [ ] blank lines to the bottom of the first page.
Count the labels to make sure [FLOWSYMB] is the 20th labeled item:

[ ]
[ ]
[ ]
[ ]
[FLOWSYMB]$S=FLOWSYMB
**FLOWSYMB
Save, exit, and reload the menu.

Select **[FLOWSYMB]**   This should flip to the symbol page.

You won't be able to get back to the first page menu unless you reload the menu. You could add a **name to the top of the first page and a $S=name at the bottom of the second page. However, AutoCAD offers a better way to get to any previous menu page. You use a $S= without a name. AutoCAD saves the eight last-used menu page names. So you can step back through each one by repeatedly executing a $S= item.

At the bottom of your **FLOWSYMB page, add a [ ] as a blank, and a $S= item. You can call it anything, but we recommend using the label [Last].

Command: **MNU**   Edit TEST.MNU.

Count labels and make sure [Last] is the 19th labeled item.

```
[SM VALVE ]^C^C^CLAYER S OBJ02 ;INSERT FLOWSMVL \1 ;\COPY L ;M @
[]
[  Last    ]$S=
```

Save, exit, and reload the menu.

Select **[FLOWSYMB]** *then* **[LAST]**

Now you can flip back and forth, but the [FLOWSYMB] label remains at the bottom of the screen when you flip to the second page. This is not harmful, but it points out that once menu items are activated, they remain active until they are displaced. With some thought, you can use this feature to design sophisticated menus, replacing only portions of your menu pages at a time. For now, just add another [ ] to the second page to force the [LAST] label to overwrite the [FLOWSYMB] label.

➥ *NOTE: Do not use a semicolon as a <RETURN> following a page name call. In some cases, such as "$S=NAME;+" AutoCAD will not recognize it as a <RETURN>. Use a space, "$S=NAME +" for example.*

Command: **MNU**   Edit TEST.MNU, add [ ]:

```
[]
[]
[  Last    ]$S=
```

Save, exit, and reload the menu. Test it.

You can select the last menu page and get cleanly back to the original menu. At this point, the labels and paging items in your TEST.MNU should look like this. (We don't show the rest of the macro code.)

```
[CIRCLE   ]                    **FLOWSYMB
[TEXT     ]                    [FlowSymb ]
[BUBBLE   ]                    [-------- ]
[]                             [AGITATOR ]
[LEADER   ]                    [ARROW    ]
[LEADER-> ]                    [CHECK V  ]
[<-LEADER ]                    [DOT      ]
[]                             [DRAIN    ]
[OppENDpt ]                    [GATECLOS ]
+                              [GATEOPEN ]
[1stENDpt ]                    [INCREASE ]
[1st-PLpt ]                    [METER    ]
[]                             [MOTOR    ]
[PIPE-VLV ]                    [PUMP     ]
+                              [REDUCE   ]
[PIPE*VLV ]                    [SAMPLER  ]
+                              [SHOWER   ]
[DUP LAYR ]                    [SM VALVE ]
+                              []
[]                             []
[]                             [  LAST   ]$S=
[]
[]
[FLOWSYMB ]$S=FLOWSYMB
```

Having made page changes, let's now turn to look at a complete menu structure using different devices.

Structuring the Menu

Your menu structure is determined by your page structure and what devices you assign those pages to. So far, you have used the *screen* device. Different devices have strengths and weaknesses which your menus should take advantage of. Let's assign menu items to the different devices so that you can see how the devices work.

Menu Devices

The devices available to you are: SCREEN, TABLET, BUTTONS, PULL-DOWN, ICON, and AUXilary. The screen is the default device. If you do not assign a device name in a menu file, AutoCAD assigns the macros to the screen. The BUTTONS menu assigns macros to mouse or digitizer puck buttons. The TABLET menu assigns commands to your digitizer tablet. The POP devices define the pull-down menus. An

AUXiliary device is any other electronic box that plugs into your computer. There are only one or two on the market, and they require an ADI driver. You can define PULL-DOWN and ICON menus with Release 9, 10, and later versions of AutoCAD.

Assigning Pages to Devices

AutoCAD treats devices much the same as page names. Each device has a unique name identified by the three consecutive asterisks preceding it, like ***SCREEN. AutoCAD supports 18 such devices. Each of the four areas on the tablet is counted as a device, and there are ten pull-down areas on the screen which AutoCAD considers as separate devices.

You can send any menu page to its device with a page change call from any device. You have seen how this works with $S= for the screen menu. The next exercises show you how to direct menu pages to other devices, starting with the tablet.

Tablet Menu

We assume that you have a digitizer tablet. If you do not have a tablet, you won't have access to the tablet items. If you do not have a tablet, you should just read this section.

If you have a digitizer tablet, photocopy the Tablet Menu illustration and tape it on your tablet anywhere outside the screen pointing area. We will reconfigure for one tablet menu area in the next exercise.

The reconfiguration will affect only the ACADDG.OVL and ACAD.CFG files you copied into the \CA-ACAD directory. It won't change your normal AutoCAD setup.

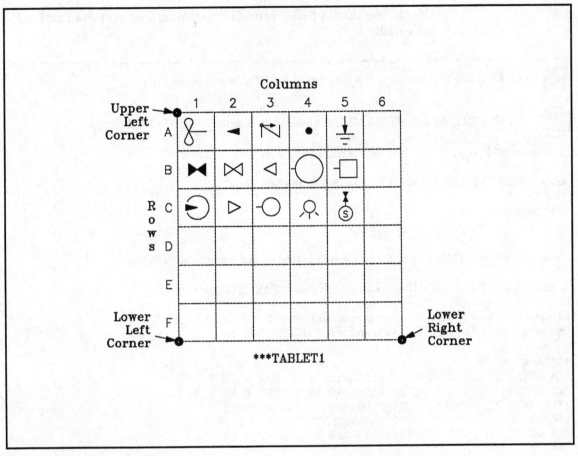

Tablet Menu

Assigning Menu Pages to a Tablet

```
Command: TABLET                          Tape on the TABLET MENU. Reconfigure:
Option (ON/OFF/CAL/CFG): CFG
Enter number of tablet menus desired (0-4) <4>: 1
Digitize upper left corner of menu area 1:                    Pick.
Digitize lower left corner of menu area 1:                    Pick.
Digitize lower right corner of menu area 1:                   Pick.
Enter the number of columns for menu area 1: 6
Enter the number of rows for menu area 1: 6
Do you want to respecify the screen pointing area? <N> Y
                          Or NO if you don't need to respecify.
Digitize lower left corner of screen pointing area:          Pick.
Digitize upper right corner of screen pointing area:         Pick.
```

If you have the CA DISK, you can stop typing. Just examine TEST.MNU as we edit.

COPY CA05.MNU to TEST.MNU and examine TEST.MNU as we edit.

COPY TEST.MNU to MY05A.MNU for backup, and continue editing TEST.MNU.

Command: **MNU**   Edit TEST.MNU.

Add a ***SCREEN device label as the first line of the file:

```
***SCREEN
[CIRCLE   ]^C^C^CMULTIPLE CIRCLE
```

Delete the [FLOWSYMB] line at the bottom of the first page for a total of 19 items.

Replace the old **FLOWSYMB page label with the ***TABLET1 device label.
Delete the [FlowSymb] and [------] lines.
Divide it into three groups of five items each and number them IA through 6C.
Delete the lines following [6C] at the end of the TEST.MNU file:

```
***TABLET1
[1A AGITATOR ]^C^C^CINSERT FLOWAGIT \1 ;\COPY L ;M @
[2A ARROW    ]^C^C^CINSERT FLOWARRO \1 ;\COPY L ;M @
[3A CHECK V  ]^C^C^CINSERT FLOWCHKV \1 ;\COPY L ;M @
[4A DOT      ]^C^C^CINSERT FLOWDOT \1 ;\COPY L ;M @
[5A DRAIN    ]^C^C^CINSERT FLOWDRAN \1 ;\COPY L ;M @
[6A ]
[1B GATECLOS ]^C^C^CINSERT FLOWGATC \1 ;\COPY L ;M @
[2B GATEOPEN ]^C^C^CINSERT FLOWGATO \1 ;\COPY L ;M @
[3B INCREASE ]^C^C^CINSERT FLOWINC \1 ;\COPY L ;M @
[4B METER    ]^C^C^CINSERT FLOWXMTR \1 ;\COPY L ;M @
[5B MOTOR    ]^C^C^CINSERT FLOWMOTR \1 ;\COPY L ;M @
[6B ]
[1C PUMP     ]^C^C^CINSERT FLOWPUMP \1 ;\COPY L ;M @
[2C REDUCE   ]^C^C^CINSERT FLOWRED \1 ;\COPY L ;M @
[3C SAMPLER  ]^C^C^CINSERT FLOWSAMP \1 ;\COPY L ;M @
[4C SHOWER   ]^C^C^CINSERT FLOWSHOW \1 ;\COPY L ;M @
[5C SM VALVE ]^C^C^CINSERT FLOWSMVL \1 ;\COPY L ;M @
[6C ]
```

Save, exit, and reload the menu.

Select **[5C SM VALVE]**   The third tablet row, fifth column (box 5C).
Command: INSERT Block name (or ?): FLOWSMVL   Executes the macro.

The flow symbols are installed on the tablet. The first five boxes across each of the top three rows contain the symbols. Box 5C has the block, FLOWSMVL. Since tablet locations depend on the file position of the menu items, we recommend that you always number and label items, even blank ones.

A ***BUTTONS Menu

Next, create and load some buttons macros. The following exercise assumes that you have a ten-button cursor with a pick button and nine assignable buttons. If you have fewer than ten, or if you have a mouse, you won't be able to access all the macros. Choose which ones you want to include, changing the macro's menu order to suit your preference.

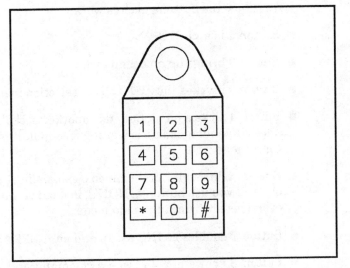

Ten-Button Cursor

Making a ***BUTTONS Menu

Command: **MNU**   Edit TEST.MNU

 If you have the CA DISK, you just need to temporarily change your [2 OSNAPS] button so it reads like the [2 OSNAPS] line below.

 Add a ***BUTTONS label, and the nine menu macros shown below, to the top of TEST.MNU:

```
***BUTTONS
[1 RETURN   ];
[2 OSNAPS   ]$S=OSNAPS
[3          ]AUTO \\
```

```
[4 SUSPENDS]\\
[5         ]NONE \\
[6         ]INT,ENDP \\
[7         ]INSERT \\
[8 LINE    ]^C^C^CLINE \
[9 MULTIPIK]\M NON @ NON @ NON @ NON @ NON @ NON @ NON @ ;\
```

Save, exit, and reload the menu.

Select **[Button 8]**	Draw some lines. The button enters LINE and first point.
Select [ ]	Draw other entities to test each button, except button 2. Undo and repeat for each.
Command: **ERASE**	Clean up.

Here is how the buttons macros work:

■ Button 1 is a <RETURN>.

■ Button 2 brings up an osnap menu.

■ Button 3 invokes the AUTO object selection mode.

■ Button 4 picks a point, but adds another backslash. If you use it while another pending macro is waiting for input, it picks but lets the macro continue to wait.

■ Buttons 5 through 7 are common osnaps. Choose the ones you use most often. If you use button 5, NONE, instead of the normal pick button, it overrides any running osnap mode.

■ Button 7 doubles as INS osnap and an INSERT command.

■ Button 8 shows how to issue a command and simultaneously pick a point.

■ Button 9 picks multiple items at one point with a single pick. It does not work with AutoCAD version 2.6.

Buttons 4 through 7, and 9, use a double backslash, \\, to keep any pending macros waiting.

Buttons are the most intimate and personal of the menu devices. Experiment to find what you like. You can't fit all the osnaps on the buttons device, so here is a comprehensive screenfull for your screen menu.

Adding Osnaps to the Screen Menu

Command: **MNU**

Examine the menu text and then do the test.

Add a page of osnaps just above the ***TABLET1 label. The last item returns to the default "root" screen:

```
**OSNAPS
[Osnaps    ]
[]
[ENDPOINT ]ENDP $S= $B=BUTTONS
[MIDPOINT ]MIDP $S= $B=BUTTONS
[INTERSCT ]INT $S= $B=BUTTONS
[PERPEND  ]PERP $S= $B=BUTTONS
[]
[NEAR     ]NEA $S= $B=BUTTONS
[INSERT'N ]INS $S= $B=BUTTONS
[NODE PT. ]NODE $S= $B=BUTTONS
[]
[CENTER   ]CEN $S= $B=BUTTONS
[TANGENT  ]TAN $S= $B=BUTTONS
[QUADRANT ]QUA $S= $B=BUTTONS
[]
[NONE     ]NON $S= $B=BUTTONS
[QUICK    ]QUICK,\
[]
[  root   ]$S=SCREEN $B=BUTTONS
```

Save, exit and reload your menu.

Select **[Button 2]**	It calls a screen menu of the osnaps.
Select **[Button 8]**	Start a line.
Select **[PERPEND]**	Pick a point.
	It osnaps and jumps back with $S= to the first screen page.

The $B=BUTTONS is not needed yet, but we put it in to save adding it later. Experiment with the buttons and screen menus, trying other buttons and osnaps with AutoCAD commands.

Menu Page Order

The order of your ***devices and **pages are important. You can place the pages within a device section in any order you want, but you need to be careful not to duplicate any page names in a menu file. If you do, AutoCAD will only recognize the first name. Menu pages are compiled for the device section under which they are listed.

Device labels are specially reserved names that AutoCAD uses to default load the first page following the device label. When AutoCAD loads a menu, it looks for each device label. AutoCAD loads each device with those items that follow its label, up to the next ***device or **page. Device labels also tell AutoCAD how to compile the following section of pages. Certain items compiled for one device will not function properly if their page is activated by another device. For example screen menu items with long labels, incorrectly compiled as pop device pages, will not display properly.

Switching Between Menu Pages

In addition to menu device sections, a key to menu structure is which $ codes call what pages. Organization will help you keep them straight.

Each device has a code which sends menu pages to a particular device:

CODE	ACTION
$S=	Screen menus
$P1= thru $P10=	Pull-down screen menus 1 thru 10
$B=	Buttons menu
$T1= thru $T4=	Tablet areas 1 thru 4
$I=	Icon menus
$A1=	Aux Box 1

Menu Device Code

A name following the code, like $B=ANYNAME, will send the named page to that device. You've used $S=SCREEN to load ***SCREEN to the screen, but any menu item can load or restore any page to its device.

In the buttons menu exercise example, button 2 loads the **OSNAPS menu to the screen. The osnaps items use $S= (without a name) to restore the previous menu page to the screen. Previous page loading is device-specific, reloading the previous page that was loaded to its device without affecting any other device.

If you duplicate menu labels in sections intended for different devices, you will get the wrong page on one device or the other and some items may not display correctly. AutoCAD will find the first occurring label regardless of device.

➡ *NOTE: You can deliberately duplicate a page, say, to override a page of the standard ACAD.MNU with a modified page. Just be sure the modified page precedes the original in the file. Also make sure you precede the modified page with its intended ***device label to tell AutoCAD how to compile it. Duplicate device labels are okay, but the first page following the first device label will be the default page for that device.*

Suspended Commands and Menu Macros

The AutoCAD menu observes the same command suspension rules as the AutoCAD command processor. If AutoCAD receives filtering modes, like osnaps and point filters, it applies the filter to the current command. For example, when AutoCAD is paused for point input by a backslash in the menu, it suspends filling a macro backslash until it receives more input. In other words, these filters suspend and do not *use up* backslashes present in the macro. Let's look at suspended commands by making another menu page, this one for the point filters.

Making a Point Filter Menu Page

Command: **MNU**

 Examine the menu text.

 Add this page above the **OSNAPS line:

```
**PTFILTERS
[Ptfilter ]
[]
[   X of   ].X $S= $S= $B=BUTTONS
[   Y of   ].Y $S= $S= $B=BUTTONS
[   Z of   ].Z $S= $S= $B=BUTTONS
[  XY of   ].XY $S= $S= $B=BUTTONS
[  XZ of   ].XZ $S= $S= $B=BUTTONS
[  YZ of   ].YZ $S= $S= $B=BUTTONS
[]
[   0,0    ]0,0 $S= $S= $B=BUTTONS
[    @     ]@ $S= $S= $B=BUTTONS
[]
[]
[]
[]
[]
[]
```

```
[]
[  root   ]$S=SCREEN $B=BUTTONS
```

> You'll have to wait to try these until you add an item to access them.

Use button 2 to make a menu page toggle. Currently, your button 2 calls up the OSNAPS screen. Add a "$B=ALT-BUT" to modify the button itself, then add an **ALT-BUT page menu. This is diagrammed in the facing page illustration at the beginning of this chapter.

 Even if you have the CA DISK, change [2 OSNAPS] to read:

```
[2 OSNAPS ]$S=OSNAPS $B=ALT-BUT
```

 If you don't have the CA DISK, add the one line **ALT-BUT page just above ***SCREEN:

```
**ALT-BUT 2
[PTFILTER alt. def. of 2 button]$S=PTFILTERS $B=BUTTONS
```

Save, exit, and reload the menu.

Notice that the **ALT-BUT label is followed by the number 2. The number is not part of the label name. The number tells AutoCAD to begin loading that page at that numbered position of the device. In this case, the position is button 2. This method of offsetting the loading position of a menu page applies to all devices. Negative numbers start at the bottom of the ***device. Use this basic technique to toggle individual menu items, or to toggle partial menus. The button and screen toggle menu system is shown in the Buttons and Screen Toggling illustration at the beginning of the chapter.

Restoring Menu Pages

Your only access to the **PTFILTERS page is by picking button 2 twice, first flipping the screen to **OSNAPS, then to **PTFILTERS. Since this flips two screen menus, you have to use two $S= items per line in your **PTFILTERS menu to return to the previous screen menu. When a point filter item is selected, the previous screen menu restores. The $B=BUTTONS insures that the buttons menu is also restored.

Select **[Button 8]**		Start a line.
Select **[Button 2]**		$S=OSNAPS $B=ALT-BUT invisibly toggles the screen to the OSNAPS and toggles button 2 to $S=PTFILTERS $B=BUTTONS.
Select **[Button 2]**		$S=PTFILTERS $B=BUTTONS toggles the screen to **PTFILTERS and restores button 2 to $S=OSNAPS $B=ALT-BUT.
Select **[X of]**		It restores the screen and original button 2, then:
From point: .X of		Pick X component of point.
(need Y):		Pick Y component.
Select **[Button 2]**		Do it several times to see it flip-flop.

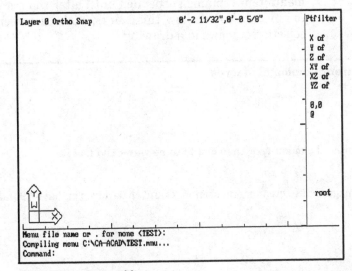

Point Filters Screen Menu

Each time you hit button 2, the screen menu pages flip-flop back and forth. Why? Because when you select button 2, the screen is changed to the osnaps page and the button menu is changed to redefine button 2. Hitting button 2 again or selecting an osnap option resets the button menu back to the original definitions.

Macros and AutoCAD's Transparent Commands

As AutoCAD matures, the ability of commands to coexist improves. A key to coexistence is transparency. Transparency means that a command can act or a mode can be set without cancelling another currently active command. Menu page changes, osnaps and point filters are always transparent. You may need to call other transparent commands in the middle of AutoCAD commands in your menu. Some common transparent commands are: 'GRAPHSCR, 'HELP, 'RESUME, 'SETVAR, 'TEXTSCR,

'ZOOM, 'PAN, and 'VIEW. You make these commands transparent by preceding the command with an apostrophe.

➨ *NOTE: In menus, you can always precede transparent commands with an apostrophe. It can't hurt if you aren't in another command, and always works if you are.*

When a transparent command is called, AutoCAD interrupts the current command, processes the transparent command completely, then resumes the original command. If a menu item is currently suspended by a backslash and a transparent command is issued, the \ is not filled. The menu item remains suspended until after the transparent command is completed. To see how this works, make a screen menu that gives a selection of views in a drawing.

Making Transparent Command Macros

Command: **MNU**

Just examine the menu text, then create some views and test it.

Add this page to the screen menu section. Count to be sure you have 19 [labeled] items:

```
**TRANVIEW
[TranView ]
[]
[  All    ]'VIEW R A $S=
[   A1    ]'VIEW R A1 $S=
[   A2    ]'VIEW R A2 $S=
[   A3    ]'VIEW R A3 $S=
[   A4    ]'VIEW R A4 $S=
[   B1    ]'VIEW R B1 $S=
[   B2    ]'VIEW R B2 $S=
[   B3    ]'VIEW R B3 $S=
[   B4    ]'VIEW R B4 $S=
[]
[]
[]
[]
[]
[]
[]
[  root   ]$S=SCREEN
```

Replace the 19th item at the bottom of your **ROOT page with:

[TRANVIEW] $S=TRANVIEW

Save, exit, and reload. [TRANVIEW] should appear at the bottom.

Command: **VIEW**	Define several views, corresponding to the menu view names. View "A" for All was in your prototype drawing.
Command: **CIRCLE**	Start any command.
Select **[TRANVIEW]**	The TranView page should appear.
Select **[ ]**	Select a view name that you defined. It is restored.
Select **[TRANVIEW] [All]**	It restores view A.

➡ *NOTE: Do not begin transparent command macros with <^C>s. The <^C> cancels any pending command. If you issue a transparent command, like 'ZOOM, when no other command is pending, 'ZOOM functions as a normal ZOOM. The leading apostrophe causes no problem. AutoCAD does not permit transparent commands that cause a regeneration.*

Pull-Down Menus — AutoCAD's Special Interface

Pull-down menus are specially implemented AutoCAD menus that pull down (some say *pop up*) to overlay a portion of your display. They are dynamic in nature. They only appear when they are opened. They disappear as soon as another action is taken. Unlike the screen menu, pull-downs *borrow* temporary space from the drawing area.

Each pull-down menu is a separate device in the menu file. There are ten positions on the display for pull-downs, so there are ten device names: ***POP1 through ***POP10. Like other devices, the labels identify the defaults. You can access any number of pages. Like the screen page code $S=, pull-downs are loaded using $P1= through $P10= page codes. The ten positions are shown in the screen shot of Pull-Down Menu Locations.

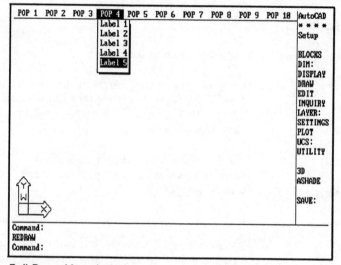

Pull-Down Menu Locations

Pull-downs are different from other devices. They need to be *opened* to be used. Using $P2=*name* loads **name to the P2 position, but it does not display it. You must use an asterisk in combination with a $P code to tell AutoCAD to open a pull-down. $P2=* causes AutoCAD to display whatever is currently loaded to the POP2 device. Menu item toggling also works with pull-downs, but you need to remember to explicitly open them if you want them displayed.

You also can *open* a pull-down by moving the pointer up to the status area of the display. Then you pick it to pull down the menu currently loaded to that portion of the status line.

The following exercise puts transparent SETVARS on the first page of POP1. The second page is for 3D system variables which we will add in the chapter on 3D customizing. For now, the second page contains only blank labels, but demonstrates how multiple pages are called and displayed. We are sure that you will think of many other useful applications for pull-downs. Our SETVARS illustrate the usefulness of pull-down item labels for displaying information. Because POP1 is the leftmost device, you can use nearly the whole display screen width for your item labels. You can also display more than eight characters in the menu bar labels on the status line. It grows as wide as needed, but long menu labels may restrict the number of pull-down menus that your display has space for.

Putting SETVARs on a Pull-Down Menu

```
Command: SETVAR            If not sure, see if you can use pull-downs.
Variable name or ?: POPUPS
POPUPS = 0 (read only)     A "0" means no.
POPUPS = 1 (read only)     A "1" means OK, then:

Command: MNU
```

 Just examine the menu text and then test the pull-down menu.

Add this page at the bottom of TEST.MNU:

```
***POP1
**P1-SETVARS
[System Vars]
[APERTURE BOX SIZE - Target box height (entered in pixels)]'SETVAR APERTURE
[BLIPMODE - Toggles drawing blip marks off/on. 0=off, 1=on]'SETVAR BLIPMODE
[HIGHLIGHT - Toggles highlighting of entities. 0=off, 1=on]'SETVAR HIGHLIGHT
[POINT MODE/SIZE - Alters point display and size. ]$I=POINTS $I=*
[MIRROR TEXT - Toggles mirroring of text off/on. 0=off, 1=on]'SETVAR MIRRTEXT
[SKETCH WITH POLYLINE - Sketch creates lines or polylines. 0=lines,
1=pline]'SETVAR SKPOLY
[SNAP ROTATION ANGLE - Changes the snap rotation angle]'SETVAR SNAPANG
[SNAP INCREMENT - Changes snap increment. Give X,Y spacing.]'SETVAR SNAPUNIT
[PICK BOX SIZE - Object pick box size (entered in pixels)]'SETVAR PICKBOX
[--]
[3D System Variables]$P1=P1-3DVARS $P1=*
**P1-3DVARS
[3D System Vars]
[--]
[--]
[--]
[--]
[--]
[--]
[--]
[--]
[Standard System Vars]$P1=P1-SETVARS $P1=*
```

Save, exit, and reload your menu. Play with the menu.

Move the cursor to highlight [System Vars] at the top left of the screen and:

```
Pull down [System Vars]                Pick it to pull it down.
Select [APERTURE BOX SIZE - Target box height (entered in pixels)]
'SETVAR                                The pull-down disappears.
```

```
Variable name or ? <POPUPS>: APERTURE
New value for APERTURE <10>: 30
```

Select something with an osnap to see it, then UNDO or set Aperture back to 10.

Flip between pages 1 and 2 to see how they work.

➡ *NOTE: If you are designing pull-down menus on a high resolution display and intend them to be usable on other displays, don't use your full character width. Many displays are limited to only 80 characters.*

```
┌─────────────────────────────────────────────────────────┬────────┐
│ System Vars                                              │CIRCLE  │
│ APERTURE BOX SIZE - Target box height (entered in pixels)│        │
│ BLIPMODE - Toggles drawing blip marks off/on. 0=off, 1=on│LE      │
│ HIGHLIGHT - Toggles highlighting of entities. 0=off, 1=on│        │
│ POINT MODE/SIZE - Alters point display and size.         │ER      │
│ MIRROR TEXT - Toggles mirroring of text off/on. 0=off, 1=on│ER-> │
│ SKETCH WITH POLYLINE - Sketch creates lines or polylines. 0=lines 1=plines ADER│
│ SNAP ROTATION ANGLE - Changes the snap rotation angle    │MDpt    │
│ SNAP INCREMENT - Changes snap increment. Give X,Y spacing.│MDpt   │
│ ──────────────────────────────────────────              │PLpt    │
│ 3D System Variables                                      │        │
│                                                          │─PIPE-VLV│
│                                                          │ PIPE*VLV│
│                                                          │ DUP LAYR│
│  ┌─Y                                                     │        │
│  │ └─                                                    │TRANVIEW │
│  │W  ─┐                                                  │        │
│  └────┼>                                                 │        │
│ Menu file name or . for none <TEST>:                     │        │
│ Compiling menu C:\CA-ACAD\TEST.mnu...                    │        │
│ Command:                                                 │        │
└─────────────────────────────────────────────────────────┴────────┘
```

A Pull-Down Menu Selection

The pull-down menu selection called POINT MODE/SIZE item isn't ready yet. The $I= that it contains calls the ***ICONS device. Obviously, you need to create an icon menu.

Icon Menus and Slide Libraries

Icons are menus that use groups of AutoCAD slides as graphic labels. They show pictures to assist your users in choosing items.

Icons work like pull-downs. You need to load the device with a $I=pagename and then display it with $I=*. However, icons use the label [ ] differently. Icon labels supply AutoCAD with the name of the slide to show in the box. Each label corresponds to one box on the screen. The boxes are automatically arranged in groups of 4, 9, or 16. The label format is:

```
[library_file_name(individual_slide_name)]
```

AutoCAD evaluates these labels when the page is popped to the screen. If you put a space as the first character in the label, AutoCAD treats it like an ordinary label. AutoCAD displays any label text in that item's screen box instead of a slide. You can use this to show a "MORE" to the user, guiding the user to access additional pages of icons.

Icon menus use slide libraries created by AutoCAD's SLIDELIB.EXE program. Keep your images simple when making icons. Small slides display much faster than complex ones. The following exercise example uses a library of slides showing all the PDMODEs (Point Display MODEs). The slide library file is named POINT.SLB. Each slide is numerically named by its PDMODE. If you have the CA DISK, you already have POINT.SLB.

If you don't have the CA DISK, you can do this exercise without making all of the slides. If you just make the first few, only the first few icon menu items will work.

Making Slide Libraries

Just read this sequence. The slide library is already on the disk.

 Make slides and a library file, POINT.SLB:

Command: **ERASE**	Clean up your screen.
Command: **ZOOM**	Center at 0,0, height of 2.25.
Command: **'SETVAR**	
Variable name or ?: **PDSIZE**	Point size.
New value for PDSIZE: **-90**	Makes it 90 percent of screen size.
Command: **POINT**	Draw a point at 0,0.
Command: **TEXT**	Start point -1.5,-1, height .375, rotation 0.
Text: **0**	Enter a zero and <RETURN>.
Command: **MSLIDE**	Name the slide 0 (zero).

Do the following to make each of the point slides.

Command: **SETVAR**	
Variable name or ? <PDSIZE>: **PDMODE**	
New value for PDMODE: **1**	Enter the number of the Point Display Mode.
Command: **CHANGE**	Change the text to match the PDMODE value.
Command: **REGEN**	Regenerate to force it to display.
Command: **MSLIDE**	
Slide file <CA05>: **1**	Name the slide for the PDMODE number used above.

Repeat the above for each of the 20 PDMODES listed below.
Substitute the PDMODE value where required. Then:

Command: **ED**   Create a text file of the slide names. Call it TEMP.TXT.
                                   Use no <SPACE>s or <TAB>s. Be sure to <RETURN> after the last
                                   line.

0
1
2
3
4
32
33
34
35
36
64
65
66
67
68
96
97
98
99
100

Save, exit, and reenter AutoCAD.

Command: **SHELL**   We assume SLIDELIB.EXE is in the \ACAD directory.

DOS Command: **\ACAD\SLIDELIB POINT < TEMP.TXT**
SLIDELIB 1.1 (2/10/88)
(C) Copyright 1987, 1988 Autodesk, Inc.
All Rights Reserved   If no errors, it created POINT.SLB.

➡ *NOTE: The SLIDELIB.EXE program is not friendly and forgiving.
Extra characters, even invisible spaces, will make your slide library
unusable. AutoCAD sees every character, even if you can't. SLIDELIB
takes its input slide name list from the keyboard unless you redirect it
from a file. The exercise uses the < redirection symbol to input from
TEMP.TXT.*

Now that you have the slide library, you're ready to make an icon menu. This menu is called by the [System Vars] pull-down menu. It graphically displays the PDMODE slides. When you select one, it SETVARs PDMODE, and prompts for PDSIZE (Point Display SIZE).

Making an Icon Screen of PDMODEs

Command: **MNU**

 Just examine the menu text, then test the icon menu.

Edit TEST.MNU and add to the bottom:

```
***ICON
**POINTS
[POINT DISPLAY OPTIONS]
[point(0)]'SETVAR PDMODE 0 'SETVAR PDSIZE
[point(1)]'SETVAR PDMODE 1 'SETVAR PDSIZE
[point(2)]'SETVAR PDMODE 2 'SETVAR PDSIZE
[point(3)]'SETVAR PDMODE 3 'SETVAR PDSIZE
[point(4)]'SETVAR PDMODE 4 'SETVAR PDSIZE
[point(32)]'SETVAR PDMODE 32 'SETVAR PDSIZE
[point(33)]'SETVAR PDMODE 33 'SETVAR PDSIZE
[point(34)]'SETVAR PDMODE 34 'SETVAR PDSIZE
[point(35)]'SETVAR PDMODE 35 'SETVAR PDSIZE
[point(36)]'SETVAR PDMODE 36 'SETVAR PDSIZE
[point(64)]'SETVAR PDMODE 64 'SETVAR PDSIZE
[point(65)]'SETVAR PDMODE 65 'SETVAR PDSIZE
[point(66)]'SETVAR PDMODE 66 'SETVAR PDSIZE
[point(67)]'SETVAR PDMODE 67 'SETVAR PDSIZE
[point(68)]'SETVAR PDMODE 68 'SETVAR PDSIZE
[ MORE]$I=MOREPTS $I=*
+
**MOREPTS
[ADDITIONAL POINT DISPLAY OPTIONS]
[point(96)]'SETVAR PDMODE 96 'SETVAR PDSIZE
[point(97)]'SETVAR PDMODE 97 'SETVAR PDSIZE
[point(98)]'SETVAR PDMODE 98 'SETVAR PDSIZE
[point(99)]'SETVAR PDMODE 99 'SETVAR PDSIZE
[point(100)]'SETVAR PDMODE 100 'SETVAR PDSIZE
[ PREVIOUS]$I=POINTS $I=*
[  ]
[  ]
[  ]
[  ]
```

Save, exit, and reload the menu.

Test the icon menu.

Pull down **[System Vars]**
Select **[POINT MODE/SIZE - Alters point display and size.]**

The POINT DISPLAY OPTIONS icon menu displays.

Select **[point(0)]**   Highlight the top left little box and pick.
Command: 'SETVAR   The menu disappears and sets the mode:
Variable name or ? <APERTURE>: PDMODE
New value for PDMODE <100>: 0
Command: 'SETVAR Variable name or ? <PDMODE>: PDSIZE
New value for PDSIZE <-90.0000>: **-12**   Enter size. Negative means % screen height.

 Delete TEST.MNU.

 Rename TEST.MNU to MY05.MNU.

Command: **QUIT**

A macro following an icon menu label works just like any other macro. The [MORE] line is an example of using a text label in an icon screen. The [MORE] macro loads the second page of points to the icon device, then pops it to the screen. The extra [ ]s in the second page force the page past nine items. Without the blanks, the page would display as 3 x 3 items and not match the 4 x 4 items in the main page.

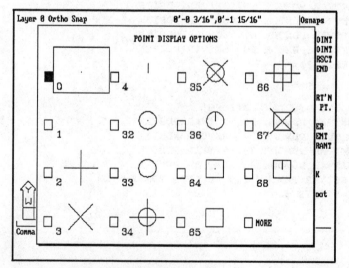

Icon Menu Called From a Macro

Summary of Menu Devices

Designing an effective menu system depends on your application. If you are uncertain about layout, use a simple tree structure. Use branches for different operations. Here are some tips for using different devices.

The SCREEN menu is convenient and right in your line of vision. The screen menu offers dynamic flipping of visible pages with definable labels. You can even swap individual items within a menu page. Use screen menus for logical organization and to order your work flow.

BUTTONS menus use the mouse or digitizer puck buttons. Having user-defined macros at the fingertips is one of AutoCAD's best features. Buttons are perfect for items which affect the picking of points and objects, since picking naturally uses the cursor.

The TABLET menu can divide your digitizing tablet into four rectangular areas, each containing a different set of commands. Tablet menus offer the advantage of using templates to visually indicate macros and commands. Tablet menus are fairly static. If you change overlays very often you will make mistakes. If you plan to market your developed system, you probably need to follow the AutoCAD standard. If not, lay out your own tablet menu to your best advantage.

PULL-DOWN menus are good for single-pick menu actions since they disappear after each pick. However, you can have an item recall its menu for multiple picks. Pull-downs also are good for giving users a descriptive text in a menu item label.

ICON menus, like tablets, are excellent graphic reminders of your symbols. They are less static and more flexible than tablets.

An AUXILIARY device is another electronic box that has the same advantages as an extra digitizing tablet without the ability to act as a pointing device.

Don't neglect the keyboard when you design your menus. You can assign commands to control keys or to two- or three-character abbreviations using macro utilities like ProKey, PRD+, or even AutoLISP. Once you learn the abbreviations, you can access any command with quick one-handed typing.

You now have menu pages and devices to work with. The next step is to build a menu system. We'll start developing our menu system in the next chapter.

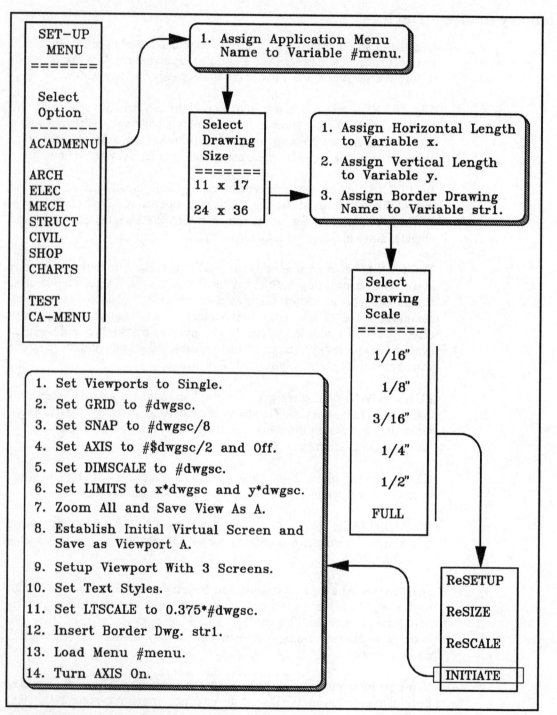

```
SET-UP
MENU
=======

Select
Option
-------
ACADMENU

ARCH
ELEC
MECH
STRUCT
CIVIL
SHOP
CHARTS

TEST
CA-MENU
```

1. Assign Application Menu Name to Variable #menu.

```
Select
Drawing
Size
=======
11 x 17

24 x 36
```

1. Assign Horizontal Length to Variable x.
2. Assign Vertical Length to Variable y.
3. Assign Border Drawing Name to Variable str1.

```
Select
Drawing
Scale
=======
1/16"

1/8"

3/16"

1/4"

1/2"

FULL
```

1. Set Viewports to Single.
2. Set GRID to #dwgsc.
3. Set SNAP to #dwgsc/8
4. Set AXIS to #$dwgsc/2 and Off.
5. Set DIMSCALE to #dwgsc.
6. Set LIMITS to x*dwgsc and y*dwgsc.
7. Zoom All and Save View As A.
8. Establish Initial Virtual Screen and Save as Viewport A.
9. Setup Viewport With 3 Screens.
10. Set Text Styles.
11. Set LTSCALE to 0.375*#dwgsc.
12. Insert Border Dwg. str1.
13. Load Menu #menu.
14. Turn AXIS On.

```
ReSETUP

ReSIZE

ReSCALE

INITIATE
```

A Menu System for Drawing Setup

CHAPTER 6

A Menu System

GETTING WHAT YOU ORDERED, AND ORDERING WHAT YOU GOT

Writing menu macros is a simple task. Structuring your menu macros into a working system takes a little more time and effort. This chapter shows you how to make a setup menu, called CA-SETUP.MNU, and an applications menu, called CA-MENU.MNU. Structuring these two menus will provide you with a menu model for your own applications.

The Benefits of Developing a Menu System

There is a common set of tasks that custom menus can perform. Tools to set up a drawing for border sheet size and drawing scale are basic to any menu system. If you work on different paper sizes at a variety of scales, you can automate your setup to deal efficiently with the different paper sizes and scales. You can plan and control scale of text and symbols, and dimension and annotate components as easily as you draw lines. You also can automate your layering scheme with menu macros. A setup menu lets you avoid the same old routine and make fewer setup mistakes.

Besides standardizing and automating your setup routine, a custom menu system tells your users what is available in your system. You can control access to screen menus to ensure that you get your drawing set up in the way your programs expect to find it. You will find that you draw more accurately and efficiently.

If you examine the following menus, you will find that they divide into two groups: general drafting macros and application-specific macros. We will follow this basic two-part breakdown as we organize menus throughout the rest of the book.

How-To Skills Checklist

The exercises in this chapter show you how to:

❑ Make a setup menu for border sheets, scales, grids and snaps.

❑ Use SETVAR to establish drawing settings.

❑ Automate loading of application menus.

❑ Organize an application screen menu.

❑ Use screen menu page footers.

❑ Make a standard text screen menu.

❑ Use a subset of your application menu as a development TEST.MNU.

❑ Use menu page access entry points to control your drawing environment.

❑ Use AutoLISP to help set up menus.

Menus and AutoLISP Tools

MENUS

The CA-SETUP.MNU is a menu file containing routines to initialize a new drawing. The root page selects the application menu to load.

DWG is a screen page to select drawing size.

SCALE is a screen page of supported plot scales.

[INITIATE] is the main CA-SETUP.MNU macro. It sets up the drawing with the correct limits, snaps and grids, inserts the border sheet, and loads the application menu.

CA-MENU.MNU is the application menu.

ROOT is the main applications page. It gives access to application- and task-specific branches.

TEXT is a typical menu page with standard text sizes and styles.

AutoLISP TOOLS

[INITIATE] is a macro that contains AutoLISP functions to help perform setup. We defer an AutoLISP discussion until the next chapter, but test the waters a bit now.

In addition to these menus, you will save a subset of the CA-MENU, called MAIN.MNU, to use as a development menu template for the rest of the book. Each chapter has its own CAnn.MNU menu, such as CA06.MNU. If you have the CA DISK, you have them all. If not, this template saves repetitive work. You will do your development and testing work in a temporary TEST.MNU file, then permanently copy it to the real menu file name.

Automating a Setup Menu

Setup is common to all drawings. What does a setup menu do? It does as much as possible. A setup menu shifts control from the prototype drawing to the menu. It provides a selectable drawing environment. A good setup menu, like CA-SETUP, does the following:

- Determines drawing scale.

- Determines drawing limits.

- Determines linetype scale.

- Establishes text styles.

- Sets GRID, SNAP, and AXIS.

- Sets DIMSCALE equal to #DWGSC, an AutoLISP variable.

- Uses AutoLISP variables to save settings.

- Sets an initial screen menu.

- Inserts a border drawing.

- Does an expanded ZOOM to establish virtual screen size.

- Resets VIEW A (All).

- Loads application menus.

Once the drawing is set up, these settings usually do not change. We recommend that you keep your setup menu separate from your application menus. This menu separation lets you lead your user through setup to get to your application menu.

The Setup Menu CA-SETUP.MNU

The book's setup menu is a basic four-page sequential screen menu. It starts the user with a menu showing the application choices available. Later, you can use the book's menu model to substitute your own labels and applications.

If you have the CA-DISK, you have the CA-SETUP.MNU. Examine CA-SETUP as you edit, and ignore the items that haven't been created yet.

If you do not have the CA-SETUP.MNU, you need to create it. To create the menu, make a 20-line template page. The first line should contain **.

Follow this line with 19 [ ]s. This template is created in the following exercise. Copy and edit the template to write each screen page. The template insures that each menu page has exactly 19 items, so they will align on the screen.

Making CA-SETUP.MNU

Enter selection: **1**   Begin a NEW drawing named CA06.

 Copy CA-SETUP.MNU to TEST.MNU, examine the exercise, then test it.

Start a new file named TEST.MNU, create the menu, then test it.

Command: **MNU**   Edit TEST.MNU, make your 20-line template:

```
**
[]
[]
[]
[]
[]
[]
[]
[]
[]
[]
[]
[]
[]
[]
[]
[]
[]
[]
[]
```

Copy the template page to make four pages, then make the first page read:

```
***SCREEN
[ SET-UP ]
[  MENU  ]
[=======]
[]
[ Select ]
[ Option ]
[--------]
[ACADMENU]^C^C^C(setq #menu "ACAD");$S=DWG
```

```
[]
[ARCH     ]^C^C^C(prompt "Architectural Menu is not available yet!^M");
[ELEC     ]^C^C^C(prompt "Electrical Menu is not available yet!^M");
[MECH     ]^C^C^C(prompt "Mechanical Menu is not available yet!^M");
[STRUCT   ]^C^C^C(prompt "Structural Menu is not available yet!^M");
[CIVIL    ]^C^C^C(prompt "Civil Menu is not available yet!^M");
[SHOP     ]^C^C^C(prompt "Shop Drawing Menu is not available yet!^M");
[CHARTS   ]^C^C^C(prompt "Charts Menu is not available yet!^M");
[]
[TEST     ]^C^C^C(setq #menu "TEST");$S=DWG
[CA-MENU  ]^C^C^C(setq #menu "CA-MENU");$S=DWG
```

Save and exit to AutoCAD.

Command: **MENU**   Reload the new TEST menu. Test all items.

Select **[CIVIL]**   Inactive items issue an AutoLISP prompt, like:
Command: (prompt "Civil Menu is not available yet!
1> ")
Civil Menu is not available yet!
Lisp returns: nil

Select **[TEST]**
Command: (setq #menu "TEST")   If you have the CA DISK, it also flips pages.
Lisp returns: "TEST"

The first page of the menu lets you select an application. Notice, there is a "^M" inside the prompt strings. The menu interpreter reads the "^M" as a special menu character and issues a <RETURN>. This <RETURN> cleans up the prompt, forcing the "nil" to a separate line.

When you complete the menu pages in this chapter, you will have three active selections: [ACADMENU], [CA-MENU], and [TEST]. Each menu item saves the name of the application menu selected, TEST, CA-ACAD, or the standard ACAD menu. These menu items use the AutoLISP function SETQ to save the menu name in an AutoLISP variable, #MENU. After saving the selected menu item name, the menu changes to a menu page of border sheet sizes.

➡ *NOTE: In the book, we set units in the prototype drawing and in specific exercises where needed. In a real application, you might wish to add units settings to each of the application selections. For example, a mechanical selection loading a menu named MECH.MNU would become:*

```
[MECH     ]^C^C^CUNITS 3 4 1 4 0 N (setq #menu MECH);$S=DWG
```

The border sheet menu establishes the drawing size. It stores the drawing size along with the appropriate border block name. The size and block are stored as the AutoLISP variables X, Y, and STR1. Create the border sheet menu.

Making a Border Sheet Page

 Continue to examine the menu, then test it.

Continue doing the exercise.

Command: **MNU**   Edit TEST.MNU and add the following below the first screen page.

```
**DWG-DOC
[This selection establishes the drawing size and saves it as a variable.]
[The final limits will be determined by a scale factor in the next selection.]
**DWG
[ Select ]
[ Drawing]
[  Size  ]
[=======]
[]
[11 x 17 ](setq x 17.0) (setq y 11.0) (setq str1 "SHEET-B");$S=SCALE
[]
[24 x 36 ](setq x 36.0) (setq y 24.0) (setq str1 "SHEET-D");$S=SCALE
[]
[]
[]
[]
[]
[]
[]
[]
[]
[]
[]
```

Save, exit, and reload the menu.

Test both sizes. First:

```
Select [TEST] [11 x 17]
Command: (setq x 17.0) 17.000000          All this scrolls by.
Command: (setq y 11.0) 11.000000
Command: (setq str1 "SHEET-B")
Lisp returns: "SHEET-B"                    It flips pages if you have the CA DISK.
```

Although this exercise only provides two sheet sizes, B and D, you can add additional sheet sizes. If you have the CA DISK, you will find two border drawings: SHEET-B.DWG and SHEET-D.DWG in your CA-ACAD directory. Each border drawing contains a complex border on layer BDR00BDR, and a simple outline reference border on layer REF00BDR. You can freeze the complex border layer and use the reference outline on layer REF00BDR. Please note that our drawing borders have very wide margins. These margins are meant to accommodate a variety of plotters. You can adjust the margins to fit your plotter.

Notice the **DWG-DOC page on the border sheet menu page. **DWG-DOC is a dummy page. It shows how to include non-functional items as additional documentation in your menu files.

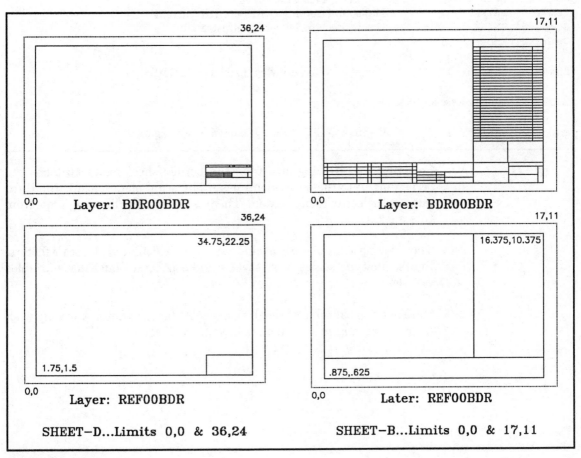

Border Drawings

If you are not using the CA-DISK, you will have to create the border drawings.

Making Border Drawings

 If you have the CA DISK, skip this sequence.

Create the simple outline reference border for both sheets.

```
Command: QUIT
Enter selection: 1          Begin a NEW drawing named SHEET-B=.

Command: LIMITS            Set 17 x 11 limits.
Command: LAYER             Make and set layer REF00BDR current.
Command: PLINE             Draw the simple border illustrated.
Command: END


Enter selection: 1          Begin a NEW drawing named SHEET-D=.
```

Repeat the same process for 36 x 24.

```
Enter selection: 1          Begin a NEW drawing named CA06 again.
```

Selecting the drawing size from the border sheet menu switches the screen menu to the scale menu page. The scale menu page is the third page in the setup menu system. The user selects the drawing scale from this menu.

The drawing scale menu contains a set of pre-calculated plot scale factors, limits, linetype scales, text style standards, and dimension variables settings.

Here is a typical table of the drawing scale factors. Later, you may wish to add or eliminate scale factors in your own menu.

DRAWING FACTORS

DRAWING SCALE	SCALE FACTOR	HORZ LIMITS	VERT LIMITS	LTSCALE	TEXT HEIGHT				
					1/16"	3/32"	1/8"	3/16"	1/4"
FULL	1	3'	2'	.375	.0625	.09375	.125	.1875	.25
3"	4	12'	8'	1.5	.25	.375	.5	.75	1
1 1/2"	8	24'	16'	3	.5	.5625	1	1.5	2
1"	12	36'	24'	4.5	.75	1.125	1.5	2.25	3
3/4"	16	48'	32'	6	1	1.5	2	3	4
1/2"	24	72'	48'	9	1.5	2.25	3	4.5	6
3/8"	32	96'	64'	12	2	3	4	6	8
1/4"	48	144'	96'	18	3	4.5	6	9	12
3/16"	64	192'	128'	24	4	6	8	12	16
1/8"	96	288'	192'	36	6	9	12	18	24
1/16"	192	576'	384'	72	12	18	24	36	48

Drawing Factors

The scale selections save the scale value as the global variable #DWGSC, then flip the menu to the **INITIATE page. There, the setup menu closes with an [INITIATE] macro which establishes the drawing settings by running several AutoCAD commands. It zooms, inserts the border, and then exits to the application menu that you selected on the first menu page. If you change your mind about your setup, you can return to previous menu pages to change your selection. [ReSCALE], for example, returns you to the drawing scale page.

Making a Drawing Scale Menu

 Examine the menu text.

 Add the menu text as shown.

Command: **MNU**   Edit TEST.MNU and add **SCALE and **INITIATE pages:

```
**SCALE
[ Select ]
[ Drawing]
[ Scale  ]
[========]
[]
[  1/16" ](setq #dwgsc 192.0);$S=INITIATE
[]
[   1/8" ](setq #dwgsc 96.0);$S=INITIATE
[]
[  3/16" ](setq #dwgsc 64.0);$S=INITIATE
[]
[   1/4" ](setq #dwgsc 48.0);$S=INITIATE
[]
[   1/2" ](setq #dwgsc 24.0);$S=INITIATE
[]
[   FULL ](setq #dwgsc 1.0);$S=INITIATE
[]
[]
[]
**INITIATE
[]
[ReSETUP ]^C^C^C$S=SCREEN
[]
[ReSIZE  ]^C^C^C$S=DWG
[]
[ReSCALE ]^C^C^C$S=SCALE
[]
[INITIATE]^C^C^CVPORTS SI GRID !#dwgsc ^GSNAP (/ #dwgsc 8) AXIS (/ #dwgsc 2);+
AXIS OFF SETVAR DIMSCALE !#dwgsc LIMITS 0,0 (list (* x #dwgsc) (* y #dwgsc));+
REGENAUTO ON ZOOM A REGENAUTO OFF VIEW S A ZOOM .75X;+
VPORTS S A ;3 V ;J ;(setq count -1 var (vports));+
(while (and var (setq alist (nth (setq count (1+ count)) var)));+
(and (equal 0.333 (caadr alist) 0.01) (equal 0 (cadadr alist) 0.01);+
(setq var nil alist (setvar "CVPORT" (car alist))))) !alist;+
(setq count -1  var (vports));+
(while (and var (setq alist (nth (setq count (1+ count)) var)));+
(and (equal 0 (caadr alist) 0.01) (equal 0 (cadadr alist) 0.01);+
(setq var nil alist (setvar "CVPORT" (car alist)))));+
VPORTS 3 H ;J ;(setq count -1  var (vports));+
```

```
(while (and var (setq alist (nth (setq count (1+ count)) var)));+
(and (equal 0 (caadr  alist) 0.01) (equal 0.333 (cadadr alist) 0.01);+
(setq var nil alist (setvar "CVPORT" (car alist))))) !alist VPORTS S CA Y ;R A;+
STYLE STANDARD ROMANS (* 0.125 #dwgsc) ;;;;;+
STYLE STD1-16 ROMANS (* 0.0625 #dwgsc) ;;;;;+
STYLE STD3-32 ROMANS (* 0.09375 #dwgsc) ;;;;;+
STYLE STD3-16 ROMANS (* 0.1875 #dwgsc) ;;;;;+
STYLE STD1-4 ROMANS (* 0.25 #dwgsc) ;;;;;+
STYLE STD1-8 ROMANS (* 0.125 #dwgsc) ;;;;;+
LTSCALE (* 0.375 #dwgsc) INSERT !str1 0,0 !#dwgsc ;;MENU !#menu ^GAXIS ON
[]
[]
[]
[]
[]
[]
[]
[]
[]
[]
[]
```

Save, exit, and reload the menu.

Here is how the [INITIATE] macro works. First, [INITIATE] sets VPORTS to SIngle to ensure a full screen configuration for the following settings. Then it sets GRID to the drawing scale #DWGSC. One grid space on screen will equal one inch on the plot. It sets SNAP to 1/8 of #DWGSC, AXIS to 1/2 of #DWGSC, and DIMSCALE to #DWGSC. Next, [INITIATE] uses AutoLISP to recalculate the limits, toggles REGENAUTO on to avoid a possible "About to regen -- proceed? Y" prompt, and does a ZOOM All. After the ZOOM All, VIEW S A saves view A (for All) and Zoom .75x zooms out to allow a healthy margin around the drawing edges. VPORTS S A saves the single setup as A.

[INITIATE] re-establishes the viewport configuration we set earlier in the CA-PROTO prototype drawing. This is necessary to force settings such as SNAP and GRID across all viewports. Unfortunately, it can't be automated without the AutoLISP that follows VPORTS S A. It's not as complex as it looks since it just repeats the same code three times to select three viewports as the macro sets the screen up. However, we'll save an explanation for the book INSIDE AutoLISP.

Then [INITIATE] resets the standard text styles for the drawing plot scale. An AutoLISP calculation provides the height of the text. Next, the [INITIATE] macro inserts the border sheet, saved as STR1, and scales it to the current scale. Last, the [INITIATE] macro loads a new menu file using the menu name that was selected by the user on the first menu page. This selected menu name is stored in the #MENU variable.

☞   *The #DWGSC variable is required by many menu items and AutoLISP routines throughout the book. It should always be set by starting up with the CA-SETUP menu.*

Now let's test the setup menu.

TEST.MNU With the CA-SETUP Menu

To make sure there are no errors in the setup menu, test the menu by selecting each item on each menu page. You should be in drawing CA06 with the setup TEST.MNU loaded.

Testing the Setup Menu and Updating CA-PROTO.DWG

Select **[ACADMENU]**   You see:
Command: (setq #menu "ACAD")   Saves menu name.

Lisp returns: "ACAD"

If OK, it flips to the Select Drawing
Size screen menu.

Select **[11 x 17]**
Command: (setq x 17.0) 17.000000
Command: (setq y 11.0) 11.000000
Command: (setq str1 "SHEET-B")
Lisp returns: "SHEET-B"

Saves X limit.
Saves Y.
Saves border name.
If OK, you get a page of scales and [INITIATE].

Select **[1/16"]**
Command: (setq #dwgsc 192.0) 192.000000
Lisp returns: nil

Saves plot scale and presents
the **INITIATE page.

Select **[INITIATE]**

GRID, SNAP, AXIS, SETVAR, LIMITS, REGENAUTO, VPORTS,
VIEW, STYLE and LTSCALE scroll by. It INSERTs the 11 x 17 border.
MENU loads ACAD.MNU, which was saved as #MENU.

Command: **U**

Type U to Undo and return to first page of setup TEST.MNU.

Select **[TEST] [24 x 36] [FULL]**
Select **[INITIATE]**

It scrolls and reloads the TEST Menu.

Command: **U**
Command: **QUIT**

Undo it. Test the rest of the items.

If you have the CA-DISK, [INITIATE] will find the CA-MENU file when it
loads the CA-MENU.MNU file.

If you don't have the CA DISK, you need to create the CA-MENU file
(later in this chapter) before it can load.

If you want to see how much work the setup menu does for you, you can
echo the setup sequence to your printer (if available) with the <^Q> toggle
before executing the setup menu. Another <^Q> toggles the printer off.

Some of the settings that the setup menu makes were previously set in
the prototype drawing, so we had temporary defaults to work with.
Scale-dependent settings, such as SNAP and GRID, are handled much
better by the setup menu. Since these settings are independent in each
viewport, the viewports must be reset for each scale and sheet size. A
setup menu or AutoLISP program is the only logical way to do this. Since
this book doesn't cover true AutoLISP commands and functions, the
viewports menu code in [INITIATE] gets a little lengthy. In the book,
INSIDE AutoLISP (New Riders Publishing), we use a SETVP function to
efficiently reset viewports.

When the entire menu is tested, add CA-SETUP to the prototype drawing so that it will be the default menu.

 Even if you have the CA DISK, add CA-SETUP to the prototype drawing.

Adding the CA-SETUP Menu to CA-PROTO

Enter selection: **2**   Edit the EXISTING drawing CA-PROTO.

 Delete TEST.MNU.

 Rename TEST.MNU to CA-SETUP.MNU.

Command: **MENU**   Load the CA-SETUP menu.
Command: **END**

Controlling Access to Your Menu Pages

Knowing when to take and when to release control of your menu system to your users is part of the customization process. Your initial drawing setup relied purely on the prototype drawing to establish your drawing environment. By creating a setup menu and the start of an applications menu, you shifted control of the drawing environment to these menus.

Understanding where to establish your control points and how to manage the drawing data gives you control of the environment. The intent is not to limit the user, but to make drawing easier and consistent. Your users will make fewer mistakes with layers, colors, and linetypes, and with sizing inserted blocks if you manage these operations at control points in your application menus.

The control point that you have started with is switching menu pages. Page changing is a natural custom control point. You can make your menu page display the current environment or change the environment in preparation for the next set of commands. You can run a series of setup and checking commands in the stage between a user's selecting a menu item and the presentation of a supporting screen page. Some control steps to consider are:

- Make or set a layer, and store the current one.

- Change the text style.

- Set the grid and snap.

- Load AutoLISP commands.

- Set AutoCAD system variables or AutoLISP variables.

- Save the drawing.

- Perform a zoom.

- Save or restore a view.

- Set up, save or restore viewports or UCSs.

- Display status information in screen status line or menu boxes, or command line prompts.

- Update a time log.

These are common tasks performed at control points. You've already seen several examples in the [INITIATE] macro. The dimensioning menu in Chapter 10 also provides examples of most of these. But right now, in the CA-MENU, you will use page access to control a layer setting. You also will make sure the #DWGSC variable is reset if the drawing is ended or restarted. #DWGSC, like many of these controls, requires a little AutoLISP.

Application Menus

Your application-specific menu pages will form the core of your menu system. They may not be the largest portion, but they are the most important. The application menu in this book *is the book*. The book's application menu pages are designed to show a range of applications rather than a single pure application, but the menu structure is typical of any application menu.

This book's menu has a primary tree structure. The default **ROOT screen page provides access to the individual menu pages that you make as you work through the book.

Making the Main Application Screen

Enter selection: **1**   Begin a NEW drawing, again named CA06.DWG.
                                The CA-SETUP menu should automatically load. It was set in the
                                previous exercise.

Copy CA-MENU.MNU to TEST.MNU, examine the menu text, then test it.

Begin a new menu file TEST.MNU, add the menu text and test it.

Command: **MNU**   Edit the new TEST.MNU.

Make a "**" and 19 line "[ ]" template as before, copy it twice, then edit the first page to:

```
***SCREEN
**ROOT
[CA-MENU ]
[]
[FLOWLINE]^C^C^CLAYER S OBJ01;;$S=FOOTER $S=FLOWLINE +
(if #dwgsc nil (setq #dwgsc (getvar "DIMSCALE")))
[]
[--------]
[TEXT    ]
[SPECIALS]
[ANNOTATE]$S=FOOTER $S=ANNOT LAYER S ANN02;;+
(if #dwgsc nil (setq #dwgsc (getvar "DIMSCALE")))
[DIMS    ]
[HATCH   ]
[--------]
[]
[TITLEBLK]
[3D      ]
[EXAMPLES]$S=FOOTER $S=EXAMPLES +
(if #dwgsc nil (setq #dwgsc (getvar "DIMSCALE")))
[]
[EDIT-LSP]LSP (load "TEST")
[EDIT-MNU]MNU MENU TEST
[]
```

Add one more short page:

```
**FOOTER -1
[  root  ]$S=SCREEN LAYER S 0 ;SNAP ON GRID ON ORTHO ON
```

Change the ** at the top of the second template page into the **EXAMPLE** page, like:

```
**EXAMPLES
[Examples]
[]
```

Save, exit, and reload the TEST menu.

Test some selections to see how they work.

Select **[EDIT-MNU]**	Puts you in your text editor in TEST.MNU. Exit to AutoCAD.
Select **[EDIT-LSP]**	Puts text editor in a new TEST.LSP file. Exit back to AutoCAD.
Select **[EXAMPLES]**	It flips to the Examples page.
Command: (if #dwgsc nil (setq #dwgsc (getvar "DIMSCALE")))	
Lisp returns: nil	And sets #DWGSC, if needed.
Select **[root]**	It returns to the CA-MENU page.

The LAYER and "(if #dwgsc nil..." expressions in the [ANNOTATE] and [FLOWLINE] items, and the [EXAMPLES] settings are examples of page access control. The LAYER command ensures that the proper layer is current before changing pages. The #DWGSC expression sets scale to the current DIMSCALE system variable, if it is not already set.

The **FOOTER page is our technique for returning to the root page. Each time a selection from the Main Menu is made, it places an entry at the *bottom* of the screen, letting you get back to the Main Menu. The -1 loads the page from the bottom of the device. Use this technique to reduce code and make menus easy to update.

The pages have 19 items to allow room for the footer. We held the total screen menu length to 20 lines to make the menu compatible with all displays. If you need to make your menus compatible with unknown displays, you should do the same. If your screen displays more lines, the footer will be at the bottom, following a blank area.

➤ *NOTE: There are several other ways to handle menu page changing and page footers to return to the root page. The ACAD.MNU returns to the root with its [AutoCAD] item, at the top of the root **S page. All other pages either start loading at the third line, leaving [AutoCAD] exposed, or they restore it with a $S=S when they are finished. The ACAD.MNU standard footer is the **X page. It is a nearly empty 20-line page, with only three items, [_LAST_], [DRAW], and [EDIT], at the bottom. It is designed to be overlaid by the typical menu page. This technique requires most ACAD.MNU page changes to include both $S=S and $S=X calls.*

You will use the current menu, called MAIN.MNU, as your development template menu for the rest of the book. At the start of each chapter, copy MAIN.MNU to start a new TEST.MNU. If you have the CA DISK, you already have MAIN.MNU so you can skip the following sequence. If you do not have the CA DISK, you need to copy the current TEST.MNU to the name MAIN.MNU.

Making a Development Menu Template MAIN.MNU

  Skip this sequence.

  Copy TEST.MNU to MAIN.MNU.

Command: **ED**   Edit MAIN.MNU and test it.

Change the **ROOT page [CA Menu] label to [CA00TEST], and strip the code following the
[FLOWLINE] and [ANNOTATE] labels. Their pages aren't in the test menus.

```
***SCREEN
**ROOT
[CA00TEST]
[]
[FLOWLINE]
[]
[--------]
[TEXT    ]
[SPECIALS]
[ANNOTATE]
[DIMS    ]
[HATCH   ]
[--------]
[        ]
```

The rest is unchanged.
Save MAIN.MNU and exit to AutoCAD.

Command: **MENU**   Load MAIN and test it.
Select [   ]   Test each item.
                                         Only the [EXAMPLES], [EDIT-MNU], [EDIT-LSP], and [root] items
                                         should function like they did before.

Despite the best of intentions, you are likely to build your menus in fits
and starts, merging and reorganizing them as you go. We are going to
merge the macros and menus that you created in the last chapter. This
merging will create the book's CA-MENU.MNU, the master menu that
you can add to throughout the book. (The CAMASTER.MNU on the CA
DISK is a copy of the final CA-MENU.)

If you have the CA DISK, you already have CA-MENU.MNU. Read along
but skip the following exercise.

If you don't have the CA DISK, you will get some practice appending and
merging files with your text editor.

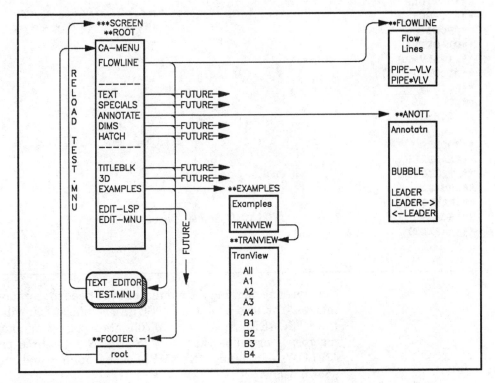

The CA-MENU Menu

You don't have to type MNU to edit the TEST.MNU. The [EDIT-MNU] item you wrote in the last exercise automatically edits TEST.MNU, and then reloads it when you reenter AutoCAD.

Merging Menu Files

Select **[EDIT-MNU]**   Edit TEST.MNU.

 Just read the menu merging exercises.

 Merge the following files.

Merge the entire MY05.MNU file into the TEST.MNU.
Merge and rename them in the order shown below.

Be careful to get all the macros on the menu pages. Only the names of the **pages and ***devices to be merged are shown.

```
***BUTTONS
**ALT-BUT 2
***POP1
**P1-SETVARS
**P1-3DVARS
***ICON
**POINTS
**MOREPTS
***SCREEN
**ROOT
**FOOTER
**EXAMPLES
**PTFILTERS
**OSNAPS
**TRANVIEW
***SCREEN                   MY05.MNU screen page.
***TABLET1
```

Save it.

You are done merging the menus, but you need to reorganize some of your macros. You also have two ***SCREEN labels. You will change most of the ***SCREEN menu from MY05 into a page of annotation and leader macros. Reorganize the old ***SCREEN into three pages,**ANNOT, **FLOWLINE, and **EXAMPLES, by adding and moving the lines shown below.

 Continue reading the exercise sequences.

 Do the following menu edits.

Change the ***SCREEN label from the MY05 menu to read **ANNOT.

Add an [Annotatn] label at the top and add blank [ ]s to make 19 items in the page.

Replace the [CIRCLE], [TEXT], [OppENDpt], [1stENDpt], [1stPLpt] and [DUP LAYR] items with [ ] blanks.
The additions and changes are shown in **bold**:

```
**ANNOT
[Annotatn ]
[]
[]
[]
[BUBBLE   ]^C^C^CCIRCLE \24 SELECT L ;TEXT S STD3-16 M @ 0 \+
LINE @ \ ID MID,QUI @ TRIM P ;END,QUI @ ;
[]
```

```
[LEADER   ]^C^C^CORTHO ON PLINE \\^O\ INSERT C:/CA-ACAD/ARROW @ 96 ;MID @ ^O
[LEADER-> ]^C^C^CORTHO ON PLINE \W 0 0 \^O\W 0 6 L -18 W 0 0 ;
[<-LEADER ]^C^C^CPLINE \\;PEDIT L E M @ X X ERASE L ;PLINE @ W 0 6 L 18 W 0 0 L 1
[]
[]                      The rest of the 19 items are [ ] blanks.
```

Move the [PIPE-VLV] and [PIPE*VLV] items (9 lines) from above to a new **FLOWLINE page.
Add the new **FLOWLINE, [Flow] and [Lines] labels and [ ] blanks to make 19 items (not all
[ ] blanks are shown).

```
**FLOWLINE
[  Flow   ]
[  Lines  ]
[]
[PIPE-VLV ]^C^C^CLAYER M OBJ02 C RED ;;+
LINE \\;INSERT /CA-ACAD/VALVE @ 16 ;DRAG \+
LINE ;\;INSERT ;@ 16 ;DRAG \+
LINE ;\;INSERT ;@ 16 ;DRAG \+
LINE ;\;INSERT ;@ 16 ;DRAG \+
LINE ;\;INSERT ;@ 16 ;DRAG
+
[PIPE*VLV ]*^C^C^CLAYER M OBJ02 C RED ;;+
LINE \\;INSERT /CA-ACAD/VALVE @ 16 ;DRAG \
[]
[]
[]
```

Move [TRANVIEW] to the **EXAMPLES page. Make sure the labeled items and [ ] blanks total
19 items:

```
**EXAMPLES
[Examples]
[]
[TRANVIEW] $S=TRANVIEW
[]
```

Find the **TRANVIEW page. Now it is accessed through the **EXAMPLES page. Add a second
$S= to the end of **each** item to return it to the previous menu before EX.MPLES. A typical line
will be:

```
[  All   ]'VIEW R A $S= $S=
```

Save, exit and return to AutoCAD. TEST.MNU should reload automatically.

Note that the [TEXT], [SPECIALS], [DIMS], [HATCH], [TITLEBLK], and [3D]
items are inactive.

Make sure the TEST.MNU is reloaded. Print out the TEST.MNU file so
you can study it as you test it. Test all the page changes and see that the
screen positions match those shown in the CA-MENU illustration.

Testing the CA-MENU Test Menu

Select **[ANNOTATE]**	It brings up Annotatn. Try some of the macros again.
Select **[root]**	To get back to CA-MENU.
Select **[FLOWLINE]**	It brings up Flow Lines. Make sure the screen changes correctly.
Select **[root]**	To get back to CA-MENU.
Select **[Button 2]**	It calls the OSNAPS and PTFILTERS toggling screens.
Select **[ ]**	Continue testing each of the items.
Select **[EDIT-MNU]**	Edit TEST.MNU if you get any errors.

 Delete TEST.MNU.

 Rename TEST.MNU to CA-MENU.MNU.

You will be happy to know the most tedious part of putting menus together is finished. You have roughed out a menu structure with a number of functional sections filled in. It is organized for the rest of the exercises in the book. From now on, you will create and work with menu pages in small TEST.MNU sections.

How to Work in TEST.MNU Menus

The next exercise is an example of how to edit a typical chapter menu in the book. Each new menu page is designed so that it *plugs into* the CA-MENU structure. Doing each chapter's development in a temporary TEST.MNU file makes menu editing easier, menu reloading faster, and protects the CA-MENU from editing errors. We will give you instructions at the end of each chapter for merging the chapter's test menu with the CA-MENU. Some chapters contain only simple example macros and AutoLISP material that you will not need to merge into the CA-MENU.

If you have the CA DISK, you already have the menus for each chapter. These are copies of MAIN.MNU with new menu pages added for the chapter. These menus are named for their corresponding chapters, like CA06.MNU and CA07.MNU.

If you don't have the CA DISK, we will ask you to copy the MAIN.MNU to a new TEST.MNU, edit it and add new pages. Always remember to rename the previous TEST.MNU to save it. Use the MAIN.MNU template to keep your test menus short and easy to use.

Making a Standard Text Screen Menu

Your version of the prototype drawing has several standard text styles. The **TEXT menu page automates the changing of styles when you enter text. If you have the CA DISK, you already have this menu, called CA06.MNU. You do not need to edit it, but you can examine the menu with your editor.

Creating the **TEXT Screen

Copy CA06.MNU to TEST.MNU, examine it, then test it.

Copy MAIN.MNU to TEST.MNU and edit as shown below.

Select **[EDIT-MNU]**   Edit the TEST.MNU.

Replace [CA00TEST] with [CA06TEST] and add the statements shown to the [TEXT] label.

```
***SCREEN
**ROOT
[CA06TEST]
[]
[FLOWLINE]
[]
[--------]
[TEXT     ]$S=TEXT $S=TXTFOOTER
```

Edit **FOOTER to **TXTFOOTER and add the following text.

```
**TXTFOOTER -1
[  root  ]$S=SCREEN LAYER S 0 ;SNAP ON GRID ON ORTHO ON STYLE STD1-8 ;;;;;;;
```

Edit the example page by adding the following material and changing **EXAMPLES to **TEXT. Make sure labels and [ ] blanks total 19 items.

```
**TEXT
[Standard]
[Textmenu]
[]
[  1/4    ]^C^C^CLAYER S TXT02;;DTEXT S STD1-4
[  3/16   ]^C^C^CLAYER S TXT02;;DTEXT S STD3-16
[  1/8    ]^C^C^CLAYER S TXT01;;DTEXT S STD1-8
[  3/32   ]^C^C^CLAYER S TXT01;;DTEXT S STD3-32
[  1/16   ]^C^C^CLAYER S TXT01;;DTEXT S STD1-16
[]
```

Save, exit, and return to AutoCAD. The menu should reload.

Test each text height. Each should set layer and start Dtext with its style.

Select **[TEXT]**

 Delete TEST.MNU.

 Rename TEST.MNU to MY06.MNU.

Command: **QUIT**

Appending the Chapter Menus

The CAMASTER.MNU file on the CA DISK includes all the important menu pages which you will develop in the following chapters. If you don't have the CA DISK, you will find instructions at the end of each chapter for combining the chapter menu with your CA-MENU.MNU. If you combine your chapter menus, your CA-MENU will match the CAMASTER.MNU file at the end of the book. The following section provides instructions on merging menus. This format will be used throughout the rest of the book.

Integrating the Text Menu

If you don't have the CA DISK, add the text menu to CA-MENU by appending and changing the following lines:

■ Insert the **TXTFOOTER and **TEXT page of your MY06.MNU in the SCREEN section of the CA-MENU.MNU file, just above the TABLET1 section.

■ Change the [TEXT] label on the **ROOT page of the CA-MENU to:

```
[TEXT    ]$S=TEXT $S=TXTFOOTER
```

Here is the Chapter 6 menu.

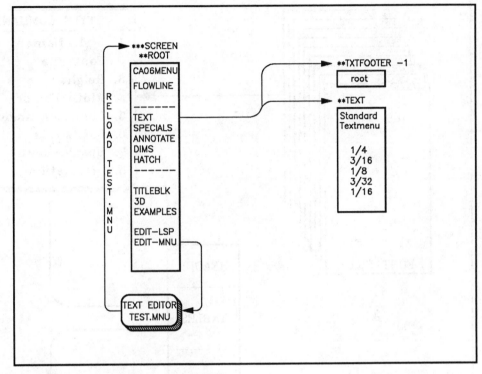

The Chapter 6 Menu Added to CA-MENU

Summary

A well-designed menu does more than just chain commands together. It can change a generic CAD program into a custom application tailored to your specific needs. Think about the users of the menu when you lay out your design. Label your menus with names that your users are familiar with, not AutoCAD terms. For example, if you create a macro to use the CHANGE command to specifically edit text, give it a label like [EditText] instead of [Change--T]. Remember, the users need to know what the macro does, not what commands it uses.

Users are less intimidated by a well-designed system. They will learn the system quickly, create accurate, uniform drawings, and reduce the time they spend on housekeeping chores to maintain the system environment.

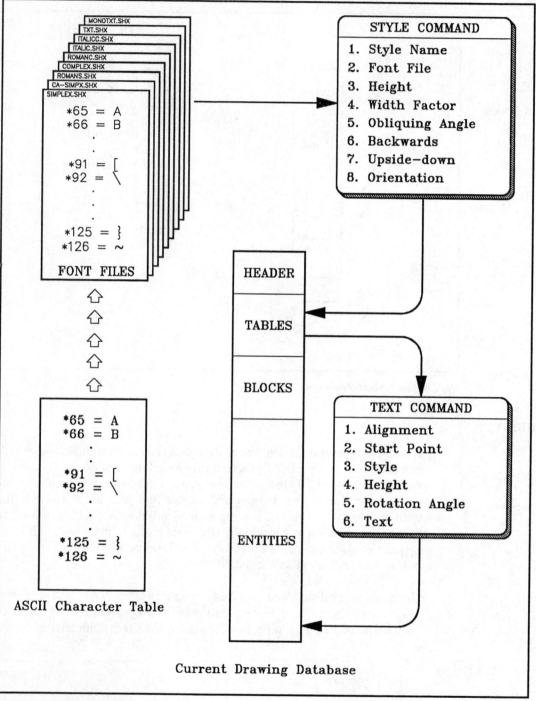

Text Style and Font Organization

CHAPTER 7

Text Styles and Fonts

ADDING CHARACTER TO YOUR DRAWINGS

AutoCAD's text styles and fonts offer a unique avenue to customization. Use fonts and styles to manipulate drawing text size and to stylize script characters. In this chapter, we will give you the basics you need to alter AutoCAD's standard font files, create your own characters, and integrate them with standard AutoCAD fonts.

AutoCAD Text Fonts

A font is a set of specific characters that make up a type style. The main text of this book, for instance, is set in Century Schoolbook font. AutoCAD perceives each of its font characters as a collection of vectors. We'll use the term *vector* instead of line so we don't confuse the vector stroke of a text entity with the line entity.

AutoCAD's fonts are stored as ASCII shape files with the .SHP extension. These files generally contain descriptions of each printable character of the keyboard. They tell AutoCAD to draw vectors for given lengths, in certain directions, to create each character. To use a font shape file in AutoCAD, you need to choose the file through the STYLE command. AutoCAD will prompt you for certain aspects such as spacing, slant, and proportion. These may be changed or accepted by hitting the RETURN key at each prompt. Once you define the font style for AutoCAD, you can use it for any text, dimensions, or annotations in your drawing. Rather than using the .SHP file, AutoCAD requires a compiled version of the file with an .SHX extension. The standard .SHP and .SHX files are provided on your AutoCAD disk set. If you want to change a character of an existing shape file or create a new shape file, you must first modify or create an .SHP file with your text editor and then compile it into an .SHX file. Unlike menus, which recompile automatically, the compiling process must be done manually using option 7 of the Main Menu.

Although worth doing, there are no easy ways to customize fonts. Font customization requires you to make your own shapes by defining new vectors for the characters you want and controlling their placement, size, and alignment. This chapter shows you how to create new characters, either from scratch or by using references to existing characters and recompiling them. It may seem tedious at first, but you'll like the results.

The Benefits of Customizing AutoCAD Text Fonts

Text is one of the most widely used AutoCAD entities, yet it is seldom customized. What can you do with a font? You can make your own dimension fractions, switch your drawings from printed to handwritten script, or create your own company logo.

Why not just use a block and insert it each time you need a special character? One simple reason is you cannot place blocks inside a string of text. Say you need a 0 with a slash through it to indicate a zero instead of the letter O. You can't go around and insert a block everywhere the text is supposed to show the zero. And wouldn't you like a good way of subscripting and superscripting the formulas and fractions in your drawings? You can solve both of these problems with font customization.

With font customization, fonts and styles give your drawing a distinctive, professional look. You can overcome any limitations of AutoCAD's standard text characters by creating special characters. And you can create characters to show fractions in your drawings.

How-To Skills Checklist

Here are the skills that you will acquire working through font customization. You will learn how to:

❏ Use the STYLE command, make new styles, and change style definitions.

❏ Make a ballot box character, like the one at the beginning of this line.

❏ Make a center line CL symbol as a text font character.

❏ Make fractions.

❏ Make bigfont characters and integrate bigfonts into your standard styles.

Macros, AutoLISP Tools, and Programs

MACROS

**SPECIALS is a menu page that types in special characters.

FILES

CA-ROMAN.SHP is a bigfont shape file containing a center line character, a ballot box, a subscript, a superscript, and a set of fractions in 1/16 increments.

AutoCAD Styles

Text is a matter of style. AutoCAD gives you many choices. The STYLE command lets you alter the appearance of any set of font characters. Let's start with the default prototype settings (name your drawing with an equal sign). Try the default TXT text font and define a ROMANS simplex style for comparison.

The STYLE and CHANGE commands also allow you to redefine existing text in the drawing. This exercise shows how AutoCAD can update restyled text on the screen with the CHANGE command.

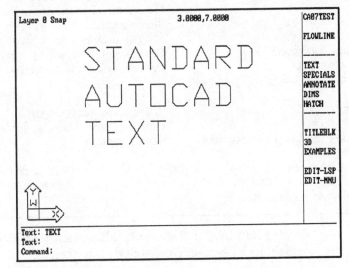

Some Standard Text

Changing Text Size Using the STYLE Command

```
Enter selection: 1              Begin a NEW drawing named CA07=.
```

 Copy CA07.MNU to TEST.MNU.

 Copy MAIN.MNU to TEST.MNU.

```
Command: MENU                   Load the menu TEST.
Command: <Snap on>              Toggle snap on with <^B> or <F9>.

Command: DTEXT                  Pick point 3,7 height 1, rotation 0 degrees.
Text: STANDARD                  Hit return to continue text line.
Text: AUTOCAD
Text: TEXT                      Return twice to accept.

Command: STYLE
Text style name (or ?) <STANDARD>: SLANT         Name of style in this drawing.
Font file <txt>: ROMANC         The font character set to ROMANC.SHX.
Height <0>: .5                  A value presets the height, or 0 lets it vary.
Width factor <1.00>: 0.8        Less than 1.0 squeezes the characters.
                                More than 1.0 expands the characters.
Obliquing angle <0>: 10         Slants characters: - for left, + for right.
Backwards? <N> <RETURN>         Or Yes draws them backwards, like a mirror.
Upside-down? <N> <RETURN>       Or Yes puts characters upside down.
Vertical? <N> <RETURN>          Or Yes defines a vertically oriented style.
SLANT is now the current text style.

Command: CHANGE                 Change the text height.
Select objects:                 Pick the second string, hit two <RETURN>s.
Enter text insertion point: <RETURN>    Same point.
Text style: STANDARD
New style or RETURN for no change: SLANT         Give a new style name.
New rotation angle <0>: <RETURN>                 Same angle.
New text <AUTOCAD>: <RETURN>
```

Typing **STYLE ?** will show you all currently defined styles. Your screen should look like the Slanted Style illustration.

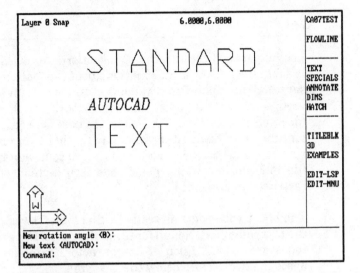

A Slanted Style

In the prototype drawing for the book, you used STYLE to preset text height to get the same height every time text is used. This makes text handling easier in menus and AutoLISP programs. The book assumes fixed height styles throughout. Using a fixed text height not only saves answering the text height question, but reduces errors and standardizes drawings. In the exercise above, the STANDARD style had variable height, but SLANT was preset to 0.5 units. Since SLANT was preset, the change command did not prompt for height. If you changed it back to STANDARD, it would prompt for height.

Examining the ROMANS.SHP Font

You will be working with one of the AutoCAD support files, ROMANS.SHP. Locate ROMANS.SHP in your \ACAD directory or in the \SOURCE subdirectory from your original AutoCAD support disks. Once you've found it, copy the file to the \CA-ACAD subdirectory, but rename it ROMAN.SHP.

Looking at ROMAN.SHP

Command: **DUP**   Copy ROMANS.SHP, even if you have the CA DISK.
SOURCEfile(s) TARGETfile(s): **\ACAD\ROMANS.SHP \CA-ACAD\ROMAN.SHP**

Command: **ED**
File to edit: **ROMAN.SHP**   Look at the top of the ROMAN.SHP file.

```
*0,4,Simplex roman     Copyright 1987 by Autodesk, Inc.
21,7,2,0
```

Looking at the first line, the *0 code alerts AutoCAD to the fact that this is a font file and gives information about the font strokes. The second line says that an upper case or tall lower case character (ascender) extends 21 vectors above the base line (the *above* code), a lower case letter (descender) goes 7 vectors below the base line (the *below* code) and the font may be drawn either in a side by side manner, or it can be drawn vertically (the 2 *mode* code). The final 0 code signals the end of the font file information. If the mode code is 0 instead of 2, then the font is restricted to horizontal.

The above code controls scale. In this font, 21 vectors equal one unit in the text command. Not all fonts are the same. For example, the TXT.SHP codes are 6,2,2,0. Each of its characters extends six vectors above or descends two vectors below the base line.

AutoCAD also needs to know how much space to put between successive lines of text. This is called a *line feed* and is treated just like any other character in the font file. Look in the file to find the line feed character.

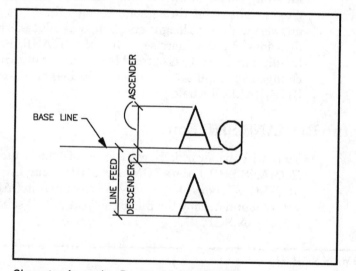

Character Ascender, Descender, and Baseline

The next two lines define the line feed character to be 34 units. The ASCII 10 line feed character is followed by the number 9. The 9 indicates the number of character definition codes to follow, each separated by a comma, and instructs AutoCAD to move down 34 vector lengths.

```
*10,9,1f
2,8,0,-34,14,8,30,34,0
```

Quit your text editor and exit back to AutoCAD.

Before you can use the ROMAN.SHP shape file that you copied from ROMANS.SHP, you must have AutoCAD compile the shapes. AutoCAD makes a .SHX file from the .SHP file.

Compiling Shape Files

Command: **QUIT**   You must use the Main Menu to compile ROMAN.SHP, creating ROMAN.SHX, to use it.

```
Enter selection: 7           Compile shape/font file ROMAN.
Enter NAME of shape file (default C:CA07): ROMAN
Compiling shape/font description file
Compilation successful. Output file ROMAN.shx contains 4926 bytes.
Press RETURN to continue: <RETURN>
```

We'll explain the line feed in detail, but first let's look at character height and spacing graphically. To examine or design characters, it helps to set up snap and grid to correspond to the character height. Since the ROMANS font is designed with a character height of 21 vectors to one drawing unit, we'll use a text height in the drawing of 21. Then, with the default snap of one unit, one snap increment will be one vector. Also, set grid to three, so seven grid increments total the 21-vector character height. That makes it easy to count vectors.

Graphic Character Inquiry

```
Enter selection: 1           Begin a NEW drawing again named CA07=.

Command: MENU                Load the menu TEST.

Command: GRID                Set to 3.
Command: LIMITS              0,0 to 72,56.
Command: ZOOM                All.
Command: UCS                 Set Origin to 21,34.
Command: UCSICON             Set to ORigin.
Command: <Ortho on>          Toggle ortho on.

Command: STYLE               Define new style ROMAN using font ROMAN.
                             Take all the defaults.
```

```
Command: DTEXT          Pick point 0,0, height 21, rotation 0 degrees.
                        The DTEXT box cursor is 21 units square.
Text: Ag                Hit return to continue text line.
Text: A                 Return twice to accept and exit.
                        Each A is 21 units high, and the line feed spacing is 34.

Command: DIST           Pick from the bottom of one A to the bottom of the other.
                        Distance = 34.0000, the line feed.
Command: DIST           Pick from the bottom of one A to its top.
                        Distance = 21.0000, the character height above.
Command: DIST           Pick from the base line of the g to its bottom.
                        Distance = 7.0000, the below value.
```

Now let's look closer at the line feed definition. The first line was:

```
*10,9,lf
```

Font characters are identified by a decimal number from 1 through 256, like the *10 above. Each number tells AutoCAD to draw a different text character. The number and the associated character it draws are standardized by the ASCII code system. The ASCII line feed code is 10. AutoCAD does not define this system, it just adheres to it. You can find the standard ASCII character set in almost any book on DOS or BASIC. When you look them up, refer to the ASCII decimal value for the character, not the *hex* value.

The 9 signifies that the actual line feed definition contains 9 byte code values. The lf is just a name to identify it. You can name your characters whatever you like.

The second line of the line feed is its character definition:

```
2,8,0,-34,14,8,30,34,0
```

The 2 is the pen up code, used because line feed must be invisible. The 8 signifies that the next two codes are an X,Y displacement, so 8,0,-34 means move 0 vectors to the right and 34 vectors down. That is exactly what we saw above, when we measured the line feed with DIST. This can optionally be written as 8,(0,-34) to make it clearer.

The 14 code signifies that the next command is only executed if the style is vertical. If so, the 8,30,34 moves back up 34 vectors and 30 to the right. The final 0 ends the shape character code.

➡ *TIP: Adjusting the line feed definition can create a font style that allows your text to coincide with the ruling lines commonly found in pre-printed forms.*

Making a Ballot Character

The next exercise will show you how to develop your first shape character, a ballot box. First, design a ballot character in the drawing. It's as simple as drawing a box, with extra lines on the bottom and right sides to give the appearance of a shadow. Draw a 16-unit box (over the top A character for comparison). Then create the shape in ROMAN.SHP. It will be our ASCII character 200. You separate all fields within a definition by commas. Parentheses improve readability, but they are not required. Parentheses are ignored by the shape compiler.

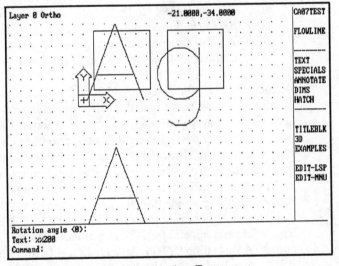

Ballot Box Drawn With Lines and as Text

Designing the Ballot Box

Command: **COLOR**	Set yellow current to see better.
Command: **LINE**	From 3,3; up 16; right 16; down 16; and Close.
Command: **ED** File to edit: **ROMAN.SHP**	Add the ballot to the end of the ROMAN.SHP file, following shape 129, kdiam.

```
*200,21,ballot
2,8,(3,3),1,9,(0,16),(16,0),(0,-16),(-16,0),(0,0),2,8,(17,-3),0
```
　　　　　　　　　　　　　<RETURN> after the last line.

Save and exit your editor back to AutoCAD.

```
Command: END            To recompile at the Main Menu.

Enter selection: 7      Compile shape/font file ROMAN.

Enter selection: 2      Edit EXISTING drawing CA07.

Command: TEXT           Start point 21,0, default height and rotation.
Text: %%200             This is the escape code for ASCII 200.
                        It draws a box.
```

➥ *NOTE: AutoCAD gives you an error message when compiling a shape file if there are errors in the font file. The most common causes of errors are trailing spaces on lines, missing or extra returns at the end of the file, and incorrect byte counts in the offending shape header. Sometimes the messages are misleading. If the cause is not obvious, look for all of these causes, and look at the line or definition just before or after the line number indicated by the error message.*

AutoCAD only sees characters 10, and 32 to 128, as standard keys on the keyboard. If you want to enter ASCII characters above 128, you need to type them in a special way. Characters above 128 are referenced by an ASCII number, preceded by a double percent %% sign. You may also be able to enter the characters as an "Alt code," depending on your system configuration. To enter <ALT 200>, hold down either your <ALT> or <ALT> and <LEFT-SHIFT> keys while you type the number 200 *with the numeric keypad keys*, then release. The advantage to this method is that you can see the character as you type in DTEXT, instead of seeing %%**200**. The %% is not special for ASCII numbers above 128. You also can type a capital A by typing %%**65**. AutoCAD treats all %%nnn (where nnn is the ASCII number) codes the same. On most DOS-based systems, you can also use alternate key entry.

The ballot box should be just like the one we drew with LINE. Examine its shape definition. There is nothing new, compared to the line feed definition, except the 1 (pen down) and 9 (continuous X,Y pairs) codes.

Each asterisk marks the beginning of a new item in the file. The 200 is the ASCII number for the font character, and 21 tells AutoCAD how many bytes of data to expect for the character definition.

`*200,21,ballot`	The BALLOT shape header.
`2,`	Deactivate pen (pen up).
`8,(3,3),`	Move up 3 and right 3.
`1,`	Activate pen (pen down).
`9,`	Interpret X,Y pairs until 0,0.
`(0,16),`	Draw 16 vectors up.
`(16,0),`	Draw 16 vectors to the right.
`(0,-16),`	Draw 16 vectors down.
`(-16,0),`	Draw 16 vectors to the left.
`(0,0),`	End of X,Y pairs.
`2,`	Deactivate pen (pen up).
`8,(17,-3),`	Move right 17 vectors and down 3 vectors.
`0`	End of shape.

AutoCAD doesn't care where you break the lines of the shape file. You can write the same definition all on one line, or on many short lines similar to the annotated listing above. Unfortunately, you can't include the comments in the file.

The 0, 1, 2, 8, and 9 codes are four of the 15 font definition codes. The entire set of instruction codes follows:

FONT DEFINITION INSTRUCTION CODES

AutoCAD's font definition language has 15 key instruction codes. Look at the table to see what each one means.

AutoCAD FONT DEFINITION INSTRUCTION CODES	
0	Marks the end of a shape definition.
1	Places the pen in a down position.
2	Lifts the pen up.
3	Scales vector lengths by dividing by next number.
4	Scale vector by multiplying by next number.
5	Saves the current location in memory. (Pushes.)
6	Recalls the previously saved location. (Pops.)
7	Draws a subshape character given by next number in file.
8	XY movement as given by next two numbers in file.
9	Followed by series of X,Y displacements. Ended by (0,0).
10	Octant arc defined by next two numbers in file.
11	Fractional arc defined by the next five numbers.
12	Arc defined by following X,Y displacement and bulge.
13	Followed by series of X,Y & bulge arcs. Ended by (0,0).
14	Vertical flag to process next command if vertical style.

Font Definition Instruction Codes

In the shape file, many of these codes determine how the next value is interpreted. For example, in the line feed:

```
2,8,0,-34,14,8,30,34,0
```

The 8 causes the 0 and -34 to be read as X,Y, displacements. The 14 causes the following 8 code to be read only if the style is vertical, and since the following 30 and 34 belong to the 8, they are also ignored for horizontal fonts.

➡ *NOTE: In the AutoCAD Reference Manual, these codes are shown as the hexadecimal numbers 001 through 009 and 00A through 00E. However, the standard AutoCAD text .SHP files use the corresponding 0 through 9 and 10 through 14 decimal values. All shape definition values can be in either decimal or hexadecimal, but the convention used in the standard shape files is to use decimal values for all X,Y and instruction codes, and hexadecimal for vector length and direction codes. Hexadecimal is base 16. Digits 1 through 9 are the same as base 10, then A=10, B=11, C=12, D=13, E=14, F=15, 10=16, 11=17, ... 1F=31, 20=32 and so forth. In shape files, a value with a leading zero is interpreted as hexadecimal, and without a leading zero as decimal.*

Font Vector Codes

In addition to X,Y displacements, you can also use vector length and direction codes. To get vector directions, AutoCAD uses 16 predefined vector directions, 0 through F. Using this hexadecimal-based numbering system to define vector direction makes it easier to deal with 16 directions. The Vector Direction diagram shows the vector directions. The standard vector lengths also are hexadecimal, from 01 up to a maximum of FF (255 decimal).

Notice that the vector endpoints in the diagram form a square, not a circle. All diagonal vectors are stretched to force their length to one vector unit in either the X or Y axis, and to one-half or one unit in the other axis. Therefore, the 1 vector is at 26.5651 degrees, not 22.5 degrees.

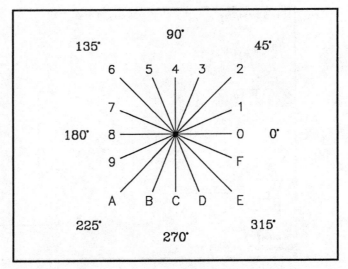

Vector Directions

Using the Instruction and Vector Codes

Let's add shadow to our BALLOT, using the vector codes and the push, pop, and fractional multiply and divide codes. Continue in the CA07 drawing, using the box you drew earlier to design the shadow.

Designing for Shadow

Command: **ERASE**	Clean up by erasing the As and g, but leave the BALLOT lines and ballot character.	
Command: **ZOOM**	Window -3,-3 to 45,24.	
Command: **SNAP**	Set to 0.5 units.	
Command: **ID**	Osnap INT to the lower left corner (3,3).	
Command: **LINE**	From @1,-1 to @16,0 to @0,16.	
Command: **LINE**	From @-.5,.5 to @0,-16 to @-16,0.	

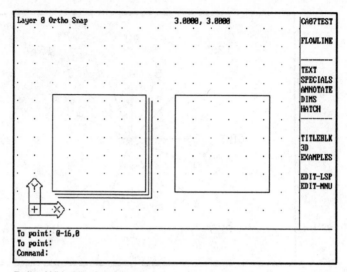

Ballot With Shadow Lines

So, from the start/end point of the original box, you need to make a pen move one vector down and to the right in the up position, then draw right 16 and up 16, then move one-half unit up and to the left in the up position, then draw down 16 and left 16. But how do you move a half vector? You use the divide code to change the interpretation of all following input. Dividing by two causes one vector to move one-half length.

Add the code just before the last pen up move, so the additions start and stop at the lower left corner of the box. The code to add to the ballot shape is:

5,	Save (push) current location.
01E,	Down and to the right one vector in E.
1,	Pen down.
0F0,	F (15) vectors in 0 direction.
010,	One vector in 0 direction
0F4,014,	F vectors in 4, and one in 4.
2,	Pen up.
3,2,	Divide by 2.
016,	One vector (really 1/2) up and to the left.
4,2,	Multiply by 2 (back to normal).
1,	Pen down.
0FC,01C,	F plus one vector in C direction.
0F8,018,	F plus one in 8 direction.
2,	Pen up.
6,	Restore (pop) saved position (lower left).

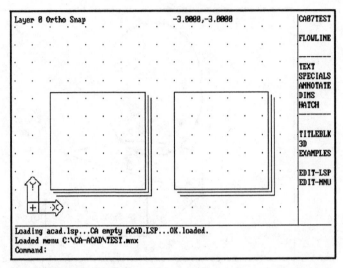

The Updated Ballot Box

Vector, Push, Pop, and Fractional Coding

```
Command: ED
File to edit: ROMAN.SHP     Change byte number and add definition to ballot.

*200,41,ballot
2,8,(3,3),1,9,(0,16),(16,0),(0,-16),(-16,0),(0,0),2,
5,01E,1,0F0,010,0F4,014,2,3,2,016,4,2,1,0FC,01C,0F8,018,2,6,8,(17,-3),0
                            Check the <RETURN> after the last line.
```

Save and exit your editor back to AutoCAD.

```
Command: END             To recompile at the Main Menu.
Enter selection: 7       Compile shape/font file ROMAN.
Enter selection: 2       Edit EXISTING drawing CA07.
                         Voila. The ballot shape is automatically updated.
```

Combining Characters

In addition to making new characters from scratch, you can also combine existing characters into new ones. Instruction code 7 causes the following code to be interpreted as a reference to another shape in the file. For example, 7,67 draws a C (ASCII code 67) at the current pen position. Using subshapes is easier than duplicating definitions and makes a font file compact and easy to update. Now, let's make a new font character, a capital C with an L superimposed over it to indicate a center line.

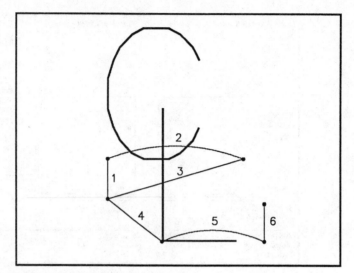

Center Line Diagram

Making a Center Line Character

The next exercise will show you how to combine existing characters to create a center line character. The book builds on this basic exercise to help you create special fractions for dimensioning. The center line font character does not create new vectors and shapes. It references the C character, 7,67, and the L character, 7,76 present in the file to create the character shape. First, design the character in the drawing editor, then code it.

Designing the Center Line Character

Command: **ERASE**	Clean up by erasing everything.
Command: **ZOOM**	Window -3,-9 to 27,33.
Command: **SNAP**	Set to 1 unit.
Command: **DTEXT**	Start point 0,6 height 21 and rotation 0.
Text: **C**	Enter the C, then pick the point 7,-6 for the L.
Text: **L**	And <RETURN> twice to accept.

DTEXT is perfect for designing combined characters because you can easily backspace and reselect points. See the Center Line Diagram for the code sequence. The code for adding the center line character is:

*150,13,CenterLine	ASCII number 150 with 13 byte values.
2,5,	Pen up, then save (push) starting point.
064,	Move up 6 in the 4 direction (see 1).
7,67,	Subshape 67, capital C (see 2).
6,	Restore (pop) starting point (see 3).
008,7,-6,	Right 7 and down 6 from start point (see 4).
7,76,	Subshape 76, capital L (see 5).
064,	Back to base line, 6 in 4 direction (see 6).
0	End definition.

The push and pop codes make all character positions relative to the start position in our design drawing. Notice that there are no pen down codes in the definition. The pen is automatically placed down at the start of each character definition, including subshapes. That is why most shapes start with a pen up 2 code, for their initial offset.

The Center Line Character

Coding the Center Line Character

```
Command: ED
File to edit: ROMAN.SHP     Add to the end of your file, just before *200,41,ballot.

*150,13,CenterLine
2,5,064,7,67,6,008,7,-6,7,76,064,0     Hit <RETURN> at the end of the line.
```

Save and exit your editor back to AutoCAD.

```
Command: END                To recompile at the Main Menu.
Enter selection: 7          Compile shape/font file ROMAN.
Enter selection: 2          Edit EXISTING drawing CA07.

Command: DTEXT              Start point 27,0 height 21 rotation 0.
Text: %%150                 Or <ALT 150> or <SHIFT-ALT> <150>.
                           <RETURN> twice to accept.
```

The resulting character should look just like the C and L that you used in designing it. Another valuable use of combined characters is to create a set of fractions.

Developing Special Fraction Characters

Many dimensions and annotations require fractions. AutoCAD's standard character set lacks fractions. Rather than live with this limitation, you can make special fractions for your dimensions. Let's start by making the fraction 1/8. Then you can copy and edit it to easily make a full set. Again, you use characters that are already defined in the font file, such as ASCII code 49 for 1, and the code 47 for the forward slash character. Since the design and coding process is the same as for the center line, we'll just give you the code in the following exercise, defining the 1/8 fraction as ASCII code 151.

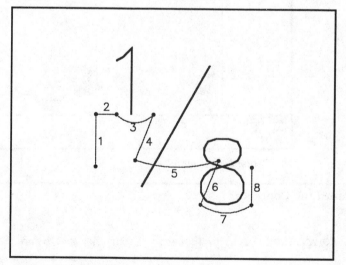

A Special 1/8 Fraction

Making a 1/8 Fraction

Command: **ED**   Edit the ROMAN.SHP file.

Near the bottom of the file, just above *200,41,ballot, add:

```
*151,29,oneeight
2,0F4,3,06,4,05,020,7,49,3,05,4,06,0CB,7,47,0CB,3,06,4,05,7,56,3,05,4,06,094,0
```

Save and exit, be sure to <RETURN>.

The following table shows the definition in an easier-to-follow form. The *See* # annotations refer to the Special 1/8 Fraction vector diagram to help you follow the vector directions.

*151,29,oneeight	Defines it as ASCII 151 with 29 bytes.
2,	Lift pen with 2 instruction.
0F4,	Move F vectors (15) in the 4 direction. See 1.
3,06,4,05,	Divide by 6, multiply by 5. A 5/6ths scale for the following strokes.
020,	Move 2 vectors in the 0 direction. See 2.
7,49,	Call the ASCII 49 subshape "1". See 3.
3,05,4,06,	Reverse the scale factor by 6/5 to normal.
0CB,	Move C vectors (12) in the B direction. See 4.
7,47,	Insert ASCII 47 "/". See 5.
0CB,	Move C vectors (12) in the B direction. See 6.
3,06,4,05,	Flop the scale factors back to 5/6.
7,56,	Call the subshape "8" (ASCII 56). See 7.
3,05,4,06,	Reset the scale factor to normal.
094,	Move 9 vectors in the 4 direction. See 8.
0	End the shape with the 0 code.

Command: **ERASE**   Erase the center lines.
Command: **END**   End the drawing.

```
Enter Selection: 7                                    Compile shape/font description.
Enter NAME of shape file (default ca07): ROMAN        File named ROMAN.

Enter selection: 2              Restart the drawing and test it.
                                The ROMAN style should be current, defined with the ROMAN font.
Command: DTEXT                  Use either %%151 or <ALT 151>.
```

➡ *NOTE: You can substitute the fraction characters in dimensions by typing the dimension text with the fraction code at the dimension text prompt.*

The fraction definition uses the 3 (divide) and 4 (multiply) scale factor codes to scale the characters so they are drawn slightly smaller than normal characters. The 3,06,4,05, first divides the vector length by 6, then multiplies that length by 5, creating a vector length that is 5/6 the size of the normal vector. Only integers are acceptable input.

You always need to reset the scale factors at the end of the shape. If you don't, AutoCAD will draw the next character with the last scale calculated.

Before going on to create a full set of fractions, wouldn't it be nice if you could create a single set of combined characters like this, and use them in several different fonts? You can, with bigfont shape definition.

Bigfonts

A *bigfont* character is a character that has a number above the ASCII limit of 256. Bigfont characters were developed so AutoCAD could work with non-ASCII foreign language character sets, and sets with more than 256 characters in the language. The Japanese KANJI character set is an example. Bigfonts require two key strokes for each character. Instead of typing something like %%151 for the 1/8 character, you might call a bigfont character by ~1, a tilde followed by a regular character.

Bigfonts are stored in shape font files that are handled in a special way by AutoCAD. AutoCAD's special handling lets you append your font characters to any font file already in use with your system. You can append bigfonts without modifying existing font files.

Using bigfonts to make special characters lets you use the stroke style of any existing compiled font file. For example, if your current text style uses the ROMANS.SHX file, you can direct your special characters to use the 1, 8, and slash characters from the ROMANS file. Your special character definitions are independent of the font strokes and font file you use.

Bigfont definitions also override duplicate standard font characters. If you redefine your zero, ASCII 48, in a bigfont file to put a slash through the zero, the slashed zero will override the standard zero character of any font that is loaded along with it.

Bigfont Files

A bigfont file starts with a header that alerts AutoCAD to the special file format. The line:

```
*BIGFONT 20,1,126,126
```

identifies the file as a bigfont file. The header has four pieces of information that tell AutoCAD how to treat the contents of the file.

The first number, 20, is the number of character definitions in the file. It doesn't have to be exact, but it does have to be within 10 percent of the actual number. The second number, 1 in our example, tells AutoCAD how many successive keyboard pairs, issued as input, it takes to *sense* a complete character. You only need a single pair of characters to call a bigfont character. However, fonts like the KANJI set need two pairs (4 keys) to call a single character. You might key in a KANJI character as ~M~C.

The tilde flags the beginning of a paired key set. The tilde is an *escape* character. It instructs AutoCAD to treat the character that follows it with special meaning. The escape character can be any character you wish. It should be a character that you use infrequently, but is accessible on the keyboard. There are not many good keys to choose from. Some choices are:

```
`       Reverse apostrophe.
|       Vertical bar.
~       Tilde.
```

The book uses the tilde. The tilde has an ASCII code of 126. AutoCAD needs to know which character you have defined as the escape character. This information is contained in the header label for the file. The code 126 must appear as the fourth and fifth item of the header line to define the tilde as a single pair and double pair character set.

You will need more codes, so try to plan ahead. Try to devise a system to help you remember them. The book uses an easy one. Tilde will be your escape character, and the numerators of the fractions will be the numbers along the top of the keyboard. This works until you run out of keys and spill over onto the QWERTY keys! Here is the book's bigfont map.

BIGFONT CHARACTER MAP			
Key	Fraction	ASCII Code	Bigfont Number
~1	1/16	49	32305
~2	1/8	50	32306
~3	3/16	51	32307
~4	1/4	52	32308
~5	5/16	53	32309
~6	3/8	54	32310
~7	7/16	55	32311
~8	1/2	56	32312
~9	9/16	57	32313
~0	5/8	58	32314
~q	11/16	113	32369
~w	3/4	119	32375
~e	13/16	101	32357
~r	7/8	114	32370
~t	15/16	116	32372
~B	Ballot	66	32322
~C	Center Line	67	32323
~S	Superscript	83	32339
~s	subscript	115	32371
~~	tilde	126	32382

Bigfont Character Map

➡ *NOTE: All keys are lower case, except ballot, center line, and superscript.*

You still need your font definition lines in the file, the same as for a normal font. The 21,7,2,0 (above, below, modes, 0) are the same as in the ROMANS font code. The book uses the header:

```
*0,4,SPECIALS  Customizing AutoCAD
21,7,2,0
```

The above and below size of a font determines its compatibility with the bigfont. Both the font and bigfont must be close to the same size. Of the standard AutoCAD fonts, ROMANS, ROMANC, ROMANT, and ITALIC are all compatible with an above, below size of 21,7, but TXT and MONOTXT have an incompatible size of 6,2.

We will use the existing definition of the 1/8 special fraction and give it a new code number. To compute the number you assign to a special character in a bigfont file, take the ASCII code of your escape code character, 126 in this case, and multiply it by a constant factor 256. This yields 32256. This number is called the base offset.

There are 256 characters in the ASCII set. Each of the 256 ASCII characters can be an escape character for a character set. Each character set can have up to 256 characters. This yields 256 times 256 potential characters, a total of 65,536.

The book's base offset is 32256. Its set of 256 potential characters starts at the 32256th position in the 65,536 total. For each character in your set, you add the base offset to the value of the ASCII character that is used for the second key of the pair. For a 1/8 character, we use a ~2 combination. Since 2 is ASCII 50, the code is 32256+50 or 32306.

Because you use the regular tilde as the escape character, you have to recreate a tilde in your upper level of characters. The ASCII code for tilde is 126, so 32256+126 is 32382. Including a tilde in your bigfont ensures that you can type it if you ever need to. To get a tilde, type ~~.

Integrating Special Characters as Bigfonts

   Examine the CA DISK file CA-ROMAN.SHP.

   Copy ROMAN.SHP to CA-ROMAN.SHP.

Command: **ED**   Edit CA-ROMAN.SHP.

You don't need the standard ROMANS characters, except for the tilde (ASCII 126). Delete all lines above the *150,11,CenterLine line except for:

```
*126,49,ktilde
2,14,8,(-9,-12),064,1,024,8,(1,3),021,020,02F,8,(4,-3),02F,020,
021,023,2,8,(-18,-2),1,023,021,020,02F,8,(4,-3),02F,020,021,
8,(1,3),024,2,8,(8,-12),14,8,(-17,-4),0
```

Enter the header lines.
Renumber *150 to *32323, for ~C, and add a -C to indicate that it is called by ~C.
Renumber *150 to *32322, for ~B, and add a -B to indicate that it is called by ~B.
Renumber the 1/8 font character from 151 to 32306, for ~2, and add a -2. It is called by ~2.

Renumber the tilde *126,49,ktilde to **32382**
Rearrange the order of the definitions to match their codes.
You should have:

```
*BIGFONT 20,1,126,126
*0,4,SPECIALS  Customizing AutoCAD
21,7,2,0
*32306,29,oneeight-2
2,0F4,3,06,4,05,020,7,49,3,05,4,06,0CB,7,47,0CB,3,06,4,05,7,56,3,05,4,06,094,0
*32322,41,ballot-B
2,8,(3,3),1,9,(0,16),(16,0),(0,-16),(-16,0),(0,0),2,
5,01E,1,0F0,010,0F4,014,2,3,2,016,4,2,1,0FC,01C,0F8,018,2,6,8,(17,-3),0
*32323,13,CenterLine-C
2,5,064,7,67,6,008,7,-6,7,76,064,0
*32382,49,ktilde
2,14,8,(-9,-12),064,1,024,8,(1,3),021,020,02F,8,(4,-3),02F,020,
021,023,2,8,(-18,-2),1,023,021,020,02F,8,(4,-3),02F,020,021,
8,(1,3),024,2,8,(8,-12),14,8,(-17,-4),0
```

To make the rest of the fractions, use the following procedure:

1. Copy both lines of the 1/8 definition 15 more times.

2. Change the *32306,29,oneeighth-2 to the appropriate code and description.

3. Substitute the appropriate 7,nn, ASCII codes for the 7,49, "1" and/or 7,56, "8."

4. For characters without a 1 for the numerator, delete the **020,** code before the **7,49,** numerator code. It adjusts for the narrower character. When you delete the **020,** you must change the **29,** the number of bytes in the definition line, to **28.**

5. For the characters with a 16ths denominator, put both byte pairs **7,49,7,54,** in place of the **7,56, "8"** code. You must add **2** (bytes) to the **28** or **29** (number of bytes in the definition line), making it **30** or **31.**

6. For characters with numerators of 11, 13, or 15, put both byte pairs **7,49,7,nn,** where nn is 49, 51 or 53, in place of the **7,49, "1"** code. You must add **2** more bytes, making it **32** or **34.**

To make the 1/4 fraction, for example, use the subshape ASCII 52 for 4, in place of subshape ASCII 56.

After you add the rest of the special fractions to the CA-ROMAN.SHP file, you will have:

Command: **ED**   Edit your CA-ROMAN.SHP file to:

```
*BIGFONT 20,1,126,126
*0,4,SPECIALS  Customizing AutoCAD
21,7,2,0
*32305,32,onesixteenth-1
2,0F4,020,3,06,4,05,020,7,49,3,05,4,06,0CB,7,47,0CB,3,06,4,05,7,49,7,54,
3,05,4,06,094,0
*32306,29,oneeighth-2
2,0F4,3,06,4,05,020,7,49,3,05,4,06,0CB,7,47,0CB,3,06,4,05,7,56,3,05,4,06,094,0
*32308,29,onequarter-4
2,0F4,3,06,4,05,020,7,49,3,05,4,06,0CB,7,47,0CB,3,06,4,05,7,52,3,05,4,06,094,0
*32309,32,fivesixteenth-5
2,0F4,020,3,06,4,05,020,7,53,3,05,4,06,
0CB,7,47,0CB,3,06,4,05,7,49,7,54,3,05,4,06,094,0
*32310,28,threeeighths-6
2,0F4,3,06,4,05,7,51,3,05,4,06,0CB,7,47,0CB,3,06,4,05,7,56,3,05,4,06,094,0
*32311,32,sevensixteenth-7
2,0F4,020,3,06,4,05,020,7,55,3,05,4,06,
0CB,7,47,0CB,3,06,4,05,7,49,7,54,3,05,4,06,094,0
*32312,29,onehalf-8
2,0F4,3,06,4,05,020,7,49,3,05,4,06,0CB,7,47,0CB,3,06,4,05,7,50,3,05,4,06,094,0
*32313,32,ninesixteenth-9
2,0F4,020,3,06,4,05,020,7,57,3,05,4,06,
0CB,7,47,0CB,3,06,4,05,7,49,7,54,3,05,4,06,094,0
*32304,28,fiveeighths-0
2,0F4,3,06,4,05,7,53,3,05,4,06,0CB,7,47,0CB,3,06,4,05,7,56,3,05,4,06,094,0
*32369,34,elevsixteenth-q
2,0F4,020,3,06,4,05,020,7,49,7,49,3,05,4,06,
0CB,7,47,0CB,3,06,4,05,7,49,7,54,3,05,4,06,094,0
*32375,28,threequarters-w
2,0F4,3,06,4,05,7,51,3,05,4,06,0CB,7,47,0CB,3,06,4,05,7,52,3,05,4,06,094,0
*32357,34,thirteensixteenth-e
2,0F4,020,3,06,4,05,020,7,49,7,51,3,05,4,06,
0CB,7,47,0CB,3,06,4,05,7,49,7,54,3,05,4,06,094,0
*32370,29,seveneighths-r
2,0F4,3,06,4,05,030,7,55,3,05,4,06,0CB,7,47,0CB,3,06,4,05,7,56,3,05,4,06,094,0
*32372,34,fifteensixteenth-t
2,0F4,020,3,06,4,05,020,7,49,7,53,3,05,4,06,
0CB,7,47,0CB,3,06,4,05,7,49,7,54,3,05,4,06,094,0
*32322,41,ballot-B
2,8,(3,3),1,9,(0,16),(16,0),(0,-16),(-16,0),(0,0),2,
5,01E,1,0F0,010,0F4,014,2,3,2,016,4,2,1,0FC,01C,0F8,018,2,6,8,(17,-3),0
*32323,13,CenterLine-C
2,5,064,7,67,6,008,7,-6,7,76,064,0
*32382,49,ktilde
2,14,8,(-9,-12),064,1,024,8,(1,3),021,020,02F,8,(4,-3),02F,020,
021,023,2,8,(-18,-2),1,023,021,020,02F,8,(4,-3),02F,020,021,
8,(1,3),024,2,8,(8,-12),14,8,(-17,-4),0
```

For good measure, add some subscript and superscript codes at the end. They are simple pen up moves:

```
*32339,5,superscript-S
2,8,(0,18),0
*32371,3,subscript-s
2,8,(0,18),0
```
                              Check the <RETURN> after the last line.

Save, exit to the AutoCAD Main Menu, and recompile the CA-ROMAN file.

Using Bigfonts With AutoCAD

Let's integrate the bigfonts, then make a menu page so they're easy to use.

You can integrate a bigfont file into your system using the AutoCAD STYLE command. At the font file prompt, answer with both the standard font file you use, like ROMANS, and the new CA-ROMAN file. Separate the font names by a comma.

Integrating Bigfonts

```
Enter selection: 2          Re-enter your drawing and test it.

Command: STYLE
Text style name (or ?) <ROMAN>: CA-ROMAN
New style.
Font file <txt>: ROMANS,CA-ROMAN          Give both names. Default the rest.
CA-ROMAN is now the current text style.

Command: ERASE             Erase everything.
Command: ZOOM              Zoom Window -3,-9 to 120,75.
```

Add the following menu, then test everything.

```
Select [EDIT-MNU]          Edit the TEST.MNU.
```

Make the following changes to the root menu.

```
***SCREEN
**ROOT
[CA07TEST]

[SPECIALS]$S=FOOTER $S=SPECIALS
```

Relabel the **EXAMPLES page to **SPECIALS and add the following:

```
**SPECIALS
[Specials]
[TEXT     ]^C^C^CTEXT
[ 1/16 ~1]~1$S= $S=
[  1/8 ~2]~2$S= $S=
[ 3/16 ~3]~3$S= $S=
[  1/4 ~4]~4$S= $S=
[ 5/16 ~5]~5$S= $S=
[  3/8 ~6]~6$S= $S=
[ 7/16 ~7]~7$S= $S=
[  1/2 ~8]~8$S= $S=
[ 9/16 ~9]~9$S= $S=
[  5/8 ~0]~0$S= $S=
[11/16 ~q]~q$S= $S=
[  3/4 ~w]~w$S= $S=
[13/16 ~e]~e$S= $S=
[  7/8 ~r]~r$S= $S=
[15/16 ~t]~t$S= $S=
[  CL  ~C]~C$S= $S=
[Ballot~B]~B$S= $S=
```

Save, exit, reload the menu and test it.

Select **[SPECIALS]**
Select **[TEXT]**   Start point 0,45 height 3 rotation 0.
Text: Select one of the fraction characters.
                                 Test them all.

Use DTEXT to try the subscripts and superscripts. Remember, the DTEXT command only accepts keyboard input and will not accept input from the menu. But if you type these codes in DTEXT, like ~S and ~s, you see the text in the drawing as you type, like the <ALT nnn> method.

Command: **DTEXT**   Try the sub- and superscripts.
Start point or Align/Center/Fit/Middle/Right/Style: **0,20**
Height <3.0000>: **<RETURN>**
Rotation angle <0>: **<RETURN>**
Text: **NORMAL ~SSUPERSCRIPT ~sNORMAL ~sSUBSCRIPT ~SNORMAL**

Command: **QUIT**

Delete TEST.MNU.

Copy TEST.MNU to MY07.MNU.

```
Layer 0 Ortho Snap                    3.0000, 20.0000       CA07TEST

                                                            FLOWLINE

                                                            ─────────
                                                            TEXT
                                                            SPECIALS
1/16 1/8 3/16 1/4 5/16 3/8 7/16 1/2 9/16 5/8 11/16 3/4 13/16 7/8  ANNOTATE
                                                            DIMS
15/16 ℃□                                                    HATCH

                                                            ─────────
                                                            TITLEBLK
                                                            3D
NORMAL  SUPERSCRIPT   NORMAL   SUBSCRIPT   NORMAL EXAMPLES

                                                            EDIT-LSP
                                                            EDIT-MNU




Rotation angle <0>:
Text: NORMAL ~SSUPERSCRIPT ~sNORMAL ~sSUBSCRIPT ~SNORMAL
Command:
```

Fractions, Subscripts and Superscripts

Notice that the menu needs no spaces between the ~ text codes and the $ page change codes.

What else can you do with bigfonts? You could add a slash-zero character to your bigfont file to redefine the normal zero character. You can even use a bigfont to define standard boilerplates and notes. You can string characters, words, or phrases together as a single bigfont character. Then, each time the standard boilerplate changes, you modify the shape file and your drawing files will automatically be updated during their next plotting or editing session.

Integrating the Specials Menu

If you don't have the CA DISK and want to add the text menu to CA-MENU:

- Insert the **SPECIALS page of your MY07.MNU in the ***SCREEN section of the CA-MENU.MNU file just above the ***TABLET1 section.

■ Change the [SPECIALS] label on the **ROOT page of the CA-MENU to:

`[SPECIALS]$S=SPECIALS $S=FOOTER`

Here is the chapter's menu.

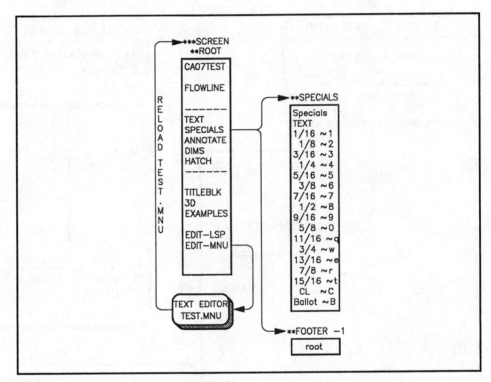

The Chapter 7 Menu Added to CA-MENU

Summary Notes

There are no easy ways to customize text. If you need special text characters, you have to *get down and dirty* and create them. But if you do need a custom font, it can make the difference between ordinary and sharp, efficient presentations. Just remember that a custom font must accompany the drawing when it is displayed or plotted.

Special linetypes, hatches, and fills can also make your drawings sparkle. Let's move on to look at their customization.

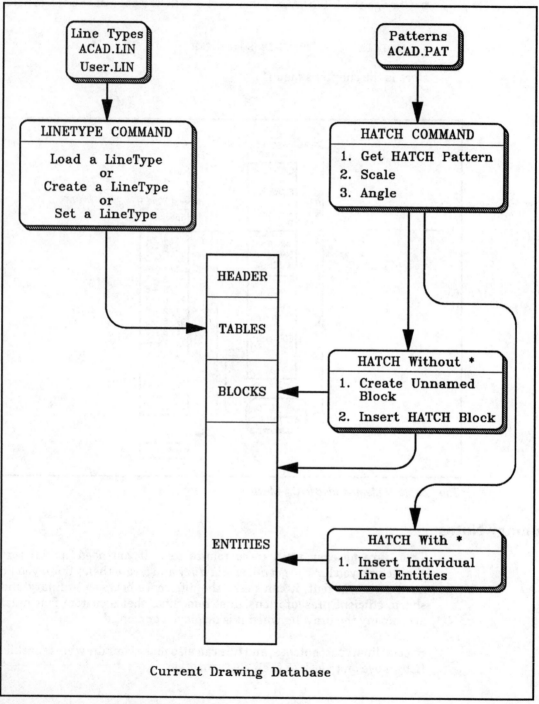

Linetype and Hatch Organization

CHAPTER 8

Linetypes, Hatches, and Fills

THE TOOLS TO ADD THE PIZAZZ TO YOUR DRAWINGS

You can add visual excitement, clarity, and meaning to your drawings by using patterned lines, textured areas, and solid fills. You can increase the impact even more by creating your own patterns. This chapter shows you how to customize linetypes, hatch patterns, and irregular fills.

The Benefits of Customized Hatches and Fills

There are two basic benefits to customizing your hatches and fills. First, custom linetypes and hatches can extend your drawing tools to indicate materials or components. Second, you can speed up your materials labeling process by combining macros with hatches.

How-To Skills Checklist

In this chapter, you will learn how to:

❑ Create linetypes and control their scales.

❑ Write hatch patterns using a development box and making AutoCAD do the hatch calculations.

❑ Put together a screen menu that uses basic blocks to hatch irregular areas.

Macros and Hatch Patterns

MACROS

**HATCH is a screen page with irregular hatch fill blocks.

[CONCRE] is a macro which calls the concrete hatch pattern definition.

[CHECKP] is a macro which calls the checkered plate hatch pattern definition.

HATCH PATTERNS

CONCRE is a hatch pattern definition which draws concrete.

CHECKP is a hatch pattern definition which draws checkered plates.

Patterns of Dots and Dashes

In AutoCAD's world, a *linetype* pattern is a set of instructions used to draw a broken line. A *hatch* pattern adds angles and spaces to the line-drawing instructions. You write a numeric pattern which describes a dash-dot sequence. The dash-dot pattern you define tells AutoCAD how long each dash is and how far to skip between the dashes.

There are two basic controls present with patterns. They are *pen up* and *pen down* motions of the graphics pen. It doesn't matter whether you are dealing with screen vectors or plotting vectors, the terms, pen up and pen down, are used generically to mean the pen is actively drawing a segment or is skipping a segment. A negative number in the code string, for instance, means *lift* the pen up and move in the up position for a specified distance.

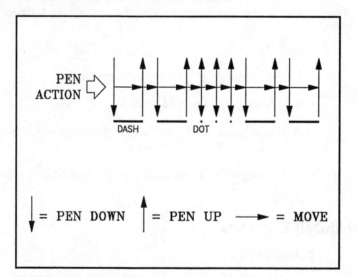

Dash and Dot Patterns

Linetypes

You can apply the linetype pattern to all drawing entities except text, traces, and solids. AutoCAD applies a dash-dot pattern along the length or circumference of an entity. It automatically adjusts the beginning and ending portion of the line pattern to make it fit equally between the end points of segments. If the line length or circumference is too short, the linetype draws as if continuous.

Linetypes are stored in a default library support file called ACAD.LIN. AutoCAD provides a Create option to the LINETYPE command to define linetypes. You can also edit the ACAD.LIN file with any ASCII text editor and create other *name*.LIN files.

To help you get a feel for working with linetypes, let's create a simple linetype called DASH3DOT. DASH3DOT has one-unit long dashes and three dots, each dot separated by a quarter unit space.

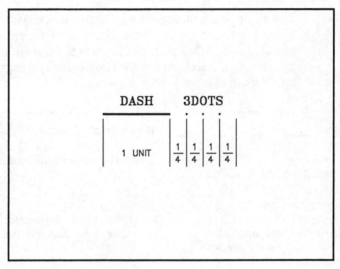

DASH3DOT Linetype

Creating a DASH3DOT Linetype

`Enter selection:` **1**   Begin a NEW drawing named CA08.

    Copy CA08.MNU to TEST.MNU.

Copy MAIN.MNU to TEST.MNU.

`Command:` **DUP**   Copy your ACAD.LIN file from your AutoCAD directory
                    to \CA-ACAD\CA-ACAD.LIN.

Select **[TEST] [24 x 36] [FULL] [INITIATE]**   It should bring up TEST.MNU.

`Command:` **LAYER**   Freeze ?????BDR (the border).

```
Command: LINETYPE          Use the linetype command to create a new pattern.
?/Create/Load/Set: C
Name of linetype to create: DASH3DOT      The name for the linetype definition.
File for storage of linetype <ACAD>: CA-ACAD          Your copy of the standard file.
Wait, checking if linetype already defined...
```

After AutoCAD verifies that the linetype definition does not already exist, you are prompted for a description of the line pattern. It helps to use a visual reminder with underscores and periods, as well as a narrative description in parentheses, to describe the pattern.

The numerical values defining the pen up and down motions are preceded by an *alignment* code. Currently, the alignment code is limited to only one: *A*. AutoCAD automatically puts the code in for you. This is followed by a positive number for a pen down dash, a negative number for a pen up blank, and a zero value for a dot.

```
Descriptive text: ___ . . . ___ . . . ___ . . . ___    (Dash with 3 dots)     Enter description.

Enter pattern (on next line):          Enter the pattern definition:
A,1,-0.25,0,-0.25,0,-0.25,0,-0.25

New definition written to file.
?/Create/Load/Set: L                   Linetypes must be loaded before use.
Linetype(s) to load: DASH3DOT          Or enter * to load all linetypes.
File to search <CA-ACAD>: <RETURN>
Linetype DASH3DOT loaded.
?/Create/Load/Set: <RETURN>
```

Here is how the pattern is put together. The definition starts with a one-unit dash. Then, it lifts the pen one-quarter unit and puts the pen back down to draw a dot. Dots are drawn by giving a zero-unit length. The other two dots are drawn in the same way. The four -0.25 pen up codes make the four blank segments of the pattern. The sequence ends by moving over another quarter unit, ready to repeat with another dash.

Scaling Linetype Patterns

Linetype patterns are influenced by a global AutoCAD scale factor. The LTSCALE command sets and applies this factor to the unit values of the linetype pattern definition. We normally suggest you use a linetype scale factor of *0.375 times the plotting scale factor*. For a 1/8-inch drawing, the plotting scale (DIMSCALE variable) is 96.0, making LTSCALE equal to

36.0. However, to make it easier to see one-unit relationships in linetypes, set LTSCALE to 1 for the following exercise.

To see how AutoCAD matches the pattern definition to entities, draw a few lines and circles on a layer using the new linetype.

Adjusting Line Scale

```
Command: LTSCALE              Change for a 1:1 relationship to the linetype definition.
New scale factor <0.3750>: 1

Command: UNITS                Set to decimal units, 4 places.
Command: SNAP                 Set to 0.25.

Command: LAYER                Make layer TEST with color green for the linetype. Then:
?/Make/Set/New/ON/OFF/Color/Ltype/Freeze/Thaw: LT
Linetype (or ?) <CONTINUOUS>: DASH3DOT
Layer name(s) for linetype DASH3DOT <TEST>: <RETURN>
?/Make/Set/New/ON/OFF/Color/Ltype/Freeze/Thaw: <RETURN>

Command: ZOOM                 Zoom left corner 0,0 and height 6.
Command: LINE                 Draw 4 lines, 1, 2, 3.5 and 4 units long.

Command: CIRCLE               Now draw 3 circles with 0.25, 0.5, and 1-unit radius.
```

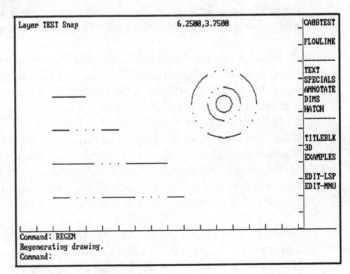

Linetype Pattern Adjusting

Look at the set of lines to see how AutoCAD fits the linetypes. When the line segment or circle is too small, AutoCAD displays the linetype as if continuous. AutoCAD can't fit the pattern to the one-unit long line. It starts to fit the pattern to the two-unit line, applying the space(s) equally between the line's endpoints. The 3.5-unit line shows how AutoCAD makes the adjusted ends longer until there is sufficient space to fit in at least one set of dots. The entire line pattern appears when the line is four units long.

Now, look at how AutoCAD applies the pattern to circles. The 0.25-radius circle (circumference 1.57 units) shows no linetype breaks. The 0.5-radius circle with a circumference of 3.1416 shows two sets of dots. The 1-unit radius circle shows three sets of dots at 120-degree intervals.

➡ *TIP: Linetypes work poorly with spline or curve fit polylines because each segment is usually so short that it draws as if continuous. The best solution is to use a unique color and assign it to a plotter linetype if your plotter supports multiple linetypes.*

Hatch Patterns

Hatch patterns also follow the concept of a pen up/down motion. However, hatch patterns have several differences. While a linetype has an alignment code, hatches are aligned by the snap base point of the drawing. Unlike a linetype, hatch patterns are families of patterned lines forced to specific angles. Hatch patterns are not applied to entities but instead create new entities to fill in bounded areas.

Hatches can create blocks or individual line entities. To create individual lines, precede the hatch pattern name with an asterisk (much like you did with the INSERT* command for blocks). If you don't use the asterisk, an unnamed block is created for each hatch insertion. These blocks actually have hidden names like *X1 or *X2. Leaving hatches as blocks saves no file space, since each already has a unique block definition which includes the individual lines within it. Exploding a hatch temporarily doubles the entity count, but then the block definition is automatically purged the next time the drawing file is loaded. There are no commands to help create hatch patterns, but you will develop a customized one later.

Hatch patterns are stored in the ACAD.PAT file. If AutoCAD doesn't find a pattern in the ACAD.PAT file, it looks for a file *name*.PAT, where *name* is the hatch pattern name. Unlike linetypes, you cannot tell AutoCAD what file to look for in a pattern library. *Be careful not to overwrite your original ACAD.PAT file in your ACAD directory.*

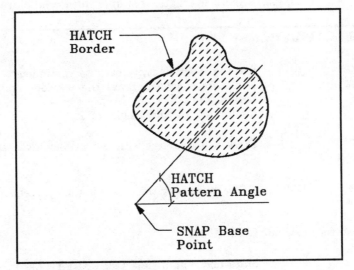

Hatch Pattern Components

A typical entry in a hatch pattern file may look like:

```
45, 0.125,0.125, 0.25,0.25, 0.25,-0.25
```

where each line has items in the format:

```
Angle, X origin, Y origin, X offset, Y offset, dash-1, dash-2
```

The angle tells AutoCAD which direction to draw the lines, 45 degrees in the example. The next two fields, X origin and Y origin, control the starting point of the line segment. This is not an AutoCAD coordinate, but rather a relative distance from the current snap base point of the drawing. The X offset and Y offset control the increments from the origin point to repeat the line. The last part of a hatch definition is the dash-dot pattern.

When AutoCAD draws a hatch, each linetype in the pattern continues at the specified angle in both directions until it hits a boundary. It dashes and dots according to the pattern. Each line is repeated parallel to itself. The origin of each repeat is offset from the previous line by the X offset and Y offset values, and the dash-dots are applied to that line. The X,Y offset is measured perpendicular to the angle of the line, like a rotated axis. Each line is repeated parallel until it fills the boundary being hatched. Groups of parallel lines created by each line of the hatch pattern are referred to as families of lines.

The next exercise creates a simple checkered plate hatch pattern.

Making a Checkered Plate Pattern

```
Command: LAYER            Set the layer linetype back to continuous.
Command: ERASE            Get a fresh screen. Erase the previous entities.
Command: SNAP             Set to 0.1
Command: ZOOM             Center 0.5,0.5 and height of 2.

Command: PLINE            Draw a 1 x 1 box with a polyline. Close the last segment.
From point: 0,0
```

You have the CHECKP.PAT file. Examine it, then use it in the next sequence.

Do the following to create CHECKP.PAT.

```
Command: ED               Start and edit a new CHECKP.PAT file in \CA-ACAD directory.
                          Enter the lines:

*CHECKP, Checkered Plate
0, 0,.09375, .25,.25, .25,-.25
90, .125,.21875, .25,.25, .25,-.25        <RETURN>
```

Save, exit, and return to AutoCAD.

Be sure to <RETURN> at the last line or you'll get: "Bad pattern definition file:" when you try to use it. If you don't <RETURN>, you may also crash AutoCAD.

```
Command: HATCH                        Try it.
Pattern (? or name/U,style): CHECKP   Type the name.
Scale for pattern <1.0000>: .5
Angle for pattern <0>: 45             Rotate the pattern.
Select objects: L                     The pline is last.
```

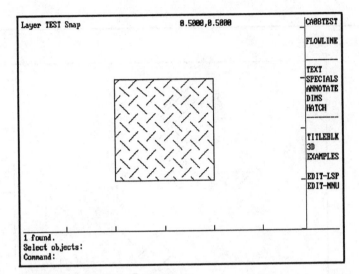

The Checkered Plate Pattern

Even though you defined the pattern with 0- and 90-degree angles, you can rotate the pattern to get a desired effect. We made the pattern at 0 and 90 degrees to avoid calculating angles.

This exercise didn't show you how to figure out the origins and offsets. The next exercise shows you how to compute the origins and offsets as you develop a concrete hatch pattern.

Making a Hatch Pattern

The following concrete hatch pattern example will give you a handy technique for creating seemingly complex, irregular patterns with little effort. The challenge presented by non-regular hatch patterns is to wade through a set of calculations to make the pattern appear random.

You can make hatches appear random by developing a tiny pattern and applying it at a larger scale. The following exercise helps you develop a simple concrete hatch pattern. If you have the disk and don't want to perform the exercise, you can use the concrete pattern, CONCRE.PAT, as-is or append it to your ACAD.PAT file. In the book, INSIDE AutoLISP, we automate the whole hatch generation process using AutoLISP.

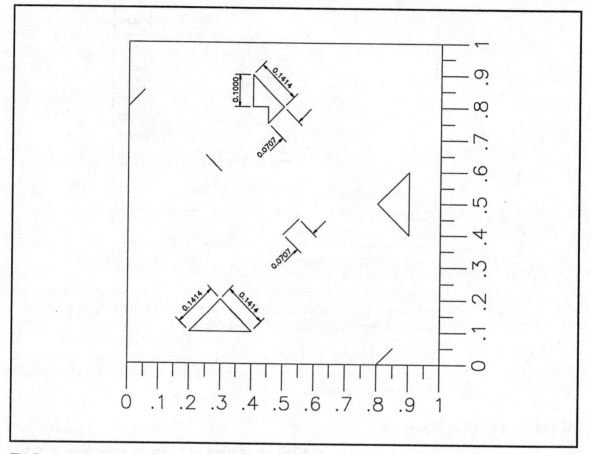

The Proposed Hatch Pattern

The concrete hatch pattern is shown in the Proposed Hatch Pattern illustration. If you have the CA DISK, you have the CONCRE.PAT file, but you'll learn more about hatches by going through the process of creating the pattern from scratch. Once you've decided on your pattern, you need to put it together. The exercise will step you through copying the pattern and boxes to make a four-box window pane image. Use all four boxes and the objects within them to calculate the pattern.

Developing a Concrete Hatch Pattern

Command: **ERASE**   Clean out the previous hatch pattern, but leave the 1 x 1 box.
Command: **LINE**   Draw the pattern as dimensioned in the illustration above.
Command: **ZOOM**   Center 2,1 with height 4.
Command: **ARRAY**   Select the 1 x 1 box and pattern. Make 2 rows x 2 columns.
Command: **COPY**   Copy the polyline box again, to the bottom right corner
                       of the array. This test box is used to develop the pattern.
Command: **PLINE**   Draw a 2 x 2 test box, lower left corner at the lower left
                       of the previous 1 x 1 test box. Close last segment.

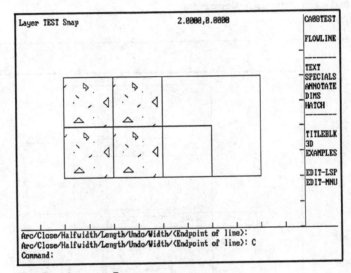

The Development Boxes

➥ *NOTE: The rest of this exercise flips in and out of the text editor to create the pattern. In actual practice, we recommend that you write down the lines to enter. Go through all the measurements first, then edit the ACAD.PAT file. To speed up your pattern development, set up a drawing area and let AutoCAD calculate the distances and angles.*

You need to create a header for the hatch pattern so that AutoCAD knows it by name and can describe it. Then, create the pattern definitions. You need to write one definition line for each member of the hatch pattern family.

Start with the dots in the pattern. Since there are three dots, you will have to write three lines. They are much like linetypes. Use DIST to measure the distances and offsets from 0,0 to each of the points. The first dot is located 6/10ths of a unit over and 2/10ths of a unit up from the origin of the pattern. The origin at coordinate 0,0 is for convenience. The X origin and Y origin are .6 and .2 respectively. The line starts at .6,.2. Here is the start of the definition sequence:

Command: **DUP**   Copy the ACAD.PAT file from your ACAD directory to the
                          CA-ACAD directory.

Command: **ED**   Edit the ACAD.PAT file.

Add this header and first definition line to the end:

```
*CONCRE, Customizing AutoCAD Concrete
0, .6,.2, 0,1, 0,-1
```

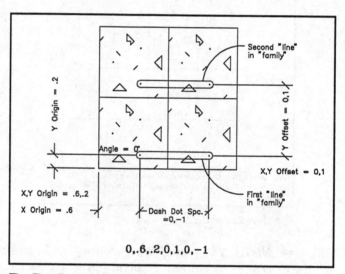

The First Dot Line Family

The origins and offsets are shown in the First Dot Line Family drawing.

In the first line, the first entry, **0**, is the angle, which we keep at 0 when defining dots. The **.6,.2** is the X,Y origin of the first dot, from 0,0. The **0,1** is the X,Y offset to the parallel patterns in the family.

An X offset of 0 makes the next line's endpoint start perpendicular to the first. Any other value would stagger the starting origin for dashed and dotted lines. The dotted line repeats parallel at every one-unit interval, so the Y offset is set to 1. The last two items, **0,-1**, are the dash-dot measurements. 0 means put the pen down to draw a dot. The -1 means lift the pen and move it over one unit before making the dot.

Repeat the same steps for the next two dot patterns. The only difference is the X,Y origin of the first dot of the line. Make sure you <RETURN> after the last line each time you add to the ACAD.PAT file. Do not add any blank lines.

Add these two lines:

```
0, .2,.5, 0,1, 0,-1
0, .6,.7, 0,1, 0,-1
```

Save, exit, and return to AutoCAD.

Command: **HATCH**   Type ? to see the listing.

Command: **HATCH**
Pattern (? or name/U,style) <CHECKP>: **CONCRE**   Use 1:1 scale, 0 angle,
                                                            select the 2 x 2 test box.

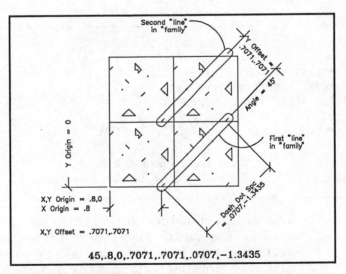

The First Dash Line Family

The hatch pattern should be identical to the dots in your sample dimensioned pattern. Next, make the isolated dash segments. First measure the distances. The origins and offsets are shown in the First Dash Line Family illustration.

Measuring the perpendicular distance between the line in the sample box and its sister line in the box to the right, you get a Y offset of 0.7071. The X offset of the lines is also 0.7071 because the line is on a 45-degree angle.

If you measure the distance from the endpoint of the first line, .85, to the start of the next line in the upper right box, 1.8,1, AutoCAD will return 1.3435, the pen up part of the line.

Command: **ED**   Edit the ACAD.PAT file.

Add the line below:

```
45, .8,0, .7071,.7071, .0707,-1.3435
```

The **45** means the line is at a 45-degree angle. It is 0.0707 units long (2/(sqrt of 2)). The **.8,0,** means the first one starts at an X,Y origin of .8,0 in the sample box. The **.7071,.7071** values show the family X,Y offset. The **.0707,-1.3435** defines a pen down dash of .0707.

The other three isolated dash line definitions are determined in the same manner.

Add these three lines:

```
45,  .5,.4,  0.7071,.7071,  .0707,-1.3435
135, .3,.6,  0.7071,.7071,  .0707,-1.3435
45,  0,.8,  0.7071,.7071,  .0707,-1.3435
```

Save, exit, and return to AutoCAD.

Command: **ERASE**   Erase the previous test hatch.
Command: **HATCH**   Test the updated pattern, selecting the 2 x 2 test box.

Your pattern should match part of the sample pattern shown in the Concrete Dots and Lines illustration. You've done the hard part. While creating a hatch pattern requires a little patience, the technique is straightforward using the methods we've shown. Finish up by writing the code for a five-sided aggregate stone and then two triangles.

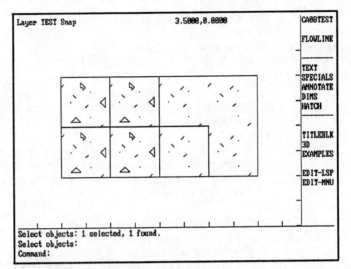

Concrete Dots and Lines

Look at the figure in the Five-Sided Aggregate illustration. Measure the short 45-degree line first. It starts at .45,.75. It has the same X and Y offsets you used with the earlier dashed lines.

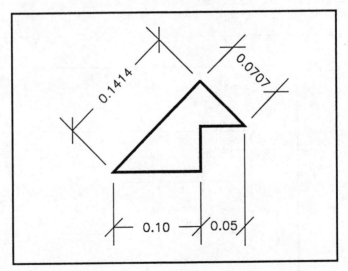

Five-Sided Aggregate

Command **ED**   Edit the ACAD.PAT file.

Add the short 45-degree line, then these other four lines:

45, .45,.75, 0.7071,.7071, .0707,-1.3435
> The short vertical line starts at the same point,.45,.75. The dash is .05 long and the pen up length is .95 (1 unit minus .05). So the line is defined as:

90, .45,.75, 0,1, .05,-.95

> The horizontal line starts at .45,.8, is .05 long, and runs at an angle of 180 degrees. You could choose the other endpoint and have it run at zero degrees, but you can't give a negative length. It means pen up! The line is defined as:

180, .45,.8, 0,1, .05,-.95

> The long vertical line is defined as:

90, .4,.8, 0,1, .1,-.9

> The closing side runs at 135 degrees, starts at .5,.8, has a dash length of .1414, and a pen up length of 1.2728. Use DIST to measure it. The perpendicular distance is 0.7071, making the definition:

135, .5,.8, 0.7071,.7071, .1414,-1.2728

Save, exit, and return to AutoCAD.

Command: **ERASE**   Erase the previous hatch.
Command: **HATCH**   Test the updated pattern, selecting the 2 x 2 test box.

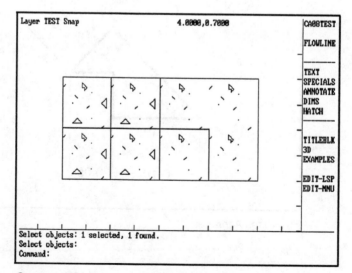

Concrete With Aggregate Added

```
Command: ED                    Edit the ACAD.PAT file.
```

Measure the triangles and add the lower left triangle.

```
0,  .2,.1, 0,1,  .2,-.8
45, .2,.1, 0.7071,.7071, .1414,-1.2728
135, .4,.1, 0.7071,.7071, .1414,-1.2728
```

Add the middle right triangle as:

```
90, .9,.4, 0,1, .2,-.8
45, .8,.5, 0.7071,.7071, .1414,-1.2728
135, .9,.4, 0.7071,.7071, .1414,-1.2728          Remember that last <RETURN>!
```

Save, exit, and return to AutoCAD.

Putting all this together, you have a concrete hatch pattern. The final definition is shown below.

```
*CONCRE, Customizing AutoCAD Concrete
0,  .6,.2, 0,1,  0,-1
0,  .2,.5, 0,1,  0,-1
0,  .6,.7, 0,1,  0,-1
45, .8,0, 0.7071,.7071, .0707,-1.3435
45, .5,.4, 0.7071,.7071, .0707,-1.3435
135, .3,.6, 0.7071,.7071, .0707,-1.3435
45, 0,.8, 0.7071,.7071, .0707,-1.3435
45, .45,.75, 0.7071,.7071, .0707,-1.3435
90, .45,.75, 0,1, .05,-.95
180, .45,.8, 0,1, .05,-.95
90, .4,.8, 0,1, .1,-.9
135, .5,.8, 0.7071,.7071, .1414,-1.2728
0,  .2,.1, 0,1, .2,-.8
45, .2,.1, 0.7071,.7071, .1414,-1.2728
135, .4,.1, 0.7071,.7071, .1414,-1.2728
90, .9,.4, 0,1, .2,-.8
45, .8,.5, 0.7071,.7071, .1414,-1.2728
135, .9,.4, 0.7071,.7071, .1414,-1.2728
```

Now try the pattern. Your screen should look like the Final Pattern illustration when you are done.

Testing the CONCRE Pattern

Command: **ERASE**   Erase the previous hatch.
Command: **HATCH**   Test the updated pattern, selecting the 2 x 2 test box.

Final Pattern

The INSIDE AutoLISP book shows you how to create a hatch generator program which can make this same hatch pattern in about five percent of the time! Achieving a more irregular appearance comes at great expense to hatch size, speed and your time. Deviating from 45- or 60-degree angular increments gets very complex; so does mixing 45- and 60-degree angles in a single pattern.

Partial and Irregular Fills

Hatches do not have block-like efficiency in their drawing data storage unless they are copied or arrayed. Large areas do not require a complete area fill. You can get around hatch inefficiencies by using s_andard *irregular* shaped blocks as hatch boundaries, stretching scale to fit, and only partially filling large areas. This saves data storage space.

You can automate this process by making a custom screen page to insert and hatch irregular boundary blocks. The following exercise shows how to make a hatch menu. Put asterisks at the beginning of the macros to auto-repeat.

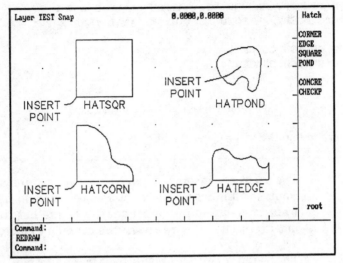

Irregular Boundaries

If you don't have the CA DISK, you need to make four 1 x 1 hatch boundaries. These are shown in the Irregular Boundaries illustration. You need to wblock the hatch boundaries with the names shown in the diagram.

Making a Hatch Menu

You have the hatch boundaries, just examine the text in the exercise.

On layer 0, draw and WBLOCK the four boundaries before proceeding.

Command: **ERASE**   Erase to clean up the screen.
Command: **ZOOM**   Zoom with the left corner at 0,0 and a height of 6".

Select **[EDIT-MNU]**   Edit the TEST.MNU.

Change the [CA00TEST] label at the top of the screen.
Change the [HATCH] label on the root menu.

```
[CA08TEST]
[HATCH]^C^C^CLAYER M HAT01 C 3 ;;$S=HATCH $S=FOOTER
```

Change the ****EXAMPLES** page as shown below.

```
**HATCH
[ Hatch  ]
[]
[CORNER  ]*^C^C^CINSERT HATCORN \C \\HATCH \\\L ;ERASE P ;
```

```
[EDGE    ]*^C^C^CINSERT HATEDGE \C \\HATCH \\\L ;ERASE P ;
[SQUARE  ]*^C^C^CINSERT HATSQR \C \\HATCH \\\L ;ERASE P ;
[POND    ]*^C^C^CINSERT HATPOND \C \\HATCH \\\L ;ERASE P ;
[]
[CONCRE  ]*^C^C^CHATCH CONCRE
[CHECKP  ]*^C^C^CHATCH CHECKP
[]
[]
```

Count [ ]s for 19 items total.

Save, exit, and return to AutoCAD. The menu should reload.

The macros to insert the hatch boundaries automatically start the hatch command and erase the boundary block once the hatch is complete. If you want to create multiple boundaries before hatching, simply cancel the macro with a <^C> or reselect the boundary macro.

The boundary blocks provide tools to render small areas of large surfaces. When a large surface requires a hatch to indicate the material it is made of, you normally just hatch portions rather than the complete surface. This provides a more pleasing appearance and room for notes and dimensions. You can combine the boundary blocks to fit irregular shapes and also insert on a reference layer that is turned off at plot time.

The following exercise shows how to use the boundaries to partially hatch a large rectangular concrete surface.

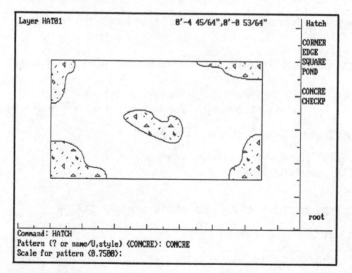

Constructed Concrete Block

Command: **PLINE**   Draw a rectangle from 1,1.5 to 1,5 to 7.5,5
to 7.5,1.5 and close.

Select **[HATCH]** *then* **[CORNER]**
Command: INSERT Block name (or ?): HATCORN
Insertion point: Pick a corner on the rectangle.
X scale factor <1> / Corner / XYZ: C Other corner: Drag it to the desired shape.
Rotation angle <0.00>:   Rotate to align with rectangle.
Command: HATCH
Pattern (? or name/U,style): *Cancel*   Cancel the rest of the macro.

Repeat the corner pattern at each corner.

Select **[POND]**   Put a freeform shape in the center.

Select **[CONCRE]**
Command: HATCH Pattern (? or name/U,style): CONCRE
Scale for pattern <1.0000>: **.75**
Angle for pattern <0.00>: **<RETURN>**
Select objects: Select the five boundary blocks and <RETURN>. You will see the
boundary blocks fill in with the concrete pattern.

Play around with some other boundaries and hatch patterns, then quit your drawing.

Command: **QUIT**

Delete TEST.MNU.

Rename TEST.MNU to MY08.MNU.

REName **\CA-ACAD\ACAD.PAT** to **CA-ACAD.PAT** for backup.
If you want the patterns for general use, copy the modified ACAD.PAT file from the CA-ACAD
directory back into your ACAD directory.

You can also create single patterns as individual files with matching
names, such as CHECKP.PAT and CONCRE.PAT from the CA DISK.

Integrating the Hatch Menu

If you don't have the CA DISK and want to add the hatch menu to
CA-MENU:

■ Insert the **HATCH page of your MY08.MNU to the end of the
***SCREEN section in the CA-MENU.MNU file, just above the
***TABLET section label.

■ Change the [HATCH] label on the **ROOT page of the CA-MENU to:

`[HATCH]^C^C^CLAYER M HAT01 C 3 ;;$S=HATCH $S=FOOTER`

The chapter's menu is shown below.

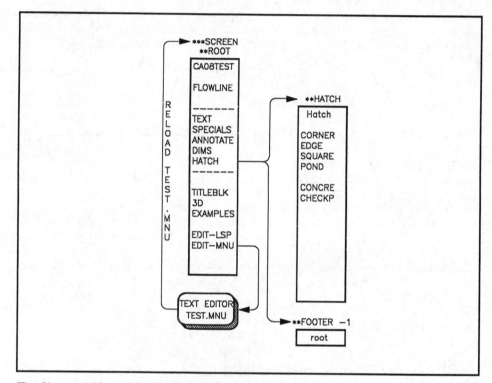

The Chapter 8 Menu Added to CA-MENU

Summary

When you create a pattern, set a snap and grid so all the lines and dots align to some reasonable increment. The smaller the increment, the larger and slower the hatch will be. Draw your lines and dots, trying to make as many lines as possible align with other lines. This creates more efficient patterns. Write down your measurements as you go.

You can get a solid filled area by using closely spaced hatch lines, but it takes a lot of drawing data and file space. An alternative for 2D work, even for irregular areas, is to use filled entities such as wide polylines, donuts, and solids. Align and overlay them in any combination that works. However, in 3D, solid fills that are not parallel to your current view do not display or plot.

Hatches don't show up in AutoShade unless you give the lines a thickness. Explode the hatch and use CHPROP to assign the thickness.

To make a nearly invisible linetype, define it as a dot at each end with a huge pen up segment in between. The definition is A,0,-31999. When you use it, all it draws are endpoints with blanks between.

This marks the end of customizing linetypes and hatches. It's time to use some AutoLISP!

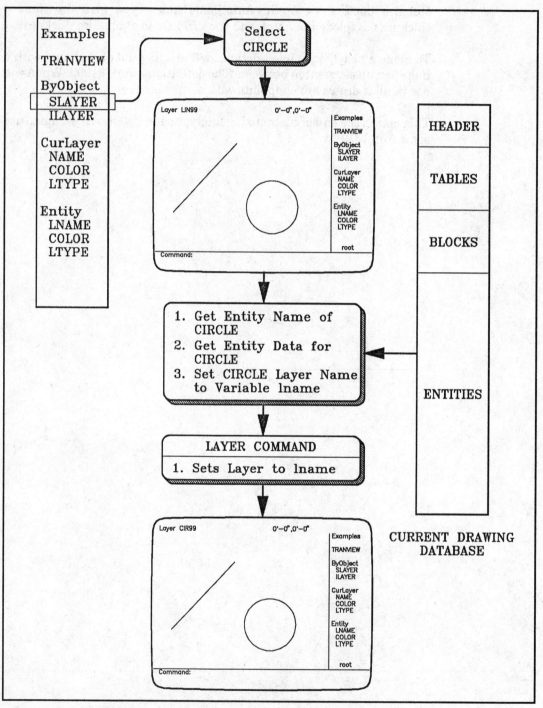

Set Layer Menu Macro

CHAPTER 9

A Little AutoLISP

MUSCLE MACROS

Until now, our macros have been mostly straight sequences of standard AutoCAD commands. This chapter shows you how to add AutoLISP to your menu macros.

What Is AutoLISP?

AutoLISP is a dialect of the LISP language. AutoLISP was derived from XLISP and is a program that coexists with the AutoCAD program within the AutoCAD system. Like every programming language, AutoLISP provides general programming tools to structure the flow of a program, to manipulate program data, and to input and output data to computer devices.

In addition to these general tools, AutoLISP has AutoCAD-specific tools. These tools let it access and update AutoCAD's drawing entity data, access AutoCAD's tables for blocks, layers, views, styles, UCSs, viewports, and linetypes, and control AutoCAD's graphics screen and device input.

Although many of the macros you created are powerful and complex, they are primarily just a *fast typist* entering sequences of standard AutoCAD commands. AutoLISP turns your macros into an *intelligent typist* who can make calculations and logical decisions, and add control to your macro. AutoLISP macros can act like custom commands, prompting, instructing, and providing choices and defaults just like AutoCAD's standard commands. This chapter introduces AutoLISP in macros. The next book in our series, INSIDE AutoLISP, teaches the writing of AutoLISP programs, offering even more power and control.

The Benefits of Using AutoLISP

What are the benefits of using AutoLISP?

AutoLISP is your direct pipeline to AutoCAD. With it, you have access to AutoCAD drawing entities, reference tables, and to passing data in and out of AutoCAD. By using AutoLISP in your menu macros, you can save data in variables, process that data, and send it back to AutoCAD. Points, distances, and other values can be stored, calculated, compared, and used to draw with. You can control your drawing environment through AutoCAD system variables by storing the system variables, prompting with drawing status, and changing and restoring the settings. You can change system settings transparently during commands for more responsiveness. You can access and extract entity data, use the data in programs, and even modify entities transparently.

How-To Skills Checklist

In this chapter, you will learn how to:

❑ Use AutoCAD system variables.

❑ Use AutoLISP variables.

❑ Extract information about the drawing and use it in macros.

❑ Learn AutoLISP syntax, function names, and arguments.

❑ Add AutoLISP routines to your menu.

❑ Pass AutoLISP data back to AutoCAD.

❑ Get user input using AutoLISP.

❑ Use the rubber band feature of AutoCAD in AutoLISP.

❑ Build AutoLISP lists and retrieve any element from them.

❑ Access the entity database using selection sets, entity names, and entity data.

❑ Use entity data in a macro.

❑ Look up AutoCAD table data.

Menus and AutoLISP Macros

Menus Using AutoLISP

In this chapter, you will experiment with a few macros in a temporary test menu, then add two pages to the CA-MENU.

**EXAMPLES receives eight useful drawing data-access macros to deal with layers, colors and linetypes.

**PTFILTERS is expanded to store and restore five user-defined point values.

Macros Using AutoLISP

[RECT] and [RECTANG] are two versions of AutoLISP macros that take two corner input points and draw a polyline rectangle.

[Point 1] is one of five macros that stores and restores defined point values.

[SLAYER] sets the current layer to the layer of a selected entity.

[ILAYER] isolates the layer of a selected object, turning all other layers off.

[Curlayer] is a set of macros, [NAME], [COLOR], and [LTYPE], that returns the name, color, and linetype of the current layer.

[Entity] is a set of macros, [LNAME], [COLOR], and [LTYPE], that returns the layer name, color, and linetype of the current entity.

AutoLISP Tools

The Shadow Box exercise is a series of hands-on expressions that takes two corner input points, inserts text, and draws a shadow box with round corners around the text. The rectangle macros are derived from these expressions.

Shadow Boxing With AutoLISP

The first exercise will just warm you up a bit, hopefully without any bruises. It is a bit of hands-on AutoLISP, typed directly at the AutoCAD command line, that shows the power of the GET functions, SETQ and GETVAR, and the COMMAND function. There are many menu macros that are impossible to write without these basic AutoLISP functions. This exercise will be quick, without much explanation. Look at it carefully and in the following sections, we will explain the functions. We will also extract parts of this first shadow box to develop into menu macros.

Let's move on to this exercise. It shows you how to enter AutoLISP variables and expressions by typing them directly into the drawing editor. It explains our format for interpreting the AutoLISP responses that you see at the command line.

Creating a Shadow Box

Let's start by using AutoLISP to develop a series of LISP expressions which create a shadow box around two lines of text. In the exercise sequence, you will see the words *Lisp returns:*. We use this to show AutoLISP's backtalk. You won't see *Lisp returns:* on your screen, but you should see the line or lines that follow it.

Start a new drawing called CA09. Type the input shown in bold. Don't panic if AutoLISP returns a 1> during the input. This is just AutoLISP's way of telling you that it needs another right parenthesis. Keep typing the input as shown and it should come out okay. Input the drawing points as the exercise requests. After you get the shadow box and text drawn, we will look very closely at each part of these AutoLISP expressions.

Drawing With AutoLISP

Enter selection: **1**   Begin a NEW drawing named CA09.

Copy CA09.MNU to TEST.MNU.

Copy MAIN.MNU to TEST.MNU.

Select **[TEST] [24 x 36] [FULL] [INITIATE]**   It should bring up TEST.MNU.
Command: **LAYER**   Freeze ?????BDR, the borders.
Command: **ZOOM**   Zoom Left at 0,0 with height 12".
Command: **STYLE**   Create a new 1/2" fancy style.
Text style name (or ?) <STD1-8>: **CPX1-2**
New style.
Font file <txt>: **ROMANC**
Height <0'-0">: **1/2**
Width factor <1.00>: **<RETURN>**   Default the rest.

The AutoLISP sequence is designed to use the default text height to calculate polyline width, but the TEXTSIZE system variable isn't updated by the STYLE command. Enter some text to set TEXTSIZE, then try the first four expressions. The first two expressions get and store corner point values for use by later expressions. The second two expressions calculate the other corner points. The LL's are the letters LL, not the number eleven.

Command: **TEXT**	Use the CPX1-2 style to enter some test text.
Command: **ERASE**	Then erase to clean it up.

```
Command: (setq ll (getpoint "Pick LL corner: "))
Pick LL corner: 3,2                     Pick or enter the point.
Lisp returns: (3.0 2.0 0.0)

Command: (setq ur (getcorner ll "Pick UR corner: "))
Pick UR corner: 9,6                     Enter the point.
Lisp returns: (9.0 6.0 0.0)

Command: (setq ul (list (car ll) (cadr ur)))
Lisp returns: (3.0 6.0)

Command: (setq lr (list (car ur) (cadr ll)))
Lisp returns: (9.0 2.0)
```

If you make a mistake on an expression, <^C> to cancel and re-enter it.

If you keep getting a 1>, type a closing parenthesis) and a <RETURN>, then hit <^C> and try inputting the AutoLISP variables and expressions again.

In AutoLISP, opening parentheses in expressions must have matching closing parentheses. Failure to close a parenthesis will give you a prompt like 1> or 2>. The AutoLISP error prompt form is n> where *n* indicates how many closing parentheses are missing.

AutoLISP opening quotation marks must have matching closing quotation marks. If you get an n> error prompt and adding additional parentheses doesn't help, then you left out a quotation mark. Type a single " and then type as many)) as you need. The hardest part of AutoLISP is getting matching pairs of parentheses and quotation marks!

You have now stored four points of a rectangle. Use AutoLISP to draw a polyline. The polyline width is based on a percentage of the current text height.

```
Command: (command "pline" ll "w"
1> (/ (setq tx (getvar "textsize")) 3) "" lr ur "w" 0 "" ul "c"))
Lisp returns: nil                 After executing the PLINE command.
```

The text size is stored in a variable for use in other expressions. Next, calculate the point on the screen where the text should be positioned. Then add the two lines of text using AutoLISP.

```
Command: (setq pt (polar l1 (angle l1 ur) (/ (distance l1 ur) 2)))
Lisp returns: (6.0 4.0 0.0)

Command: (command "text" "c" pt 0 "CUSTOMIZING")
Lisp returns: nil                        After executing the TEXT command.

Command: (command "text" "" "AutoCAD")
Lisp returns: nil                        After executing the TEXT command.

Command: (command "fillet" "r" tx "fillet" "p" l1)    Round the corners of the polyline.
Lisp returns: nil                        After executing the FILLET command.
```

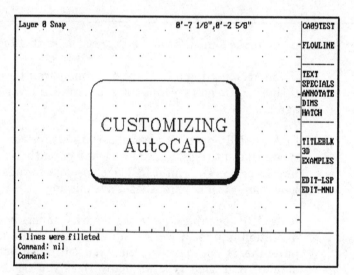

Shadow Box Drawn With AutoLISP Expressions

If all went well, you should have a shadow box outlining the text, "CUSTOMIZING AutoCAD."

Of course, any AutoCAD user could easily draw this without AutoLISP! But, after we explain these expressions, we'll automate this in a menu macro and add some flexibility to the text input.

AutoLISP Variables and Expressions

When AutoLISP was first introduced into the AutoCAD program, it wasn't even called AutoLISP. It was just called "Variables and Expressions" for building macros. Don't let AutoLISP intimidate you. Just think of AutoLISP as it was originally introduced, providing variables and expressions for your macros.

Variables

AutoLISP uses variables. A *variable* represents something that is not constant, something that changes its value. You use variables all the time. You multiply your tax *rate* by your *income* and (if it were only that simple) send the result to the IRS. Rate and income are variables.

AutoLISP lets you substitute variables in place of constant values. You attach a value to a variable name. You can attach the information to the variable name explicitly in a macro, or you can attach the information by having a user supply the information. You can use the variable names within AutoLISP expressions to perform calculations and make logical decisions.

In the shadow box exercise, LL (for the lower left corner point) was a variable. It got a value from the GETPOINT expression that asked the user for a point. This value was later passed to the PLINE command as one of the corners of the rectangle.

```
Command: (command "pline" ll "w"...
```

AutoCAD's System Variables

When you change the settings or values of snap, osnap, ortho, or when you just pick a point, AutoCAD saves the newly set condition, value, or point as a system variable. You have already used the SETVAR command to set system variables. You can see all of the current system variable settings with the SETVAR command and a question mark.

Using SETVAR to Look at System Variables

```
Command: SETVAR
Variable name or ? <DIMSCALE>: ?          Gives a listing.
```

```
ACADPREFIX   "C:\ACAD\"                          (read only)
ACADVER      "10"                                (read only)
AFLAGS       0
ANGBASE      0.00
ANGDIR       0
APERTURE     6
AREA         0.0000                              (read only)
ATTDIA       0
ATTMODE      1
ATTREQ       1
AUNITS       0
AUPREC       2
AXISMODE     1
AXISUNIT     0'-0 1/2",0'-0 1/2"
BACKZ        0'-0"                               (read only)
BLIPMODE     1
CDATE        19890107.122419201                 (read only)
CECOLOR      "BYLAYER"                           (read only)
CELTYPE      "BYLAYER"                           (read only)
CHAMFERA     0'-0"
CHAMFERB     0'-0"
-- Press RETURN for more --
```

The SETVAR Display

See the system variables table in Appendix C for a complete listing, along with descriptive comments on the variables.

Variable Data Types

You can access system variables and create new variables with names of your own with AutoLISP. If you look closely at the list of system variables in Appendix C, you will see three types of variables: *string*, *integer*, and *real*. (*Points* are lists of reals.) System variables and any AutoLISP variables that you may create are one of these types.

■ *String* variables have text values placed in quotes to identify the value as a string. For example, the system variable ACADPREFIX is currently "C:\ACAD\." The values "3.1," "SHEET-D," "pline," "-1234," and "The quick brown fox..." are all strings.

■ *Integers* are positive or negative whole numbers without fractions, decimal places or decimal points. AutoCAD often uses values of 0 and 1 to indicate whether a system variable toggle, like SNAPMODE and ORTHOMODE, is turned off (0) or on (1). Integers must be between -32768 and +32767. Larger and smaller values cause errors without warning. The values 1, 3234, and -12134 are valid integers.

■ *Reals* are positive or negative numbers with decimal points. In AutoLISP, you cannot begin or end a real with a decimal. If the value is less than 1.0, you must put a 0 before the decimal point (0.123) or you will get "error: invalid dotted pair." Examples of real system variables are FILLETRAD, TEXTSIZE, and AREA. Unlike integers, real values are not limited to certain numbers. However, AutoLISP formats reals in scientific notation when the values are very large or very small. Valid reals look like 1.0, 3.75218437615, -71213.7358 and 1.234568E+17.

■ *Points* are really AutoLISP lists. A list is one or more values of any variable type grouped within parentheses. The shadow box GETPOINT and GETCORNER expressions returned point lists. The LASTPOINT system variable is a point list with a value such as: (6.5 1.5 0.0).

Using system variables, you can control many AutoCAD drawing editor settings. You have changed these system settings with the SETVAR command, and you have used the transparent 'SETVAR command to change settings in the middle of another AutoCAD command. You can change some, but not all, of the system variable settings. Certain variables are indicated as *read only* meaning you can only extract, not update, their values.

How to Use AutoLISP to Get and Set System Variables

You can also access AutoCAD's system variables with AutoLISP's GETVAR and SETVAR functions. GETVAR is a function, not a command. SETVAR is the name of an AutoLISP function and also the name of the AutoCAD command. A simple example of using a system variable is a macro to retrieve the name of the current layer with (getvar "CLAYER") and pass it along to a command that can use it.

```
[CH:LAYER ]^C^C^CSELECT AU \CHPROP P ;LAYER (getvar "CLAYER") LAYER \;
```

The [CH:LAYER] macro uses the getvar "CLAYER" to get and enter the current layer name as a default to the CHPROP command. Look at the macro above. It has the effect of presenting the current layer as a default for the CHPROP command.

The shadow box expressions used the TEXTSIZE system variable to get the current text height. Try some GETVAR and SETVAR functions by typing the input shown in the following exercise.

Using GETVAR and SETVAR to Get and Set System Variables

Continue in your CA09 drawing.

Command: **LAYER**   Set the layer named OBJ01 current.

```
Command: (getvar "CLAYER")          Get the current layer value.
Lisp returns: "OBJ01"               The value, the layer name.

Command: (setvar "ORTHOMODE" 1)     Reset the ortho value to on.
Lisp returns: 1

Command: (setvar "CLAYER" "0")      Try to reset layer.
error: AutoCAD rejected function    You can't. It's read only.
Lisp returns: (SETVAR "CLAYER" "0") The offending AutoLISP function.
```

In previous chapters, you used and set several system variables in macros. The flaw in those macros was that settings were left changed, with their original settings not restored. You can write macros that use the GETVAR and SETVAR functions to get, save, and then restore your drawing settings.

Expressions

An AutoLISP expression begins with an opening parenthesis and ends with a closing parenthesis. AutoLISP expressions can contain other AutoLISP expressions. You must nest each expression in its own pair of parentheses.

A typical AutoLISP expression has this syntax:

```
(function argument)
```

Here are the rules for the expression game:

- Every expression has opening and closing parentheses.

- Every expression has a function name. The name must immediately follow the opening parenthesis.

- Expressions can be nested, with each balancing its opening and closing parentheses.

- Every expression gets evaluated (executed) and returns a result. The result is the last evaluated value, which may be nil.

- Everything in AutoLISP is either T (true) or nil. If something has no value, it's nil. If it has a value, it's true (non-nil).

Functions and Arguments

A *function* is a subroutine that tells AutoLISP what task to perform.

Tasks include addition, subtraction, multiplication, or division. A function may have any number of arguments or no arguments. The divide function /, DISTANCE, POLAR, SETQ, and along with other functions were used in the shadow box exercise.

An *argument* provides data to the function. Arguments may be variables, constants, or other functions. Some arguments are flags or optional parameters that alter the action of the function. If a function is defined to accept an argument, you must provide the function with a value for the argument. The angle function in the shadow box exercise takes two points as arguments, LL and UR.

You'll find a complete description of all the AutoLISP functions in Appendix C. Refer to Appendix C to check your syntax and correct types of arguments.

How AutoCAD and AutoLISP Communicate

The opening and closing parentheses allow AutoCAD to distinguish between AutoCAD commands and AutoLISP expressions. Each time AutoCAD detects an opening parenthesis, it passes the entire expression to AutoLISP. AutoLISP evaluates the expression and returns the result to AutoCAD. AutoCAD uses the result and continues.

AutoCAD can cause a problem within AutoLISP when AutoCAD wants a literal text string. There are two places where AutoCAD wants a literal text string: when prompting for text, or prompting for an attribute. A system variable called TEXTEVAL controls the situation. Setting TEXTEVAL to 1 (On) forces AutoCAD to send the expression to AutoLISP for evaluation and print the results instead of the expression itself.

Using Math Functions in AutoLISP

AutoLISP has several built-in math functions. In calculating the polyline width for the shadow box exercise, you used a divide function in the expression:

```
(/ (setq tx (getvar "textsize")) 3)
```

This expression divides the text height by three to give you the polyline width value.

When you talk about AutoLISP functions, you say (+ 1 2) evaluates to 3. In algebra, the same function is expressed as 1 + 2 equals 3. This addition example has two arguments, both constants. Arguments are the data for the function. Some AutoLISP math functions, like + - * and /, can have any number of arguments. Some functions require a specific number or type of argument, and some take optional parameters or flags. Here is a list of built-in math functions that you can use in your macros:

```
MATH FUNCTION              DESCRIPTION
(/ arg1 arg2 arg3 ... )    ARG1 divided by ARG2
                             divided by ARG3 ...
(* arg1 arg2 arg3 ... )    ARG1 times ARG2 times ARG3 ...
(+ arg1 arg2 arg3 ... )    ARG1 plus ARG2 plus ARG3 ...
(- arg1 arg2 arg3 ... )    ARG1 minus ARG2 minus ARG3 ...
(1+ arg)                   ARG plus 1
(1- arg)                   ARG minus 1
(abs arg)                  Absolute value of ARG
(exp arg)                  e to the ARG power
(expt base power)          BASE to the POWER
(gcd arg1 arg2)            Greatest Common Denominator
                             of ARG1 and ARG2
(log arg)                  Natural log of ARG
(max arg1 arg2 arg3 ... )  Maximum of arguments
(min arg1 arg2 arg3 ... )  Minimum of arguments
(rem arg1 arg2 arg3)       The remainder only of:
                             ARG1 divided by ARG2 ...
(sqrt arg)                 SQuare RooT of ARG
```

AutoLISP Math Functions

How AutoLISP Evaluates Expressions

AutoLISP evaluates expressions left to right at the same nesting level. When a nested expression is encountered, the entire nested expression is evaluated left to right before the next expression on the right. One good thing about having all these parentheses is that you never write a formula that evaluates in a different order than you expect.

If all the arguments are integers, the results will be an integer and any fractional part will be dropped. If any argument is a real, the result will be a real. Try some math functions and look at nesting. Type the functions at the command line.

Using AutoLISP Math Functions

```
Command: ERASE                              Erase the shadow box to clean up the screen.
Command: (+ 1 2.0)                          Returns a real.
Lisp returns: 3.0


Command: (/ 3 2)                            Drops the .5 remainder.
Lisp returns: 1


Command: (* 5 (- 7 2))                      The (- 7 2) expression is nested and evaluated first.
Lisp returns: 25


Command: (setq a 1)                         Assigns the value 1 to a variable.
Lisp returns: 1


Command: (+ (setq a (* a 3)) (+ a 2))       Assigns variable before second expression.
Lisp returns: 8


Command: (+ (+ a 2) (setq a (* a 3)))       Uses variable, then reassigns it.
Lisp returns: 14
```

Making Your Own Variables and Expressions

You create variables by giving a value to a symbol. In the shadow box exercise command, you assigned a point to the symbol LL (for lower left) with the expression (setq ll (getpoint ...)).

AutoLISP automatically assigns a data type when you create a variable. AutoLISP variables are completely independent of AutoCAD system variables and their names may duplicate AutoCAD system variable names. Each time you use the variable name or refer to the variable name in a macro, program, or expression, the program replaces the variable name with the most recent value assigned to that name.

Variables can be any printable combination of letters and numbers except those reserved because of their special meanings in AutoLISP. There also are some ill-advised characters that may confuse or interfere with AutoLISP when you use them in menu macros. Avoid using the following characters:

```
RESERVED AND ILLEGAL CHARACTERS:   . ' " ; ( ) or <SPACE>
AutoLISP FUNCTIONS:         ~ * = > < + - /
ILL-ADVISED CHARACTERS: ? ` ! \ ^ or any control character.
```

The ATOMLIST

You should not use AutoLISP function names as variable names. The ATOMLIST is an AutoLISP variable that stores all defined functions and variable names. You can see these functions by looking at AutoLISP's ATOMLIST.

```
Command: !ATOMLIST
(A INTERS GRREAD GRTEXT GRDRAW GRCLEAR UPORTS TRANS HANDENT TBLSEARCH TBLNEXT EN
TUPD ENTMOD ENTSEL ENTLAST ENTNEXT ENTDEL ENTGET SSMEMB SSDEL SSADD SSLENGTH SSN
AME SSGET ANGTOS RTOS COMMAND OSNAP REDRAW GRAPHSCR TEXTSCR POLAR DISTANCE ANGLE
INITGET GETKWORD GETCORNER GETINT GETSTRING GETORIENT GETANGLE GETREAL GETDIST
GETPOINT MENUCMD PROMPT FINDFILE GETENV SETUAR GETUAR  TERPRI PRINC PRIN1 PRINT
WRITE-LINE READ-LINE WRITE-CHAR READ-CHAR CLOSE OPEN STRCASE ITOA ATOF ATOI CHR
ASCII SUBSTR STRCAT STRLEN PAUSE PI MINUSP ZEROP NUMBERP FLOAT FIX SQRT SIN LOG
EXPT EXP COS ATAN 1- 1+ ABS MAX MIN NOT OR AND > >= /= = <= < ~ GCD BOOLE LSH LO
GIOR LOGAND REM * - + ASSOC MEMBER SUBST LENGTH REVERSE LAST APPEND CDDDDR CDDDA
R CDDADR CDDAAR CDADDR CDADAR CDAADR CDAAAR CADDDR CADDAR CADADR CADAAR CAADDR C
AADAR CAAADR CAAAAR CDDDR CDDAR CDADR CDAAR CADDR CADAR CAADR CAAAR CDDR CDAR CA
DR CAAR CDR CAR CONS COND LISTP TYPE NULL EQUAL EQ BOUNDP ATOM NTH PAGETB PICKSE
T ENAME REAL FILE STR INT SYM LIST SUBR T MAPCAR APPLY LAMBDA EVAL *ERROR* / QUI
T EXIT _UER UER IF UNTRACE TRACE DEFUN FOREACH REPEAT WHILE PROGN FUNCTION QUOTE
READ LOAD SETQ SET MEM UMON ALLOC EXPAND GC ATOMLIST)

Command:
```

The ATOMLIST

AutoLISP will list all user-defined variables, functions, and function names if you type !ATOMLIST. The exclamation point tells AutoCAD to return the value of the AutoLISP variable that follows it.

Looking at the ATOMLIST

Command: **<F1>**	Flip to the text screen.
Command: **!ATOMLIST**	You will see the ATOMLIST display.

A few of these functions are used exclusively by the AutoLISP evaluator and are not intended for users. The rest of the functions are documented in the AutoLISP Programmer's Reference, and most are used in examples in the book, INSIDE AutoLISP (New Riders Publishing).

When you type your variable names, upper or lower case makes no difference. Try to keep your names under six characters since names over six characters require more memory. Don't begin a variable name with a number.

```
INVALID VARIABLE NAMES:                              VALID NAMES:
123 (represents an integer number)                   PT1
10.5 (represents a constant real value of 10.5)      txt
ANGLE (redefines the AutoLISP function ANGLE)        ANGL
A(1) (contains invalid characters)                   A-1
OLD SUM (contains space)                             OLD_SUM
```

How to Assign Values to Variables

SETQ binds a stored value to a variable name. In algebra, you write y=3, but in AutoLISP you enter **(setq y 3)**. Both the equal sign of the algebraic expression and the SETQ of the AutoLISP expression are functions. Each function binds (sets) the value 3 to the variable y. The opening (left) and closing (right) parentheses form the expression.

After binding a value to a variable name, you can use an exclamation point to supply that value to AutoCAD. The exclamation point identifies the word that follows as an AutoLISP symbol, usually a variable name. When AutoCAD sees the ! character, it passes the variable name to AutoLISP. AutoLISP interprets it and passes its value back to the AutoCAD command processor. You can also use the new variables in other AutoLISP expressions.

Using SETQ to Set and ! to Use AutoLISP Variables

Command: **(setq y 2)**   Set variable Y to the integer value 2.
Lisp returns: 2

Command: **!Y**   Send Y's value to AutoCAD.
Lisp returns: 2

Command: **(setq x 3)**
Lisp returns: 3

Command: **(+ x y)**   Use the values in an addition expression.
Lisp returns: 5

Well, you can create variables, assign values to them, and use the values in functions. How do you use these simple variables and expressions to improve and enhance your macros?

Using GET Functions for Macro Input

One area where AutoLISP can enhance your macros is to get (and control) the input for macro commands. Use the GET family of AutoLISP functions to get drawing input. There is a get function for each major data type. All of the arguments to get functions are optional. The get functions can have a prompt argument to ask a question, or to give an instruction. The prompt can be any text string. All the GET functions require a backslash to pause for input when used in a menu macro.

Here is the complete list of GET functions that you have to work with:

GET FUNCTIONS	EXPLANATION
(getangle basept promptstring)	Returns angle from 2 points or typed input.
(getcorner basept promptstring)	Returns 2nd corner of a rubber-banded rectangle.
(getdist basept promptstring)	Returns distance from 2 points or typed input.
(getint promptstring)	Integer.
(getkword promptstring)	Returns one of a list of predefined key words.
(getorient basept promptstring)	Like GETANGLE but handles non-East base angle setting.
(getpoint basept promptstring)	Point.
(getreal promptstring)	Real.
(getstring flag promptstring)	String. If FLAG is True, it accepts <SPACES> in string and requires <RETURN> to enter.

AutoLISP GET Functions

You've already seen the GETPOINT and GETCORNER functions in the shadow box expressions:

```
Command: (setq ll (getpoint "Pick LL corner: "))
(setq ur (getcorner ll "Pick UR corner: "))
```

The "Pick LL corner:" is the GETPOINT prompt string. The LL value it gets was then used by GETCORNER as its base point for its rubber band box. Try a couple of other input functions to get the hang of it. Type the input at the command line.

Using GET Functions for Input to Macros

```
Command: (getangle "Enter angle: ")
Enter angle: 30                      Or pick two points to show an angle.
Lisp returns: 0.523599               AutoLISP uses and returns angles in radians, not degrees.
                                     There are 2 x PI radians in 360 degrees. One degree = 180/PI.

Command: (* (getangle "Enter angle: ") (/ 180 pi))   PI is predefined.
Enter angle: 30
Lisp returns: 30.0

Command: (setq pt1 (getpoint "Enter point: "))       Save a point.
Enter point:                                         Pick a point.
Lisp returns: (2.0 2.0 0.0)

Command: (getangle pt1 "Enter angle: ")   Use pt1 as base point for rubber-banding.
Enter angle:                              Pick a point.
Lisp returns:  0.96007

Command: (getangle pt1 "Enter angle: ")
Enter angle: 30                          Or you can type it.
Lisp returns: 0.523599

Command: (getstring "Enter word: ")
Enter word: This                         The first <SPACE> enters it.
Lisp returns: "This"

Command: (getstring T "Enter sentence: ")   T is predefined.
Enter sentence: This is a sentence.         It allows <SPACES>.
Lisp returns: "This is a sentence."

Command: (getcorner pt1 "Enter other corner: ")   Use the base point, pt1.
Enter other corner: (5.4375 4.875 0.0)            It rubber bands a rectangle.
```

If you followed the sequences, you noticed that the input automatically becomes the data type requested. Invalid responses that are not the requested data type are rejected. GETSTRING will accept numbers as string data, and GETREAL will accept integers, but it converts the integers to floating-point reals. Use GETDIST instead of GETREAL because you can enter distance either by picking points, with optional rubber-banding, or by typing values. GETDIST treats distance as a real data type. You can input either decimal or current units, but the input is automatically converted to decimal.

If you use an integer, like 96, within an AutoLISP expression where it expects a real, like 96.0, AutoLISP converts it to 96.0. If you give an

AutoLISP GETREAL or GETDIST function input like 96.0, 96. or 96, AutoLISP accepts and converts these values to 96.0. However, if you use a real within an AutoLISP expression that expects an integer, like the ITOA function, it will cause an error.

GETPOINT accepts point input in X and Y coordinates. A Z coordinate is returned if either of two conditions are meet. The AutoCAD FLATLAND variable is set to 0, meaning AutoCAD is in full 3D mode, or the INITGET function initialized GETPOINT to accept and return Z values. Recall that a point in AutoLISP is simply a list of two (or three) reals, like (1.5 2.0 6.75).

How to Use Base Point Arguments and Rubber-Banding in Macros

The GETDIST, GETANGLE, GETORIENT, and GETPOINT functions can use an optional base point argument. GETCORNER must have a base point. AutoCAD uses rubber band lines when you show a distance or angle by selecting points. Rubber-banding lets you dynamically display a distance in the coordinates box on the screen. Remember that the distance<angle is displayed in the relative distance coords mode. The GETDIST, GETANGLE, GETORIENT, and GETPOINT functions all rubber band input when two points are input or a base point is set. Use an optional base point if you need to tie the point down.

Placing a GET function without a base point in the middle of an ordinary AutoCAD command interferes with the normal command's rubber-banding. Try this:

Testing the GETPOINT Function

```
Command: LINE
From point:                              Pick a point.
To point: (getpoint "Pick it: ")
Pick it:                                 Your rubber-banding is gone.
```

When you use the keyboard, the GET functions automatically pause for input. However, you need to use the backslash character \ to pause a macro for input. Two AutoLISP get functions pose a problem when you use the backslash method of pause control. The GETDIST and GETANGLE functions offer the user the choice of picking two points or typing the distance<angle. Typing the input requires only one backslash. If you pick two points, you need two backslashes. If you use these functions, you need to plan ahead and prompt for the input format expected. Base points help avoid this because they need only typed input or one pick point.

Using GET Functions in Menu Macros

Let's resurrect the shadow box example as a menu macro. Try the first two lines. Then add to the macro in several stages as we proceed through additional functions.

If you are using the CA DISK, you have these macros in their various stages of development in the menu file called CA09.MNU. Copy this file to the CA-ACAD directory, look at it with your text editor, and test it in the exercises. If you are not using the disk, you will need to create the file and the macros.

GET Functions in a [RECT] Macro

 Just examine the macros.

Create the macros.

Select **[EDIT MNU]**   Edit TEST.MNU.

Change [CA00TEST] to [CA09TEST] and add [RECT] to the second [ ] on the **EXAMPLES page.

```
***SCREEN
**ROOT
[CA09TEST]

**EXAMPLES
[Examples]
[]
[RECT      ]^C^C^C(setq ll (getpoint "Pick LL corner: "));\+
(setq ur (getcorner ll "Pick UR corner: "));\+
PLINE !LL .X !UR !LL !UR .X !LL !UR C;
[]
```

Save TEST.MNU and exit to AutoCAD.

Let's examine the [RECT] macro, then test it. GETPOINT gets the first (lower left) corner and SETQ saves it as LL. The backslash after GETPOINT makes the macro pause for AutoLISP input, just like pausing for AutoCAD command input. Follow the AutoLISP expression with a semicolon (for <RETURN>) prior to the backslash. Then GETCORNER gets the opposite (upper right) corner, using LL as the anchor for a rubber band rectangle. It is saved as UR. Instead of calculating the other corners with CAR and CADR (like the shadow box which will be explained later), we used the alternative method of drawing the polyline with XYZ point filters. The second (lower right) corner gets its X coordinate from UR and its Y from LL, in the sequence .X !UR !LL. In menus, as in typing AutoLISP variables at the command line, you feed variable names to AutoCAD by preceding them with an exclamation mark, like !LL.

Try [RECT] now:

```
Select [Examples] [RECT]                     Draw a rectangle.
Command: (setq ll (getpoint "Pick LL corner: "))
Pick LL corner: 2,1
Lisp returns: (2.0 1.0 0.0)
Command: (setq ur (getcorner ll "Pick UR corner: "))
Pick UR corner: 6,5
Lisp returns: (6.0 5.0 0.0)

Command: PLINE              And !LL .X !UR !LL !UR .X !LL !UR C; draws it:
From point: !LL
Current line-width is 0'-0"
Arc/Close/Halfwidth/Length/Undo/Width/<Endpoint of line>: .X of !UR (need Y):
!LL
Arc/Close/Halfwidth/Length/Undo/Width/<Endpoint of line>: !UR
Arc/Close/Halfwidth/Length/Undo/Width/<Endpoint of line>: .X of !LL (need Y):
!UR
Arc/Close/Halfwidth/Length/Undo/Width/<Endpoint of line>: C
```

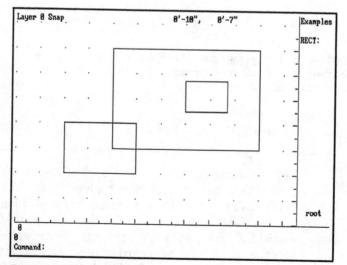

Rectangles Drawn With [RECT]

The shadow box used the LIST, CAR and CADR functions to calculate the UL and LR corners. Let's make a version called [RECTANG] that uses these functions. Remember in AutoLISP, points are lists, so let's look at lists to see how they work.

How AutoLISP Lists Work

A *list* is a group of elements of any data type, treated as one expression and stored as a single variable. An AutoLISP list may contain any number of reals, integers, strings, variables, or even other lists. Anything between an opening parenthesis and its corresponding closing parenthesis is a list. If this sounds hauntingly familiar, it is. Any expression is a list! Lists organize and process groups of information. Several system variables are lists. The LIMMAX (upper right Limits) system variable, for example, is a list. You just saw AutoLISP return the LL point list as (2.0 1.0 0.0) in the [RECT] exercise.

Points Are AutoLISP Lists

```
Command: (getvar "LIMMAX")
```
Lisp returns: (36.0 24.0) The upper right point of the limits.

Other examples of AutoLISP lists are ("A" "B") and ("NAME" 10.0 "DESK" "WS291A").

How to Use List Functions

AutoLISP has many list manipulation functions. [RECT:] uses the functions LIST, CAR, and CADR. LIST is simple. It just makes a list of its arguments. Since a list is a group of elements, you need a way to extract the element that you want. CAR is shorthand for the first element of a list, and CADR is the second element. These were used in the shadow box. Let's try them in [RECTANG]:

Building a [RECTANG] Macro

Select [EDIT MNU]   Edit TEST.MNU. Copy and add:

```
[RECTANG ]^C^C^C(setq ll (getpoint "Pick LL corner: "));\+
(setq ur (getcorner ll "Pick UR corner: "));\+
(setq ul (list (car ll) (cadr ur)));+
(setq lr (list (car ur) (cadr ll)));+
(command "pline" ll lr ur ul "c");
[]
```

Save TEST.MNU and exit to AutoCAD.

```
Select [Examples] [RECTANG]
Command: (setq ll (getpoint "Pick LL corner: "))
Pick LL corner:                                    Pick any point.
Command: (setq ur (getcorner ll "Pick UR corner: "))
Pick UR corner:                                    Pick any point.

Command: (setq ul (list (car ll) (cadr ur)))
Lisp returns: (2.375 4.75)                          Or your UL corner.

Command: (setq lr (list (car ur) (cadr ll)))
Lisp returns: (8.375 1.75)                          Or your LR corner.

Command: (command "pline" ll lr ur ul "c")         Draws the rectangle with PLINE.
```

In the [RECTANG] example, (list (car ll) (cadr ur))) created a new point from the CAR (first element) of LL and the CADR (second element) of UR. The CAR function extracted the X coordinate of the lower left GETPOINT and the upper right GETCORNER points.

The similar CDR function returns a list of all elements *except* the first element.

Using the Quote Function to Build Lists

The QUOTE function, which can be abbreviated as a single quotation mark ', is also important. Unlike the LIST function which evaluates its contents before forming a list, QUOTE suppresses the evaluation of its expression(s). When it forms a list, it includes its contents literally.

Let's look again at LIST, CAR, CADR, the similar CDR, and at the QUOTE function. Type the input at the command line to see how these functions work.

Manipulating Lists

```
Command: (setq test (list 1 2 3.0))     Make a list.
Lisp returns: (1 2 3.0)

Command: (car test)
Lisp returns: 1                          The first element.

Command: (cdr test)
Lisp returns: (2 3.0)                    The rest of the list. All but the first element.

Command: (cadr test)                     The second element...
Lisp returns: 2                          the CAR of the CDR.
```

```
Command: (nth 2 test)
Lisp returns: 3.0
```
The third element.

```
Command: (setq test (list r s t))
```
Evaluates R, S, and T which are all unassigned symbols (variables) with value nil.

```
Lisp returns: (nil nil nil)
```
Then it makes a list of three nils.

```
Command: (setq test (quote (r s t)))
Lisp returns: (R S T)
```
Returns the unevaluated symbols.

```
Command: (setq test '(r s t))
Lisp returns: (R S T)
```
QUOTE abbreviated.

Other List Functions

AutoLISP has other functions to manipulate lists; among them are CAAR, CADDR, CADAR, and Nth. You can use the Nth function to access any element of a list, like (nth 2 '(a b c d)) which returns c. But watch the numbering because Nth counts 0, 1, 2, 3 . . . (*not* 1, 2, 3 . . .). This is typical computer counting. Watch your 0's and 1's carefully with AutoLISP functions. All AutoLISP functions do not count the same way.

LAST, REVERSE, LENGTH, APPEND, and CONS are more list manipulation functions. LAST will give you the last element of a list. REVERSE flips the order of the list. LENGTH returns its length. APPEND takes any number of arguments, each a list, and merges them into a single list. CONS adds a new first element to a list. See INSIDE AutoLISP (New Riders Publishing) for information on using these and the other list functions.

Passing Data to AutoCAD With the COMMAND Function

AutoLISP can instruct AutoCAD to do anything that you can type at the command prompt. The key is the COMMAND function which lets you run AutoCAD commands within an AutoLISP statement. You've seen the COMMAND function in the shadow box exercise and the [RECTANG] macro.

```
(command "pline" ll lr ur ul "c")
```

The rules for using the COMMAND function are simple.

■ Put AutoCAD commands, options, and text in quotes.

■ Do not use GET input functions within a COMMAND function.

■ Do not precede your variable names with an exclamation point.

■ Use only true AutoCAD commands. You can't issue C: commands defined by AutoLISP with DEFUN.

AutoLISP takes each item of the COMMAND's argument list and sends it to AutoCAD after first evaluating arguments that contain AutoLISP variables or expressions. Variables can be used anywhere in the statement to supply AutoCAD with data. Quoted "strings" are taken as literal input by AutoCAD. Variables which are preceded by a single quotation mark (') are not evaluated, and expressions which evaluate to the symbol T or nil will cancel like a <^C>. Unquoted words are taken as AutoLISP variables. You can nest other expressions and built-in AutoLISP functions within the COMMAND function. They will be evaluated and their returned value passed to AutoCAD.

Of course, AutoCAD will reject the command input if there are errors in syntax or data type. AutoCAD doesn't care where the command data comes from, but it must be correct input for the command.

Each item of the command list must be one complete instruction to AutoCAD. You cannot enter half an AutoCAD command word, like ERA and later add the SE to get ERASE. You also must treat each instruction separately. AutoCAD treats (command "CIRCLE 5,5 0.25") as one erroneous instruction, not three instructions. Here is the correct format, with examples, for the COMMAND function.

```
COMMAND FUNCTION              EXAMPLE
(command item1 item2...)   (command "CIRCLE" "5,5" 0.25)
                           (command "CIRCLE" '(5  5) "0.25")
```

You can quote numbers like "0.25," but it is clearer to leave them in unquoted form like 0.25. Don't use unquoted leading or trailing decimal points, like .25 or 25., or you will get an invalid dotted pair error. Points can be lists like '(5 5) or strings like "5,5". Any value can be passed as a variable.

You can interrupt a command sequence. AutoCAD is independent of AutoLISP. You can let AutoCAD do half of a job then let AutoLISP intervene and finish the job or pass control back to AutoCAD. Try an example with the CIRCLE command.

Using the COMMAND Function

```
Command: (command "CIRCLE")
CIRCLE 3P/2P/TTR/<Center point>: nil
3P/2P/TTR/<Center point>: 5,5              Pick a point.
Diameter/<Radius>: (command 0.25)          Supply the radius.
Lisp returns: 0.25000000000000
```

The AutoLISP COMMAND sends the CIRCLE command to the AutoCAD command interpreter. AutoCAD issues the prompt for the command. Since the COMMAND function always returns a nil after evaluation, AutoCAD sees the nil, does not understand it, and reissues the "3P/2P/TTR/<Center point>:" prompt. Although a nil *within* the COMMAND function cancels like a <^C>, a *returned* nil is generally ignored.

You can send AutoCAD the <RETURN> and the <^C> cancel codes. When AutoLISP sees "" (null string), it sends a <RETURN>. A nil sends a <^C> (cancel). Try using a "", then try a nil.

Strings

[RECT] used a simple string prompt, like "Pick LL corner: " in a GETPOINT. In many cases, you need to manipulate and combine strings of text to form a prompt. One good example is to provide your users with default names during questions. For example, here is a [CH:LAYER] macro which permits a name other than the current layer to be entered and used as a default:

```
[CH:LAYER ]^C^C^CSELECT AU \;+
(setq ln (getstring (strcat "Enter layer name <" (getvar "clayer") ">: ")));\+
(if (= ln "") (setq ln (getvar "clayer")));+
CHPROP P ;LAYER ln LAYER \;
```

STRCAT is a function that takes any number of string arguments and combines them into a single string. In this example, it uses GETVAR to obtain the current layer and forms the prompt string "Enter layer name <0>: " to show the user the current layer name as a default. Here are several other string handling and associated functions:

STRING FUNCTIONS	EXPLANATION
ITOA	Converts Integers TO Strings.
STRCASE	Converts UPPER/lower case.
SUBSTR	Extracts portions of strings.
STRLEN	Returns the length of a string.
RTOS	Converts REALs TO STRings.
ANGTOS	Converts ANGles TO STRings.
ATOF	Converts an ASCII string representation of a real TO Floating point (a real).
ATOI	Converts an ASCII representation of an integer TO an Integer.
ASCII	Returns the ASCII value of the first character of a string.
CHR	Converts the integer value of an ASCII character to a string consisting of that character.

String Functions

Adding Logic to Your Macros

Every program has a flow, direction, or logic which it follows. You can use a branch in your macros to direct your AutoLISP program to execute in a predictable order. Conditional statements are your branching tools for controlling your AutoLISP programs. The following overview will give you an idea of the kinds of decisions you can have your programs make and react to.

Conditional Program Branching

AutoLISP has two branching functions, IF and COND. All branching conditions need a conditional test to perform a branch. These conditional test expressions usually use *logical* and *relational* operators, like the equal to =, greater than > or less than < symbol. A conditional test may use any AutoLISP expression.

Using Nil and Non-Nil in Conditional Tests

Remember, if something in AutoLISP has no value, it's nil. If it has a value, it's T (true, non-nil). AutoLISP's conditional functions work on a nil or a non-nil basis. Non-nil means that as long as there is some value, the condition *passes* the test. Since everything is either nil or T, any expression can act as a conditional test.

Logical Operators

A logical operator is a function that determines how two or more items are compared. The basis for comparison is whether something is nil or non-nil. Logical operators return either a T (non-nil) or a nil (false) condition. The basic functions for logical operations are AND, OR and NOT.

The table below gives examples for the logical operations. As you look at the table, A and B are True (non-nil) and C is nil.

LOGICAL FUNCTIONS	WILL RETURN
(and a b c)	nil
(and a b)	T
(and b (getpoint "Pick: "))	Depends on input
(or c a b)	T
(or c)	nil
(not (or a b))	nil
(not c)	T

AutoLISP Logical Functions

Both the AND and the OR functions can take any number of arguments. The AND function returns nil if any of its arguments are nil, otherwise, it returns T. The OR function returns T if any of its arguments are non-nil, otherwise it returns nil. Reading this carefully explains why, with no arguments, (and) is T, but (or) is nil!

OR stops evaluating and returns T as soon as it sees the first non-nil atom. In the same way, AND quits evaluating and returns nil as soon as it encounters a nil argument. You need to be careful when you put other functions inside AND or OR. Whether an argument is evaluated depends on the values of preceding arguments.

NOT is simple. NOT takes a single argument and returns the opposite. NOT returns T if its argument is nil, OR returns nil if its argument is non-nil.

Relational Operators

A *relational* operator is a function that evaluates the relationship between two or more items. Relational operators include: *less than*, *greater than*, *equal to*, and *not equal to*.

The basis for comparison is whether something is nil or non-nil. Relational operators return either a T if the expression is true (non-nil), or return nil if the expression is false. The greater than and less than functions take any number of arguments. The first argument is compared to each following argument. Other relationals take only two arguments. Generally, the arguments may be any data type; the arguments are compared to see if they are numerically greater than, less than, or equal to.

In the following examples, X is '(A B C), Y is 1.5 and Z also is '(A B C). AutoLISP function>= AutoLISP function.

EXAMPLE	READ AS	RETURNS
(< 2 y)	2 is less than Y -- false	nil
(> 2 y 3)	2 is greater than Y or 3 -- false	nil
(<= 1.5 y)	1.5 is less than or equal to Y	T
(>= 2 y)	2 is greater than or equal to Y	T
(= 1.5 y)	1.5 is equal to Y	T
(equal 1.5 y)	1.5 evaluates to same as Y	T
(eq z x)	Z is identical to X -- false	nil
(equal z x)	Z evaluates to same as X	T
(/= 2 y)	2 is not equal to y	T

AutoLISP Relational Functions

Except for eq, equal, = and /=, these operations may have multiple arguments, comparing the first argument to all other arguments. Use the eq function to test lists to see if they are SETQed (bound) to the same object. Eq generally is equivalent to the = and equal functions for numerical and string comparisons.

How to Use the IF Structure

The simplest and most frequently used program branch is the IF structure, sometimes called *if-then-else*. In plain English, AutoLISP thinks, "If the condition is T, then execute the first expression, else (if it is nil) execute the second expression." Look at this expression:

```
(if test "YES" "NO")
```

```
EXAMPLE                    IF TEST IS
(if test
  "YES"                    TRUE, then returns:    "YES"
  "NO"                     nil, else returns:     "NO"
)
```

IF has two possible paths in the example. Assume the variable TEST has a value. The *if* condition test is true and the *then* statement is executed, which returns the value of "YES." The *else* statement, an optional statement of the IF structure, is executed in the opposite case only when the condition is not true.

The PROGN Structure

Limiting IF statements to only a single *then* and a single *else* statement is confining. If you want to execute several statements, AutoLISP provides PROGN. PROGN groups multiple AutoLISP expressions into one expression, notifying AutoLISP to treat the next series of statements as one statement. The PROGN's structure is:

```
(progn arg1 arg2 arg3 ...)
```

The arguments can be any number of valid AutoLISP expressions. PROGN is commonly used to execute multiple arguments as the *then* or *else* of an IF function, for example:

```
(if test "YES" (progn (setvar "ORTHOMODE" 0) "NO"))
```

```
EXAMPLE                    IF TEST IS
(if test
  "YES"                    TRUE, then returns:    "YES"
  (progn                   nil, else sets ortho off and
    (setvar "ORTHOMODE" 0)
    "NO"                   returns:   "NO"
  )
)
```

PROGN always returns the last atom evaluated by the last expression within it. We often use this combined with PRINC to provide a *clean* exit from AutoLISP expressions. The PRINC function, called without arguments, returns nothing (actually an ASCII 0 null character).

Cleaning Up the [RECTANG] Macro With PROGN and PRINC

The [RECTANG] macro returned several values while calculating, and a nil at the end. We can suppress these by nesting the whole thing in a PROGN, ended by a PRINC. Try this whether you have the CA DISK or not.

A Cleaner [RECTANG] Macro

Select **[EDIT MNU]**   Edit TEST.MNU.

Add the PROGN and PRINC. Remove the backslashes after both GET functions.

```
[RECTANG ]^C^C^C(progn (setq ll (getpoint "Pick LL corner: "));+
(setq ur (getcorner ll "Pick UR corner: "));+
(setq ul (list (car ll) (cadr ur)));+
(setq lr (list (car ur) (cadr ll)));+
(command "pline" ll lr ur ul "c") (princ));
```

Save TEST.MNU and exit to AutoCAD.

Select **[Example] [RECTANG]**   And test it.
                                          All the returned values are gone.

That cleaned it up a bit, but the contents of the menu file itself, and the PLINE command dialogue still appear. These also can be suppressed, using the CMDECHO and MENUECHO system variables. MENUECHO is explained in the last chapter of this book, and CMDECHO is explained in INSIDE AutoLISP (New Riders Publishing).

The PROGN made the entire macro into a single expression, so the backslash pauses for input are no longer needed. The entire expression was read before the GET functions prompted for input.

Using IF and PROGN to Store and Recall Points

In AutoCAD's 3D world, complex objects are often composed of primitive entities that lack the ability to store key points. In particular, many desirable object snaps do not exist in complex objects. For example, 3D spheres constructed of 3D faces or 3D polylines do not store their center points. One solution is to save the center point in an AutoLISP variable. A name associated with the point variable and a simple screen macro can help control the use of each such variable.

Add the macro to store and recall points to the **PTFILTERS page of the CA-MENU.MNU file. The point filters are called by button number two on your pointing device. To avoid errors, we must initialize the string variables at the button call on the **ALT-BUT 2 page.

Storing and Recalling 3D Points

 Copy CA-MENU9.MNU to TEST.MNU and examine the macros.

 Rename TEST.MNU to MY09.MNU, copy CA-MENU.MNU to TEST.MNU, and create the macros.

Select **[EDIT MNU]**   Edit TEST.MNU.

Add the bold text to the **ALT-BUT 2 buttons menu page.

```
**ALT-BUT 2
[PTFILTER alt. def. of 2 button](if #st1 nil +
(setq #st1 "Point 1" #st2 "Point 2" #st3 "Point 3" #st4 "Point 4" +
#st5 "Point 5")) $S=PTFILTERS $B=BUTTONS
```

Add, copy and edit the bold text to the **PTFILTERS screen menu page.

```
[    @      ]@ $S= $S= $B=BUTTONS
[]
[Point 1  ](setq #pt1 +
(if (setq tpt (getpoint (strcat (progn (print #pt1) "") #st1 ": "))) +
(progn (setq #st1 (getstring T "Point name: ")) tpt) #pt1));\
[Point 2  ](setq #pt2 +
(if (setq tpt (getpoint (strcat (progn (print #pt2) "") #st2 ": "))) +
(progn (setq #st2 (getstring T "Point name: ")) tpt) #pt2));\
[Point 3  ](setq #pt3 +
(if (setq tpt (getpoint (strcat (progn (print #pt3) "") #st3 ": "))) +
(progn (setq #st3 (getstring T "Point name: ")) tpt) #pt3));\
[Point 4  ](setq #pt4 +
(if (setq tpt (getpoint (strcat (progn (print #pt4) "") #st4 ": "))) +
(progn (setq #st4 (getstring T "Point name: ")) tpt) #pt4));\
[Point 5  ](setq #pt5 +
(if (setq tpt (getpoint (strcat (progn (print #pt5) "") #st5 ": "))) +
(progn (setq #st5 (getstring T "Point name: ")) tpt) #pt5));\
[]
[   root   ]$S=SCREEN $B=BUTTONS
```

Save, exit, and return to AutoCAD. The menu should reload.

The IF expression added to the second button **ALT-BUT2 page is quite simple. The point macros will fail with a bad argument when they test their #ST strings unless the #ST variables have a string value. So #ST variables are initialized the first time that button 2 is used to call the point filters menu. This happens only once because of the IF test. *If* #ST1 is true (it already has a value), *then* the if returns nil and does nothing, *else* #ST1 is nil so the SETQ expression is evaluated, setting all the #ST variables to string values.

The [Point 1] macro allows you to store and recall a point. It acts just like a calculator's store and recall buttons. This macro can be executed at any time, even inside a command. When you execute the macro, you are prompted for a point. You can either enter a new point or hit <RETURN> to accept the current point saved. If you enter a new point by either typing or picking it, you are prompted for a point name. The point name is a string of text provide as your reminder of the point's use. This text is displayed along with the current point list each time the macro is executed. Try the simple exercise below to see how it works, then we'll examine the code.

```
Command: POLYGON          Create a five-sided polygon.
Number of sides: 5
```

Press button 2 on your pointing device twice to get the point filters menu.

```
Lisp returns: "Point 5"    As the initialization code scrolls by.
Edge/<Center of polygon>: [Point 1]    Select from screen menu.
                           LISP code scrolls by and the prompt is displayed for the point.
nil Point 1:               Pick any point.
                           LISP code scrolls by and the prompt is displayed for the point name.

Point name: CENTER OF POLYGON          Label the point.
Inscribed in circle/Circumscribed about circle (I/C): C
Radius of circle:                      Pick a point.

Command: MOVE             Select L to move the polygon.
Base point or displacement: [Point 1]    Select the macro.
                           The value (yours will differ) and prompt are displayed:

(6.5 3.25 0.0) CENTER OF POLYGON: <RETURN>          Accept the default point.
                           LISP code scrolls by and the point is entered.
Second point of displacement:          Pick any point.
```

Finding the center of a polygon can be a difficult task, but the point store/recall can save it during creation. Lets examine it:

```
[Point 1  ](setq #pt1 +
(if (setq tpt (getpoint (strcat (progn (print #pt1) "") #st1 ": "))) +
(progn (setq #st1 (getstring T "Point name: ")) tpt) #pt1));\
```

The [Point 1] macro is one big IF inside a SETQ. It's our first complex expression, so let's break it down to examine the thought process behind creating it. First, what does it do? *If* you enter a new point, *then* it saves the point, asks for a new name, and returns the point, *else* it just returns the old point.

Now, how does it do this? Ignore the STRCAT (which creates a *prompt*) for a moment, and examine the IF *test* expression.

(setq tpt (getpoint *prompt*)) — If GETPOINT receives a point, it returns the value (True). If it receives a <RETURN>, it returns nil. Thus, a true point value or a nil is assigned to TPT (our temporary point) and returned as the *test* result by SETQ.

(if *test* **(progn ...tpt) #pt1))** — If the test returned true (a new point), *then* the PROGN is evaluated to get its name and return the name value TPT, *else* the #PT1 returns the old point value. Now, look at the *then* PROGN.

(progn (setq #st1 (getstring T "Point name: ")) tpt) — The GETSTRING prompts for and returns the point name, which is set to #ST1 for use by the next execution of the macro. The PROGN is simply used to group the SETQ-GETSTRING and #TPT as a single *then* expression which returns #TPT's value. Now, look at the SETQ that encloses the entire macro.

(setq #PT1 (if ...)) — Whether the IF returns the old #PT1 or new TPT value, the point is saved as #PT1 by SETQ, which returns its value to AutoCAD as the final result of the macro. Finally, let's go back and examine the STRCAT prompt for the GETPOINT.

(strcat (progn (print #pt1) "") #st1 ": ") — The prompt must be a single string, but we want it to include the current point value as well as its #ST1 name string. STRCAT combines any number of strings, but it's very difficult to format the point value (a list data type) as a string. The PRINT function can print any data type to the screen, but it returns the same data type, which would choke STRCAT. So our trick is to put the PRINT #PT1 in a PROGN along with a "" (null string), so the PROGN returns a string value to STRCAT. STRCAT then combines "", the value of #ST1, and ": " as the prompt string.

The [Point 1] macro ends in a backslash so that if it is used in the middle of a pending menu item, it will pause correctly.

The COND Structure

COND works much like IF, except COND can evaluate any number of test conditions. Think of COND as a kind of multiple IF routine. Once COND finds the first condition that is non-nil, it processes the statement(s) associated with that condition. COND only processes the first non-nil condition.

The general format is shown below.

```
(cond
   (first test-condition  first statements ... )
   (second test-condition second statements ... )
   ... more tests and statements ...
   (T last-statements ... )
)
```

COND takes any number of lists as its arguments. Each argument must be a list containing a test followed by any number of expressions to be evaluated. COND interprets the first item of each list as that list's test condition. It evaluates all of the expressions within the first non-nil list.

Since COND looks for the first non-nil condition, you want to make sure you test the most likely conditions before you test the least likely conditions. Putting your most likely non-nil conditions first increases your program's speed. The COND function is a good way to make programs branch based on a series of conditions. You can make the last test a test that is always non-nil, like the symbol T. Its expression will be evaluated if none of the others are non-nil. This is good for error prompts.

Program Looping Structures

Like many other programming languages, AutoLISP has several methods to cause a series of program steps to loop, executing over and over again. You can use these looping structures to reduce the number of statements in the program, continue a routine until a user action terminates it, converge on a mathematical solution, or batch process a list of data. We will mention two of these tools: the REPEAT and WHILE structures.

The REPEAT Structure

AutoLISP's REPEAT is a simple looping structure. Consider using REPEAT if your macros need to repeat some task. The REPEAT function executes any number of statements a specific number of times. All of its expressions get evaluated, but they get evaluated once each loop. REPEAT returns the value of the last expression on the last loop.

Here is the general format and an example.

```
(repeat number   statements to repeat ... )
```

You can type a simple repeating statement at the AutoCAD command line.

Using a REPEAT Loop in AutoLISP

```
Command: (repeat 5 (prompt "\nDo some stuff"))
Do some stuff
Do some stuff
Do some stuff
Do some stuff
Do some stuffnil

Command:
```

The WHILE Program Structure

The function WHILE loops like REPEAT, except WHILE is open-ended, terminated by a conditional test. WHILE continues to loop through its series of statements until the condition is nil:

```
(while condition    statements to execute ... )
```

Unlike the IF function, WHILE does not have an alternate *else* set of statements to execute if the condition fails the test. However, like COND and REPEAT, WHILE lets you include an unlimited number of statements in the loop. WHILE allows an indefinite but controllable number of loops. Each loop of a WHILE function tests the condition and, if non-nil, evaluates each of the statements included within the closing parenthesis. WHILE returns the last evaluation of the last completed loop. If no loops are completed, it returns nil.

WHILE is good for validating input, looping until the input meets the test. You also can use the function for program iteration. Iteration means that a loop is continued until the results of one or more expressions, calculated within the loop, determine whether the loop is terminated. The conditional test for an iteration usually contains some variable whose value gets changed during the course of the loop. Try the following at the keyboard.

Using a WHILE Loop Function

Command: **(setq count 0)**
Lisp returns: 0

Command: **(while (< count 10) (princ count) (setq count (1+ count)))**
012345678910   WHILE function counts from 0 to 9 and displays each number.
                                AutoLISP returns the value of COUNT (10) at the end of the WHILE
                                loop.

➡ *TIP: GET functions are often put in a WHILE loop to test input; for*
example, to see if the input is a member of a list.

A Little Entity Access

Some of AutoLISP's more powerful customization features come from its
access to AutoCAD's drawing database. Let's take a quick peek at
AutoCAD's database using AutoLISP's entity access.

Every AutoCAD entity, whether a line, arc, or circle, has a name that is
recognized by AutoCAD. Since the names change every time a drawing is
entered from AutoCAD's main menu, you don't even want to try to
remember them. Instead, use AutoLISP's entity functions to ask for the
names of entities from the database. Getting entity data lets you
manipulate the data directly or use the data in your macros. Type the
following input at the command line.

Using ENTLAST and ENTGET Functions to Get Entity Data

Command: **ERASE**   Erase everything to clean up.
Command: **LAYER**   Set the layer OBJ01 current.
                                    Turn layer 0 off.
Command: **TEXT**   Enter normal left text at point 3.5,4.0:
Text: **This is text.**

Command: **(setq ent (entlast))**   Get the last entity's "name" with ENTLAST.
Lisp returns: <Entity name: 60000A14>   Yours may be different.

Command: **(setq edata (entget ent))**   Look at its data with ENTGET.
Lisp returns: ((-1 . <Entity name: 60000A14>) (0 . "TEXT") (8 . "OBJ01") (10 3.5
4.0 0.0) (40 . 0.5) (1 . "This is text.") (50 . 0.0) (41 . 1.0) (51 . 0.0) (7 .
"CPX1-5") (71 . 0) (72 . 0) (11 0.0 0.0 0.0) (210 0.0 0.0 1.0))

The entity name lets AutoLISP refer to and manipulate the entity. The
ENTGET function looks up the data associated with the name you
provide. You can even erase entities that you can't see by feeding

AutoCAD entity names. AutoCAD's standard object selection depends on visibility, but you can bypass visibility using entity names.

How Entity Data Is Stored

Entity data is returned in a list format with special groups of DXF (Drawing eXchange Format) codes that flag which type of data is contained in the sublist. Each sublist has two parts. The first part is the DXF code, and the second is the data value. The integer 0 is a code for the entity type in the example above. You can see that the type is listed as TEXT. The 8 is a code for layer, and the layer is listed as OBJ01. The 10 is the code for the start (insert) point which is 3.5 4.0. (Left, aligned, and fit text use the 10 code for their insert points and the 11 code for their alignment codes. Right, middle, and centered text use the 11 for insert points and 10 for alignment. For entities like lines, the 10 and 11 codes are the start and endpoints. The 40 code is the height, the 1 code is the text value, the 50 is the rotation, the 41 is the width factor, the 51 is the oblique angle, the 7 is the style, the 71 and 72 codes are text justification and generation flags, and the 210 is for 3D.

These codes have differing meanings with different entities. Generally, any default data is not stored or listed. The leading integers in the parentheses are used to identify the type of data so that AutoLISP can process it. You can grab and manipulate any part of any drawing entity's data. The sky's the limit. That is why AutoLISP is such a powerful tool. It gives you direct access to the AutoCAD drawing database.

Extracting Entity Data

The DXF code (always an integer) allows you to access the inner parts of an entity list by association. In effect, you say, "Give me the sublist that has a 10 DXF code." AutoLISP will look at the entity list, find the sublist that has the matching 10 code, and return that sublist. AutoLISP's ASSOC function gives you the ability to associate lists. Try extracting some data by typing the following input:

Using the ASSOC Function to Extract Entity Data

Command: **(assoc 1 edata)**   Get the text group.
Lisp returns: (1 . "This is text.")

Command: **(cdr (assoc 1 edata))**   Extract the data from the text group.
Lisp returns: "This is text."

Since the association list still contains the DXF code, you need to strip this code before passing the list to AutoCAD. The CDR (the list less the first item) function is perfect for this.

Getting Data From AutoCAD's Tables

AutoCAD keeps items like blocks, layers, styles, linetypes, UCSs, viewports, and view names in reference tables. AutoLISP's TBLSEARCH function can look through a table and return information from it.

The TBLSEARCH function needs two pieces of information: the table to search and the name of the item to look for. Try two searches.

Using TBLSEARCH for a Quick Look at AutoLISP Table Access

```
Command: (tblsearch "LAYER" "OBJ01")
Lisp returns: ((0 . "LAYER")(2 . "OBJ01")(70 . 0)(62 . 3)(6 . "CONTINUOUS"))

Command: (tblsearch "STYLE" "CPX1-5")          Looks up style "CPX1-5."
Lisp returns: ((0 . "STYLE") (2 . "CPX1-5") (70 . 0) (40 . 0.5) (41 . 1.0) (50 .
0.0) (71 . 0) (42 . 0.5) (3 . "ROMANC") (4 . ""))
```

➤ *NOTE: If you select a block insert, you get the information for the insert, not the entities within it. A block's entities are accessible by getting an entity name through table access and accessing it through entity access. This is explained in INSIDE AutoLISP (New Riders Publishing).*

Let's add a few useful entity and table access functions to the **EXAMPLE page of the CA-MENU menu.

AutoLISP Entity Access Macros

Select **[EDIT MNU]**   Edit TEST.MNU.

Add the following to the **EXAMPLES page of the ***SCREEN section:

```
**EXAMPLES
[Examples]
[]
[TRANVIEW]$S=TRANVIEW
[]
[ByObject]
[ SLAYER ]^C^C^C+
(setq lname (cdr (assoc 8 (entget (car (entsel))))));\LAYER S !lname ;
[ ILAYER ]^C^C^C+
```

```
(setq lname (cdr (assoc 8 (entget (car (entsel))))))));\LAYER S !lname OFF * ;;
[]
[CurLayer]
[ NAME     ](getvar "CLAYER")
[ COLOR    ](cdr (assoc 62 (tblsearch "LAYER" (getvar "CLAYER"))))
[ LTYPE    ](cdr (assoc 6 (tblsearch "LAYER" (getvar "CLAYER"))))
[]
[Entity ]
[ LNAME    ](cdr (assoc 8 (entget (car (entsel)))))
[ COLOR    ](cdr (assoc 62 (entget (car (entsel)))))
[ LTYPE    ](cdr (assoc 6 (entget (car (entsel)))))
[]
[]
```

Save, exit, and return to AutoCAD. The menu should reload.

To test it, create a variety of entities on several layers.
Select **[EXAMPLES] [CA-LAYER]**   Then try each item, selecting various entities.

Here is a brief description of these menu macros:

[SLAYER] — sets the current layer to the layer of the selected entity.

[ILAYER] — isolates the layer of the selected entity, turning all other layers off.

[NAME] — returns the current layer's name.

[COLOR] and **[LTYPE]** — returns the color and linetype of the current layer. Current layer color and linetype are available through the STATUS command, but these macros show you how you can access the same values through AutoLISP.

[Entity] [LNAME], **[COLOR]**, and **[LTYPE]** — returns the layer, color, or linetype of the entity that you select.

It's time to quit and save our menus.

Command: **QUIT**

 Delete TEST.MNU. Rename CA-MENU9.MNU to CA-MENU.MNU

 Rename TEST.MNU to CA-MENU.MNU.

Integrating the Chapter 9 Menu

You do not need to integrate the MY09 menu into the CA-MENU. If any of the rectangle macros in this chapter are useful to you, add them to your own menus. You've already saved the rest of your menu work in CA-MENU.MNU.

Here is this chapter's CA-MENU9.MNU menu.

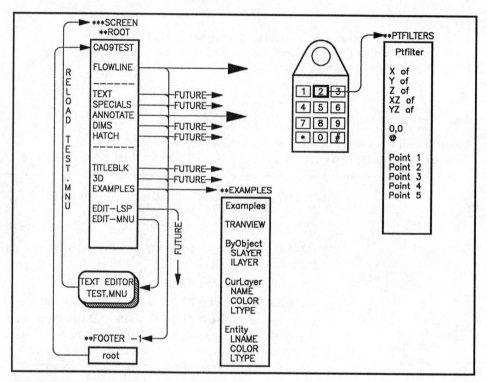

The CA-MENU9 Menu

AutoLISP Summary

Here are some summary tips and techniques for using variables and expressions to integrate AutoLISP into your menu macros.

Use AutoLISP to create intelligent macros to replace repetitive menu macros. AutoLISP variables can eliminate menu selections that depend on drawing scale. When possible, calculate values to feed to AutoCAD commands, rather than pausing for user input. Add prompts to menu macros to clarify use. Coordinate input with backslashes. When you think about improving your macros with AutoLISP, use our examples as idea lists.

This is the end of the book's basic tools section for menus and macros, and a little AutoLISP. In INSIDE AutoLISP (New Riders Publishing), we will extend this power, showing you how to add more control, how to establish automatic drawing setup in an ACAD.LSP file, how to write and save AutoLISP programs, and how to create AutoLISP C: commands that act like AutoCAD's commands. In the last two chapters of this book, let's apply what we've learned to developing custom systems for 3D drawing and dimensioning.

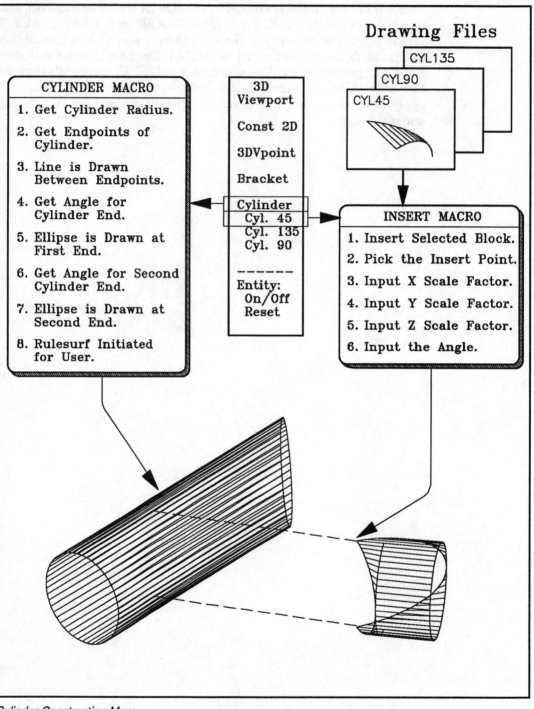

Cylinder Construction Menu

CHAPTER 10

Customizing for 3D

THE VOYAGE TO 3D SPACE

You can customize AutoCAD's 3D world to harness its powers. Developing specific routines to standardize, automate, and control features like the User Coordinate System (UCS), Viewports, entity creation, and editing will add to your 3D success.

This chapter will show you how to add and adjust settings in your prototype drawing, develop commands that revert 3D drawings to 2D views, automate changes to the UCS, and combine 3D entities to create complete 3D drawings. Finally, overall customization requires some finishing touches to complete your system. We will show you how to use system variables to control your drawing in 3D.

The Benefits of Developing 3D Tools

Even the simplest three-dimensional part can take minutes to draw. A well-constructed macro, can eliminate the time-consuming task of determining UCS planes, changing system variables, calculating entity intersections, and more.

Since most AutoCAD users traditionally need a 2D hard copy of a drawing, an effective, simple system of creating 2D views from a 3D drawing is given in this chapter. Associated views are automatically updated each time the 3D drawing is redefined.

Just a few 3D tools specific to your needs will provide a comfortable work environment for your 3D drawings.

How-To Skills Checklist

The exercises in this chapter show you how to:

❑ Add standard viewports, views, and UCS settings to your prototype drawing.

❑ Make multiple view plans from 3D drawings.

❑ Automate the 3DMESH command to create complex objects.

❑ Work with cylinders, cylinder intersections, and 3D building blocks.

❑ Control editing of 3D drawings and work around interfering objects.

Menus and Macros

MENUS

**3D is the main menu for working with the book's 3D macros and tools.

**P2-END-SAVE is a pull-down menu with standardized save and end routines.

**P1-3DVARS is a pull-down menu providing instant access to the AutoCAD system variables which control 3D mesh creation.

MACROS

[**Const 2D**] creates plan, side, and front view reference drawings for simultaneous viewing or individual plotting.

[**3DVpoint**] is a replacement macro for the VPOINT command. It uses DVIEW to provide enhanced control of eye-to-target viewing.

[**Bracket**] shows how a simple macro can create complex 3D parts. The macro controls the 3DMESH command to create any size bracket.

[**Cylinder**] is an effective tool and a demonstration of how to use UCS, point filtering, and a little AutoLISP to make cylinders. Cylinders are common to many piping, industrial, and mechanical applications. A series of 3D intersection cylinders and a method of determining intersections are also incorporated into the 3D menu.

[**Entity:**], [**On/Off**] and [**Reset**] are related macros that selectively turn entities on and off during 3D edit operations. They operate much the same way as turning layers on and off.

Creating a 3D Work Environment

It is going to take time to develop all the tools you need for 3D. However, the things you need to do will generally fall into the following categories.

■ Establish viewports for 3D.

■ Create and define common UCSs.

■ Make corresponding UCS/Views.

■ Add 3D system variables control.

■ Develop macros to edit and create 3D parts.

■ Convert 3D drawings to 2D for hard copy output.

Start by making the required adjustments to your prototype drawing.

Modifying the Prototype Drawing for 3D

Even if you have the disk, you need to make just a few adjustments to your prototype drawing to accommodate better control of 3D commands. We will create and save a viewport configuration with four viewports. Each viewport has a different view: either plan, front, side, or 3D. Add and save a view and UCS to correspond to each viewport.

Viewports for 3D Constructions

Adding 3D Viewports to the Prototype Drawing

Enter selection: **2**   Edit an EXISTING drawing named CA-PROTO.

Command: **UCSICON**	Turn on.
Command: **GRID**	Turn grid off.
Command: **UCS**	Save current UCS as PLAN.
Command: **UCS**	Rotate the X axis 90 degrees.
Command: **UCS**	Save UCS as FRONT.
Command: **UCS**	Rotate the Y axis 90 degrees.
Command: **UCS**	Save UCS as SIDE.
Command: **UCS**	Set UCS to World.

Command: **VPORTS**   Divide screen into four equal viewports.

Make lower left viewport active.

Command: **VPOINT**   Set viewpoint to 0,-1,0.
Command: **VIEW**   Save view as FRONT.

Make lower right viewport active.

Command: **VPOINT**   Set viewpoint to 1,0,0.
Command: **VIEW**   Save view as SIDE.

Make upper right viewport active.

Command: **VPOINT**   Set viewpoint to -.5,-1,.5.
Command: **VIEW**   Save view as 3DVIEW.

Make upper left viewport active.

Command: **VIEW**   Save view as PLAN.
Command: **VPORTS**   Save as 3DCONST.
Command: **VPORTS**   Make viewport into a SIngle screen.
Command: **GRID**   Turn grid on.
Command: **END**

Establishing 3D construction viewports requires a lot of setting up. By building the viewports into your prototype drawing, you avoid this process in future drawings. Although the point of origin for the various UCS settings and the saved views may not be exactly what your next drawing requires, all that you need to do is change the point of origin or view magnification and save them back to the same names.

The 3D Menu

The 3D menu is the starting place for adding custom 3D commands and macros to your system. Some selections of the menu presented here have other submenus associated with them. As the chapter progresses, so does the menu system.

If you don't have the CA DISK, you will be editing the CA-MENU.MNU. This will provide an example of developing new menu pages in the master menu. If you have the disk, all the menus and macros are in the CA-MNU10 menu file. The CA-MNU10 menu includes all the menus we have developed so far, including Chapter 10. Examine the menu as you edit, and ignore those items that haven't been covered yet.

Setting up the 3D Menu

Enter selection: **1**   Begin a NEW drawing named CA10.

 Copy CA-MNU10 to TEST.MNU and examine the remaining sequence.

 Copy CA-MENU.MNU to TEST.MNU and add the preliminary 3D menu page.

Set up the drawing with the following setup menu selections.

Select **[TEST] [11 x 17] [FULL] [INITIATE]**
Select **[EDIT-MNU]**   Edit TEST.MNU.

Add the bold text to the [3D] label on the root menu page.

```
[3D]^C^C^C(if #dwgsc nil (setq #dwgsc (getvar "DIMSCALE"))) +
LAYER N REF3D C 1;;;$S=FOOTER $S=3D
[EXAMPLES]
```

Go to the screen menu section of the menu and add the following labels above ***TABLET1.

```
**3D
[   3D    ]
[Viewport ]^C^C^CVPORTS R 3DCONST
[]
[]
[]
[]
[]
[]
[]
[]
[]
[]
[]
[]
[]
[]
[]
[]
[]
***TABLET1
```
Save, exit, and return to AutoCAD. The edited menu should reload.

Test the 3D menu and the 3D construction viewports with the simple exercise below. You will use the SOLID command to create a simple angle bracket in 3D.

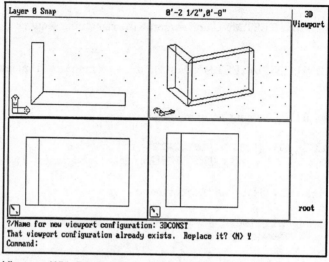

Viewport With Bracket

Testing the 3D Menu and Prototype Drawing

Select **[3D]** *then* **[Viewport]**	Screen shows four viewports.
Command: **LAYER**	Freeze layer ?????BDR to get rid of the border. Set layer OBJ01 current.
Command: **GRID**	Set grid to 1 in each viewport.
Command: **SNAP**	Set snap to 1/2 in each viewport.

Make the upper left viewport active.

Command: **FILL**	Turn fill off.
Command: **ZOOM**	Zoom center at 4,8-1/2 and 4" high.
Command: **SOLID**	
First point:	Pick absolute point 2,9-1/2.
Second point:	Pick absolute point 2-1/2,9-1/2.
Third point:	Pick absolute point 2,7.
Fourth point:	Pick absolute point 2-1/2,7-1/2.
Third point:	Pick absolute point 6,7.
Fourth point:	Pick absolute point 6,7-1/2
Third point: **<RETURN>**	
Command: **CHPROP**	Change the thickness of the solids to 2-1/2.
Command: **ZOOM**	Zoom extents and then .75X in the other three viewports.
Command: **VPORTS**	Resave viewport configuration as 3DCONST.

Your screen should show four different views of the same part.

➥ *TIP: When adding thickness to entities, it may be faster to draw the entity and then change its thickness with CHPROP.*

Creating Multiple View Drawings From 3D Objects

Although 3D construction offers a new approach to drawing and design, sooner or later you will need a 2D hard copy. Traditional 2D methods of representing parts are still required. You can create a 2D drawing from a 3D part simply by duplicating the part at the required views. The following macro helps create a plan, front, and side view drawing of any 3D part without using AutoLISP.

Creating a Macro for Multiview Drawings

Examine the macro shown below.

Add the bold text to the 3D menu page.

Select **[EDIT-MNU]**   Edit TEST.MNU.

```
[Viewport ]
[]
[Const 2D ]^C^C^CBLOCK;PLAN;\BOX;\\;UCS;O;@;INSERT;PLAN;@;;;;+
UCS;X;90;BLOCK;FRONT;@;L;;OOPS;UCS;Y;90;BLOCK;SIDE;@;L;;UCS;W;+
INSERT;*PLAN;\;;INSERT;FRONT;\;;;INSERT;SIDE;\;;;
```

Create a 2D drawing of the bracket.

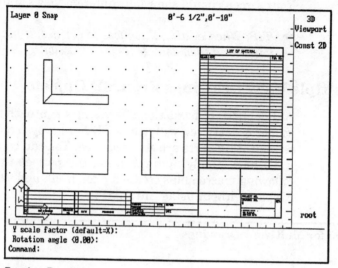

Bracket Drawing

Creating a Multiview Drawing

```
Command: LAYER          Thaw layer ?????BDR to get back the border.
Command: VPORTS         Make upper left viewport into a single screen.
Command: ZOOM           Zoom all.
```

Select **[3D]** *then* **[Const 2D]**

Supply the following input to the prompts as the commands scroll by.

```
Insertion base point: 2,7  Corner of the bracket.
First corner:              Pick first corner of window.
Other corner:              Pick second corner to enclose the two solids.
Insertion point:           Pick absolute point 2,7.
Insertion point:           Pick absolute point 2,3.
Insertion point:           Pick absolute point 8,3.
```

The macro creates three blocks of the part. The front and side blocks are nested blocks of the PLAN block. The PLAN block is inserted with an asterisk so it can be edited. Any editing would be done on the part in the plan view. After editing, you can update the front and side views by blocking the plan view of the part back to PLAN, redefining the block reference. Try a simple edit with the exercise below and then look at the drawing from a different point of view to see how it was constructed.

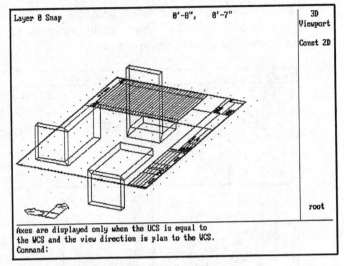

The Drawing From a Different Viewpoint

Editing the Multiview Drawing

Command: **STRETCH**	Stretch the horizontal leg in the plan view 1" to the right.
Command: **BLOCK**	Redefine the PLAN block with the same 2,7 insert point.
Command: **OOPS**	Bring the plan view back.
Command: **REGEN**	Regen updates the front and side views.
Command: **VPOINT**	Set viewpoint to -1,-.5,.5

Improve the macro by exploding the plan block after insertion, then you can DRAG to position the block. Also, you can automatically produce other views by using different menu labels to insert each view as needed. Viewing parts in 3D is critical to working effectively in 3D space.

Viewing Objects in 3D Space

With AutoCAD Release 10, a new command, DVIEW, was added. DVIEW expands your control over viewing a drawing. The old VPOINT command allows changes to the eye point location but always keeps a target point of 0,0,0. DVIEW gives control over both the eye and target point when establishing your view of the drawing. VPOINT also regenerates the view to the extents of the drawing. DVIEW displays the view based on the camera-to-target distance.

The following macro is a simple but effective replacement for the VPOINT command. The macro stores two point values and supplies them to the

DVIEW Points option. The macro requests X,Y points first, then a Z value. This lets you pick the exact point of view by specifying a target and camera position. The viewpoint is regenerated with the target in the center of the current viewport.

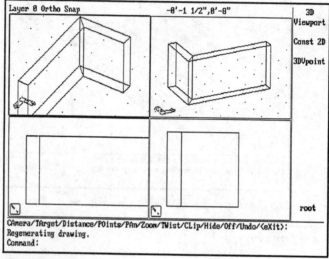

3D View of Bracket

Establishing 3D Viewpoints With DVIEW

Examine the macro shown below and test it.

Add the bold text to the 3D menu page.

Select **[EDIT-MNU]**   Edit TEST.MNU.

```
[Const 2D]
[]
[3DVpoint ]^C^C^C(setq #target (getpoint "Enter target location "));.XY;\+
(setq #camera (getpoint "Enter camera location "));.XY;\+
DVIEW;;PO !#TARGET !#CAMERA;;
[]
```

Save, exit, and return to AutoCAD. The menu should reload.

Command: **ERASE**   Erase all of the drawing except for the bracket shown in plan.
Select **[Viewport]**   To restore the 3DCONST viewport.

Make the upper left viewport active and test the improved viewpoint macro.

Select **[3D]** *then* **[3DVpoint]**   Try viewing the bracket from different angles.

As you run the macro, you'll notice that the standard AutoCAD DVIEWBLOCK (the house) is presented on the screen. This may confuse users of your custom system. You can improve this routine by defining a new DVIEWBLOCK with no entities and turning BLIPMODE off during the macro execution. You could also accept the current eye and target point values as defaults. Going a step farther, you could make block icons and temporarily insert them at the eye and target points during prompts.

Working With 3D Entities

AutoCAD really is a 2D entity system that can draw in any 3D plane. Take a good look at the AutoCAD drawing database. You will see that the only 3D entities are 3DPOLY, 3DFACE, and the obsolete 3DLINE (all lines are now 3D). A complete 3D system could have entities such as SPHERE, BOX, TRIANGLE, CONE, and so on. Using a LIST-type command and selecting *sphere* could then generate a measurement report showing volume, surface area, and center point. However, AutoCAD has chosen to depict 3D in a way that offers more flexibility for irregular shapes, and leave measurements to AutoLISP routines. So how does AutoCAD draw what appears to be 3D objects?

Almost exclusively, AutoCAD uses a mesh to represent 3D entities. Macros and AutoLISP commands calculate the points of a mesh based on the shape of the object to draw. Unlike the LINE and CIRCLE commands, AutoCAD's 3D mesh commands, REVSURF, RULESURF, EDGESURF, and TABSURF can be thought of as routines that determine mesh points based on the data you supply. However, these 3D commands always create polyline mesh entities.

3D mesh commands require control entities to establish path curves, rotation axes, and direction vectors. This chapter's 3D menu creates a unique layer for these entities called REF3D. REF3D specifies the layer for use as a 3D construction layer where linetype and line width are not important.

Let's take a look at AutoCAD's standard 3D drafting tools for 3D shapes by loading the AutoCAD standard menu and bringing up the 3D icon menu. If you wish, try some of the 3D commands on your own.

Looking at AutoCAD's 3D Commands

Command: **MENU**   Load the menu ACAD.

| *Select* [**DRAW**] | From the pull-down menus. |
| *Select* [**3D Construction...**] | At the bottom. |

The icon menu provides access to the standard menu entities and a number of special shapes like pyramid, dome, and torus. These are created by AutoLISP commands that prompt for geometric information and then generate shapes with the MESH commands.

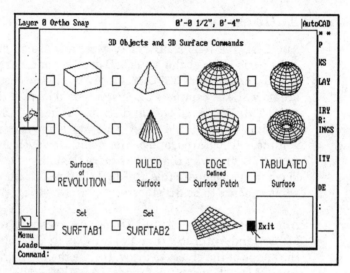

AutoCAD's 3D Icon Menu

Now it's time to create your own commands.

Direct Mesh Generation

The 3DMESH command can be used to create your own mesh routines. The difference between 3DMESH and the other mesh commands (like REVSURF) is that you have to calculate and supply the mesh points.

Calculating Mesh Points

As you'll see in the next macro, you can do alot of 3D without AutoLISP. Instead of calculating every point of a mesh, the [Bracket] macro uses a combination of AutoLISP variables, XYZ point filtering, and relative @ point references. Point filtering is used here to mix and match coordinates of the key points for input to the 3DMESH command. One type of use for this macro is to draw extruded aluminum angles. You could expand the macro to draw metal studs, channels, and runners. Let's develop the [Bracket] macro.

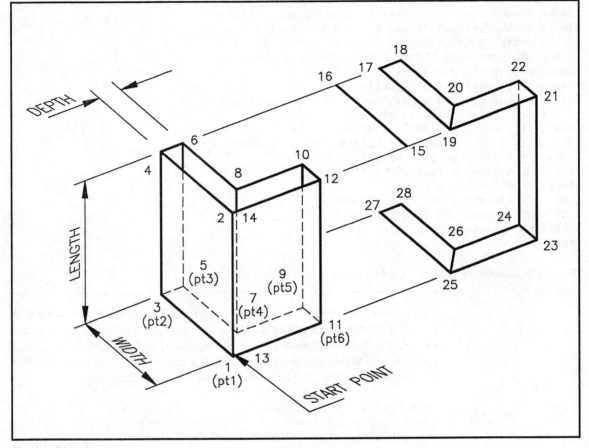

Bracket Diagram

3D Bracket Macro with 3DMESH

Command: **MENU**   Load the TEST.MNU.

  Examine the menu text shown below.

  Make the bold additions to the 3D menu page.

Select **[EDIT–MNU]**   Edit TEST.MNU.

```
[3DVpoint ]
[]
[Bracket  ]^C^C^C+
(setq length (getdist "Enter bracket length: "));\+
(setq width (getdist "Enter bracket width: "));\+
(setq depth (getdist "Enter bracket depth: "));\+
(setq pt1 (getpoint "Enter bracket start point: "));\+
(setq pt2 (polar pt1 (/ PI 2) width)) +
(setq pt3 (polar pt2 0 depth)) +
(setq pt4 (polar pt3 (* PI 1.5) (- width depth))) +
(setq pt5 (polar pt4 0 (- width depth))) +
(setq pt6 (polar pt5 (* PI 1.5) depth)) +
3DMESH 14 2 !pt1 .XY @ !length !pt2 .XY @ !length +
!pt3 .XY @ !length !pt4 .XY @ !length +
!pt5 .XY @ !length !pt6 .XY @ !length +
!pt1 .XY @ !length @ +
.XY !pt2 !length @ .XY !pt3 !length +
.XY !pt1 !length .XY !pt4 !length +
.XY !pt6 !length .XY !pt5 !length +
!pt6 !pt5 !pt1 !pt4 !pt2 !pt3
```

Save, exit, and return to AutoCAD. The menu should reload.

The macro looks complex but it is really quite simple. The first section gets the start point and the distances for the sides of the part. It stores each of the bracket dimensions in variables called LENGTH, WIDTH, and DEPTH. The starting point is stored in the variable PT1 and is located on the outside corner of the bracket (see the Bracket diagram).

```
[Bracket  ]^C^C^C+
(setq length (getdist "Enter bracket length: "));\+
(setq width (getdist "Enter bracket width: "));\+
(setq depth (getdist "Enter bracket depth: "));\+
(setq pt1 (getpoint "Enter bracket start point: "));\+
```

The center section uses the POLAR function and the PI variable to calculate the six corner points of the L-shaped base of the part. The calculated points all lie on the current UCS plane. The diagram shows each point variable name and the location on the bracket.

```
(setq pt2 (polar pt1 (/ PI 2) width)) +
(setq pt3 (polar pt2 0 depth)) +
(setq pt4 (polar pt3 (* PI 1.5) (- width depth))) +
(setq pt5 (polar pt4 0 (- width depth))) +
(setq pt6 (polar pt5 (* PI 1.5) depth)) +
```

The last step is to start the 3DMESH command with a 14 by 2 mesh size and supply the vertex points in the correct order. The order is shown on the diagram as 1, 2, 3, and so on. The macro first draws the body of the part in a clockwise direction using vertexes 1 through 14. This is done by supplying the calculated base points (PT1 thru PT6) and then using XYZ filters on the same points to get the top vertex. For example, to get the coordinate at vertex 4, the X and Y coordinates of PT3 are matched with the LENGTH variable of the bracket for the Z coordinate.

```
3DMESH 14 2 !pt1 .XY @ !length !pt2 .XY @ !length +
!pt3 .XY @ !length !pt4 .XY @ !length +
!pt5 .XY @ !length !pt6 .XY @ !length +
!pt1 .XY @ !length @ +
```

After the body is drawn, the top and bottom ends are capped. A single edge is created between locations 15 and 16 which overlays vertexes at 2 and 4. This is done to move the vertex to the end corner and maintain a single entity. The ends are capped in a continuous order (vertexes 17 thru 28), creating one overlapping face on the edge of the part.

```
.XY !pt2 !length @ .XY !pt3 !length +
.XY !pt1 !length .XY !pt4 !length +
.XY !pt6 !length .XY !pt5 !length +
!pt6 !pt5 !pt1 !pt4 !pt2 !pt3
```

Using the mesh to create this part offers a lot of advantages over other methods. You can create an infinite number of variations on the part with different dimensions, it can be edited freely, and it is still a single entity.

Test the macro with the exercise below. Redraw the same bracket you created earlier with the two solids, but this time use the [Bracket] macro.

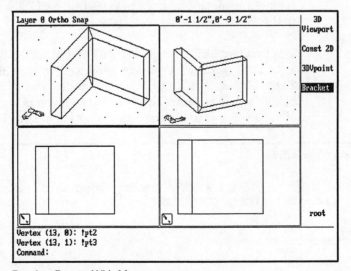

Bracket Drawn With Macro

Bracket Drawn With 3DMESH Macro

Make the upper left viewport active.

```
Command: ERASE           Erase all the entities in the drawing.

Select [3D] then [Bracket]
Enter bracket length: 2.5
Enter bracket width: 3
Enter bracket depth: .5
Enter bracket start point: 2,7

Command: QUIT            You will use a new drawing for the rest of the chapter.
```

The part is always drawn square to the current X and Y axis. You can position the part by first establishing a UCS or by adding a MOVE and ROTATE to the end of the macro.

Improvements to the macro could include the capability to input different length widths and edges for each leg. You could also draw the part at the correct angle by using the GETANGLE function and incorporating the angle in the polar calculations.

Adding 3D System Variables

Before we move on to more 3D mesh constructions, we need to add some system variables to the menu to control how the 3D mesh commands generate meshes. These system variables are most important in controlling mesh density. These system variables are accessed with a call to the POP1 device.

The first two SETVARS, SURFTAB1 and SURFTAB2, control tabulated and generated surfaces that are produced by the REVSURF, RULESURF, TABSURF, and EDGESURF commands. The SURFTYPE, SURFU, and SURFV settings control how a surface mesh is applied to the boundaries of a 3D polygon using the Smooth option of the PEDIT command.

Adding 3D System Variables

```
Enter selection: 1       Begin a NEW drawing named CA10 again.
Select [TEST] [24 x 36] [1/2"] [INITIATE]

Command: ERASE           Erase all of the border.
```

Examine the menu text shown below.

Make the bold changes to the pop1 menu.

Select [EDIT-MNU]   Edit TEST.MNU.

```
**P1-3DVARS
[3D System Vars]
[--]
[M TabSurfs - Number of tabulations/mesh density in M direction]'SETVAR SURFTAB1
[N TabSurfs - Number of tabulations/mesh density in N direction]'SETVAR SURFTAB2
[--]
[Smooth Surface Type - 5=Quadratic B-spline 6=Cubic B-spline 8=Bezier]+
'SETVAR SURFTYPE
[M Surface Density   - smooth surface density in M direction]'SETVAR SURFU
[N Surface Density   - smooth surface density in N direction]'SETVAR SURFV
[--]
[Spline Fit Polyline/Surface Fit Mesh/3DFACE Invisible Edge Control](progn +
(prompt "1=Display frame/Invisible edges 0=Don't display frame/Invisible edges");+
(princ));'SETVAR SPLFRAME
[--]
[--]
[Standard System Vars]$P1=P1-SETVARS $P1=*
```

Save, exit, and return to AutoCAD. The menu should reload.

The SPLFRAME system variable controls a number of aspects in AutoCAD. For polygon meshes, the SPLFRAME setting controls the type of curve fit algorithm applied to the polygon. AutoCAD provides quadratic and cubic B-spline surface fitting and Bezier surface fits.

➡ *NOTE: The menu selection for setting the SPLFRAME system variable includes the PRINC, PROGN, and PROMPT functions to display information on the command line. This is a good technique to use with any menu macro since the top one or two lines of the command line are not used by the command being executed. You will see this in more detail in the next chapter.*

Creating 3D Cylinders and Intersections

A cylinder is a 3D object. Using a cylinder to represent a pipe, tube, or some other cylindrical object poses no particular problem if the ends are square (cut at 90 degrees). However, many cylinders intersect other objects at different angles. Constructing intersections between cylinders and other parts requires cylinders with beveled ends. The beveled ends create an elliptical surface at the end of the cylinder.

In AutoCAD, you can produce an ellipse with the required beveled end, either by using the ELLIPSE command or by using a polyline after a PEDIT operation. Once an ellipse is generated for both ends, use the RULESURF command to create a final one-piece beveled cylinder. The ellipses define the mesh.

RULESURF, applied to any closed polyline, starts its ruling lines at the last vertex and works backwards to the first vertex. It is almost impossible to generate rulesurf meshes between two different types of entities (such as a polyline ellipse and a circle). The usual result is a twisted alignment of the rule lines, an effect desirable in some cases but not for cylinders. Even drawing a surface between two circles can result in the twisted image if the zero-degree quad points are not exactly aligned.

The easiest solution is to always use the ELLIPSE command for each end of the cylinder, since an ellipse can represent a circle as well as an ellipse. The tricky part is calculating the shape of the ellipses and aligning them to avoid *the twist*. The cylinder macro given below shows how to do this.

The following [Cylinder] macro is mostly an exercise in UCS control and point handling, with a little trigonometry to determine the elliptical shapes. The macro uses XYZ to calculate points.

A 3D Cylinder Macro

Examine the menu text shown below.

Make the bold additions to the 3D menu page.

Select **[EDIT-MNU]**   Edit TEST.MNU.

```
[Bracket  ]
[]
[Cylinder ]^C^C^C(setq clayer (getvar "CLAYER")) LAYER S REF3D;;+
UCS D TEMPUCS;UCS S TEMPUCS;+
(setq rad1 (getreal "Enter radius of cylinder: "));\+
(setq pt1 (getpoint "Pick first point: "));\+
(setq pt2 (getpoint pt1 "Pick second point: "));\+
LINE !pt1 !pt2;;UCS E L;+
(setq ang (getangle '(0 0) "Enter angle of cut: "));\+
(setq rad2 (abs (/ rad1 (sin ang))));+
(setq ang (- (/ (* ang 180) pi) 90));+
UCS Z !ang UCS Y 90 ELLIPSE C 0,0 .Y 0,0 !rad1 !rad2;+
UCS R TEMPUCS;UCS O !pt2;UCS Z !pt1 !pt2;+
```

```
(setq ang (getangle '(0 0) "Enter angle of cut: "));\+
(setq rad3 (abs (/ rad1 (sin ang)))));+
(setq ang (- (/ (* ang 180) pi) 90));+
UCS Z !ang UCS Y 90 ELLIPSE C 0,0 .Y 0,0 !rad1 !rad3 LAYER S !clayer;;+
UCS R TEMPUCS RULESURF
[]
```

Save, exit, and return to AutoCAD. The menu should reload.

The [Cylinder] macro starts off by saving the current layer and establishing the 3D reference layer. It then deletes the UCS named TEMPUCS. Since AutoCAD gives a warning message if you try to redefine an existing UCS, we automatically delete it to make sure it does not exist.

```
[Cylinder ]^C^C^C(setq clayer (getvar "CLAYER")) LAYER S
REF3D;;+
UCS D TEMPUCS;UCS S TEMPUCS;+
```

The next section gets user input. The cylinder radius and two endpoints are obtained. A line is drawn between the two points and the UCS is set to the plane of the line, using the Entity option.

```
(setq rad1 (getreal "Enter radius of cylinder: "));\+
(setq pt1 (getpoint "Pick first point: "));\+
(setq pt2 (getpoint pt1 "Pick second point: "));\+
LINE !pt1 !pt2;;UCS E L;+
```

The UCS is set to the line prior to requesting the first bevel angle so that a rubber band line can indicate the angle of the bevel cut.

```
(setq ang (getangle '(0 0) "Enter angle of cut: "));\+
```

The ellipse consists of a major and minor radius. One radius is supplied by the user. The second radius is determined by calculating the hypotenuse of the radius of the cylinder at the angle of cut.

```
(setq rad2 (abs (/ rad1 (sin ang))));+
```

The angle is converted to degrees from radians and 90 degrees is subtracted. This is so the angle can be sent to AutoCAD commands in the proper form.

```
(setq ang (- (/ (* ang 180) pi) 90));+
```

Now the tricky part. The Z axis of the UCS is rotated to the bevel angle. This places the X axis at the angle of the bevel. The Y axis is rotated 90 degrees, making it perpendicular to the plane of the construction line.

This places the UCS in a plane at the end of the line that will contain the ellipse. Once the UCS is established, the ellipse is easy to draw. Since the origin of the UCS is also the center of the ellipse, the ellipse is placed at 0,0. The RAD1 and RAD2 variables supply the radii for the ellipse.

```
UCS Z !ang UCS Y 90 ELLIPSE C 0,0 .Y 0,0 !rad1 !rad2;+
```

Next, the UCS is repositioned to the other end of the line and a new bevel angle is obtained. The process is repeated to calculate the new beveled end. The second ellipse is drawn and the saved layer is set current.

```
UCS R TEMPUCS;UCS O !pt2;UCS Z !pt1 !pt2;+
(setq ang (getangle '(0 0) "Enter angle of cut: "));\+
(setq rad3 (abs (/ rad1 (sin ang))));+
(setq ang (- (/ (* ang 180) pi) 90));+
UCS Z !ang UCS Y 90 ELLIPSE C 0,0 .Y 0,0 !rad1 !rad3 LAYER S
!clayer;;+
```

Finally, the original UCS is restored and the RULESURF command is started.

```
UCS R TEMPUCS RULESURF
```

Finish the RULESURF by picking the ellipse at each end of the line. The cylinder is complete.

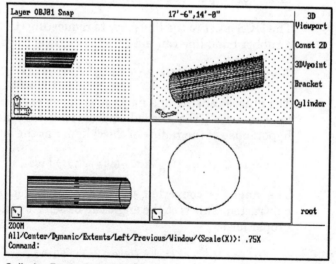

Cylinder Drawn With Macro

Drawing a Cylinder With the Macro

Select [3D] *then* [Viewport]   Screen shows four viewports.

Command: **LAYER**   Set layer OBJ01 current.
Command: **GRID**   Set grid to 12 in each viewport.
Command: **SNAP**   Set snap to 6 in each viewport.

Make the upper left viewport active.
Command: **ZOOM**   Window from 0,0 to 40',25'.

Pull down [System Vars] *select* [3D System Variables]
Select [M TabSurfs ....]   Set SURFTAB1 to 48.

Select [Cylinder]
Enter radius of cylinder: **25**
Pick first point: Pick absolute point 4',16'.
Pick second point: Pick polar point @14'-0"<0.00
Enter angle of cut: **90**
Enter angle of cut: **67.5**
Select first defining curve.   Pick one ellipse.
Select second defining curve.   Pick the other ellipse.

Command: **ZOOM**   Zoom extents then .75X in the other three viewport.

Our example prepared the cylinder for an adjoining cylinder at 45 degrees. This requires calculating the miter angle for the connecting ends.

When indicating the angle of cuts, the 0.0 base angle is along the line from the first point to the second point. To calculate the angle of bevels, you add half of the bevel angle to one cylinder end and subtract the other half from the adjoining beveled end. In the example of a 45-degree bevel, 22.5 is subtracted from 90 to get 67.5 degrees. The next segment will need 22.5 added to 90 degrees for a total of 112.5 degrees.

You could improve the macro by making it loop to draw a series of connected cylinders. It could support working with an existing ellipse or automatically draw a line from the ellipse's center to its circumference to indicate the UCS X axis at the time it was created. This would help align the UCS to the cylinder for a possible future edit. An enhanced version of the macro could be converted to AutoLISP to provide these features with better error trapping and user assistance.

Controlling Redraw During Display Changes

The Cylinder macro is unnecessarily slow due to the many redraws that occur in each viewport. We created the macro this way so you could see each operation performed. Macros that change the UCS can function faster if you eliminate the redraws. You can suppress redraws by turning the display settings off. To do this, change the following SETVAR commands.

> AXISMODE — Set to 0 (off).
>
> GRIDMODE — Set to 0 (off) in each viewport.
>
> UCSICON — Set to 0 (off) in each viewport.
>
> UCSFOLLOW — Set to 0 (off) in each viewport.

Using the SETVAR command does not erase a currently displayed grid, axis or ucsicon. It just disables updating until a redraw is performed.

➡ *NOTE: If AXIS is on, a redraw will be performed in all viewports even though the axes are not visible. If multiple viewports are set, turn the axes off with the AXISMODE system variable since AutoCAD disables the AXIS command while using VPORTS.*

Try creating a cylinder with the display settings turned off.

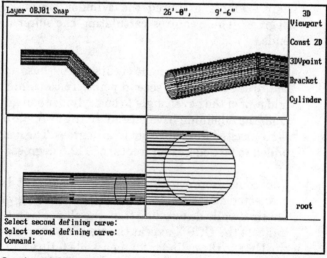

Continued Cylinder

Creating the Cylinder With Redraw Disabled

Command: **SETVAR**	Set AXISMODE to 0 (off).
Command: **SETVAR**	Set GRIDMODE to 0 (off) in each viewport.
Command: **SETVAR**	Set UCSICON to 0 (off) in each viewport.

Make sure the upper left viewport is active.

Select **[Cylinder]**	Add another cylinder.
Enter radius of cylinder: **25**	
Pick first point:	Pick absolute point 18',16'.
Pick second point:	Pick polar point @10'<315.00
Enter angle of cut: **112.5**	
Enter angle of cut: **90**	
Select first defining curve.	Pick one ellipse.
Select second defining curve.	Pick the other ellipse.

Adding Cylinder Intersection

You can use the cylinder macro to produce cylinders which can be joined end to end. Having the ability to create intersecting cylinders gives you the beginnings of a usable application menu.

The cylinder intersection parts you created in Chapter 3 and a little trigonometry are all you need to create intersecting cylinders. The first step is to add macros to the 3D menu so you can access the parts.

Automating the Cylinder Blocks

 Examine the menu text shown below, the blocks are on the disk.

Make the bold additions to the 3D menu page and make sure you create the blocks in Chapter 3.

Select **[EDIT-MNU]**	Edit TEST.MNU.

```
[Cylinder ]
[]
[ Cyl. 45 ]^C^C^CINSERT CYL45 \XYZ
[ Cyl.135 ]^C^C^CINSERT CYL135 \XYZ
[ Cyl. 90 ]^C^C^CINSERT CYL90 \XYZ
```

Save, exit, and return to AutoCAD. The menu should reload.

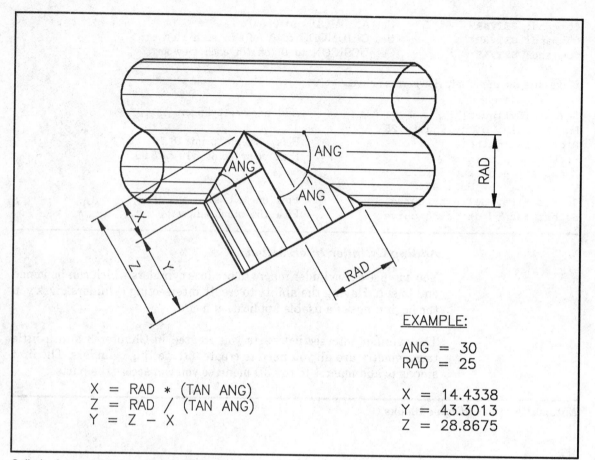

Cylinder Intersection Diagram

EXAMPLE:

ANG = 30
RAD = 25

X = RAD * (TAN ANG)
Z = RAD / (TAN ANG)
Y = Z - X

X = 14.4338
Y = 43.3013
Z = 28.8675

The process of creating what appears to be a complex intersection is really quite simple. The intersection is controlled by the insertion scale factors of the three cylinder end blocks. The process is to calculate the values required to insert the parts. After that, you insert the parts using the XYZ option of the INSERT command. Negative values are used to avoid changing the UCS in lieu of flipping the Z axis. The Cylinder Insertion diagram shows how to calculate the insert values. The following exercise steps you through the example.

Insert	X Scale	Y Scale	Z Scale	Angle
1. CYL45	25	43.3013	25	30
2. CYL45	25	43.3013	−25	30
3. CYL45	−25	14.4338	25	30
4. CYL45	−25	14.4338	−25	30
5. CYL90	−25	28.8675	25	30
6. CYL90	−25	28.8675	−25	30

Exercise Insert Values

Building an Intersecting Cylinder

Make the upper left viewport active.
Use the table above to get values for each insert shown below.

Select **[Cyl. 45]**	Pick a point in the center of the cylinder at ①.
Select **[Cyl. 45]**	Pick point ① again.
Select **[Cyl. 45]**	Pick point ① again.
Select **[Cyl. 45]**	Pick point ① again.
Select **[Cyl. 90]**	Use Osnap node and pick point ②.
Select **[Cyl. 90]**	Use Osnap node and pick point ② again.
Command: **ZOOM**	Magnify each viewport to examine the construction.

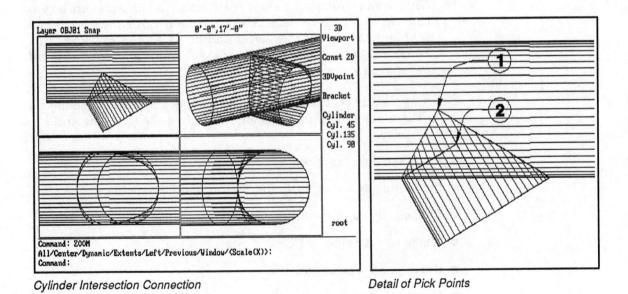

Cylinder Intersection Connection   *Detail of Pick Points*

Cylinders and Beyond

The cylinder routines presented here are limited to connecting cylinders of the same diameter with coincident center lines. By developing a few more cylinder blocks for transitional conditions like changes in diameter, and by adjusting for offsets in center lines, you could develop a system that handles virtually any condition.

The cylinder parts were created with other applications in mind.

➡ *NOTE: The cylinder block parts were created with RULESURF and produced nonparallel lines. This results in a block that gives the illusion of distortion. You could create blocks with parallel lines by using 3DMESH to select points that align on the two arcs.*

Controlling Entity Display

A three-dimensional drawing is like a paradise island. Both are great to see but once you have to work on them, life is a little less fun. The problem of obscured entities in AutoCAD increases in the 3D world because the entity you may want lies behind other entities. You have seen this even in 2D drawings when one entity is drawn over the top of another. Selecting the first entity is impossible because AutoCAD looks from last to first in the entity database during selection.

➡ *TIP: You can reverse the order of the database, making the entities you want the first entities AutoCAD sees. Simply COPY the entities you want over the tops of themselves and do an ERASE Previous. This creates new entities at the bottom of the database and deletes the old ones that were deeper in the database.*

Selecting obscured entities for entry can become a difficult and annoying task. There are several methods for eliminating the offending entities, these involve

■ Block and insert routines.

■ Controlling layers with On, Off, Freeze, and Thaw options.

■ Temporarily moving entities.

■ Changing your view or UCS.

■ Erasing and oopsing entities.

■ Deleting and restoring entities with AutoLISP.

You can automate any or all of the above suggestions. Some are more secure than others. The first five are straightforward; we will explain the last suggestion. Think of deleting and restoring entities with AutoLISP as sort of a *hide* option for entities, much like word processors can selectively hide paragraphs of text. Hiding allows you to make something invisible and restore the visibility later.

The following macros, called [Entity], [On/Off] and [Reset], turn AutoCAD entities off and on.

These macros use the ENTDEL function of AutoLISP to erase an entity from the display screen, yet keep the entity alive in the database. The AutoCAD ERASE command does the same thing, but entities cannot be selectively restored after an ERASE command. With AutoLISP, individual entities can be erased and restored any time during the *current drawing session*. Along with ENTDEL, we will introduce a few more AutoLISP functions and some tricks, such as indirect variable access in the following menus.

Entity on and off control is a temporary, limited application system for hiding entities. It consists of three macros:

[Entity:] — Allows you to select an entity and assign it to an AutoLISP variable. You can select an infinite number of entities to control.

[On/Off] — Turns all selected entities on or off depending on their current state.

[Reset] — Turns all selected entities on and removes them from the variable list, allowing you to start over again.

Add the macros to the **3D menu.

An Entity ON/OFF Macro

 Examine the menu text shown below.

 Make the bold additions to the test menu.

Select **[EDIT-MNU]**   Edit TEST.MNU.

Add the bold text to the root menu.

```
[3D          ]^C^C^C(if #entnum nil (setq #entnum 0)) +
(if #dwgsc nil (setq #dwgsc (getvar "DIMSCALE"))) +
LAYER M REF3D C 1;;;$S=FOOTER $S=3D
```

Add the bold text to the 3D menu page.

```
[ Cyl. 90 ]
[]
[-------- ]
[Entity:  ](setq #entnum (1+ #entnum)) (setq tv (strcat "M" (itoa #entnum)));+
(set (read tv) (car (entsel "Pick entity: ")));\
[  On/Off ](setq temp 0);+
(while (< temp #entnum) (setq temp (1+ temp) tv (eval (read (strcat "M";+
(itoa temp))))) (if tv (entdel tv)))
[  Reset  ]^C^C^C(setq temp 0) (command "ERASE");+
(while (< temp #entnum) (setq temp (1+ temp) tv (eval (read (strcat "M";+
(itoa temp))))) (if tv (command tv (entdel tv))));+
(command "" "OOPS") (setq #entnum 0);+
[]
```

Save, exit, and return to AutoCAD. The menu should reload.

Several important AutoLISP functions like EVAL, READ, 1+, SET, ITOA, and ENTSEL are used here for the first time. We'll describe the functions as they occur in the following explanation.

Examine the [Entity:] macro below. The first expression uses the 1+ function to increment the entity countervariable, #ENTNUM. The second expression uses STRCAT to combine "M" with the string that the ITOA function converts from #ENTNUM and assigns to a temporary variable named TV. The third expression uses the ENTSEL function to have you select an entity. This returns a list of the entity name and the point by which it was selected. The CAR function separates the entity name from the point so it can be assigned to a variable.

SET is a variation of the SETQ function. Unlike SETQ, the SET function evaluates the first argument before assigning a value to the second argument. The READ function is required to convert the quoted string stored in the TV variable to a non-quoted symbol.

```
[Entity:  ](setq #entnum (1+ #entnum)) (setq tv (strcat "M"
(itoa #entnum)));+
(set (read tv) (car (entsel "Pick entity: ")));\
```

The following [On/Off] macro uses the WHILE function to loop through the numbers 1 to #ENTNUM and constructs a string like "M1," "M2", and so on. The string is converted to a symbol Mn which is used to determine the entity name stored with that symbol. The entity name is then stored in the TV variable. Finally, if TV has an entity name, the ENTDEL function deletes the entity from the drawing. The next section provides a more complete description.

```
[  On/Off ](setq temp 0);+
(while ( temp #entnum) (setq temp (1+ temp) tv (eval (read
(strcat "M";+
(itoa temp))))) (if tv (entdel tv)))
```

Indirect Variable Access

The key element to the routines above is the ability to have one variable point to another variable. This technique is called *indirect variable access*, made possible with the EVAL and READ functions. Entities are stored by name in variables called M1 through Mn where n is any integer. Another variable, #ENTNUM, stores the number of entities currently selected. The variable TV (temporary variable) indirectly points to the data stored in the Mn variable. Initially, TV stores a string "Mn" which is converted to a variable with the READ function in the (read tv) expression. AutoLISP sees the result as Mn.

Doing an EVAL Mn returns the data stored in that variable. Changing the temporary variable value by using STRCAT to build a variable name that can be manipulated with numbers like M1, M2,...Mn allows access to unlimited variables. The variable TEMP is a counter to control the loop and is used to increment the indirect variable Mn.

It is impossible for AutoLISP to determine if an entity is currently deleted. The [Reset] macro uses the same *while* loop structure as the [On/Off] macro uses to supply the ERASE command with the stored entities. The trick here is that (command tv (entdel tv)) supplies the entity names to the ERASE command both before and after the ENTDEL is evaluated. This insures that the entity has been selected by the ERASE command and can be restored either by OOPS or ENTDEL.

Testing the Entity ON/OFF Macros

Select **[Entity:]**
Pick entity: Pick the main cylinder.

Select **[Entity:]**
Pick entity: Pick any cylinder part.

Select **[On/Off]**   The two entities are deleted.

Select **[Entity:]**
Pick entity: Pick another cylinder part.

Select **[On/Off]**   The first two entities are restored and the last one is deleted.

Select **[Reset]**   All the entities are restored.

You could make some additional improvements to the macros by putting the entity selection in a *while* loop for more than one selection at a time. You could add a new macro to remove an entity from the variable list. You could also disallow selecting the same entity twice.

➡ *WARNING: Do not end the drawing while entities are turned off.*

Entities removed with ENTDEL are erased. ENTDEL can also unerase them, but if you end your drawing without restoring the entities, they are permanently gone. This is probably not what you would want. Next we will show you how to reduce the risk of this event.

Final System Controls

You have seen how you can control many aspects of the 3D drawing process from initial creation to simple control over what layer gets used when.

Controlling the Ending of a Drawing.

Ending a drawing can be just as important as its beginning. Ending should leave the drawing ready to plot unless you intend to make further edits. You need to turn reference layers off, restore any entities hidden by ENTDEL, and set layer 0 as current. You can customize your ending by adding a pull-down menu to automate the final steps in preparing to end the drawing. Add the following page to your menu system under the POP2 device.

Creating a Custom End Menu

 Examine the POP2 menu text.

 Go to the bottom of the POP1 menu and add the following macros shown in bold.

Select **[EDIT-MNU]**   Edit TEST.MNU.

```
[--]
[Standard System Vars]$P1=P1-SETVARS $P1=*
***POP2
**P2-END-SAVE
[End / Save]
[SAVE Default]^C^C^CSAVE;;
[SAVE New File]^C^C^CSAVE
[--]
[QUIT Verify]^C^C^CQUIT
[--]
[END For Plot]^C^C^C(setq temp 0) (command "ERASE");+
(while (< temp #entnum) (setq temp (1+ temp) tv (eval (read (strcat "M";+
(itoa temp))))) (if tv (command tv (entdel tv))));+
(command "" "OOPS");+
LAYER S 0 F REF*;;FILL ON
[END For Edit]^C^C^CEND
```

Save, exit, and return to AutoCAD. The menu should reload.

The [End for Plot] selection insures the drawing is ready for plotting at a later time. The [End for Edit] leaves the drawing at its current settings so you can return to the drawing at the point you left off. If you plot from the editor, develop macros in your system to consider the same possibilities as the end macros.

➤ *TIP: Editing an existing drawing always starts with the root page of the menu. It is good practice to develop end sequences to establish the environment required for the root page so the drawing is set up correctly when you return to it.*

That completes the menu editing for this chapter. Use the new end macro to complete the last exercise.

A Controlled Ending

   Delete TEST.MNU

Copy TEST.MNU to MY10.MNU and CA-MENU.MNU

Turn some entities off with the Entity ON/OFF macro to test the ending sequence.

Pull down **[End / Save]**
Select **[END For Plot]**   The entities should be restored before ending.

Exit AutoCAD.

You can make a more controlled ending by using AutoCAD's DEFINE and UNDEFINE commands. This lets you create new commands in AutoLISP that replace AutoCAD's standard commands. Creating a new END command would insure a correct end to a drawing even if END is typed from the keyboard.

You can even initialize the creating or editing of a drawing using the ACAD.LSP file and S::STARTUP functions of AutoLISP. These features can automatically perform AutoLISP functions and AutoCAD commands each time a drawing is brought into the editor. However, all of this requires a little more knowledge of AutoLISP and is, unfortunately, beyond the scope of the first level of customization in CUSTOMIZING AutoCAD. The book, INSIDE AutoLISP, covers this and the full AutoLISP language.

Here is the chapter's menu.

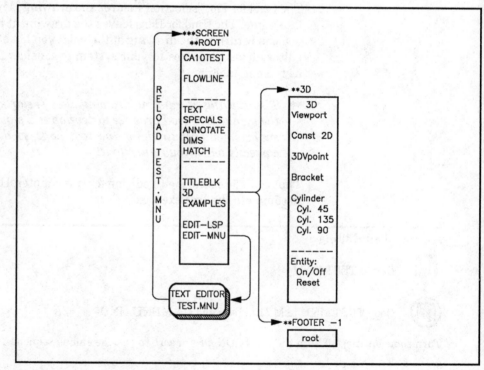

Chapter 10 Menu

Summary

Here are a few last ideas for customizing 3D.

Use a viewport to show a perspective view. You can't draw or edit in that viewport, but any editing you do in the other viewports will also appear in perspective.

Create and store a number of 3D views in perspective or parallel view. Make a macro that calls a script to display each stored view for a fixed number of seconds. As you edit the drawing, you can see your changes by replaying the script.

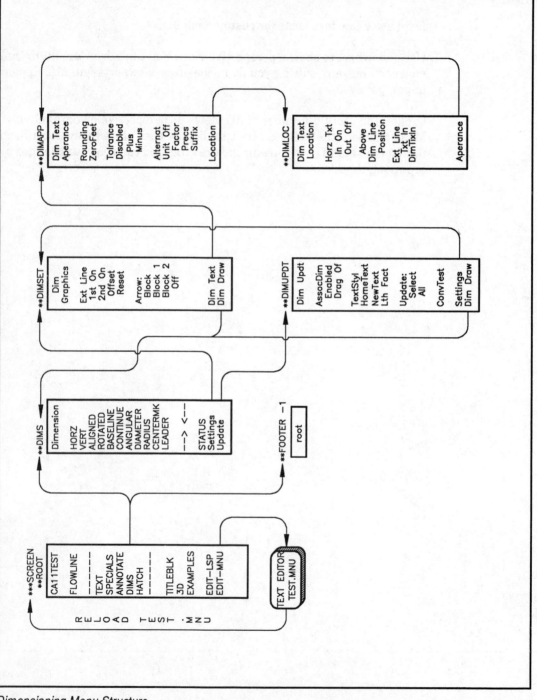

Dimensioning Menu Structure

CHAPTER 11

Efficient Dimensioning With AutoCAD

Taming Dimensioning

You can customize dimensioning to provide a faster, more tailored system of dimensioning with AutoCAD. This chapter shows you how and introduces a complete set of enhanced dimensioning features. This chapter shows you how to customize AutoLISP macros to simplify the use of dimension commands. In addition to giving you a dimensioning menu, this chapter will help you gain the knowledge you need to create efficient, informative, and maintainable menu structures.

Dimensioning Tools

AutoCAD's dimensioning tools and commands enable you to create a wide variety of dimension formats. Each command relies on a group of system settings to control text position, extension line placement, arrow/tick mark sizes and other features. AutoCAD is capable of generating associative dimensions — special entities that are automatically updated as drawing conditions vary.

This chapter assumes that you have a basic knowledge of AutoCAD's dimensioning commands. Many of the macros developed here use these dimensioning system variables. You will find the variables listed in the AutoCAD System Variables Table in Appendix C.

The Benefits of Customized Dimensions

Taking control of AutoCAD's dimensioning ties your system together and provides flexibility for a wide variety of applications. Custom dimensioning systems eliminate the trial and error approach to dimension variable setup. You can develop predefined setups that determine the appearance, style, and location of each dimension. A little dimensioning organization can make your system respond to the challenges of different conditions present in each drawing. Your overall benefit is greater control, fewer frustrations, and faster drawing production time.

How-To Skills Checklist

The exercises on dimensioning show you how to:

❏ Plan a menu system, organize the contents of a menu, and develop it.

❏ Overlay pages of menus on the same screen to dynamically update menu options.

❏ Read and understand how AutoLISP processes a LISP expression.

❏ Use AutoLISP to create intelligent macros which are sensitive to user settings in the current drawing.

❏ Build informative prompts that give defaults and show current values.

Macros and Menus

In this chapter, we formally introduce you to menu toggles. Mini-pages of macros are used to build complete screen menus. The complete menus are:

MENUS

DIMS contains the AutoCAD dimension draw commands and custom macros we develop in this chapter.

DIMSETT presents system variables that adjust the graphic look of dimensions.

DIMLOC accesses the system settings used to alter the location of dimension text.

DIMAPP is a menu for dimension text appearances. It works with AutoCAD's dimension system settings to shape your dimension text with rounding values, alternate dimension types, and tolerances.

DIMUPDT is composed of macros that update associative dimensions quickly. It has routines to manage separate dimension line and text layers.

DIM????-ON and **DIM????-OFF** are groups of mini-pages that serve as the mechanism for toggling menu options. There are over ten toggling groups in this chapter's menu.

Simple Dimension Subcommands

When you ask AutoCAD to dimension, it enters a dimensioning mode. The normal "Command:" prompt is changed to a "Dim:" prompt to reflect this new mode. The AutoCAD DIM or DIM1 command activates the dimension mode. All dimensioning commands are then *subcommands* of the dimension mode. They work within the dimension mode, but not outside of it at the "Command:" prompt. The dimension mode is deactivated with the EXIT command, or in the case of the DIM1 command, is automatically deactivated. Dimensions come down to four basic measurements: linear distance, angular rotation, circle diameters, and curve radii. AutoCAD uses the measurements to create several type of dimensions: **Linear** (includes HORizontal, VERtical, ALIgned, ROTated, BASeline and CONtinue), **ANGular, CENter, DIAmeter,** and **RADius.**

Dimensions are made up of several components, most of which are configured by the dimensioning system variables (DIMVARS). Let's review the parts of a dimension: dimension lines, Extension lines, Dimension text, Arrows/ticks and blocks, Center marks, Leaders and text, Dimension tolerances, Dimension limits, and Alternate unit dimension values.

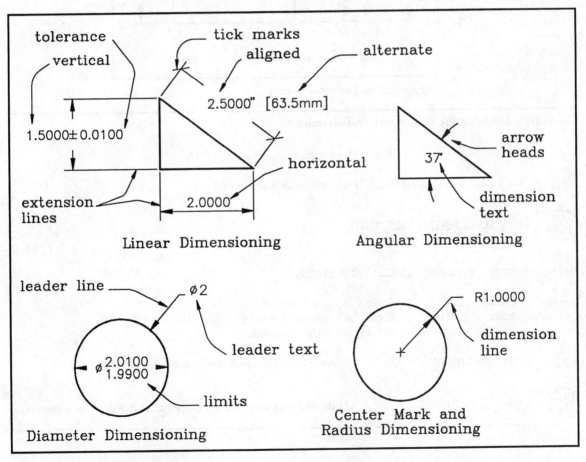

Dimension Types and Components

Setting Up for Dimension Customization

Let's draw a simple part to dimension, then examine the dimensioning setup in our CA-PROTO prototype drawing.

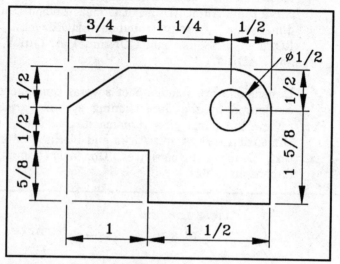

Simple Part for Dimension Testing

Creating a Drawing for Dimension Development

Enter selection: **1**   Begin a new drawing named CA11.

COPY CA11.MNU to TEST.MNU and examine it as we edit.

COPY MAIN.MNU to TEST.MNU.

Select **[TEST]** **[24 x 36]** **[FULL]** **[INITIATE]**

Command: **LAYER**   Freeze layer ?????BDR.
Command: **ZOOM**   Zoom Left, corner 0,0 and height 4.
Command: **LAYER**   Set layer OBJ02 current.

Command: **INSERT**   Insert *CA11DIM at 0,0 with scale 1 and rotation 0.

Command: **PLINE**   Draw the part and add the circle (don't draw the dimensions).

A Simple DIM Menu

The basic part of any custom dimensioning menu is AutoCAD's dimension draw commands. Since you use these commands more frequently than the dimension settings, you will want to place them on a single, easily accessible page. Create a screen menu with the dimension commands. Use the * repeating macro facility of AutoCAD's menu interpreter to make continuous looping macros.

The CA11.MNU included on the CA DISK is the complete menu system which we will develop in this chapter. You will notice more labels and macros than seen in the first exercises. Ignore these until labels and macros are introduced later in the chapter.

The Dimension Draw Menu

Examine the macros below and then test the menu.

Add the new macros to the menu and test it.

Select [EDIT-MNU]   Edit TEST.MNU.

Add the bold text to the [DIMS] label on the root menu page.

```
[ANNOTATE]
[DIMS     ]^C^C^CLAYER M DIM01 C CYAN;;;+
(if #dwgsc nil (setq #dwgsc (getvar "DIMSCALE"))) $S=FOOTER $S=DIMS
[HATCH   ]
```

Change **EXAMPLES to **DIMS and add these labels and macros:

```
**DIMS
[Dimension ]
[]
[HORZ     ]*^C^C^CDIM1 HORIZONTAL
[VERT     ]*^C^C^CDIM1 VERTICAL
[ALIGNED  ]*^C^C^CDIM1 ALIGNED
[ROTATED  ]*^C^C^CDIM1 ROTATED
[BASELINE ]*^C^C^CDIM1 BASELINE
[CONTINUE ]*^C^C^CDIM1 CONTINUE
[ANGULAR  ]*^C^C^CDIM1 ANGULAR
[DIAMETER ]*^C^C^CDIM1 DIAMETER
[RADIUS   ]*^C^C^CDIM1 RADIUS
[CENTERMK ]*^C^C^CDIM1 CENTER
[LEADER   ]*^C^C^CDIM1 LEADER
[]
```

```
[ ]
[ ]
[STATUS   ]^C^C^CDIM1 STATUS
[ ]
[ ]
```

Save TEST.MNU and exit to AutoCAD. Try the menu.

Select: **[DIMS] [DIAMETER]**   Dimension the circle.

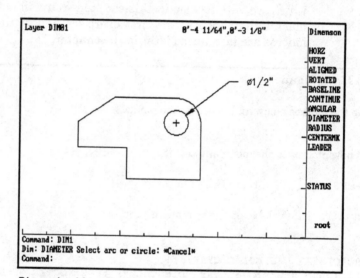

Dimension Menu Screen

Creating an Intelligent Menu

Although using the menu is better than typing commands at the keyboard, it is still primitive. There is a lot more to dimensioning than just creating simple dimension macros. But before you create a complex menu application, take the time to consider what your menu needs to provide, how you want to access it, and how it should be organized. We will use this dimensioning chapter to show the logic and thought process of designing a complete menu.

Let's begin by reviewing what is already established by the book's setup. The prototype drawing establishes architectural units as the default units and presets other dimension variables for consistency with these units. The preset system variables are:

DIMASZ — The arrow head size is set to 3/16".

DIMCEN — The center mark is set to 1/16".

DIMDLI — The dimension line increment is set to 3/8".

DIMEXE — The extension line extension is set to 3/16".

DIMEXO — The extension line offset is set to 3/32".

DIMTXT — The dimension text is set to 1/8" high.

If you want to prevent your users from changing these variables, don't include them in your menu. If you want your users to modify them, then include them, but add a reset macro. The reset macro should change these variables back to the values set in your prototype drawing.

DIMSCALE is one of the most important dimension system variables. It controls the scale of all scalar dimension variables, and is generally set to the drawing plot scale. We use it to control all scale-related aspects of the drawing. DIMSCALE is set in new drawings by the [INITIATE] macro of the CA-SETUP menu. For existing drawings, it is initialized prior to making root menu page changes that depend on its value, such as [DIMS] (see below). DIMSCALE should never be reset in a drawing once scale-dependant entities like text have been added. In that case, you may want to write a RESCALE macro to resize your text.

The Dimension Menu Structure

The first consideration in menu design is to break the dimension tasks into groups. Dimensioning breaks into three logical sections: drawing a dimension, controlling the dimension appearance, and editing or updating a dimension.

Next, consider the priorities of these groups, their functions and how to access them. Our menu design includes an approach to dimensioning that is common to most applications. The menu structure we developed is shown below.

❑ **DIMS** — To Draw Dimensions (one screen page)

Access this menu page directly from the root menu because you will use it the most often. The macros use DIM1 to automatically return to the command prompt. You normally need to use other AutoCAD commands between dimensioning sessions. You want to include special macros, such as our [--> <--] for automating special or frequently used dimension sequences. Allow transparent access to supporting dimension system variables.

❑ **DIMSETT**, **DIMLOC** and **DIMAPP** — To Control Dimension Appearance (three screen pages)

Access these menu pages from the DIMS menu page. Single macro mini-pages overlay specific items on these pages. Single label macros toggle DIMVARS and display their current settings when possible.

❏ **DIMUPDT** — To Edit and Update Dimensions (one screen page)

Access this menu page from the DIMS menu page also. It includes macros to update one or all dimensions in a drawing. Mini-page macros are used to display current settings.

AutoCAD offers a wide variety of dimensioning features. We don't include every dimension setting here but we have provided enough example material to demonstrate multi-page menu development and toggles. Actual applications rarely require every dimensioning option. Examine your needs and modify the book's menu with the features you need. Here are the five pages of our finished menu.

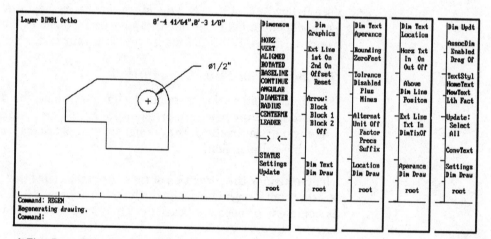

A Five-Page Dimensioning Menu

Controlling Dimension Variables

You control the look of your dimensions through AutoCAD's dimension system variables (DIMVARS).

Except for variables with string values, DIMVARS can be set by the SETVAR command or by the AutoLISP SETVAR function. However, DIMVARS are recognized during the dimension mode as subcommand names. Simply enter the DIMVAR name as a command to the "Dim:" prompt. This method allows you to change the read-only string variables.

Defaults are presented and input is filtered for proper syntax. The defaults are also formatted for the current user's units.

Transparency of the DIMVAR settings is important and gives great flexibility in altering dimensions on the fly. You don't need to cancel the current command to change settings. Keep this in mind when you design your own dimension macros.

Dimension Appearance Settings

Next, let's add a **DIMSETT screen menu page to control the graphic elements of the dimensions. These macros adjust the extension lines, dimension line offset distance, and arrow head blocks.

A Screen Menu for Dimension Graphics

 Examine the macros below and then test the menu.

 Add the new macros to the menu and test it.

Select **[EDIT-MNU]**   Edit TEST.MNU.

First add a [Settings] page call to line 18 of the **DIMS page.
Add the new **DIMSETT page following the end of the **DIMS page.

```
[LEADER    ]*^C^C^CDIM1 LEADER
[]
[]
[]
[]
[Settings]$SDIMSETT
[]
**DIMSETT
[   Dim    ]
[Graphics  ]
[]
[Ext Line  ]
[]
[]
[ Offset   ](progn (if (setq val (getdist (strcat +
"Extension line offset distance <" (rtos (getvar "DIMEXO")) ">: ") ))+
(setvar "DIMEXO" val))(princ));
[ Reset    ](setvar "DIMEXO" 3/32)
[]
[Arrow:    ]
[ Block    ](progn (setq tmp (getstring +
(strcat "Dim block name (or . for none) <" (getvar "DIMBLK") ">: ")))+
```

```
(command "dim1" "dimblk" tmp) (princ));
[ Block 1 ](progn (setq tmp (getstring +
(strcat "1st end dim block name (or . for none) <" (getvar "DIMBLK1") ">: ")))+
(command "dim1" "dimblk1" tmp) (princ));
[ Block 2 ](progn (setq tmp (getstring +
(strcat "2nd end dim block name (or . for none) <" (getvar "DIMBLK2") ">: ")))+
(command "dim1" "dimblk2" tmp) (princ));
[]
[]
[]
[]
[Dim Text]$S=DIMAPP
[Dim Draw]$S=DIMS
```

Save TEST.MNU and exit to AutoCAD.

Select **[DIMS]**	Displays the dimension draw menu.
Select **[Settings]**	To get to the dimension graphics menu.
Select **[Offset]**	Change the offset variable (DIMEXO) to 1/8".
Extension line offset distance <3/32">: **1/8**	
Select **[Reset]**	Sets DIMEXO back to 3/32" (default).

This DIMSETT menu page is not complete yet. Unless you have the CA DISK, it includes blank labels that will be filled in later with mini-page toggle macros. Let's take a few minutes to examine what we have before we move on.

[**Dim**] and [**Graphics**] are inactive labels to inform you where you are.

[**Ext Line**] is also a title, under which four extension line related items will appear. The first two are blank for now, followed by [Offset] and [Reset].

[**Offset**] allows the user to change the extension line offset distance. The [**Reset**] macro label resets the offset to the established standard default.

➡ *TIP: Indent your labels to indicate their relationship to a title. It helps the user to understand that a macro is part of a series of similar menu macros.*

Although the DIMEXO variable is preset in the prototype drawing, it is likely to change from time to time. A typical need may be to extend an extension line through the center of a circle. The [Offset] macro does this and much more.

The menu label is informative and a prompt adds more information by giving the current value as the default. Creating intelligent multi-function macros like this can keep the user from having to memorize AutoCAD's many system variable names.

Let's examine this macro in more detail.

```
[ Offset ](progn (if (setq val (getdist (strcat +
"Extension line offset distance <" (rtos (getvar "DIMEXO")) ">: ") ))+
(setvar "DIMEXO" val))(princ));
```

When you read a LISP routine, it is easiest to look at it the same way AutoLISP does. AutoLISP starts with the deepest level of parentheses and works outward from left to right. The [Offset] macro is totally enclosed in a PROGN function which contains two unique statements. The first statement sets a new DIMEXO value. The second statement is simply a PRINC function used to suppress the nil output that AutoLISP normally produces.

Examine the step-by-step breakdown of the first statement to see how it sets a new DIMEXO value. We will assume the current value is 3/32" and you want to change it to 1/8".

(getvar "DIMEXO") — This is the first function evaluated by AutoLISP because it is the innermost expression. The GETVAR returns the current value of DIMEXO which is **0.09375**. This value is then used by the RTOS function.

(rtos 0.09375) — The RTOS function is the next level out. It evaluates the substituted value returned by the GETVAR function. RTOS converts the value to a string in the user's current units, resulting in **"3/32"**. The "3/32" string value is then used by the STRCAT function in the next level.

(strcat "Extension line offset distance <" "3/32" ">: ") — The STRCAT creates a new string by combining the prompt strings with the string returned by the RTOS function. This produces a single string, **"Extension line offset distance <3/32>: "**, which creates a prompt showing the current value as the default. This prompt is used by the GETDIST function.

(getdist "Extension line offset distance <3/32>: ") — The GETDIST function uses the string to prompt you for a new offset distance. You would respond by typing 1/8, which GETDIST returns to the next level as a decimal value **0.125**. This value is passed to the SETQ function.

(setq val 0.125) — The SETQ function assigns 0.125 to the variable VAL, which is then used by the IF function.

(if val (setvar "DIMEXO" val)) — The IF function evaluates the variable VAL. If VAL has any value other than nil, the test is true and the following SETVAR function is evaluated. The SETVAR assigns the value of VAL which is 0.125, to DIMEXO.

If you had hit <RETURN> at the GETDIST prompt, SETQ would have assigned nil to the variable VAL. The IF function's test would have failed and the SETVAR function would have been skipped, leaving DIMEXO unchanged. This is how default routines work.

Creating and reading AutoLISP routines takes a little practice, but soon becomes second nature. The [Offset] macro is typical of all the dimension macros that access distance-related DIMVARS. The macro gets a distance value from the user with GETDIST. The value is stored in the variable VAL. A prompt showing the current setting of the variable in <brackets> is constructed using the STRCAT function. If the user has entered a value, the SETVAR is changed.

Since this application uses arrow heads, macros are provided to manipulate them. Tick marks are not used, so their system variables can be ignored. The arrow block macros are the same as those used in [Offset] except they use the GETSTRING function to get the block name. String type DIMVARS need additional testing. This macro will fail if the user gives a block name that is not defined. The bold text in the macro below shows how adding a little AutoLISP can be used to test the block name and verify that it exists.

```
[ Block](progn (setq tmp (getstring +
(strcat "Dim block name (or . for none) <" (getvar "DIMBLK") ">: ")))+
(if (and tmp (/= "." tmp) (tblsearch "BLOCK" tmp)) +
(command "dim1" "dimblk" tmp);+
(if (and tmp (/= "." tmp)) (prompt "Block not defined.") +
(command "dim1" "dimblk" ".")))(princ));
```

Individual DIMVAR Controls Using TOGGLES

Usually, drafters need to control one or more dimension variables repeatedly. For instance, one dimension may have the left extension line suppressed while another dimension may use a different arrow head block at each end of the dimension line.

Independent control of DIMVARS that toggle on and off can be achieved in many ways. One method might be to make a static menu with macros for all DIMVARS:

```
[DIMSE1   ]'SETVAR DIMSE1
```

This macro is very simple, but requires the user to know the DIMVAR name and how to set it on and off. A minor improvement can be achieved with two macros, one for ON and the other for OFF.

```
[EXT1  OFF]'SETVAR DIMSE1 0
[EXT1  ON ]'SETVAR DIMSE1 1
```

This method is more informative, but requires two lines and still does not tell the user the variables' current settings. It leaves the user guessing.

The best method, a surprisingly simple one, is to create a dynamically constructed screen menu composed of single line entries for each DIMVAR. We call them *mini-pages*. Essentially, each DIMVAR has two screen pages, one for OFF, the other for ON. Depending on the current setting of a DIMVAR, either the ON or the OFF page is overlaid on the screen menu. Let's create a series of ON/OFF mini-pages for some DIMVAR settings.

Creating Menu Toggles

 Examine the macros below.

Add the new macros to the menu.

Select **[EDIT-MNU]**   Edit TEST.MNU.

Add the following text to the menu page call on the dim draw menu.

```
[Settings]$S=DIMSETT (progn +
(menucmd (strcat "S=DIMSE1-" (if (zerop (getvar "DIMSE1")) "ON" "OFF"))) +
(menucmd (strcat "S=DIMSE2-" (if (zerop (getvar "DIMSE2")) "ON" "OFF"))) +
(menucmd (strcat "S=DIMSAH-" (if (zerop (getvar "DIMSAH")) "OFF" "ON"))) +
(princ))
```

Add the following single line menus below the graphics menu.

```
[Dim Text]$S=DIMAPP
[Dim Draw]$S=DIMS
**DIMSE1-OFF 5
[ 1st Off](progn (setvar "DIMSE1" 0) +
(prompt "First ext line is now ON.") (princ));$S=DIMSE1-ON
**DIMSE1-ON 5
[ 1st On  ](progn (setvar "DIMSE1" 1) +
(prompt "First ext line is now OFF.") (princ));$S=DIMSE1-OFF
**DIMSE2-OFF 6
[ 2nd Off ](progn (setvar "DIMSE2" 0) +
```

```
(prompt "Second ext line is now ON.") (princ));$S=DIMSE2-ON
**DIMSE2-ON 6
[ 2nd On  ](progn (setvar "DIMSE2" 1) +
(prompt "Second ext line is now OFF.") (princ));$S=DIMSE2-OFF
**DIMSAH-OFF 14
[  Off   ](progn (setvar "DIMSAH" 1) +
(prompt "Dims may be generated with DIFFERENT end blocks.") (princ));$S=DIMSAH-ON
**DIMSAH-ON 14
[  On    ](progn (setvar "DIMSAH" 0) +
(prompt "Dims may be generated with the SAME end blocks.") (princ));$S=DIMSAH-OFF
```

Save and return to AutoCAD.

These basic toggling menus use AutoLISP to change a variable setting and prompt the user. The prompt reflects the purpose of the DIMVAR setting and its current state. Each ON/OFF macro pair is assigned to the same line of a screen menu by placing a line number after the page name. Line 5 controls the drawing of the first extension line. Line 14 shows if different dimension blocks are on or off. Try the dimension menu.

Dimension the horizontal base of the part with the exercise below.

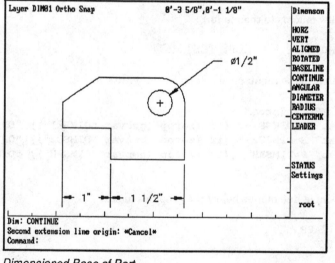

Dimensioned Base of Part

Toggling Extension Lines

Select **[DIMS]**   Displays the dimension draw macros.
Select **[HORZ]**   Prompt asks for first extension line origin.
Select **[Settings]**   Displays the dimension graphics screen and reprompts

for first extension line origin.

Complete the 1" dimension.

Select **[1st On]**   The screen menu toggles to [1st Off]. The message is displayed.
First ext line is now OFF.

Select **[Dim Draw]**   Displays the dimension draw macros.
Select **[CONTINUE]**   Select continue dimension command.

Complete the 1-1/2" dimension.

The common extension line between the two dimensions is a single line. The first extension line will remain off until you change it again. Each time you call the dimension graphics menu, the toggle will display as off, reflecting the current value. Test the other toggles.

Toggle Construction

The menu page names have been carefully planned so that AutoLISP can access individual toggle pages with one simple statement. The statements basically test each DIMVAR name, determines whether its ON (= 1) or OFF (= 0), and displays the appropriate screen page. Since each page is defined at a unique line, the toggle item falls on the underlying page at the correct line. The STRCAT function is used to build the page name. The name is then passed to the MENUCMD function, which calls the page to the screen.

The [Settings] page call determines what menu to show for the DIMSE1, DIMSE2 and DIMSAH variables. Selecting the [Settings] macro first calls the graphics menu, then immediately fills in the screen showing the current state of the dimension toggle variables.

```
[Settings]$S=DIMSETT (progn +
(menucmd (strcat "S=DIMSE1-" (if (zerop (getvar "DIMSE1")) "ON" "OFF"))) +
(menucmd (strcat "S=DIMSE2-" (if (zerop (getvar "DIMSE2")) "ON" "OFF"))) +
(menucmd (strcat "S=DIMSAH-" (if (zerop (getvar "DIMSAH")) "OFF" "ON"))) +
(princ))
```

The graphics menu consists of three toggling macros. The [Settings] macro tests each DIMVAR with the ZEROP function. ZEROP returns T (true) if the DIMVAR is 0, otherwise it returns nil. The IF function tests the value returned by the ZEROP function. If the test is T, it returns the first argument string; otherwise it returns the second, in this case ON or OFF. STRCAT creates a page name by combining the SETVAR name with the

ON or OFF string. The MENUCMD function uses the name to call the mini-page.

```
**DIMSE1-OFF 5
[ 1st Off](progn (setvar "DIMSE1" 0) +
(prompt "First ext line is now ON.") (princ) (princ));$S=DIMSE1-ON
**DIMSE1-ON 5
[ 1st On  ](progn (setvar "DIMSE1" 1) +
(prompt "First ext line is now OFF.") (princ));$S=DIMSE1-OFF
```

Each mini-page menu simply sets a DIMVAR value, gives a prompt to the user, and flips the menu page to its companion mini-page. For example, the DIMSE1-OFF menu page turns the DIMVAR off and then overwrites itself on the screen with the DIMSE1-ON menu page. The illustration below shows how the menu works.

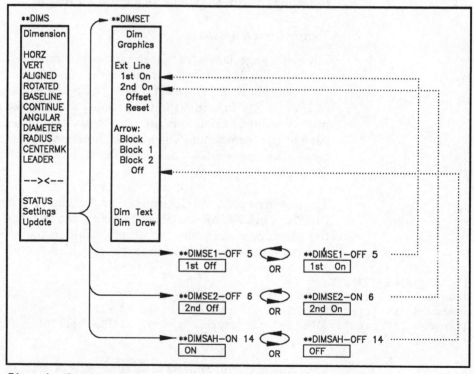

Dimension Graphics Menu

Improving Dimension Text

The next aspect of dimensioning to consider is text style, appearance, and location. One menu (given below) controls the appearance of text with rounding factors, zero-feet editing, tolerances, and alternate unit text. Another menu sets the text location, when to put the text above dimension lines, the angular orientation of text, and what to do if the text does not fit within the extension lines.

The first text adjustment is to enforce the use of the correct text style. The best way to insure this is to set the style at the root menu call.

Creating Dimension Text Menus

 Examine the macros below.

 Add the new text to the root menu page.

Select **[EDIT-MNU]**   Edit TEST.MNU.

Add the following text to the [DIMS] label on the root menu.

```
[DIMS    ]^C^C^CDIM1 STYLE STD1-8 LAYER M DIM01 C CYAN;;+
(if #dwgsc nil (setq #dwgsc (getvar "DIMSCALE"))) $S=FOOTER $S=DIMS
```

Stay in your editor.

To control text appearance, develop a screen menu and macros to set rounding factors and zero suppression. Toggles will control the use of tolerances and alternate units, and will include settings to support those features. This screen menu will be accessed from the dimension graphics menu. Let's add this menu and the related mini-page menus.

➡ *NOTE: Some menu labels have been abbreviated to display within the eight-character limit of a screen menu. You may choose to alter the dimensioning system to work as pull-down menus for longer, more informative labels. If you want to experiment, just substitute the $S= calls with $P1= calls and add a $P1=* to open the menus at the correct time. However, we don't recommend using pull-downs for menu toggles since each time a toggle is changed, the pull-down menu must be closed and then reopened.*

Continue examining or adding the following text to the [Dim Text] label on the graphics menu.

```
[Dim Text]$S=DIMAPP (progn (foreach var '("DIMTOL" "DIMALT") +
(menucmd (strcat "S=" var "-" +
(if (zerop (getvar var)) "OFF" "ON")))) (princ))
```

Add the following text to the end of the menu.

```
**DIMSAH-ON 14
[   On    ](progn (setvar "DIMSAH" 0) +
(prompt "Dims may be generated with the SAME end blocks.")(princ));$S=DIMSAH-OFF
**DIMAPP
[Dim Text ]
[Aperance ]
[]
[Rounding ](progn (if (setq val (getdist (strcat +
" ^M ^MDimension rounding value <" (rtos (getvar "DIMRND")) ">: ") ))+
(setvar "DIMRND" val))(princ));
[ZeroFeet ](progn (if (setq val (getreal (strcat +
" ^MZero-feet/inch control (0, 1, 2, 3 plus 4 or 8) ^M+
Current examples: " (rtos 0.5) "     " (rtos 6.0) "     " (rtos 12.0) "     " +
(rtos 12.06225) "^MCurrent control value <" (itoa (getvar "DIMZIN")) ">: ") ))+
(setvar "DIMZIN" val))(princ));
[]
[Tolrance]
[]
[  Plus   ](progn (if (setq val (getdist (strcat +
"Plus (upper range) tolerance <" (rtos (getvar "DIMTP")) ">: ")))+
(setvar "DIMTP" val))(princ));
[  Minus  ](progn (if (setq val (getdist (strcat +
"Minus (lower range) tolerance <" (rtos (getvar "DIMTM")) ">: ")))+
(setvar "DIMTM" val))(princ));
[]
[Alternat ]
[]
[  Factor ](progn (if (setq val (getreal (strcat +
"Alternate linear dim scale factor <" (rtos (getvar "DIMALTF") 2) ">: ") ))+
(setvar "DIMALTF" val))(princ))
[  Precs  ](progn (if (setq val (getreal (strcat +
"Alternate units decimal places <" (rtos (getvar "DIMALTD") 2) ">: ")))+
(setvar "DIMALTD" val))(princ))
[  Suffix ](progn (setq tmp (getstring (strcat +
"Alternate unit suffix string (or . for none) <" (getvar "DIMAPOST") ">: "))) +
(command "dim1" "dimapost" (if tmp tmp ".")) (princ));
[]
[Location ]$S=DIMLOC
**DIMTOL-OFF 8
[Disabled ](progn (setvar "DIMTOL" 1) +
```

```
(prompt "Dimension tolerances will be generated.")(princ));$S=DIMTOL-ON
**DIMTOL-ON 8
[Enabled  ](progn (setvar "DIMTOL" 0) +
(prompt "Dimension tolerances will NOT be generated.")(princ));$S=DIMTOL-OFF
**DIMALT-OFF 13
[Unit Off ](progn (setvar "DIMALT" 1) +
(prompt "Alternate unit dimensions will be generated.")(princ));$S=DIMALT-ON
**DIMALT-ON 13
[Unit On  ](progn (setvar "DIMALT" 0) +
(prompt "Alternate unit dimensions will NOT be generated.")(princ));+
$S=DIMALT-OFF
```

Save and return to AutoCAD.

The menu pages controlling text appearance use techniques that we have described before, but a few minor modifications have been made to improve their appearance. Before we explain the modifications, try the exercise below.

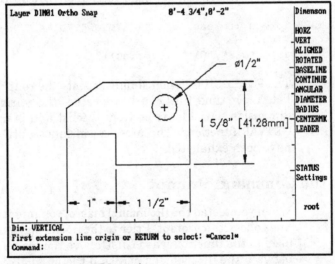

Part With Vertical Dimension

Testing the Dimension Text Macros

Select **[DIMS] [Settings]**   Get to the dimension graphics menu.

Select **[1st Off]**   Toggle first extension to [1st On].
Select **[Dim Text]**   Displays the text appearance menu.
Select **[Rounding]**   Notice the clean display at the command line and
type <RETURN> to accept the 0 default.

Select	**[ZeroFeet]**	Examine the command line display. Set value to 1.
Select	**[ZeroFeet]**	Examine the examples in the command line display to see the effect of the new setting, then set the value back to 0.
Select	**[Unit Off]**	Toggle alternate units to [Unit On].
Select	**[Suffix]**	Set suffix to mm for millimeters.
Select	**[Dim Draw]**	Display shows the dimension draw macros.
Select	**[VERT]**	Dimension the right vertical side of the part.

The initial dimension graphics menu page tested and called each toggle menu individually using the IF function. The text appearance menus are streamlined with a modification that introduces the FOREACH function. Both menus achieve the same thing. Although the FOREACH statement only calls two screen menu pages, it can call any number of menu pages with no further duplication of code. Its benefits will be more obvious in the next screen menu page when we call five screen menu pages. Shown below is the two-menu page version of FOREACH.

```
[Dim Text]$S=DIMAPP (progn (foreach var '("DIMTOL" "DIMALT") +
(menucmd (strcat "S=" var "-" +
(if (zerop (getvar var)) "OFF" "ON")))) (princ))
```

The FOREACH function simply repeats the routine for each variable in a list. Each time the loop is repeated, the variable VAR is assigned a dimension variable name from the list and is used in the STRCAT and GETVAR functions. The process continues until all elements of the list have been exhausted.

Cleaning Up the Command Prompt

When you tested the [Rounding] macro, you might have noticed two blank lines above the prompt. Prior to the [Rounding] macro, the AutoLISP code used in the function was visible above the macro prompt. The difference between the [Rounding] macro and the previous macros is the use of ^M in the prompt string. The ^M is an ASCII control character that issues a line feed to the screen. You can make AutoLISP scroll two blank lines before displaying the prompt by placing two ^Ms with a leading space in front of each prompt string. The ^M is expanded when the GET function is evaluated, causing the line feed. The AutoLISP code scrolls past the three-line command prompt area, cleaning it up.

```
[Rounding ](progn (if (setq val (getdist (strcat +
" ^M ^MDimension rounding value <" (rtos (getvar "DIMRND")) ">: ")))+
```

The DIMZIN variable has a variety of options, so it cannot be effectively implemented as a toggle. By using three prompt lines, we can present a list of valid options, an example of the current setting, and a prompt with the value of the current setting. The RTOS formats the example for each type of dimension possible.

```
[ZeroFeet ](progn (if (setq val (getreal (strcat +
" ^MZero-feet/inch control (0, 1, 2, 3 plus 4 or 8) ^M+
Current examples: " (rtos 0.5) "      " (rtos 6.0) "      " (rtos 12.0) "      " +
(rtos 12.06225) "^MCurrent control value <" (itoa (getvar "DIMZIN")) ">: ") ))+
(setvar "DIMZIN" val))(princ));
```

Change the [ZeroFeet] settings and reselect the macro to display the examples under the influence of the new setting. If the format is correct, a simple <RETURN> will keep the current settings.

Adding Intelligence to Your Toggling

The last menu provided access to certain dimension variables regardless of their current state. For example, the plus and minus tolerance selections are available even though the tolerance DIMVAR is disabled. The next menu will demonstrate how certain dimension variables can be accessed only when they have an effect in dimensioning.

We'll use the intelligent toggle technique to control the dimension text location. The DIMLOC menu is called from the text appearance menu page and allows access back and forth between them. The location menu will control whether dimension text is drawn horizontally inside or outside the extension lines and whether the text is placed within or above the dimension line. Additional controls will determine if the text is forced within the extension lines or allowed to run outside of them.

This menu will use the FOREACH function to process a list of five dimension variables.

Adding a Text Location Menu

 Examine the macros below.

 Add the new macros to the menu.

Select **[EDIT-MNU]**   Edit TEST.MNU.

Add the following text to the [Dim Text] label on the graphics menu.

```
[Location]$S=DIMLOC +
(progn (foreach var '("DIMTIH" "DIMTOH" "DIMTAD" "DIMTOFL" "DIMTIX") +
(menucmd (strcat "S=" var "-" +
(if (zerop (getvar var)) "OFF" "ON"))))(if (not (zerop (getvar "DIMTAD"))) +
(menucmd "S=DIMTVP-ON"))(princ))
```

Add the following text to the end of the menu.

```
**DIMALT-ON 13
[Unit On ](progn (setvar "DIMALT" 0) +
(prompt "Alternate unit dimensions will NOT be generated.")(princ));+
$S=DIMALT-OFF
**DIMLOC
[Dim Text ]
[Location ]
[]
[Horz Txt ]
[]
[]
[]
[Dim Line ]
[]
[]
[Ext Line ]
[]
[]
[]
[]
[]
[Aperance ]$S=DIMAPP (progn (foreach var '("DIMTOL" "DIMALT") +
(menucmd (strcat "S=" var "-" +
(if (zerop (getvar var)) "OFF" "ON"))))(princ))
**DIMTIH-OFF 5
[ In Off ](progn (setvar "DIMTIH" 1) +
(prompt "Dimension text inside extension lines will be HORIZONTAL.")(princ));+
$S=DIMTIH-ON
**DIMTIH-ON 5
[ In On ](progn (setvar "DIMTIH" 0) +
(prompt "Dimension text inside extension lines will vary.")(princ));+
$S=DIMTIH-OFF
**DIMTOH-OFF 6
[ Out Off ](progn (setvar "DIMTOH" 1) +
(prompt "Dimension text outside extension lines will be HORIZONTAL.")(princ));+
$S=DIMTOH-ON
**DIMTOH-ON 6
[ Out Off ](progn (setvar "DIMTOH" 0) +
(prompt "Dimension text outside extension lines will vary.")(princ));+
$S=DIMTOH-OFF
**DIMTAD-OFF 8
```

```
[ Within  ](progn (menucmd "S=DIMTVP-ON") (setvar "DIMTAD" 1) +
(prompt "Dimension text will be placed ABOVE dimension lines.")+
(princ));$S=DIMTAD-ON
**DIMTAD-ON 8
[ Above   ](progn (menucmd "S=DIMTVP-OFF") (setvar "DIMTAD" 0) +
(prompt "Dimension text will be placed BETWEEN dimension lines.")+
(princ));$S=DIMTAD-OFF
**DIMTVP-OFF 10
[]
**DIMTVP-ON 10
[ Positon](progn (if (setq val (getdist (strcat +
"Vertical position of text above or below dimension line <" +
(rtos (getvar "DIMTVP")) ">: "))) (setvar "DIMTVP" val))(princ));
**DIMTOFL-OFF 13
[ Txt In  ](progn (setvar "DIMTOFL" 1) +
(prompt "Dim lines will be generated for text placed outside ext lines.")+
(princ));$S=DIMTOFL-ON
**DIMTOFL-ON 13
[ Txt Out ](progn (setvar "DIMTOFL" 0) +
(prompt "Dim lines will NOT be generated for text placed outside ext lines.")+
(princ));$S=DIMTOFL-OFF
**DIMTIX-OFF 14
[DimTixOf ](progn (setvar "DIMTIX" 1) +
(prompt "Dim text will be forced between ext lines.")+
(princ));$S=DIMTIX-ON
**DIMTIX-ON 14
[DimTixOn ](progn (setvar "DIMTIX" 0) +
(prompt "Dim text will NOT be forced between ext lines.")+
(princ));$S=DIMTIX-OFF
```

Save and return to AutoCAD.

Examining the dimension text location menu reveals that the underlying page consists of nothing more than inactive labels. The actual function labels are all provided by a single screen menu. Toggles called by the FOREACH function overlay mini-page menus on the screen, filling in the appropriate items. Test the menu with the following exercise.

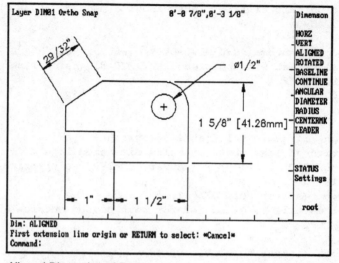

Aligned Dimension of Part

Testing the Text Location Menu

Select **[DIMS] [Settings]**   To get to the dimension graphics menu.

Select **[Dim Text]**   Go to the dimension text menu.
Select **[Unit On]**   Toggle alternate units to [Unit Off].
Select **[Location]**   Displays the dimension text location menu.

Select **[In On]**   Toggle horizontal text off within extension lines.
Select **[Within]**   Toggle text within dimension line to text above.

Select **[Dim Draw]**   Displays the dimension draw macros.
Select **[ALIGNED]**   Dimension the chamfered corner of the part.

The above exercise should have drawn the dimension text above and parallel to the dimension line. When you toggled the label [Within] to [Above], you should have noticed a [Positon] selection appear in the menu. Since position applies only to text above a dimension line, this mini-page should only be shown when text is set to *above*. This illustrates the intelligence we like to incorporate in a macro.

```
[Location]$S=DIMLOC +
(progn (foreach var '("DIMTIH" "DIMTOH" "DIMTAD" "DIMTOFL" "DIMTIX") +
(menucmd (strcat "S=" var "-" +
(if (zerop (getvar var)) "OFF" "ON")))) (if (not (zerop (getvar "DIMTAD"))) +
(menucmd "S=DIMTVP-ON")) (princ))
```

The [Location] macro completes the screen menu page by using the FOREACH function to compose the menu page calls. However, it includes a test to determine if the [Positon] macro needs to be displayed. The additional test is performed on the DIMTAD variable. DIMTAD controls whether the text is drawn within or above the dimension line. If the text is set to be drawn above the dimension line, the DIMTVP variable can specify how far above or below it should be placed. Testing DIMTAD determines what to display — a blank line or the [Positon] macro. The blank line is achieved by leaving an empty label on the DIMTVP-OFF mini-page.

```
**DIMTAD-OFF 8
[ Within  ](progn (menucmd "S=DIMTVP-ON") (setvar "DIMTAD" 1) +
(prompt "Dimension text will be placed ABOVE dimension lines.") +
(princ));$S=DIMTAD-ON
**DIMTAD-ON 8
[ Above   ](progn (menucmd "S=DIMTVP-OFF") (setvar "DIMTAD" 0) +
(prompt "Dimension text will be placed BETWEEN dimension lines.")+
(princ));$S=DIMTAD-OFF
**DIMTVP-OFF 10
[]
**DIMTVP-ON 10
[ Positon](progn (if (setq val (getdist (strcat +
"Vertical position of text above or below dimension line <" +
(rtos (getvar "DIMTVP")) ">: "))) (setvar "DIMTVP" val))(princ));
```

Dimension Update Tools

Until now, we have controlled the look and style of dimensions before they were generated. In the exercises so far, the dimensions are in a variety of styles and formats. Now we address the problem of updating dimensions after they have been placed in a drawing. The last menu page provides macros to edit or modify existing dimensions.

The DIMUPDT menu page includes two toggles that control associative dimensioning and the ability to drag during updates. The standard HOMETEXT, NEWTEXT and STYLE commands are on the menu. A modified UPDATE command has two options for changing dimensions. A user can selectively choose dimensions to update or perform a full global update. DIMLFAC is also provided to supply a dimensioning length factor. Finally, a special macro will automatically move any text placed on the dimension layer to the text layer.

The menu page will only be accessible from the DIMS menu page, but will allow access back to both the DIMS and settings menu pages.

A Screen Menu for Updating Dimensions

 Examine the macros below.

 Add the new macros to the menu.

Select **[EDIT-MNU]**   Edit TEST.MNU.

First add a screen page call after the [Settings] label of the dimension draw menu.

```
[Status   ]
[Settings]$S=DIMSETT (progn +
(menucmd (strcat "S=DIMSE1-" (if (zerop (getvar "DIMSE1")) "ON" "OFF"))) +
(menucmd (strcat "S=DIMSE2-" (if (zerop (getvar "DIMSE2")) "ON" "OFF"))) +
(menucmd (strcat "S=DIMSAH-" (if (zerop (getvar "DIMSAH")) "OFF" "ON"))) +
(princ))
[Update   ]$S=DIMUPDT (progn (foreach var '("DIMASO" "DIMSHO") +
(menucmd (strcat "S=" var "-" +
(if (zerop (getvar var)) "OFF" "ON")))) (princ))
```

Add the following screen menu pages to the bottom of the menu.

```
**DIMTIX-ON 14
[DimTixOn ](progn (setvar "DIMTIX" 0) +
(prompt "Dimension text will NOT be forced between extension lines.") +
(princ));$S=DIMTIX-OFF
**DIMUPDT
[Dim Updt ]
[]
[AssocDim ]
[]
[]
[]
[TextStyl ]^C^C^CDIM1 STYLE
[HomeText ]*^C^C^CDIM1 HOMETEXT
[NewText  ]*^C^C^CDIM1 NEWTEXT
[Lth Fact](progn (if (setq val (getreal (strcat +
"Linear dimensioning length factor <" (rtos (getvar "DIMLFAC") 2) ">: ")))+
(setvar "DIMLFAC" val)) (princ))
[]
[Update:  ]
[ Select  ]*^C^C^CDIM1 UPDATE
[ All     ]^C^C^C(if (setq ss (ssget "x" '((0 . "DIMENSION"))))+
(command "dim1" "update" ss ""))
[]
[ConvText ]^C^C^C(if (setq ss (ssget "x" (list '(0 . "TEXT") +
(cons 8 (getvar "CLAYER"))))) (command "chprop" ss "" "LA" "DIM02" "") +
(prompt "No dimension text to convert.")) (princ)
```

```
[]
[Settings]$S=DIMSETT (progn +
(menucmd (strcat "S=DIMSE1-" (if (zerop (getvar "DIMSE1")) "ON" "OFF"))) +
(menucmd (strcat "S=DIMSE2-" (if (zerop (getvar "DIMSE2")) "ON" "OFF"))) +
(menucmd (strcat "S=DIMSAH-" (if (zerop (getvar "DIMSAH")) "OFF" "ON"))) +
(princ))
[Dim Draw]$S=DIMS
**DIMASO-OFF 4
[ Disable ](progn (setvar "DIMASO" 1) +
(prompt "Generated dimensions will be associative.") (princ));$S=DIMASO-ON
**DIMASO-ON 4
[ Enabled ](progn (setvar "DIMASO" 0) +
(prompt "Generated dimensions will NOT be associative.") (princ));$S=DIMASO-OFF
**DIMSHO-OFF 5
[ Drag Of](progn (setvar "DIMSHO" 1) +
(prompt "Associative dimensions will display updated value during drags.")+
(princ));$S=DIMSHO-ON
**DIMSHO-ON 5
[ Drag On ](progn (setvar "DIMSHO" 0) +
(prompt "Associative dimensions will NOT display updated value during drags.")+
(princ));$S=DIMSHO-OFF
```

Save and return to AutoCAD.

You have used most of the routines in the above menu before. But there are a couple of routines that use somthing new. Try the following exercise, then read the explanation on the new technique.

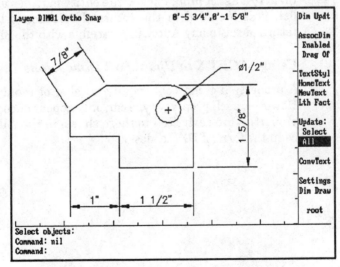

Part With Updated Dimensions

Updating the Part Dimensions

Select **[DIMS] [Settings] [Dim Text]**   Go to the text appearance menu.

Select **[Rounding]**   Set to 1/8".
Select **[Dim Draw]** then **[Update]**

Select **[Select]**   Pick the aligned dimension and return to see it updated.
Select **[All]**   To see all of the remaining dimensions updated.

The [All] selection updated all the dimensions without your selecting them. That's because we had AutoLISP select them.

Creating Selection Sets Automatically

AutoCAD edits entities by operating on a selection set. Until now, you determined the selection set by picking entities or by enclosing them in a window. AutoLISP provides the SSGET function to create selection sets of entities. SSGET uses an optional *mode* indicator to determine how a selection set is created. A *W* uses a window, *P* uses the previous set, and *L* selects the last entity. Most of the entity selection methods are available to the SSGET function. An additional mode, available only through AutoLISP, is the *X* mode.

With the X mode, SSGET searches all the drawing entities and compares them to a list of properties. If the entity matches all the properties in the list, it is included in the returned selection set. You can assign the returned set to any AutoLISP variable with the SETQ function.

Using SSGET X to Update All Dimensions

A property list can contain any number of requirements in any order. However, each property type can only appear once in each list. The entity properties are restricted to those shown in the following table and must be in the form of DXF codes.

CODE	DESCRIPTION	EXAMPLE
0	Name of the entity.	(0 . "LINE")
2	Insert block name.	(2 . "ARROW")
6	Name of linetype.	(6 . "CENTER")
7	Text style name.	(7 . "STANDARD")
8	Name of the layer.	(8 . "OBJ02")
38	Elevation.	(38 . 144.0)
39	Thickness.	(39 . 6.0)
62	Color number.	(62 . 1)
66	Attributes for block insert.	(66 . 1)
210	3D extrusion direction.	(210 1.0 0.0 -0.5)

SSGET X Property Codes

Property lists consist of one or more dotted pairs. Each pair has a DXF code preceding the data, just like an entity data list. You can create the list by placing a single quote ' in front of the list. For example:

```
(ssget "x" '((0 . "CIRCLE") (6 . "HIDDEN") (8 . "OBJ01")))
```

With this example, SSGET would create a selection set of every circle with a hidden linetype that is on layer OBJ01.

The [All] macro in the menu page simply uses SSGET X to create a selection set of all the dimensions in the drawing. SETQ assigns the selection set to the variable SS. The IF function verifies that there are dimensions in the drawing by determining if the SETQ function returned a value other than nil. If the variable contains entities, they are passed along to the UPDATE command.

```
[ All     ]^C^C^C(if (setq ss (ssget "x" '((0 . "DIMENSION"))))+
(command "dim1" "update" ss ""))
```

Creating New Dimension Features

AutoCAD's full-featured dimensioning program cannot cover every possible dimensioning need. Fortunately, creating macros with the aid of AutoLISP provides the means to create custom features.

Text on Dimension Layer Problem

Many users have complained that AutoCAD puts the dimension text on the same layer as the dimension lines. Using AutoLISP, you can create a simple solution to this problem. Assuming the dimensions are not associative (drawn with DIMASO turned off), this macro will search the drawing and change any text on the dimension layer (it must be current) to the correct text layer.

```
[ConvText]^C^C^C(if (setq ss (ssget "x" (list '(0 . "TEXT") +
(cons 8 (getvar "CLAYER"))))) (command "chprop" ss "" "LA" "TXT01" "") +
(prompt "No dimension text to convert."))(princ)
```

The macro uses SSGET X in much the same way as the [All] macro. It creates a selection set containing all the text on the current layer and then supplies the list to the CHPROP command. The macro uses LIST, CONS and GETVAR to create a filter list in the correct format. Notice the use of the single quotation mark to suppress evaluating the list.

A Custom Dimension Macro

There's an unlimited variety of dimension configurations, layouts, and requirements for users. Some are not easily addressed by AutoCAD. The following macro is an example of how to write a dimension command from scratch.

While the macro confers with AutoCAD dimensions, it does not rely on the DIM mode subcommands. It is constructed entirely of INSERT and LINE commands to form an inverted dimension. Dimension variables are accessed to draw the dimension exactly like AutoCAD's.

The macro draws the dimension lines, inserts arrow heads, allows the user to input text, and shifts it into place. It also places the text on the TXT01 layer. The macro can be improved to include extension lines, but we have kept it simple here for explanation.

Creating a Custom Dimension

 Examine the macros below and then test the menu.

 Add the new macros to the menu and test it.

Enter the following macro on the dim draw page below the [LEADER] macro.

```
[LEADER]*^C^C^CDIM1 LEADER
[]
[--> <--]*^C^C^C+
(setq ept1 (getpoint " ^MPick the left point of the dim line: "));\+
(setq ept2 (getpoint  ept1 "Pick the right point of the dim line: "));\+
(setq blsize (* (getvar "DIMSCALE") (getvar "DIMASZ")));+
(setq extlin (* (getvar "DIMSCALE") 0.375));+
(setq ang (angle ept1 ept2) dist (distance ept1 ept2));+
```

```
(command "INSERT" "DIMARROW" ept1 blsize blsize (polar ept1 (+ pi ang) 1));+
(command "LINE" ept1 (polar ept1 (+ pi ang) extlin) "");+
(command "INSERT" "DIMARROW" ept2 blsize blsize (polar ept2 ang 1));+
(command "LINE" ept2 (polar ept2 ang extlin) "");+
(setq txtstr (getstring T (strcat "Text <" (rtos dist) ">: ")));\+
(command "TEXT" "M" ept1 ept2 (if (= txtstr "") (rtos dist) txtstr));+
(command "CHPROP" "L" "" "LA" "TXT01" "");+
(setq tpt (getpoint ept1 "Text position point: "));\+
(if tpt (command "MOVE" "P" "" ept1 tpt))
```

Save and return to AutoCAD.

Create the DIMARROW block as described below.

Select **[DIMS]**	Displays the DIMS menu page.
Select **[HORZ]**	Draw any horizontal dimension on the drawing.
Command: **EXPLODE**	Explode the dimension.
Command: **ERASE**	Erase all of the dimension except for the left arrow.
Command: **SCALE**	Use the reference option to scale 3/16" to 1".
Command: **BLOCK**	Block the arrow as DIMARROW with the insertion point at the arrow point.

Before you read the explanation, try the exercise below.

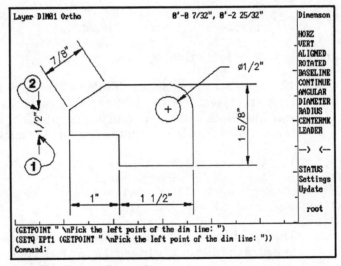

Part With Custom Dimension

Testing the Custom Dimension Macro

```
Select [DIMS]              Displays the DIMS menu page.
Select [-->  <--]          Select the custom dimension.
Pick the left point of the dim line:    Pick point ①.
Pick the right point of the dim line:   Pick point ②.
Text <1/2">: <RETURN>
Text position point:       Center the text between the arrows.
```

The custom dimension macro is the last macro in the menu system. It looks a little complex, but if you examine it in small parts, it is really pretty simple. The first two lines of the macro get two points from the user describing the left and right points of the dimension. The second line uses the first point to provide a rubber band line to assist in selecting the second point.

```
(setq ept1 (getpoint " ^MPick the left point of the dim line: "));\+
(setq ept2 (getpoint ept1 "Pick the right point of the dim line: "));\+
```

The following three lines calculate values for four variables. The variable BLSIZE stores the value of the arrow head insert scale. The length of the dimension lines is set to 3/8" for the final plot scale and is stored in EXTLIN. ANG and DIST store the angle and distance between the two pick points.

```
(setq blsize (* (getvar "DIMSCALE") (getvar "DIMASZ")));+
(setq extlin (* (getvar "DIMSCALE") 0.375));+
(setq ang (angle ept1 ept2) dist (distance ept1 ept2));+
```

The next four lines use the COMMAND function to draw the dimension lines and insert the arrow blocks. The variables are used to establish starting points, block scale, and line lengths. The POLAR function is used to determine the direction of the line and the angle of the blocks.

```
(command "INSERT" "DIMARROW" ept1 blsize blsize (polar ept1 (+ pi ang) 1));+
(command "LINE" ept1 (polar ept1 (+ pi ang) extlin) "");+
(command "INSERT" "DIMARROW" ept2 blsize blsize (polar ept2 ang 1));+
(command "LINE" ept2 (polar ept2 ang extlin) "");+
```

The final lines in the macro control the dimension text. The TXTSTR is assigned the distance between the two pick points as a default. Although not required, any text input by the user is accepted. The TEXT command is executed, placing the text in line with the arrow heads. The CHPROP command moves the text to the text layer and prompts the user to reposition the text. The last line of the macro moves the text to the selected point or leaves it unchanged if the entered text position is nil.

```
(setq txtstr (getstring T (strcat "Text <" (rtos dist) ">: ")));\+
(command "TEXT" "M" ept1 ept2 (if (= txtstr "") (rtos dist) txtstr));+
(command "CHPROP" "L" "" "LA" "TXT01" "");+
(setq tpt (getpoint ept1 "Text position point: "));\+
(if tpt (command "MOVE" "P" "" ept1 tpt))
```

Other variations of the [--> <--] macro can be created. In fact, you could ignore all of AutoCAD's dimensioning tools and develop your own system. The book, INSIDE AutoLISP (New Riders Publishing), explores this topic in detail and develops a full isometric dimensioning menu. Experiment with some variation of the custom dimension such as [-->--<--], [<--->--] or with ticks and dots [o----/--]. Most of the macro expressions will remain the same.

Testing the Dimension Menu Pages

Use the simple part drawing to test the dimension features.
Test the effect of different toggles and settings.

Delete TEST.MNU.

 Rename TEST.MNU to MY11.MNU.

Command: **QUIT**   Quit after testing the menu.

Integrating the Dimension Menu

If you don't have the CA DISK and want to add the text menu to CA-MENU:

- Insert all the dimension menus from your MY11.MNU into the ***SCREEN menu section just above ***TABLET of the CA-MENU.MNU file.

- Change the [DIMS] label on the **ROOT page of the CA-MENU to:

```
[DIMS     ]^C^C^CDIM1 STYLE STD1-8 LAYER M DIM01 C CYAN;;+
(if #dwgsc nil (setq #dwgsc (getvar "DIMSCALE")));+
$S=FOOTER $S=DIMS
```

Don't stop now. The tools developed in this chapter apply not only to dimensioning but to every feature of AutoCAD. You know all about menus, toggles, overlaying pages, and using AutoLISP in macros. Now you can apply what you've learned and expand these menus for you particular application. Let's finish up the menus.

Finalizing Your CA Menus

Your CUSTOMIZING AutoCAD menus are your starting point to time-saving application programs. Value them and develop them further. Although necessarily simple for the book, the form, style, and organization of each menu teaches the concepts you need to know about menus. We'll finish up with a few last menu controls.

Suppressing Command Line Text

You can suppress the screen *echoing* of prompts and messages by menu macros. The AutoCAD system variable MENUECHO controls the echo. It is similar to AutoLISP's CMDECHO system variable. You can set MENUECHO to 0 (normal), 1, 2, 3, 6, or 7 to control the echo. Use the CA-SETUP.MNU item [INITIATE] as your example. [INITIATE] scrolls several lines on the screen. Try cleaning it up.

Finalizing the CA-SETUP Menu

Enter selection: **1**   Begin a new drawing named INIT.

Command: **ED**   Edit your CA-SETUP.MNU file.

Add these two MENUECHO settings to the start and end of the [INITIATE] macro:

```
[INITIATE]^C^C^CSETVAR MENUECHO 3;+
CVPORTS SI GRID !#dwgsc ^GSNAP (/ #dwgsc 8) AXIS (/ #dwgsc 2);+
AXIS OFF SETVAR DIMSCALE !#dwgsc LIMITS 0,0 (list (* x #dwgsc) (* y #dwgsc));+
REGENAUTO ON ZOOM A REGENAUTO OFF VIEW S A ZOOM .75X;+
VPORTS S A ;3 V ;J ;(setq count -1  var (vports));+
(while (and var (setq alist (nth (setq count (1+ count)) var)));+
(and (equal 0.333 (caadr  alist) 0.01) (equal 0 (cadadr alist) 0.01);+
(setq var nil alist (setvar "CVPORT" (car alist))))) !alist;+
(setq count -1  var (vports));+
(while (and var (setq alist (nth (setq count (1+ count)) var)));+
(and (equal 0 (caadr  alist) 0.01) (equal 0 (cadadr alist) 0.01);+
(setq var nil alist (setvar "CVPORT" (car alist)))));+
VPORTS 3 H ;J ;(setq count -1  var (vports));+
(while (and var (setq alist (nth (setq count (1+ count)) var)));+
(and (equal 0 (caadr  alist) 0.01) (equal 0.333 (cadadr alist) 0.01);+
(setq var nil alist (setvar "CVPORT" (car alist))))) !alist VPORTS S CA Y ;R A;+
STYLE STANDARD ROMANS (* 0.125 #dwgsc) ;;;;;+
STYLE STD1-16 ROMANS (* 0.0625 #dwgsc) ;;;;;+
STYLE STD3-32 ROMANS (* 0.09375 #dwgsc) ;;;;;+
```

```
STYLE STD3-16 ROMANS (* 0.1875 #dwgsc) ;;;;;+
STYLE STD1-4 ROMANS (* 0.25 #dwgsc) ;;;;;+
STYLE STD1-8 ROMANS (* 0.125 #dwgsc) ;;;;;+
LTSCALE (* 0.375 #dwgsc) INSERT !str1 0,0 !#dwgsc ;;MENU !#menu ^GAXIS ON+
SETVAR MENUECHO 0
```

Save and exit to AutoCAD.

Command: **MENU**   Reload the CA-SETUP menu.
Select **[TEST] [24 x 36] [1/2] [INITIATE]**

Watch the initiation sequence.

[INITIATE] should run "cleaner." If you left MENUECHO on during the initiate macro, it would suppress all your application menus, including the prompts. You can toggle MENUECHO on and off for portions of a menu item. MENUECHO is usually set to a value of 1 to 3. You can override the echo setting by printing prompts to the screen. The ^P ASCII character turns the console echo on. To print items to the screen, you enclose the items in a pair of ^Ps. Once the printing is turned on with ^P, it stays on for the rest of the macro or until you turn it off with another ^P. Use this in a macro like:

```
[ ARROW ]^PINSERT^P ARROW \96.0 96.0 \
```

If MENUECHO is set to 1, only the *insert* part of the macro would be shown on the display.

```
Command: INSERT        You would still see the AutoCAD prompts,
Block name (or ?):     but the input from the macro is suppressed.
```

➡ *TIP: Print the AutoCAD command names to the screen so your users learn a little about how the macro works.*

We recommend leaving MENUECHO on and using ^P when you want to echo menu items. This produces the cleanest interface.

We hope that you will take what you have learned with this book and create your own custom system. If you wish to integrate your customized menus with the ACAD.MNU, the following section provides a minimum integration.

Integrating CA-MENU With AutoCAD's Standard Menu

Your CA-MENU is already in its final form, but you may want to integrate it with the ACAD standard menu. Although most of the

CA-MENU menu system is independent of the ACAD menu, you still need to do a few things to join them together. Here's how.

Integrating CA-MENU With the ACAD Standard Menu

Copy the original ACAD.MNU file into the \CA-ACAD directory.

Command: **ED**   Edit the copied ACAD.MNU.

Find the **S page below the ***SCREEN device name.
Add this line near the bottom of the **S page:

```
[ CA-MENU  Loads the Customizing AutoCAD menu.]MENU CA-MENU
```

Save and exit to AutoCAD.

Command: **MENU**   Load the modified ACAD.MNU.

Select **[CA-MENU]**   The CA-MENU should load.

Command: **ED**   Edit CA-MENU.

Add an [ACADMENU] item to the 19th label [ ] of the **ROOT page:

```
[ACADMENU]MENU ACAD
```

Save and exit to AutoCAD.

Command: **MENU**   Load modified CA-MENU. [ACADMENU] should be at line 19.

Select **[DIMS]**   Or any of the application menu pages.
                                    Its menu should cover [ACADMENU].

Select **[root]**   [ACADMENU] should reappear. Try several more page changes.

Select **[ACADMENU]**   The ACAD menu should load.

Command: **QUIT**

This is the minimum integration. If you want to integrate further, you can merge the two menus into one.

Merging the CA-MENU Into the ACAD Menu

You can combine the CA-MENU into the ACAD menu file. A single menu file will provide a consistent set of pull-down, tablet, button, and screen menus for your users. AutoCAD only allows one definition for each device. For example, to have the custom tablet area and AutoCAD's standard tablet areas available at the same time, you need to have them in one file. Pick and choose the sections of the CA-MENU file you want to combine. Or just combine the entire file. To do so, you need to:

- Put your custom menu first, followed by the ACAD.MNU.

- Check for duplicate ***device and **page names. Remember, if ***device and **page names are duplicated, the first occurrence overrides.

- If you modify the ACAD.MNU code, you don't want to update pages scattered through ACAD.MNU with each new release of AutoCAD. Duplicate any pages you want to modify and place the modified copies in the ACAD.MNU file above the body of the menu. Then you can delete the body of the ACAD.MNU and append the new one when you get updates.

There is a problem integrating the ACAD.MNU popup, icon, and tablet menus into a custom menu. Many of these menu items flip pages in the screen menu. These menus will scramble if the user picks a tablet or other device item that pages the screen.

Even if you don't integrate the ***SCREEN device section of ACAD.MNU, these $S=pagename screen calls may cause problems if your menu duplicates any ACAD.MNU page names. There is a solution:

- Integrate only the popup, icon, and tablet devices.

- Copy the sections to integrate to a temporary file.

- Do a search-and-replace. Replace all: $S= with: $S=QZX and save it.

- Put your menu first and append the modified temporary file.

Now if you select a tablet item that has a screen call, it will look for a non-existent screen page and do nothing. For example, the ACAD.MNU ***TABLET4 contains the submenu **TEXT1 33, which includes the macro:

```
$S=X $S=TEXT ^C^CTEXT
```

This macro calls the **TEXT screen menu. The CA-MENU also has a **TEXT screen. The example search-and-replace changes the macro to:

```
$S=QZXX $S=QZXTEXT ^C^CTEXT
```

If you make these changes, the two menus become one, fully integrating your system by making all the commands and macros available.

Authors' Farewell

This must be the end!

But don't stop here. You will find an AutoLISP function reference and more information in the appendices. We hope that you proceed along the path to customizing AutoCAD, and that we have helped you with our own ideas, information, and techniques. Expanding your application with AutoCAD customization is well worth the effort. Come join us in our other book, INSIDE AutoLISP.

Good luck customizing!

Menu Macros

CHAPTER 4

TEST.MNU
Introductory menu macro routines to create bubbles, leaders, piping lines, and miscellaneous utilities.

CHAPTER 5

**BUTTONS
CUSTOMIZING AutoCAD's default button menu, providing a number of selection options.

**FLOWSYMB
A screen menu page showing symbol library use.

**OSNAPS
A screen menu page containing object snap options.

**P1-SETVARS
A popup menu page providing a means to set system variables.

**POINTS
An icon menu providing a visual means to establish point shapes.

**PTFILTERS
A screen menu page containing XYZ point filter options.

**TRANSVIEW
A menu page containing transparent view selections.

CHAPTER 6

**DWG
A screen menu page of drawing sizes.

**ROOT
A small screen menu page used to place a footer on subsequent screen pages.

**SCALE
A screen menu page of drawing scale sizes.

**TEXT
A simple screen menu page used to set and select different text sizes.

CA-MENU.MNU
This will become the final menu created by the CUSTOMIZING AutoCAD exercises. It is structured to receive the chapter menu pages as they are created. See the CAMASTER menu for the final CA-MENU.

CA-SETUP.MNU
CUSTOMIZING AutoCAD's menu file containing routines to initialize a new drawing. **DWG is a menu page providing drawing size selection. **SCALE is a menu page used to select drawing scale and [INITIATE] routines. The [INITIATE] selection is a large macro that establishes limits, grid, snap, text styles, border sheet insertion, and loads a current application menu.

CHAPTER 7

**SPECIALS

A screen menu page used to type special characters, like fractions, for the ROMANS text font.

CHAPTER 8

**HATCH

A screen menu page with a checkered plate and concrete pattern. It includes predefined hatch border tools.

CHAPTER 9

**CA-LAYER

A screen menu page of AutoLISP macros for working with layers.

CHAPTER 10

**3D

A screen menu presenting 3D macros for drawing cylinders, creating cylinder intersections, constructing brackets, and for changing viewport configurations and view points. Entity ON/OFF macros are included to assist editing in 3D.

**P1-3DVARS

A pull-down menu to provide access to the system variables controlling 3D mesh generation.

**P2-END-SAVE

A pull-down menu to standardize the ending and saving of a drawing file.

CHAPTER 11

**DIMS

A screen menu with the AutoCAD dimensioning command and custom macros for generating special dimensions.

**DIMSETT

A screen menu to set the graphic look of dimensions. Dimension offsets, blocks and tolerances are included.

**DIM????-ON and **DIM????-OFF

A series of toggle screen menus to show the current dimension system variables settings.

**DIMAPP

A screen menu to adjust the appearance of dimension text, rounding, tolerances, and alternate dimension units.

**DIMLOC

A screen menu to control the location of dimension text, lines, and extensions.

**DIM-UPDT

A screen menu to assist in working with associated dimensions to update and convert dimensions.

Setup, Memory, and Errors

Setup Problems With CONFIG.SYS

If your CONFIG.SYS settings do not run smoothly, your only indication may be that things don't work. If you get the error message:

```
Bad or missing FILENAME
```

DOS can't find the file as it is specified. Check your spelling, and provide a full path.

```
Unrecognized command in CONFIG.SYS
```

means that you made a syntax error, or your version of DOS doesn't support the configuration command. Check your spelling.

Watch closely when you boot your system. These error messages flash by very quickly. If you suspect an error, temporarily rename your AUTOEXEC.BAT file so that the system stops after loading CONFIG.SYS. You also can try to send the screen messages to the printer by hitting <CTRL-PRINTSCREEN> as soon as DOS starts reading the CONFIG.SYS file. Another <CTRL-PRINTSCREEN> turns the printer echo off.

Problems With AUTOEXEC.BAT

Errors in AUTOEXEC.BAT are harder to troubleshoot. There are many causes. Often, the system just doesn't behave as you think it should. Here are some troubleshooting tips:

■ Isolate errors by temporarily editing your AUTOEXEC.BAT. Try using a leading colon ":" to disable a line:

```
: NOW DOS WILL IGNORE THIS LINE!
```

■ Many AUTOEXEC.BAT files have echo to the screen turned off by the command ECHO OFF or @ECHO OFF. Disable ECHO OFF to see what the AUTOEXEC.BAT file is doing. Put a leading ":" on the line.

- Echo to the printer. Hit <CTRL-PRINTSCREEN> while booting to see what is happening.

- Make sure PROMPT, PATH, and other environment settings precede any TSR (memory resident) programs in the file.

- Check your PATH for completeness and syntax. Unsophisticated programs that require support or overlay files in addition to their .EXE or .COM files may not work, even if they are in the PATH. Directories do not need to be in the PATH, unless you want to execute files in them from other directories.

- APPEND (DOS 3.3 or later) works like PATH and lets programs find their support and overlay files in other directories. It uses about 5K of RAM. All files in an appended directory are recognized by programs as if they were in the current directory. If you use APPEND, *use it cautiously*. If you modify an appended file, the modified file will be written to the current directory, NOT the appended directory. Loading an AutoCAD.MNU file from an appended directory creates an .MNX file in the current directory. AutoCAD searches an appended directory before completing its normal directory search pattern, so appended support files will get loaded instead of those in the current directory.

- SET environment errors are often obscure. Type SET <RETURN> to see your current environment settings. If a setting is truncated or missing, you probably are out of environment space. Fix it in your CONFIG.SYS file. Do not use extraneous spaces in a SET statement:

```
SET ACADCFG=\CA-ACAD ....OK. Sets "ACADCFG" to "\CA-ACAD"
SET ACADCFG =\CA-ACAD ...Wrong. Sets "ACADCFG "
SET ACADCFG= \CA-ACAD ...Wrong. Sets to " \CA-ACAD"
```

- If your AUTOEXEC.BAT doesn't seem to complete its execution, you may have tried to execute another .BAT file from your AUTOEXEC.BAT file. If you nest execution of .BAT files, the second one will take over and the first will not complete. There are two ways to nest .BATs. With DOS 3.0 and later, use:

```
COMMAND /C NAME
```

where NAME is the name of the nested .BAT file . With DOS 3.3, use:

```
CALL NAME
```

- If you are fighting for memory, insert temporary lines in the

AUTOEXEC.BAT to check your available memory. Once you determine what uses how much, you can decide what to sacrifice. Use:

```
CHKDSK
PAUSE
```

at appropriate points. Reboot to see the effect. Remove the lines when you are done. We use an alternative FREEWARE program called MEM.COM. It reports available RAM, quickly.

- If you have unusual occurrences or lockups, and you use TSRs, suspect the TSRs as your problem source. Cause and effect may be hard to pin down. For example, there is a simple screen capture program that, if loaded, locks up our word processor — even when inactive! Disable TSRs one at a time in your AUTOEXEC. Reboot and test.

These are the most common problems. See a good DOS book if you need more information.

Problems With DOS Environment Space

Running out of space to store DOS environment settings may give the error:

```
Out of environment space
```

An environment space problem also may show up in unusual ways, such as a program failing to execute, AutoLISP not having room to load, or a block insertion not finding its block. This occurs because the PATH, AutoCAD settings limiting EXTended/EXPanded memory, and AutoCAD configuration, memory, and support file settings are all environment settings.

To find out how much environment space you need:

- Type SET at the DOS prompt.

- Count the characters displayed, including spaces.

- Add the number of characters for all SET statements you wish to add. Include revisions to your AUTOEXEC.BAT and startup files, like CA.BAT.

- Add a safety margin of 10 percent.

For CUSTOMIZING AutoCAD, you need about 240 bytes (characters). DOS defaults environment size to 160 bytes or less, depending on the DOS version. The space expands if you type in settings, but cannot expand during execution of a .BAT file, including your AUTOEXEC.BAT. Loading a TSR (memory resident) program or utility such as SIDEKICK, PROKEY, some Ram disks and print buffers, the DOS PRINT or GRAPHICS commands, and other utilities freezes the environment space to the current size.

Fortunately, DOS 3.0 or later versions can easily expand the space. Add this line to your CONFIG.SYS:

```
SHELL = C:\COMMAND.COM /P /E=nnn
```

Substitute your boot drive for "C:" if your boot drive isn't C. Do not use "nnn"; replace nnn with an integer value:

- For DOS 3.0 and 3.1, nnn is the desired environment size divided by 16. If you want 512 bytes, use 32 since (512/16=32). The maximum for nnn is 62.

- For DOS 3.2 and 3.3, nnn is the actual size setting. For 512 bytes, use 512. The maximum for nnn is 32768.

If you must use DOS 2, your solutions are more difficult. You have few choices. You can modify your COMMAND.COM file to allocate a larger environment.

Using DOS 2

We do not recommend that you run AutoCAD with DOS 2. If you have reason to run with DOS 2 and you encounter environment space problems, we provide a troubleshooting technique to debug the DOS COMMAND.COM and expand your environment space to 512 bytes. Proceed at your own risk. Have someone familiar with DOS's DEBUG program help if you are on unfamiliar ground. Changing your COMMAND.COM will make the change permanent and automatic, unless you overwrite the change later.

Debugging DOS 2 COMMAND.COM

This change is for PC DOS 2.0 and 2.1 only. It assumes your boot drive is C:. To set 512 bytes:

`C:\> COPY COMMAND.COM *.20`	Make a backup. Use a name like .20 for DOS 2.0, or .21 for DOS 2.1.
`C:\> COPY COMMAND.COM *.20X`	A copy to debug. Use .20X for DOS 2.0 or .21X for DOS 2.1.

DEBUG.COM must be in a directory on the path.

```
C:\> DEBUG COMMAND.20X          Or .21X for DOS 2.1. You get a "-" prompt:
-D ECE ECF                      Display the current value:

3585:0EC0                 BB 0A
```

CAUTION: If you didn't get BB 0A as shown above, then quit now!
Type Q <RETURN> to quit. You have a different version of DOS.

```
-E ECF 20                       Replaces the value 0A with 20.
-D ECF ECF                      Check it:

3585:0EC0                 BB 20
```

If BB 20 was shown above, type W to write it. Otherwise quit instead.

```
-W
Writing 4500 bytes              Confirms the writing of xxx bytes.
-Q                              Quits, but the W saved the change.
```

If all went OK, test it:

```
C:\> FORMAT A:/S                Format a diskette with the DOS boot files.

C:\> COPY COMMAND.20X  A:*.COM  Copy the modified file to drive A.
```

Reboot the system with the diskette in drive A.

The system won't boot your CONFIG.SYS or AUTOEXEC.BAT, but it should boot up DOS correctly. If it appears okay, make a backup file of both the modified and original COMMAND.COM files. Then, copy the modified file to drive C: and reboot.

If you have any problems, reboot your system from a diskette with a copy of the original COMMAND.COM, copy the original to drive C:, and reboot again. Your system will be back to its former unchanged state.

Memory Settings and Problems

There are several DOS environment settings that deal with AutoCAD's memory usage. These settings are explained and shown in a chart of memory usage chart in the AutoCAD Installation and Performance Guide. None of AutoCAD's settings affect other programs or tie up memory when AutoCAD is not running. The AutoCAD status command shows several memory values:

```
Free RAM:  9784 bytes        Free disk: 1409024 bytes

I/O page space: 109K bytes   Extended I/O page space: 592K
                             bytes
```

"Free RAM" is the unused portion of RAM for AutoCAD to work in. "I/O page space" is RAM used by AutoCAD to swap data in and out. An I/O page value of 60K or more is adequate for most use, and we've worked (slowly!) with values under 20K.

"SET ACADFREERAM=nn" reserves RAM for AutoCAD's working space. Too small a size can cause "Out of RAM" errors, slow down spline fitting, and cause problems with AutoCAD's HIDE, TRIM, and OFFSET commands. However, a large ACADFREERAM setting reduces I/O page swap space and slows down AutoCAD. The default is 14K, the maximum depends on the system, usually about 24 to 26K. A setting larger than the maximum is equivalent to maximum. There is no magic number. Try changing ACADFREERAM to a lower or higher setting if you get errors or want to increase I/O page space.

"Extended I/O page space" is another factor that affects I/O page space. Extended memory is IBM AT-style memory above the 1 Mb mark. It is commonly used as Ram disk (VDISK), a print buffer (PRINT), and by some sophisticated programs like AutoCAD. AutoCAD uses extended memory as "Extended I/O page space" to swap its temporary files into extended RAM instead of slower disk space. Expanded memory is Intel Above Board style memory above the 640K mark. It is also known as LIM and EMS memory. It is used for RAM disks and print buffers, and is designed for page swapping. AutoCAD uses it as "Extended I/O page space."

It may take some investigation to determine which type of memory you have. You often can configure Intel Above Boards and their imitators as expanded or extended memory. Expanded memory is relatively clean, with established techniques for programs to share it. Unfortunately, extended memory lacks protection. Programs wishing to use it are not always able to tell if it is already in use by another program.

If you use extended memory and sometimes get unexplained crashes, you may have a memory conflict between programs. Crashes may appear random. Check to see what, if any, programs other than AutoCAD may be using your extended memory. In particular, check for DOS VDISK and PRINT. Check your CONFIG.SYS and AUTOEXEC.BAT. Figure out what addresses are in use so that you can set AutoCAD to avoid the conflict. If you have extended RAM, and it is used by any other program like DOS VDISK (RAM disk) or DOS PRINT, you can use "SET ACADXMEM=start,size" to avoid conflict. See your AutoCAD Installation and Performance Guide for details.

Even if you do not encounter crashes, you may want to examine your memory usage. AutoCAD uses up some free RAM to enable "Extended I/O page space." If you have 2 Mb or more of extended or expanded memory, you may need to actually restrict AutoCAD's use of it. Each Kbyte of "Extended I/O page space" reduces free RAM by 16 bytes. You also may want to restrict your extended or expanded memory use if you run SOFTWARE CAROUSEL or another multi-tasking setup.

"SET ACADLIMEM=value" configures expanded memory usage (LIM-EMS). This setting is probably not critical, since EMS avoids conflicts. If you must restrict it, or wish to reserve some of your LIM-EMS RAM for other programs to use via SHELL, refer to your AutoCAD Installation and Performance Guide.

Using CUSTOMIZING AutoCAD With a RAM Disk

Running AutoCAD from a RAM disk can be more efficient than using extended/expanded memory for I/O page space. If you want to run AutoCAD from a RAM disk, there are three things to look at: AutoCAD's program files, temporary files, and the drawing itself.

AutoCAD locates its temporary files on the same drive and directory as the drawing, unless you tell it otherwise. Using the configuration menu, select item 8 (Configure operating parameters). Then choose item 5 (Placement of temporary files). Item 5 defaults to <DRAWING>, for the drawing's directory. You can reset this to a RAM disk and locate your temporary files there. If you use a RAM disk, we recommend allowing about two times the size of your largest drawing.

Regardless of the temporary file setting, AutoCAD still locates the temporary file(s) that eventually becomes the new drawing file in the directory of the drawing file itself. This occurs because AutoCAD closes up the file(s) instead of copying it when the drawing is ended.

To speed drawing disk access, you can edit the drawing from your RAM disk. Make sure the finished drawing is copied back to a real drive. Use a menu macro, or redefine the END command for safety. If you have sufficient I/O page space, you won't gain much by putting the drawing on a RAM disk.

The easiest way to put the AutoCAD program on RAM disk is to copy all files to it. This may waste a little memory, but if you have plenty, it works. Make sure that you have set a real disk directory with SET ACADCFG=, ensuring any configuration changes are copied back to a real disk.

If you want to place AutoCAD on the RAM disk but need to make efficient use of RAM disk space, selectively copy AutoCAD program files to it. There is little advantage to putting support files or the ACAD.EXE file on a RAM disk. Start with the overlay files. They are listed in the Software Installation section of your AutoCAD Installation and Performance Guide. The most important are: ACAD.OVL, ACAD0.OVL, and ACADVS.OVL. The ACAD2.OVL and ACAD3.OVL contain ADE2 and ADE3 commands, and the ACADL.OVL is AutoLISP. If you have to decide between them, you can refer to the AutoCAD Reference Manual's appendix on commands. Decide whether you use ADE2 or ADE3 commands the most!

Make sure that the files copied to the RAM disk are not included in the \ACAD directory of your hard disk. Make an \ACAD\RAM directory to store the files. Let's assume that you have the following drives and directories:

```
C:                 Hard disk.
D:                 RAM disk.
C:\ACAD            Standard ACAD support files and
                   program files except the .OVL files.
C:\ACAD\RAM        AutoCAD .OVL files to go on RAM disk.
C:\SUPFILES        Project-specific support files.
C:\PROJECT         Working drawing project directory.
C:\CFGFILES        Specific configuration.
```

If D: is on your PATH, and you have copied the .OVL files to D:, you start AutoCAD with the following:

```
SET ACAD=SUPFILES
SET ACADCFG=CFGFILES
C:\ACAD\ACAD
```

This works fine. AutoCAD will find all its needed files. The \ACAD\ACAD explicitly tells DOS to look in the \ACAD directory for the ACAD.EXE file. AutoCAD will also look there for .OVL files and remember it for support files. AutoCAD is a smart program, and it will also search the PATH to find its other needed support files. Since D: is on the PATH, it finds its .OVLs, and remembers D: as a possible source of support files.

If your path is wrong, or a file is in neither \ACAD or D:, you will get:

```
Can't find overlay file ACAD0.OVL.
Enter file name prefix (path name\ or X:) or '.' to quit=
```

Finding Support Files

When you ask AutoCAD to find a support file, like a menu file, it searches in a particular order. Given the above settings, you would get:

```
"STUFF.mnu":  Can't open file
  in C:\PROJECT (current directory)     First the current directory.
  or C:\SUPFILES\                       Then the directory designated by SET ACAD=.
  or D:\                                 Then the .OVL directory found on PATH, if any.
  or C:\ACAD\                           Last the program directory, home of ACAD.EXE.
Enter another menu file name (or RETURN for none):
```

If you keep AutoCAD's search order in mind, it will help you avoid errors in finding the wrong support files. A common cause of finding the wrong support files is setting ACAD=*somename* in a startup batch file. Make sure to SET ACAD= to clear it at the end of the batch file. Clear your SET ACADCFG= settings.

Current Directory Errors

If you use SHELL to change directories (CD) from inside AutoCAD, you may get strange results. Parts of AutoCAD recognize the change and parts do not. New drawings will not default to the new current directory, yet drawings saved with SAVE will observe the directory change. Subsequent attempts to load support files, such as .MNX files, can cause AutoCAD to crash.

If you must change a directory on SHELL excursions, automate it with a batch file that returns to the original directory.

SHELL Errors

Here are some common errors encountered when using SHELL:

```
SHELL error swapping to disk
```

is most likely caused by insufficient disk space. Remember that AutoCAD's temporary files can easily use a megabyte of disk space.

```
SHELL error: insufficient memory for command
```

can be caused by an ill-behaved program executed during a previous shell, or before entering AutoCAD. Some ill-behaved programs leave a dirty environment behind that causes AutoCAD to erroneously believe insufficient memory exists.

```
Unable to load program: insufficient memory
Program too big to fit in memory
```

If SHELL got this far, these are correct messages. You need to modify your ACAD.PGP to allocate more memory space for program.

```
SHELL error in EXEC function (insufficient memory)
```

can be caused by the shell memory allocation being too small to load DOS. Exactly how much memory you need to allocate depends on your versions of DOS and AutoCAD, and on what you have in your CONFIG.SYS file. DOS 3.2 and later versions must have at least 25000 bytes allocated in the ACAD.PGP. Use 30000 to give a little cushion.

Common AutoLISP Errors

The AutoLISP Programmers Reference gives a complete listing of error messages. The following list gives a few hints of where and how to look for other causes.

```
error: invalid dotted pair
error: misplaced dot
```

Look for a missing or an extra quotation mark above the apparent error location. Look for " imbedded in a string where it should be \". Look for strings that exceed 132 characters. STRCAT two strings if you need to.

```
n>        prompts such as    3>
```

Look for the same quotation mark errors as shown in the dot errors example. Look for a missing closing parenthesis. If the error occurs while you are loading an .LSP file, look in the file.

```
Unknown command
```

May be caused by AutoLISP, if you have a COMMAND function containing a "". The "" tries to repeat the last command entered *at* the ACAD prompt, *not* the last command sent to ACAD via the COMMAND function.

Miscellaneous Problems

If you run under a multi-tasking environment like CAROUSEL or DESKVIEW, you may get an error claiming a file should be in a directory it never was in. For example, you may get:

```
Can't find overlay file D:\ACAD\ACAD.OVL
Retry, Abort?
```

Or any other .OVL or ACAD.EXE. Don't type an "A" until you give up. Try an "R" to retry. If that doesn't work, copy the file to the directory listed in the error message. Flip partitions. You may need to hit another "R" during the flip. Copy the file, flip back and "R" again.

```
Expanded memory disabled
```

When starting ACAD from DOS, this error message can be caused by a previously crashed AutoCAD. Sometimes a crashed AutoCAD does not fully clear its claim on expanded memory. This causes the program to think none is available. Reboot to clear it.

Insufficient File Errors

You may encounter file error messages due to AutoCAD's inability to open a file. This may be caused by too few files requested in the FILES= statement of the CONFIG.SYS file or AutoLISP's OPEN function leaving too many files open. If you repeatedly crash an AutoLISP routine which opens files, you may see the following:

```
Command: (load "test")
Can't open "test.lsp" for input
error: LOAD failed
(load "test")
```

If you know the variable names SETQed to the files, try to CLOSE them before you get the message. Otherwise, you have little choice but to QUIT AutoCAD and reboot the system to clean things up. This error can also show up as:

```
Can't find overlay file C:\ACAD\ACAD.OVL
```

Tracing and Curing Errors

You and your users are your best sources for error diagnosis. When problems occur, log them so you can recognize patterns. Here are some tips and techniques:

■ Use screen capture programs to document the text screen.

■ Dump the screen to the printer.

■ Write down what you did in as much detail as possible, as far back as you can remember.

■ Dump a copy of AutoCAD's STATUS screen to the printer.

■ Dump a copy of the screen of the DOS command SET to check settings.

Avoidance is the best cure.

Reference Tables

This appendix provides an annotated table of the AutoCAD system variables and a handy reference guide to the AutoLISP functions.

AutoCAD System Variables

Use the AutoCAD System Variables Table to determine AutoCAD drawing environment settings. The table presents all the variable settings available through the AutoCAD SETVAR command or AutoLISP SETVAR and GETVAR functions. The system variable name and the default ACAD prototype drawing settings are shown. A brief description is given of each variable and the meaning of code flags. Some variables are read-only and are noted as **<RO>**. All values are saved with the drawing unless noted with **<CFG>** for ConFiGuration, or **<NS>** for Not Saved.

AutoCAD System Variables

VARIABLE NAME	DEFAULT SETTING	DEFAULT MEANING	COMMAND NAME	VARIABLE DESCRIPTION
ACADPREFIX	"C:\ACAD\"			AutoCAD directory path **<NS>,<RO>**
ACADVER	"10"			AutoCAD release version **<RO>**
AFLAGS	0		ATTDEF	Sum of: Invisible=1 Constant=2 Verify=4 Preset=8
ANGBASE	0	EAST	UNITS	Direction of angle 0
ANGDIR	0	CCW	UNITS	Clockwise=1 Counter clockwise=0
APERTURE	10	10	APERTURE	Half of aperture height in pixels **<CFG>**
AREA	0.0000		AREA,LIST	Last computed area **<NS>,<RO>**
ATTDIA	0	PROMPTS		Insert uses: DDATTE dialogue box=1 Attribute prompts=0
ATTMODE	1	ON	ATTDISP	Attribute display Normal=1 ON=2 OFF=0
ATTREQ	1	PROMPTS		Insert uses: Prompts=1 Defaults=0
AUNITS	0	DEC. DEG.	UNITS	Angular units Dec=0 Deg=1 Grad=2 Rad=3 Survey=4
AUPREC	0	0	UNITS	Angular units decimal places
AXISMODE	0	OFF	AXIS	Axis ON=1 Axis OFF=0
AXISUNIT	0.0000,0.0000		AXIS	Axis X,Y Increment
BACKZ	0.0000		DVIEW	Back clipping plane offset - See VIEWMODE **<RO>**
BLIPMODE	1	ON	BLIPMODE	Blips=1 No Blips=0
CDATE	19881202.144648898		TIME	Date.Time **<NS>,<RO>**
CECOLOR	"BYLAYER"		COLOR	Current entity color **<RO>**
CELTYPE	"BYLAYER"		LINETYPE	Current entity linetype **<RO>**
CHAMFERA	0.0000		CHAMFER	Chamfer distance for A
CHAMFERB	0.0000		CHAMFER	Chamfer distance for B
CLAYER	"0"		LAYER	Current layer **<RO>**
CMDECHO	1	ECHO	SETVAR	Command echo in AutoLISP Echo=1 No Echo=0 **<NS>**
COORDS	0	OFF	[^D] [F6]	Update display Picks=0 ON=1 Dist>Angle=2
CVPORT	1		VPORTS	Identification number of the current viewport
DATE	2447498.61620926		TIME	Julian time **<NS>,<RO>**
DIMALT	0	OFF	DIMALT	Use alternate units ON=1 OFF=0
DIMALTD	2	0.00	DIMALTD	Decimal precision of alternate units
DIMALTF	25.4000		DIMALTF	Scale factor for alternate units
DIMAPOST	""	NONE	DIMAPOST	Suffix for alternate dimensions **<RO>**
DIMASO	1	ON	DIMASO	Associative=1 Line,Arrow,Text=0
DIMASZ	0.1800		DIMASZ	Arrow Size=Value (also controls text fit)
DIMBLK	""	NONE	DIMBLK	Block name to draw instead of arrow or tick **<RO>**
DIMBLK1	""	NONE	DIMBLK1	Block name for 1st end, see DIMSAH **<RO>**
DIMBLK2	""	NONE	DIMBLK2	Block name for 2nd end, see DIMSAH **<RO>**
DIMCEN	0.0900	MARK	DIMCEN	Center mark size=Value Add center lines=Negative
DIMDLE	0.0000	NONE	DIMDLE	Dimension line extension=Value
DIMDLI	0.3800		DIMDLI	Increment between continuing dimension lines
DIMEXE	0.1800		DIMEXE	Extension distance for extension lines=Value
DIMEXO	0.0625		DIMEXO	Offset distance for extension lines=Value
DIMLFAC	1.0000	NORMAL	DIMLFAC	Overall linear distance factor=Value
DIMLIM	0	OFF	DIMLIM	Add tolerance limits ON=1 OFF=0
DIMPOST	""	NONE	DIMPOST	User defined dimension suffix (eg: "mm") **<RO>**
DIMRND	0.0000	EXACT	DIMRND	Rounding value for linear dimensions
DIMSAH	0	OFF	DIMSAH	Allow separate DIMBLKS ON=1 OFF=0
DIMSCALE	1.0000		DIMSCALE	Overall dimensioning scale factor=Value
DIMSE1	0	OFF	DIMSE1	Suppress extension line 1 Omit=1 Draw=0
DIMSE2	0	OFF	DIMSE2	Suppress extension line 2 Omit=1 Draw=0
DIMSHO	0	OFF	DIMSHO	Show associative dimension while dragging
DIMSOXD	0	OFF	DIMSOXD	Suppress dim. lines outside extension lines Omit=1 Draw=0
DIMTAD	0	OFF	DIMTAD	Text above dim. line ON=1 OFF(in line)=0

VARIABLE NAME	DEFAULT SETTING	DEFAULT MEANING	COMMAND NAME	VARIABLE DESCRIPTION
DIMTIH	1	ON	DIMTIH	Text inside horizontal ON=1 OFF(aligned)=0
DIMTIX	0	OFF	DIMTIX	Force text inside extension lines ON=1 OFF=0
DIMTM	0.0000	NONE	DIMTM	Minus tolerance=Value
DIMTOFL	0	OFF	DIMTOFL	Draw dim. line even if text outside ext. lines
DIMTOH	1	ON	DIMTOH	Text outside horizontal ON=1 OFF(aligned)=0
DIMTOL	0	OFF	DIMTOL	Append tolerance ON=1 OFF=2
DIMTP	0.0000	NONE	DIMTP	Plus tolerance=Value
DIMTSZ	0.0000	ARROWS	DIMTSZ	Tick size=Value Draw arrows=0
DIMTVP	0.0000		DIMTVP	Text vertical position
DIMTXT	0.1800		DIMTXT	Text size=Value
DIMZIN	0		DIMZIN	Controls leading zero (see AutoCAD manual)
DISTANCE	0.0000		DIST	Last computed distance **<NS>**,**<RO>**
DRAGMODE	2	AUTO	DRAGMODE	OFF=0 Enabled=1 Auto=2
DRAGP1	10		SETVAR	Drag regen rate **<CFG>**
DRAGP2	25		SETVAR	Drag input rate **<CFG>**
DWGNAME	"TEST"			Current drawing name **<RO>**
DWGPREFIX	"C:\IA-ACAD\"			Directory path of current drawing **<NS>**,**<RO>**
ELEVATION	0.0000		ELEV	Current default elevation
EXPERT	0	NORMAL	SETVAR	Suppresses "Are you sure" prompts (See AutoCAD Reference Manual)
EXTMAX	-1.0000E+20,-1.0000E+20			Upper right drawing extents X,Y **<RO>**
EXTMIN	1.0000E+20,1.0000E+20			Lower left drawing extents X,Y **<RO>**
FILLETRAD	0.0000		FILLET	Current fillet radius
FILLMODE	1		FILL	Fill ON=1 Fill OFF=0
FLATLAND	0		SETVAR	Temporary 3D compatibility setting act like Release 9=1 R10=0
FRONTZ	0.0000		DVIEW	Front clipping plane offset - See VIEWMODE **<RO>**
GRIDMODE	0	OFF	GRID	Grid ON=1 Grid OFF=0
GRIDUNIT	0.0000,0.0000		GRID	X,Y grid increment
HANDLES	0		HANDLES	Entity handles Enabled=1 Disabled=0 **<RO>**
HIGHLIGHT	1		SETVAR	Highlight selection ON=1 OFF=0 **<NS>**
INSBASE	0.0000,0.0000		BASE	Insert base point of current drawing X,Y
LASTANGLE	0		ARC	Last angle of the last arc **<NS>**,**<RO>**
LASTPOINT	0.0000,0.0000			Last @ pickpoint X,Y **<NS>**
LASTPT3D	0.0000,0.0000,0.0000			Last @ pickpoint X,Y,Z **<NS>**
LENSLENGTH	50.0000		DVIEW	Length of lens in perspective in millimeters **<RO>**
LIMCHECK	0	OFF	LIMITS	Limits error check ON=1 OFF=0
LIMMAX	12.0000,9.0000		LIMITS	Upper right X,Y limit
LIMMIN	0.0000,0.0000		LIMITS	Lower left X,Y limit
LTSCALE	1.0000		LTSCALE	Current linetype scale
LUNITS	2	DEC.	UNITS	Linear units: Scientific=1 Dec=2 Eng=3 Arch=4 Frac=5
LUPREC	4	0.0000	UNITS	Unit precision decimal places or denominator
MENUECHO	0	NORMAL	SETVAR	Normal=0 Suppress echo of menu items=1 No prompts=2 No input or prompts=3 **<NS>**
MENUNAME	"ACAD"		MENU	Current menu name **<RO>**
MIRRTEXT	1	YES	SETVAR	Retain text direction=0 Reflect text=1
ORTHOMODE	0	OFF	[^O] [F8]	Ortho ON=1 Ortho OFF=0
OSMODE	0	NONE	OSNAP	Sum of: Endp=1 Mid=2 Cen=4 Node=8 Quad=16 Int=32 Ins=64 Perp=128 Tan=256 Near=512 Quick=1024
PDMODE	0	POINT	SETVAR	Controls style of points drawn
PDSIZE	0.0000	POINT	SETVAR	Controls size of points
PERIMETER	0.0000		AREA,LIST	Last computed perimeter **<NS>**,**<RO>**

VARIABLE NAME	DEFAULT SETTING	DEFAULT MEANING	COMMAND NAME	VARIABLE DESCRIPTION
PICKBOX	3		SETVAR	Half the pickbox size in pixels <CFG>
POPUPS	1			AUI Support=1 No Support=0 <NS>, <RO>
QTEXTMODE	0	OFF	QTEXT	Qtext ON=1 Qtext OFF=0
REGENMODE	1	ON	REGENAUTO	Regenauto ON=1 Regenauto OFF=0
SCREENSIZE	570.0000,410.0000			Size of display in X,Y pixels <NS>, <RO>
SKETCHINC	0.1000		SKETCH	Recording increment for sketch
SKPOLY	0	LINE	SETVAR	Polylines=1 Sketch with Line=0
SNAPANG	0		SNAP	Angle of SNAP/GRID rotation
SNAPBASE	0.0000,0.0000		SNAP	X,Y base point of SNAP/GRID rotation
SNAPISOPAIR	0	LEFT	SNAP [^E]	Isoplane Left=0 Top=1 Right=2
SNAPMODE	0	OFF	SNAP [^B] [F9]	Snap ON=1 Snap OFF=0
SNAPSTYL	0	STD	SNAP	Isometric=1 Snap standard=0
SNAPUNIT	1.0000,1.0000		SNAP	Snap X,Y increment
SPLFRAME	0		SETVAR	Display spline frame ON=1 OFF=0
SPLINESEGS	8		SETVAR	Number of line segments in each spline segment
SPLINETYPE	6	CUBIC	SETVAR	Pedit spline generates: Quadratic B-Spline=5 Cubic B-Spline=6
SURFTAB1	6		SETVAR	Rulesurf and tabsurf tabulations, also revsurf and edgesurf M density
SURFTAB2	6		SETVAR	Revsurf and edgesurf N density
SURFTYPE	6	CUBIC	SETVAR	Pedit smooth surface generates: Quadratic B-Spline=5 Cubic B-Spline=6 Bezier=8
SURFU	6		SETVAR	M direction surface density
SURFV	6		SETVAR	N direction surface density
TARGET	0.0000,0.0000,0.0000		DVIEW	UCS coords of current viewport target point <RO>
TDCREATE	2447498.61620031		TIME	Creation time (Julian) <RO>
TDINDWG	0.00436285		TIME	Total editing time <RO>
TDUPDATE	2447498.61620031		TIME	Time of last save or update <RO>
TDUSRTIMER	0.00436667		TIME	User set elapsed time <RO>
TEMPPREFIX	""			Directory location of AutoCAD's temporary files, defaults to drawing directory <NS>, <RO>
TEXTEVAL	0	TEXT	SETVAR	Evaluate leading "(" and "!" in text input as: Text=0 AutoLISP=1 <NS>
TEXTSIZE	0.2000		TEXT	Current text height
TEXTSTYLE	"STANDARD"		TEXT,STYLE	Current text style <RO>
THICKNESS	0.0000		ELEV	Current 3D extrusion thickness
TRACEWID	0.0500		TRACE	Current width of traces
UCSFOLLOW	0		SETVAR	Automatic plan view in new UCS=1 Off=0
UCSICON	1		UCSICON	Sum of: Off=0 On=1 Origin=2
UCSNAME	""		UCS	Name of current UCS Unnamed="" <RO>
UCSORG	0.0000,0.0000,0.0000		UCS	WCS origin of current UCS <RO>
UCSXDIR	1.0000,0.0000,0.0000		UCS	X direction of current UCS <RO>
UCSYDIR	0.0000,1.0000,0.0000		UCS	Y direction of current UCS <RO>
USERI1 - 5	0			User integer variables USERI1 to USERI5
USERR1 - 5	0.0000			User real variables USERR1 to USERR5
VIEWCTR	6.2518,4.5000		ZOOM,PAN,VIEW	X,Y center point of current view <RO>
VIEWDIR	0.0000,0.0000,1.0000		DVIEW	Camera point offset from target in WCS <RO>
VIEWMODE	0		DVIEW,UCS	Perspective and clipping settings, see AutoCAD Reference Manual <RO>
VIEWSIZE	9.0000		ZOOM,PAN,VIEW	Height of current view <RO>
VIEWTWIST	0		DVIEW	View wist angle <RO>
VPOINTX	0.0000		VPOINT	X coordinate of VPOINT <RO>
VPOINTY	0.0000		VPOINT	Y coordinate of VPOINT <RO>

VARIABLE NAME	DEFAULT SETTING	DEFAULT MEANING	COMMAND NAME	VARIABLE DESCRIPTION
VPOINTZ	1.0000		VPOINT	Z coordinate of VPOINT **<RO>**
VSMAX	12.5036,9.0000,0.0000			ZOOM,PAN,VIEW
				Upper right of virtual screen X,Y **<NS>**,**<RO>**
VSMIN	0.0000,0.0000,0.0000			ZOOM,PAN,VIEW
				Lower left of virtual screen X,Y **<NS>**,**<RO>**
WORLDUCS	1		UCS	UCS equals WCS=1 UCS not equal to WCS=0 **<RO>**
WORLDVIEW	1		DVIEW,UCS	Dview and VPoint coordinate input: WCS=1 UCS=0

<NS> Not Saved   **<CFG>** Configure File   **<RO>** Read Only

AutoLISP Function Reference Table

Each AutoLISP function is given below with a brief description of the function's action and the results returned. The number and data type of arguments are shown.

(+ *number number* ...)

Returns the sum of all numbers, as integers or real numbers depending on the values.

(– *number number* ...)

Returns the difference of the first number subtracted from the sum of the remaining numbers. An integer or real number is returned, depending on the value.

(* *number number* ...)

Returns the product of all numbers.

(/ *number number* ...)

Returns the quotient of first number divided by the product of the remaining numbers.

(= *atom atom* ...)

Returns T if atoms are numerically equal, otherwise returns nil. Only numbers and strings are valid.

(/= *atom atom*)

Returns T if atoms are numerically not equal, otherwise returns nil. Only numbers and strings are valid.

(< *atom atom* ...)

Returns T if each atom is numerically less than the following atom, otherwise returns nil. Only numbers and strings are valid.

(<= *atom atom* ...)

Returns T if each atom is numerically less than or equal to the following atom, otherwise returns nil. Only numbers and strings are valid.

KEY:

...	means additional arguments may follow.
Bold italics	are required arguments.
Light italics	are optional arguments.

(> atom atom ...)

Returns T if each atom is numerically greater than the following atom, otherwise returns nil. Only numbers and strings are valid.

(>= atom atom ...)

Returns T if each atom is numerically greater than or equal to the following atom, otherwise returns nil. Only numbers and strings are valid.

(~ number)

Returns the bitwise NOT of number.

(1+ number)

Returns number incremented by 1.

(1- number)

Returns number decremented by 1.

(abs number)

Returns the absolute value of an integer or real number.

(and expression ...)

Returns T if all expressions are true, otherwise returns nil and ceases evaluation at the first nil expression encountered.

(angle point point)

Returns an angle in radians from the X axis in a counterclockwise direction to a line between the two points.

(angtos angle mode precision)

Returns a string conversion of an angle from radians to the units specified by mode. The conversion defaults to the current units and precision unless otherwise specified with the optional mode and precision arguments.

(append list ...)

Returns a single list made up of any number of lists.

(apply function list)

Returns a value of the list after applying the function to the list argument.

(ascii string)

Returns the first character of the string as an ASCII integer character code.

(assoc item list)

Returns a list containing the item from a list of lists.

(atan *number* number**)**

> Returns the arctangent of number between -pi and pi. If the second number is provided, the arctangent of the first number divided by the second number is returned. With both numbers, direction signs are considered and the result ranges between 0 and 2pi.

(atof *string***)**

> Returns a real number converted from a string.

(atoi *string***)**

> Returns an integer converted from a string.

(atom *item***)**

> Returns T if item is not a list, otherwise returns nil.

(boole *function integer integer* ...**)**

> Returns one of 16 possible boolean operations, based on the function value, on any number of integers.

(boundp *atom***)**

> Returns T if the atom has a value, otherwise returns nil.

(cadr *list***)**

> Returns the second element in the list.

(car *list***)**

> Returns the first element in the list.

(cdr *list***)**

> Returns a list minus the first element in the list.

(c????r *list***)**

> Returns an element or list defined by the combinations of a and d characters in the expression, up to four levels deep. For example, caadr, cddr, cadar, and so on.

(chr *integer***)**

> Returns a single character string converted from the integer to the ASCII character code.

(close *file-desc***)**

> Closes a file defined by the file-desc variable. The file-desc variable must be assigned to a valid file name.

(command *argument* **...)**

> Executes AutoCAD commands; (command) alone executes a return, (command nil) executes a <^C>.

(cond **(***test* *expression* **...)** **...)**

> Evaluates expression(s) of the first non-nil test. Any number of (test expression...) lists are scanned for the test case. The value of the last-evaluated expression is returned. Cond ceases further evaluation after finding a non-nil test or after completing the list of tests.

(cons *item* *item***)**

> Returns a dotted pair in the form (item . item).

(cons *item* *list***)**

> Returns a new list with the item as the first element of the supplied list.

(cos *angle***)**

> Returns the cosine of a radian angle.

(defun *name* **(***argument* **...)** *expression* **...)**

> Creates a function with a given name. The argument list can supply variables to be passed to the function and/or variables that are local to the function. The function will evaluate the expression(s) and return the result of the last expression evaluated. Prefixing a C: to the function name will create a lisp command that acts like a standard AutoCAD command. Defining a S::STARTUP function in the ACAD.LSP file will create an automatic executing function.

(distance *point* *point***)**

> Returns a distance between two 3D or 2D points.

(entdel *ename***)**

> Deletes or restores the ename depending on its condition in the current editing session.

(entget *ename***)**

> Returns a list of data describing the entity specified by the ename.

(entlast)

> Returns the last nondeleted entity name in the database.

(entmod *list***)**

> Updates an entity in the database with a new entity data description list. Except for polyline vertexes and block attributes, the entities are redisplayed on the screen with the new data.

(entnext *ename***)**

> Returns the first nondeleted entity name in the database. If the optional ename is provided, the nondeleted entity name immediately following the ename is returned.

(entsel *prompt***)**

> Returns a list containing the entity name and the point coordinates the user picked to select the entity. The optional prompt string can provide specific instructions for entity selection.

(entupd *ename***)**

> Allows selective updating of polyline vertexes and block attribute enames after (entmod)s have been performed.

(eq *variable variable***)**

> Returns T if the first variable expression is identically bound to the second variable. Otherwise returns nil.

(equal *expression expression* *accuracy***)**

> Returns T if the first expression is equal to the second expression. Otherwise returns nil. The optional accuracy value determines how accurate two numbers must be to be considered equal.

(*error* *string***)**

> A user-definable error function. The string will contain a message describing the error.

(eval *expression***)**

> Returns the results of evaluating the expression.

(exp *number***)**

> Returns a real number of e raised to the power of number.

(expt *base power***)**

> Returns the base number raised to the power number. The value returned is an integer or real number depending on the base and power values.

(findfile *filename***)**

> Returns the filename with the path appended if the file was found in the AutoCAD library path. Otherwise returns nil.

(fix *number***)**

> Returns an integer value of the number and drops the remainder.

(float *number***)**

> Returns a real value of the number.

(foreach *name list expression***)**

> Evaluates the expression, substituting each element in the list for the defined name used in the expression.

(gcd *integer integer***)**

> Returns the greatest common denominator of two integers.

(getangle *point prompt***)**

> Returns an angle in radians. Value may be entered by a user or determined by two user-provided points. The angle is always measured counterclockwise from the X axis. An optional point value specifies the base point for a rubber-banding line. The optional prompt string can provide specific instructions for desired point values.

(getcorner *point prompt***)**

> Returns a point selected as the second corner of an AutoCAD window cursor. The optional prompt string can provide specific instructions for desired point selection.

(getdist *point prompt***)**

> Returns a user-entered distance or the calculated distance between two user-provided points. The optional point value specifies the base point for a rubber-banding line. An optional prompt can provide specific instructions for desired point selection.

(getenv *name***)**

> Returns a string value of the system environment variable setting specified by the name.

(getint *prompt***)**

> Returns an integer provided by the user. The optional prompt string can provide specific instructions for input.

(getkword *prompt***)**

> Returns a string matching the key word input by the user. Key words are specified in the (initget) function. The optional prompt string can provide specific instructions for input.

(getorient *point prompt***)**

> Returns a radian angle as input by a user or as calculated by two user-provided points. The angle is converted for a 0 base and angle direction from the X axis different from AutoCAD's standard default. The optional point value specifies the base point to show a rubber-banding line. An optional prompt string can provide specific instructions for desired point values.

(getpoint *point prompt***)**

>   Returns a point. The optional point value specifies the base point of a rubber-banding line. The optional prompt can provide specific instructions for desired point selection.

(getreal *prompt***)**

>   Returns a real number provided by the user. The optional prompt string can provide specific instructions for input.

(getstring *flag prompt***)**

>   Returns a string of up to 132 characters from the user. If the optional flag expression is not nil, spaces are allowed in the string, otherwise spaces act like a <RETURN> and end input. The optional prompt string can provide specific instructions for input.

(getvar *sysvar***)**

>   Returns the value of the AutoCAD system variable specified by the quoted sysvar variable.

(graphscr)

>   Switches from the text screen to the graphics screen on single screen systems.

(grclear)

>   Temporarily clears the graphics screen in the current viewport. Redraw will refresh the screen.

(grdraw *point point color mode***)**

>   Draws a vector between the two supplied points in the color specified. The line will be highlighted if optional mode is not 0 (zero).

(grread *track***)**

>   Reads the input device directly. If the track option is present and not nil, it returns the current mouse or digitizer cursor location.

(grtext *box text mode***)**

>   Writes text string in the text portion of the graphics screen specified by the box number. The option mode integer highlights/de-highlights the box of text. A box number of -1 writes to the status line, -2 writes to the coordinate status line, and from 0 on, writes to the menu labels, with 0 representing the top label.

(handent *handle***)**

>   Returns the entity name corresponding to the permanent handle name if handle has been enabled.

(if *test expression* *expression***)**

>   If the test is not nil, the first expression is evaluated. If the test is nil, the optional

second expression is evaluated. The function returns the value of the evaluated expression.

(initget *bits string***)**

Establishes options for GETxxx functions.

```
1 Null input is not allowed.          8  Does not check limits.
2 Zero values are not allowed.       16  Returns 3D points (default).
4 Negative values are not allowed.   32  Dashed lines used for
                                         rubber-banding.
```

The optional string defines a list of key words as acceptable input to a get??? function.

(inters *point point point point flag***)**

Returns a point value of the intersection of a line between the first two points and a line between the second two points. If the optional flag is not nil, the lines are infinitely projected to calculate the intersection.

(itoa *integer***)**

Returns a string conversion of an integer.

(lambda *argument expression* **...)**

Defines an in-line function supplying argument(s) to expression(s) for evaluation.

(last *list***)**

Returns the last element in a list.

(length *list***)**

Returns the number of elements in a list.

(list *expression***)**

Returns a list constructed from the supplied expression(s).

(listp *item***)**

Returns T if item is a list. Otherwise returns nil.

(load *filename expression***)**

Loads an AutoLISP file specified by the filename. The optional expression will be evaluated if the load function fails.

(log *number***)**

Returns a real number of the natural log of the supplied number.

(logand *integer integer* **...)**

Returns an integer of a logical bitwise AND of two or more integers.

`(logior integer integer ...)`

> Returns an integer of a logical bitwise OR of two or more integers.

`(lsh number numberbits)`

> Returns an integer of the logical bitwise shift of number by numberbits.

`(mapcar function list ...)`

> Returns the results of executing a lisp function on the elements of one or more lists.

`(max number number ...)`

> Returns the highest value in a series of numbers.

`(member item list)`

> Returns the remainder of the list starting at the item if it is found. Otherwise returns nil.

`(menucmd string)`

> Displays the menu page of a menu specified by the string. The string must include the type of menu and the page name according to menu standards.

`(min number number ...)`

> Returns the lowest value in a series of numbers.

`(minusp number)`

> Returns T if number is negative. Otherwise returns nil.

`(not item)`

> Returns T if item is nil. Otherwise returns nil.

`(nth integer list)`

> Returns the item specified by the integer position in a list.

`(null item)`

> Returns T if item is bound to nil. Otherwise returns nil. Typically used for lists.

`(numberp item)`

> Returns T if item is a number. Otherwise returns nil.

`(open filename mode)`

> Opens a file specified by filename for use specified by the mode. The modes are "r" for reading, "w" for writing, and "a" for appending.

(or expression ...)

> Returns T if one of the expressions is true. Otherwise returns nil or ceases evaluation at the first true expression encountered.

(osnap point mode)

> Returns a point value specified by the osnap mode string on the supplied point value.

pause

> The constant pause is used in the command function to wait for user input.

pi

> The constant pi is set to approximately 3.1415926.

(polar point angle dist)

> Returns a point calculated at an angle and distance from a supplied point.

(prin1 expression file-desc)

> Prints the expression to the screen and returns the expression. If the optional file-desc is supplied and the file is open for writing, output is redirected to file-desc.

(princ expression file-desc)

> Prints the expression to the screen and returns the expression, except control characters are not evaluated. If the optional file-desc is supplied and the file is open for writing, output is redirected to file-desc.

(print expression file-desc)

> Prints a newline and the expression to the screen and returns a newline and expression. If the optional file-desc is supplied and the file is open for writing, output is redirected to file-desc.

(progn expression ...)

> Evaluates a series of expressions, returning the value of the last expression.

(prompt string)

> Displays a string statement in the screen's prompt area.

(quote expression)

> Returns the expression without evaluation, a ' does the same function.

(read string)

> Returns a symbol of the first atom or list in a string.

(read-char *file-desc***)**

> Returns the ASCII character code of a single character typed at the keyboard or read from the optional file-desc.

(read-line *file-desc***)**

> Returns a string typed at the keyboard or read from the optional file-desc.

(redraw *ename mode***)**

> Redraws the current viewport unless ename is provided, in which case the entity represented by ename is redrawn. The mode option redraws the entity in four possible ways: 1 = standard redraw, 2 = reverse redraw (blank), 3 = highlight redraw, and 4 = de-highlight.

(rem *number number* ...**)**

> Returns the remainder of the first number divided by the product of the rest of the numbers.

(repeat *number expression* ...**)**

> Evaluates each expression by the number of times specified. Number must be an integer.

(reverse *list***)**

> Returns a reversed list of items in the supplied list.

(rtos *number mode accuracy***)**

> Returns a string conversion of the supplied number in the current UNITS setting unless the optional mode and accuracy override it. The mode values are:

> | | | | |
> |---|---|---|---|
> | 1 | Scientific | 4 | Architectural |
> | 2 | Decimal | 5 | Fractional |
> | 3 | Engineering | | |

(set *symbol expression***)**

> Sets a quoted symbol with value of the expression. An unquoted symbol can set values indirectly.

(setq *symbol expression* *symbol1 expression1***)**

> Sets a series symbol with value of the matching expression.

(setvar *sysvar value***)**

> Sets an AutoCAD system variable specified by sysvar to the value supplied.

(sin *angle***)**

> Returns the sin of a radian angle.

(sqrt *number***)**

> Returns the square root of number.

(ssadd *ename selection-set***)**

> Creates empty selection set when no arguments are provided. If the optional ename is provided, a selection set is created with just that ename. If an ename is provided with an existing selection set, it is added to the selection set.

(ssdel *ename selection-set***)**

> Deletes the ename from the selection set and returns the ename.

(ssget *mode point point***)**

> Uses AutoCAD's standard selection set options to return a selection set of entities from the user. The optional mode settings use predetermined selection options to automate selection without input from the user. The point values are used to establish Window and Crossing boxes. An X mode returns entities matching a filtering list based on any combination of the following group codes:

```
0   Entity type          38   Elevation (being dropped)
2   Block name           39   Thickness
6   Linetype name        62   Color number
7   Text style name      66   Attributes
8   Layer name          210   3D extrusion direction
```

(sslength *selection-set***)**

> Returns the number of entities in a selection set.

(ssmemb *ename selection-set***)**

> Returns the ename if it is in the selection set. Otherwise returns nil.

(ssname *selection-set number***)**

> Returns the entity name of the number position of the selection set.

(strcase *string flag***)**

> Returns string converted to upper case unless the optional flag evaluates to T, which converts to lower case.

(strcat *string string ...***)**

> Returns a single string by combining all the supplied strings.

(strlen *string***)**

> Returns the number of characters in the string.

(subst *item item list*)

> Returns a list with the first item replacing every occurrence of the second item in the supplied list.

(substr *string start* *length*)

> Returns a string from the start position number of the supplied string to either the end of the string or to the end of the number of characters specified by the optional length value.

T

> A constant symbol T is used as the value of true.

(tblnext *tname* *flag*)

> Returns a data description list of a table name specified by tname. If the optional flag is T, the first table data is returned, otherwise the next table entry is returned each time the function is used.

(tblsearch *tname symbol* *flag*)

> Returns a data description list of a table name specified by tname and the symbol name. If flag is T, a (tblnext) function will return the table data on the next entry.

(terpri)

> Prints a new line on the screen.

(textscr)

> Flips to the text screen on single screen systems.

(trace *function* ...)

> Prints the entry of the specified functions, indented by depth, and returns the value as a debugging aid.

(trans *point code code* *flag*)

> Returns a translated point of the supplied point from the first coordinate code to the second coordinate code. The code values are: 0 for World Coordinate System, 1 for User Coordinate System, and 2 for Display Coordinate System (screen). If the flag is not nil, the point value is treated as a 3D displacement.

(type *item*)

> Returns the type of the item such as real, integer, string, list, and so on.

(untrace *function* ...)

> Removes the trace function from the supplied function(s).

(ver)

> Returns a string with the current AutoLISP version.

(vmon)

Turns on AutoLISP's virtual paging of functions. It makes function definitions eligible to be swapped in and out of RAM to allow for the loading of more programs.

(vports)

Returns a list of the current viewport settings. The list includes the viewport numbers and values indicating corner points for each port. The active viewport is first on the list.

(while *test expression* **...)**

Evaluates the expressions as long as the test returns T (true).

(write-char *number* *file-desc*)

Writes a character specified by the ASCII character code number to the screen or to a file specified by the optional file-desc.

(write-line *string* *file-desc*)

Writes a string to the screen or to a file specified by the optional file-desc.

(zerop *number*)

Returns T if number equals 0 (zero). Otherwise returns nil.

The Authors' Appendix

How CUSTOMIZING AutoCAD Was Produced

We thought you might be interested in the hardware, software, tools, and techniques that we used to put the book together. This appendix tells a little about how the book was produced, and also tells you about some of our favorite tools and sources of information for customization.

Our Hardware

Four computers were used for development, writing, and production of the book. Three were equipped with a copy of AutoCAD provided by Autodesk, Inc. We used a Sun 386i workstation, provided by Sun Microsystems, Inc., and two IBM/PC/XT computers with Intel 286 processors and co-processors running at 10 Mhz. Each IBM computer had 2 Mb or more of Intel Above Board expanded memory. The fourth computer was used as a production printing machine, running Xerox Ventura Publisher from the Xerox Corporation.

We used Verticom M256E and H256E monitors and video cards from Verticom, Inc. The Verticoms provided 640 x 480 graphics in 256 colors. The Verticom boards are IBM CGA and PGC compatible. They can run AutoShade. We also used a VMI Image Manager 1024 video card, provided by Vermont Micro Systems, Inc. We used a Verticom two-page display system on the production workstation. Pointing was done by Hitachi Tiger Tablets and CALCOMP 2500 and 2300 digitizers. The CALCOMP digitizers came from CALCOMP. We used Logitech mice.

Final page printing and illustrations were done on an NEC LC 890 Postscript Page (laser) Printer. The NEC was provided with the help of KETIV Technologies.

Our AUTOEXEC.BAT Files

Here is Rusty's annotated AUTOEXEC.BAT file for his DOS setup. It shows a lot of our favorite tools.

`c:\boot\MAXIT /CA /DB0`	These install the extra MAXIT memory, from McGraw Hill.
`c:\boot\MAXIT /CA /DB0`	It increases DOS memory to 736 Kb.
`set ACADFREERAM=26`	Sets AutoCAD RAM.
`set LISPHEAP=34500`	
`set LISPSTACK=10000`	
`PROMPT $P$G`	Displays current directory at DOS prompt.
`PATH d:\NORTON;d:\DOS;c:\BAT;c:\UTIL;d:\MOUSE;C:\;D:\;d:\WORD`	
`d:\dos\FASTOPEN d:=84 c:=48`	Reduces disk access with DOS 3.3.
`c:\boot\SAFEPARK 15`	A utility parks the hard disk after 15 seconds.
`:  c:\boot\vloadh c:\boot\h8vdi.ker`	The ":" makes this Verticom H256 line inactive without deleting.
`ECHO ^[[1;0;59p`	An ANSI.SYS key reassignment.
`c:\boot\CTRLALT`	An invaluable cut and paste utility.
`c:\boot\SPEEDFXR -X 2 28`	Speeds up the screen text cursor.
`c:\util\MAP > MAPMEM.$`	Reads memory use map and redirects to filename MAPMEM.$.
`ask "Run Carousel? ", yn`	Uses Norton Utilities ASK to optionally run Carousel.
`if errorlevel 2 goto SETUP`	If ASK got N (No=2), go to label :SETUP
`if errorlevel 1 goto CAROUSEL`	If ASK got Y (Yes=1).
`:SETUP`	BATCH label allows optional execution of following.
`c:\util\PUSHDIR`	Initializes utility, saves current directory on a stack.
`CALL PUP rem POP restores path`	(DOS 3.3) Calls the PUP.BAT command, and returns here.
`ask "Run JOT? ", yn`	Another optional load.
`if errorlevel 2 goto CONTINUE`	Skip JOT.
`if errorlevel 1 CD\JOT`	
`1\JOT`	Installs the JOT! abbreviation macro program.
`CD\`	Back to root directory.
`:CONTINUE`	
`COPY d:\acad\RAM F:`	Loads AutoCAD to RAM disk.
`D:`	
`goto end`	Skip the rest. Don't load Carousel.
`:CAROUSEL`	
`C:\CAROUSEL\CAROUSEL`	Load The Software Carousel. This was invaluable.
`:END`	That's all!

Here is Joe's AUTOEXEC.BAT file.

`path=c:\dos;c:\acad;c:\ws;c:\norton;c:\`

```
prompt $p$g
cls
```

Directories do not need to be in the PATH, unless you want to execute files in them from other directories. Any .EXE, .COM, or .BAT program file stored in a directory in the PATH can be executed from any other directory. For example, UTIL, DOS, and NORTON are in our PATH so that we can use them.

We use several TSR (RAM resident) utilities, which are always available in the background. They typically pop up when you hit some *hotkey* and disappear when retired. We used some TSRs, including CTRLALT for text screen capture and copying, PUSHDIR to save and restore current directories, JOT to create keyboard macro abbreviations, and HotShot Graphics for AutoCAD screen captures.

Our development environment included The Software Carousel, Norton's Editor, CTRLALT, Microsoft Word, and several in-house text conversion programs developed by Pat Haessly.

Our Text Editor

A good text editor is invaluable in customizing AutoCAD. Besides creating ASCII files, it helps if your editor is comfortable, compact, quick, and easy to use. Norton's Editor was our choice as a text editor. Norton's Editor has all the following features.

■ Quick loading, compact size. Quick saving and exit. Save to another file name. Ability to handle large files. Merge files.

■ Compare text for differences.

■ Line and column number counter display. Go to line number. Row mode, including block copy and move.

■ Versatile cursor control. Versatile delete. Undelete text. Versatile block commands. Versatile search and replace.

■ Find matching punctuation, like: (([ ]]).

Perhaps the most valuable feature in Norton's Editor is the punctuation matching. It helps you find your way back out when you get lost in "Stupid Parentheses Land" within AutoLISP.

Our Multi-Tasking Interactive Environment

Some operating systems and operating system extensions let you load more than one program at a time. Concurrent ones, like Windows 386 and Deskview, can run programs in the background while you work. They require a 386 machine. Others, like The Software Carousel from Softlogic Solutions, run on PC/XT/AT machines. They can flip back and forth between programs, but only one program is active at a time.

We found The Software Carousel invaluable in writing this book. It integrated our system. On the IBM computers, we set up four "partitions." Each was like a separate computer. All four coexisted in the single system, but each could maintain its own settings and environment. The partitions were:

```
1       AutoCAD.
2       Norton's Editor and other utilities.
3       More utilities and housekeeping.
4       Microsoft Word.
```

CTRLALT ties the system together by extending across all partitions. CTRLALT is a memory-resident pop up freeware program by Barry Simon and Richard Wilson. It has many features including:

- Popup ASCII table.

- Popup Hex table.

- Popup ANSI table.

- Print.

- Cut and paste.

The cut and paste feature made the tedious and error-prone task of documenting the book's AutoCAD and AutoLISP routines easier. We could flip into AutoCAD, hit <CTRL-ALT-RETURN>, highlight part of the text screen and capture it. This captured the screens exactly as you should see them.

Of course, none of this was required on the Sun386i workstation. Multiple windows were simultaneously active, allowing us to develop, test, cut, and paste between AutoCAD and our documents. Exercises in our documents were then pasted back into AutoCAD to verify their accuracy.

Document Illustration, Formatting, and Printing

Microsoft Word was used to create the document. Xerox Ventura Publisher was used to format and print. Illustrations were done in AutoCAD. Screen images, both text and graphics, were captured and cleaned up with HotShot Graphics by SymSoft, Inc.

Tools, Sources, and Support

No one knows everything there is to know about AutoCAD. Knowing where to find AutoCAD information can help you solve many application problems. Here are other tools and resources that we'd like to share.

Advanced AutoCAD Classes

Autodesk, Inc., has authorized a hundred or more AutoCAD training centers in the United States and several foreign countries. These training centers are usually affiliated with colleges and technical institutes. Many centers have specialized and advanced courses on AutoLISP. Gold Hill Computers, the makers of Golden Common Lisp, is providing AutoLISP courses through selected authorized AutoCAD training centers. You can get information about the centers by calling Autodesk, Inc., (800) 445-5415 or (415) 332-2344. In addition, many AutoCAD dealers also teach courses that meet or exceed the quality of the authorized AutoCAD training centers.

A Brief Look at the CompuServe Autodesk Forum

Autodesk's forum on CompuServe may be the best source of support available today. The CompuServe Information Service, Compuserve, Inc., is available to anyone with a computer, modem, communications software, telephone, and password.

You join CompuServe by getting a membership kit at a computer store, software store, or bookstore. When you follow the instructions and *log on*, the CompuServe main menu "TOP" shows:

```
CompuServe                    TOP

1   Subscriber Assistance
2   Find a Topic
3   Communications/Bulletin Bds.
4   News/Weather/Sports
5   Travel
6   The Electronic MALL/Shopping
7   Money Matters/Markets
```

```
8  Entertainment/Games
9  Home/Health/Family
10 Reference/Education
11 Computers/Technology
12 Business/Other Interests

Enter choice number !GO ADESK
```

If you shortcut with GO ADESK, you get the Autodesk Top Menu:

```
Autodesk

FUNCTIONS
```

Most forums are divided into several parts:

```
1 (L)  Leave a Message
2 (R)  Read Messages
3 (CO) Conference Mode
4 (DL) Data Libraries
5 (B)  Bulletins
6 (MD) Member Directory
7 (OP) User Options
8 (IN) Instructions

Enter choice !
```

Private and weekly group two-way interactive sessions.

Announcements such as new releases are promptly posted here.

Help!

You will be interested mainly in 1 (L) Leave a Message, 2 (R) Read Messages, and 4 (DL) Data Libraries. The messages and data libraries are broken up into several subject areas. If you are only interested in AutoLISP, you can set your topic user options to ignore everything else. If you select 4 (DL) Data Libraries, you will see a list of topics:

```
Data Libraries Available:

0 ADESK File Cabinet
1 AutoCAD
2 AutoLisp
3 AutoShade
4 AutoSketch
5 AutoFlix
6 AEC
7 Wishlist
8 3rd Party Software
9 What's New!
10 Utilities / ADI
13 AutoSolid
15 Dealers only
16 Developers only

Enter Choice !2
DL 2 - AutoLISP
```

If you select 2 AutoLISP, you get a typical DL:

```
1 (DES) Description of Data Library
2 (BRO) Browse thru Files              Short descriptions filtered by keyword/date.
3 (DIR) Directory of Files
4 (UPL) Upload a New File              Contribute something you've created.
5 (DOW) Download a File                Copy a file to your system.
6 (DL)  Change Data Library            Shortcut to another DL.
7 (T)   Return to Function Menu        Back to the previous menu.
8 (I)   Instructions                   Help is always available.
```

Browsing with 2 (BRO) shows short file descriptions. You can enter keywords to search for specific topics. Read it on-line, or copy it to your computer. There are many valuable AutoLISP routines that users have donated in DL 2. Upload time is free, and you can download them for just a few dollars per hour.

You can leave a message and get a reply in less than 24 hours. Some of the most knowledgeable Autodesk people contribute. And you have the benefit of the largest CAD user group on-line. Many users will already have solved a problem you've encountered and reply.

Here are some tips that we have learned. Set options so there is no pause between messages. Figure out how to make your communications software capture text to a disk file as it scrolls on the screen. Read the messages later, offline, and formulate replies to upload later. You can download the free communications package ATO from the IBMSW (IBM SoftWare) forum. This package is designed to automate using CompuServe forums.

We recommend using the CompuServe forum. It is the best support money can buy. It averages about $6/hour of connected time and is well worth the time it takes to learn to use it.

Bulletin Boards

Many other local AutoCAD bulletin boards exist. You will find a listing, maintained by New Riders Publishing, in the Autodesk Forum on CompuServe. GO ADESK and check the library for the newest upload of the list, or contact us at New Riders Publishing, Attn: Bulletin Board.

User Groups

There are numerous AutoCAD user groups. Some of the best overall support comes from these members. You may find members, or whole groups, who share a similar application to yours. New Riders also maintains a list of user groups. GO ADESK and check for the newest upload of the list, or contact us at New Riders Publishing, Attn: User Groups.

Magazines

AutoCAD has two independent magazines.

```
CADalyst                        CADalyst Publications LTD.
Subscription Manager            282-810 W. Broadway
314 E Holly, #106               Vancouver BC Canada V5Z 4C9
Bellingham, WA 98225
(604) 873-0811


CADENCE
Circulation Dept.
POB 203550
Austin, TX 78720-3550
(512) 250-1700
```

Books

After you have worked your way through CUSTOMIZING AutoCAD, you may find that you want to learn more about AutoLISP. You can continue learning about AutoCAD customization with INSIDE AutoLISP, also written by Smith and Gesner. INSIDE AutoLISP is your ultimate guide to learning the full power of the AutoLISP language. The book describes all the AutoLISP functions and teaches each one with hands-on exercises. Hundreds of programs illustrate techniques and how to apply AutoLISP to further customize your system. Keep in mind that AutoLISP is its own dialect of the LISP language. Here are three books on the general LISP language that we found useful.

- The "bible" of LISP is Winston and Horn's LISP (Addison-Wesley).

- David Touretsky's LISP A Gentle Introduction to Symbolic Computation (Harper & Row) is a good, easy introduction to LISP.

- Tony Hasemer's Looking at LISP (Addison-Wesley) is another good reference.

Commercial Utilities

There are many utility programs to ease dealing with DOS, the computer, and, of course, your proliferating files. The best source of information and reviews on current programs are the magazines: PC Magazine, PC World, Info World, and PC Week.

Here are a few categories along with a few of our favorite programs:

Hard Disk Management and Backup

Use something more efficient than DOS BACKUP for archiving your files. We use Fastback, Fifth Generation Systems, for its speed and superb error recovery.

After you back up your hard disk, you should clean it up. Unfortunately, just deleting garbage isn't enough. DOS tends to break files into smaller and smaller chunks as time goes on. The average hard disk is probably operating at less than half of its optimum speed. The solution is weekly or monthly cleanups with an inexpensive utility like Disk Optimizer from Softlogic Solutions. We use the Disk Optimizer. We also recommend MACE from Paul Mace Software, or the SpeedDisk utility on Norton's Utilities. These programs will rearrange files for faster access.

A unique program for problem hard disks is the Disk Technician, Prime Solutions, Inc. It diagnoses and actually repairs flaky disks by maintaining a comparative record and doing a low level format on individual problem tracks. It also includes the SAFEPARK utility which we use.

If you erase a file or even a directory accidentally, there is hope of recovery if you catch it quickly. Hope is slim if you do anything that writes to the disk before recovery. The best known utility, which we use, is the NU unerase utility of Norton's Utilities. Others are: MACE, Paul Mace Software, or PC Tools, Central Point Software.

Keyboard Macros

Electronic shorthand programs, like Prokey from RoseSoft, speed entry of repetitive text and commands and reduce errors. We used Prokey extensively in the past, and still use it for some tasks. Others are Newkey, FAB Software's low cost shareware, Keyworks from Alpha Software Corp. with an optional program language, or Metro from Lotus Development Corp.

Now we use an abbreviation program, JOT!, from Beacon Software International. It expands abbreviations automatically while you type. If you type LI, for instance, it sends LINE to AutoCAD. Another is PRD Plus, Productivity Software Int'l. Some keyboard macros, like Prokey, have a similar feature, but they are not automatic and require a trigger key to expand the abbreviation.

User Interface Shells

If you hate DOS, or if you are a system manager who needs to insulate users from DOS, there are numerous DOS shells. They generally provide a point and shoot interface to DOS through menus. Norton Commander, PC Tools, and many others are available for almost any taste. Avoid memory-resident shells unless they use EMS. Otherwise, AutoCAD will probably be left RAM hungry.

General Utility Packages

There are dozens of little utilities that you may find useful even if you only manage a single system. Many utilities are available as shareware or freeware. There are several comprehensive utilities packages available commercially.

We use Norton Utilities, from Peter Norton Computing. The programs include an easy point and shoot interface, and many life-saving disk restore and cleanup tools. PC Tools, Central Point Software, has a unique directory cut and past feature which can move entire directory trees intact. But don't try it with Carousel loaded!

Other typical features include directory and file name sorting, text searching groups of files, finding files no matter where they are on the disk, changing file attributes, directory name listing, disk testing, and almost anything else that DOS forgot and we need.

Freeware and Shareware

Some of the best things in your computer's life are free, or nearly so. Most of the AutoCAD command line and text screen sections in this book were *captured* from the AutoCAD text screen by CTRLALT. This is freeware. We got it by downloading it from the IBMSW (IBM SoftWare) Forum on CompuServe. Here are some other popular utilities with asterisks indicating programs that we use.

ARC521.COM*   An ARC utility to compress and archive files into libraries. Saves
              30-65% for DWG files.
BADSEC.ARC   Finds bad sectors on hard or floppy disks.
BASERE.ARC   Is a pop up number base converter.
BC.EXE   Is a backup companion, a simple backup utility. We use FastBack.
CARUTL.ARC*   Software Carousel utilities.
COMSWT.ARC   Switches COM1: and COM2:
CTLALT.ARC*   Pop up utilities, tables, cut/paste from screen into other programs.
D.ARC*   Keeps track of files added/erased in hard disk subdirectories.
              It makes cleanup easy.
FDIR.EXE   Directory listing in user set alpha-sorted order. We use a similar

	Norton Utility, DS.
FILL.ARC*	Copies group of files on minimum number of floppies, fills each full.
GLOBAL.ARC*	Executes a DOS command, program, or .BAT file on a group of files or directories. Great for cleanup.
GUDLUK.ARC	A side-by-side text file comparison utility.
HELP.ARC	Help facility for DOS commands, functions, syntax, etc.
HIDE.ARC	Two programs to Hide or UnHide directories. Good for security.
HOTKEY.ARC	Cursor speed-up and run-on stopper.
KEYBUF.COM	Extends your keyboard buffer. Gets rid of the beeps and dropped character errors.
KEYLOC.ARC	Changes shifting keys (ctrl, alt, shift) into on/off toggles.
LOC.COM	Small, fast file finder (wildcards allowed). We use Norton's FF.
MOVE.ARC	Moves files (or subdirectories) between directories. We made our own .BAT program.
NEWER.COM*	Finds files newer (or older) than other files.
NEWKEY.ARC	Keyboard macro processor, improves macro file handling. Highly rated shareware.
NOTEPAD.COM	Small, memory-resident notepad like Sidekick.
POPDIR.COM*	Restores current directory previously saved on stack with PUSHDIR.COM. Great in .BAT files.
PWORD.ARC	Prevents booting without entering password (source incl).
QUERY.ARC*	Creates .COM file to display ASCII text.
REMIND.ARC	Daily reminder utility (demo). Shareware.
SEARCH.ARC	PATH-like access to data, overlay, etc. files. We use DOS 3.3 APPEND.
SRCH82.ARC	Fast text search and replacement program.
VDL.ARC*	Mass file delete with verification. Excellent for cleanup.
WAITEX.ARC	Loads/runs programs at appointed time.
WHATIS.ARC	Adds 60-character comments to files. We use Norton's FI.

To obtain any of these utilities, follow your CompuServe instructions.

There also is an organization called the PC Software Interest Group (PC-SIG) which maintains and distributes a large library of public domain software, freeware, and shareware. PC-SIG publishes annual catalogues and monthly updates. PC-SIG checks its software. They charge a distribution fee of about $6 per disk. This fee is in addition to any possible shareware fees. Their entire 490+ disk, 9000 program library is available on a single CD-ROM for about $200! Here is their address:

```
PC-SIG
1030 E. Duane Ave., Suite D
Sunnyvale, CA 94086
(408) 730-9291
```

Authors' Last Word and Mail Box

We had a lot of fun and learned a lot doing the book. We hope that you enjoy CUSTOMIZING AutoCAD and that you come back to the book again and again for customizing ideas. Build on our ideas. Modify and adapt the routines so that they do what you want them to do. We only ask that you give us credit for what we provide, and that you pass the credit on. We hope you will continue with your AutoCAD system customization with INSIDE AutoLISP.

If you want to correspond with us, we can be reached electronically on CompuServe. Use CompuServe's EMAIL feature to send us a message. Rusty Gesner's number is: 76310,10. Please leave your name, telephone number, the version of AutoCAD that you are using, a description of the hardware, and your comments. Send us tips and new ideas that were inspired by the book.

We will respond to you on CompuServe or by telephone as soon as possible. We try to respond within 48 hours. We scan our mail each day. Of course, you can reach us by telephone or good old-fashioned mail at the New Riders number and mail address in the back of the book.

Good luck with your customizing! See you in INSIDE AutoLISP.

Index

EXERCISE INDEX

*To complete your AutoCAD library, look for
INSIDE AUTOLISP®— another fine New
Riders book by Smith and Gesner.*

New Riders Library

INSIDE AutoCAD   **Fifth Edition**
The Complete AutoCAD Guide

D. Raker and H. Rice
750 pages, over 400 illustrations
ISBN: 0-934035-49-0 **$29.95**

INSIDE AutoCAD, the best selling book on AutoCAD, is entirely new and
rewritten for AutoCAD's 3D Release 10. This easy-to-understand book serves
as both a tutorial and a lasting reference guide. Learn to use every single
AutoCAD command as well as time saving drawing techniques and tips.
Includes coverage of new 3D graphics features, AutoShade, and AutoLISP.
This is the book that lets you keep up and stay in control with AutoCAD.

INSIDE AutoLISP
The Complete Guide to Using AutoLISP for AutoCAD Applications

J. Smith and R. Gesner
672 pages, over 150 illustrations
ISBN: 0-934035-47-4, **$29.95**

Introducing the most comprehensive book on AutoLISP for AutoCAD Release
10. Learn AutoLISP commands and functions and write your own custom
AutoLISP programs. Numerous tips and tricks for using AutoLISP for routine
drawing tasks. Import and export critical drawing information to/from Lotus
1-2-3 and dBASE. Automate the creation of scripts for unattended drawing
processing. *INSIDE AutoLISP* is the book that will give you the inside track
to using AutoLISP.

INSIDE AutoSketch
A Guide to Productive Drawing Using AutoSketch

By Frank Lenk
240 pages, over 120 illustrations
ISBN: 0-934035-20-2, **$17.95**

INSIDE AutoSketch gives you real-life mechanical parts, drawing schematics,
and architectural drawings. Start by learning to draw simple shapes such as
points, lines and curves, then edit shapes by moving, copying, rotating and
distorting them. Explore higher-level features to complete technical drawing
jobs using reference grids, snap, drawing layers and creating parts. *INSIDE
AutoSketch* will let you draw your way to success!

CUSTOMIZING AutoCAD　　Second Edition
The Complete Guide to Integrating AutoCAD With Menus, Macros and More!

J. Smith and R. Gesner
480 pages, over 100 illustrations
ISBN: 0-934035-45-8, **$27.95**

Uncover the hidden secrets of AutoCAD's 3D Release 10 in this all new edition. Discover the anatomy of an AutoCAD menu and build a custom menu from start to finish. Manipulate distance, angles, points, and hatches — ALL in 3D! Customize hatches, text fonts and dimensioning for increased productivity. Buy *CUSTOMIZING AutoCAD* today and start customizing AutoCAD tomorrow!

STEPPING INTO AutoCAD　　Fourth Edition
A Guide to Technical Drafting Using AutoCAD

By Mark Merickel
380 pages, over 140 illustrations
ISBN: 0-934035-51-2, **$29.95**

This popular tutorial has been completely rewritten with new exercises for Release 10. The book is organized to lead you step by step from the basics to practical tips on customizing AutoCAD for technical drafting. Handy references provide quick set-up of the AutoCAD environment. Improve your drawing accuracy through AutoCAD's dimensioning commands. It also includes extensive support for ANSI Y14.5 level drafting.

AutoCAD Quick Reference Guide
Everything You want to Know About AutoCAD

By Dorothy Kent
180 pages, over 50 illustrations
ISBN: 0-934035-57-1, **$11.95**

All essential AutoCAD functions and commands are arranged alphabetically and described in just a few paragraphs. Includes a command index and an appendix listing all menu commands and functions for each version of AutoCAD. Extensive cross-indexing make this the instant answer guide to AutoCAD.

The Autodesk File

Written and Edited by John Walker
608 pages
ISBN 0-934035-63-6 $24.95

The unvarnished history of Autodesk, Inc., the company behind AutoCAD. Read the original memos, letters and reports that trace the rise of Autodesk, from start-up to their present position as the number one CAD software company in the world. Learn the secrets of success behind Autodesk and AutoCAD. Must reading for any AutoCAD user or entrepreneur!

New Riders Library also includes products on Desktop Publishing

INSIDE XEROX VENTURA PUBLISHER

A Guide to Professional-Quality Desktop Publishing on the IBM PC

James Cavuoto and Jesse Berst
704 pages, 330 illustrations
ISBN 0-934035-59-8 **$24.95**

2nd Edition

The best reference guide to Ventura Publisher is now even better! *Inside Xerox Ventura Publisher*, 2nd Edition, has been completely rewritten for Ventura Publisher Version 2 and includes more of what readers have asked for: more hands-on examples, more easy-to-use charts, and more time-saving tips and tricks.

PUBLISHING POWER WITH VENTURA

The Complete Teaching Guide to Xerox Ventura Publisher

Martha Lubow and Jesse Berst
624 pages, 230 illustrations
ISBN 0-934035-61-X **$27.95**

2nd Edition

Unlock the inner secrets of Ventura Publisher Version 2 with this well-written tutorial. You'll learn how to create your own great-looking business documents by producing the "real world" documents presented in this book. These documents include reports, newsletters, directories, technical manuals, and books. Companion software is available.

DESKTOP MANAGER

ISBN: 0-934035-34-2 **$99.95**

Supports Version 1 and 2

Desktop Manager is the desktop accessory software for IBM and compatible personal computers that helps you manage your Ventura Publisher documents, running transparently from within the Ventura Publisher environment. A multifunction software utility, *Desktop Manager* provides file management, timed backup, document control, style sheet settings, and report generation. This utility program comes complete with an 180-page guide.

STYLE SHEETS FOR BUSINESS DOCUMENTS
(Book and Disk Set)

Martha Lubow and Jesse Berst
320 pages, 150 illustrations
ISBN 0-934035-22-9 **$39.95**

Supports Version 1 and 2

Introducing a cure for the common document—*Style Sheets for Business Documents*. This book and disk set contains more than 30 predesigned Ventura Publisher templates for creating top-quality business documents. Style sheets are presented for proposals, reports, marketing materials, ads, brochures, and correspondence. More than 100 pages of design tips and tricks are also included.

STYLE SHEETS FOR TECHNICAL DOCUMENTS
(Book and Disk Set)

By Byron Canfield and Chad Canty
320 Pages 150 illustrations
ISBN: 0-934035-29-6 **$39.95**

Supports Version 1 and 2

Get the maximum out of Ventura Publisher with these advanced technical document formats. This book/disk combination presents more than 25 ready-to-use templates for creating technical documents and books. Also includes techniques for creating pictures and tables, plus advanced tips for modifying formats to fit your needs.

STYLE SHEETS FOR NEWSLETTERS
(Book and Disk Set)

By Martha Lubow and Polly Pattison
320 Pages over 150 illustrations
ISBN: 0-934035-31-8 **$39.95**

Supports Version 1 and 2

This book and disk set presents more than 25 predesigned Ventura Publisher templates for creating one-, two-, three-, and four-column newsletters. Just open the chapter template, load in your own text, and print. A complete description of every style sheet and key tag for all chapter templates is also included.

For fast service, call a New Riders Sales Representative
now at (818) 991-5392

MANAGING DESKTOP PUBLISHING

By Jesse Berst
320 Pages over 150 illustrations
ISBN: 0-934035-27-X **$9.95**

The essential handbook for the modern writer and editor. *Managing Desktop Publishing* shows you how to save production time by preformatting documents. Learn to manage your files, styles and style sheets. Also presented are the elements of style you need to succeed in today's desktop publishing arena. Companion software is available.

Order from New Riders Publishing Today

Yes, please send me the productivity-boosting material I have checked below. Make check payable to New Riders Publishing.

❑ **Check enclosed.**

❑ **Charge to my credit card:**

❑ **Visa #**   ❑ **Mastercard #**

Expiration date: _____

Signature: _____

Name _____

Company: _____

Address: _____

City: _____

State _____ Zip: _____

Phone: _____

The easiest way to order is to pick-up the phone and call (818) 991-5392 between 9:00 AM and 5:00 PM PST. Please have your credit card readily available and your order can be placed in a snap!

Quantity	Description of Item	Unit Cost	Total Cost
	Customizing AutoCAD 2nd Edition	$27.95	
	Customizing ACAD Disk	$14.95	
	AutoCAD Reference Guide	$11.95	
	AutoCAD Reference Disk	$14.95	
	Inside AutoCAD 5th Edition	$29.95	
	Inside AutoCAD Disk	$14.95	
	Inside AutoLISP	$29.95	
	Inside AutoLISP Disk	$14.95	
	Inside AutoSketch	$17.95	
	Inside AutoSketch Drawing Disk	$ 7.95	
	Stepping into AutoCAD 4th Edition	$29.95	
	Stepping into AutoCAD Disk	$14.95	
	COOKIES (Put the fun back in your computer)	$ 6.95	

Send to:

New Riders Publishing
P.O. Box 4846
Thousand Oaks, CA 91360
(818)991-5392

Shipping and Handling: see information below.		
SalesTax: California please add 6.5% sales tax.		
TOTAL:		

Shipping and Handling: $3.50 for the first book and $1.00 for each additional book. Floppy disk add $1.50 for shipping and handling. Add $15.00 per book for overseas shipping and handling. If you have to have it NOW, we can ship product to you in 24 to 48 hours. For an additional $5.00 RUSH CHARGE for processing plus the actual cost of air freight, you'll be able to receive your item over night or in 2 days.

New Riders Publishing P.O. Box 4846 Thousand Oaks, CA 91360 (818) 991-5392
FAX (818) 991-9263

CA

Order from New Riders Publishing Today

Yes, please send me the productivity-boosting material I have checked below. Make check payable to New Riders Publishing.

Name _____

Company: _____

❑ Check enclosed.

❑ Charge to my credit card:

❑ Visa # _____ ❑ Mastercard # _____

Address:_____

City: _____

State_____Zip:_____

Expiration date: _____

Signature: _____

Phone: _____

The easiest way to order is to pick-up the phone and call (818) 991-5392 between 9:00 AM and 5:00 PM PST. Please have your credit card readily available and your order can be placed in a snap!

Quantity	Description of Item	Unit Cost	Total Cost
	Customizing AutoCAD 2nd Edition	$27.95	
	Customizing ACAD Disk	$14.95	
	AutoCAD Reference Guide	$11.95	
	AutoCAD Reference Disk	$14.95	
	Inside AutoCAD 5th Edition	$29.95	
	Inside AutoCAD Disk	$14.95	
	Inside AutoLISP	$29.95	
	Inside AutoLISP Disk	$14.95	
	Inside AutoSketch	$17.95	
	Inside AutoSketch Drawing Disk	$ 7.95	
	Stepping into AutoCAD 4th Edition	$29.95	
	Stepping into AutoCAD Disk	$14.95	
	COOKIES (Put the fun back in your computer)	$ 6.95	

Send to:

New Riders Publishing
P.O. Box 4846
Thousand Oaks, CA 91360
(818)991-5392

Shipping and Handling: see information below.		
SalesTax: California please add 6.5% sales tax.		
TOTAL:		

Shipping and Handling: $3.50 for the first book and $1.00 for each additional book. Floppy disk add $1.50 for shipping and handling. Add $15.00 per book for overseas shipping and handling. If you have to have it NOW, we can ship product to you in 24 to 48 hours. For an additional $5.00 RUSH CHARGE for processing plus the actual cost of air freight, you'll be able to receive your item over night or in 2 days.

New Riders Publishing P.O. Box 4846 Thousand Oaks, CA 91360 (818) 991-5392
FAX (818) 991-9263

CA

27.95